Theoretical Computer Science and Software Engineering

Theoretical Computer Science and Software Engineering

Editor: Brielle Morrison

NY RESEARCH PRESS

New York

Published by NY Research Press
118-35 Queens Blvd., Suite 400,
Forest Hills, NY 11375, USA
www.nyresearchpress.com

Theoretical Computer Science and Software Engineering
Edited by Brielle Morrison

International Standard Book Number: 978-1-64725-373-8 (Hardback)

Cataloging-in-publication Data

Theoretical computer science and software engineering / edited by Brielle Morrison.
p. cm.
Includes bibliographical references and index.
ISBN 978-1-64725-373-8
1. Computer science. 2. Software engineering. 3. Computers. I. Morrison, Brielle.
QA76 .T443 2023
004--dc23

Contents

Preface

ıe main aim of this book is to educate learners and enhance their research focus by ·esenting diverse topics covering this vast field. This is an advanced book which compiles gnificant studies by distinguished experts in the area of analysis. This book addresses ıccessive solutions to the challenges arising in the area of application, along with it; the ook provides scope for future developments.

ıe discipline which involves the study of information, computation and automation is ıown as computer science. It can be broadly divided into theoretical computer science, plied computer science and computer systems. Theoretical computer science (TCS) refers a branch of mathematics and computer science that focuses on the mathematical aspects computer science such as type theory, lambda calculus and the theory of computation. pplied computer science encompasses software engineering, Image and sound processing, ıd computer graphics. Software engineering is a subfield of computer science which focuses ı the design, development, testing, distribution and maintenance of software products. his book explores all the important aspects of theoretical computer science and software ıgineering in the present day scenario. It will also provide interesting topics for research, hich interested readers can take up. A number of latest researches have been included to ep the readers up-to-date with the global concepts in this area of study.

was a great honour to edit this book, though there were challenges, as it involved a lot communication and networking between me and the editorial team. However, the end sult was this all-inclusive book covering diverse themes in the field.

nally, it is important to acknowledge the efforts of the contributors for their excellent ıapters, through which a wide variety of issues have been addressed. I would also like to ıank my colleagues for their valuable feedback during the making of this book.

Editor

1

A New Linear Logic for Deadlock-Free Session-Typed Processes

Ornela Dardha(✉) and Simon J. Gay

School of Computing Science, University of Glasgow, Glasgow, UK
{Ornela.Dardha,Simon.Gay}@glasgow.ac.uk

Abstract. The π-calculus, viewed as a core concurrent programming language, has been used as the target of much research on type systems for concurrency. In this paper we propose a new type system for deadlock-free session-typed π-calculus processes, by integrating two separate lines of work. The first is the propositions-as-types approach by Caires and Pfenning, which provides a linear logic foundation for session types and guarantees deadlock-freedom by forbidding cyclic process connections. The second is Kobayashi's approach in which types are annotated with priorities so that the type system can check whether or not processes contain genuine cyclic dependencies between communication operations. We combine these two techniques for the first time, and define a new and more expressive variant of classical linear logic with a proof assignment that gives a session type system with Kobayashi-style priorities. This can be seen in three ways: (i) as a new linear logic in which cyclic structures can be derived and a CYCLE-elimination theorem generalises CUT-elimination; (ii) as a logically-based session type system, which is more expressive than Caires and Pfenning's; (iii) as a logical foundation for Kobayashi's system, bringing it into the sphere of the propositions-as-types paradigm.

1 Introduction

The Curry-Howard correspondence, or propositions-as-types paradigm, provides a canonical logical foundation for functional programming [42]. It identifies types with logical propositions, programs with proofs, and computation with proof normalisation. It was natural to ask for a similar account of concurrent programming, and this question was brought into focus by the discovery of linear logic [24] and Girard's explicit suggestion that it should have some connection with concurrent computation. Several attempts were made to relate π-calculus processes to the proof nets of classical linear logic [1,8], and to relate CCS-like processes to the $*$-autonomous categories that provide semantics for classical linear logic [2]. However, this work did not result in a convincing propositions-as-types framework for concurrency, and did not continue beyond the 1990s.

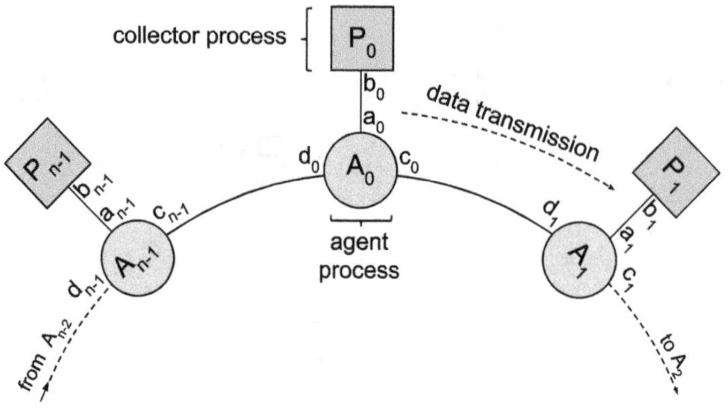

Fig. 1. Cyclic scheduler

Meanwhile, Honda *et al.* [26,27,38] developed *session types* as a formalism for statically checking that messages have the correct types and sequence according to a communication protocol. Research on session types developed and matured over several years, eventually inspiring Caires and Pfenning [12] to discover a Curry-Howard correspondence between dual intuitionistic linear logic [7] and a form of π-calculus with session types [38]. Wadler [41] subsequently gave an alternative formulation based on classical linear logic, and related it to existing work on session types for functional languages [23]. The Caires-Pfenning approach has been widely accepted as a propositions-as-types theory of concurrent programming, as well as providing a logical foundation for session types.

Caires and Pfenning's type system guarantees deadlock-freedom by forbidding cyclic process structures. It provides a logical foundation for deadlock-free session processes, complementing previous approaches to deadlock-freedom in session type systems [9,15,21,22]. The logical approach to session types has been extended in many ways, including features such as dependent types [39], failures and non-determinism [11], sharing and races [6]. All this work relies on the acyclicity condition. However, rejecting cyclic process structures is unnecessarily strict: they are a necessary, but not sufficient, condition for the existence of deadlocked communication operations. As we will show in Example 1 (Fig. 1), there are deadlock-free processes that can naturally be implemented in a cyclic way, but are rejected by Caires and Pfenning's type system.

Our contribution is to define a new logic, *priority-based linear logic* (PLL), and formulate it as a type system for *priority-based* CP (PCP), which is a more expressive class of processes than Wadler's CP [41]. This is the first Curry-Howard correspondence that allows cyclic interconnected processes, while still ensuring deadlock-freedom. The key idea is that PLL includes conditions on inter-channel dependencies based on Kobayashi's type systems [29,30,32]. Our work can be viewed in three ways: (i) as a new linear logic in which cyclic proof structures can be derived; (ii) as an extension of Caires-Pfenning type systems so that they accept more processes, while maintaining the strong logical foundation; (iii) as a logical foundation for Kobayashi-style type systems.

An example of a deadlock-free cyclic process is Milner's well-known scheduler [35], described in the following Example 1.

Example 1 (Cyclic Scheduler, Fig. 1*).* A set of agents $A_0, ..., A_{n-1}$, for $n > 1$, is scheduled to perform a certain task in cyclic order, starting with agent A_0. For all $i \in \{1, ..., n-1\}$, agent A_i sends the result of computation to a collector process P_i, before transmitting further data to agent $A_{(i+1) \bmod n}$. At the end of the round, A_0 sends the final result to P_0. Here we define a finite version of Milner's scheduler, which executes one round of communication.

$$\begin{aligned}
Sched &\triangleq ...(\boldsymbol{\nu} a_i b_i)...(\boldsymbol{\nu} c_i d_{(i+1) \bmod n})(A_0 \mid A_1 \mid ... \mid A_{n-1} \mid P_0 \mid P_1 \mid ... \mid P_{n-1}) \\
A_0 &\triangleq c_0[\mathbf{n}_0].d_0(x_0).a_0[\mathbf{m}_0].\mathsf{close}_0 \\
A_i &\triangleq d_i(x_i).a_i[\mathbf{m}_i].c_i[\mathbf{n}_i].\mathsf{close}_i \qquad i \in \{1, ..., n-1\} \\
P_i &\triangleq b_i(y_i).Q_i \qquad i \in \{0, ..., n-1\}
\end{aligned}$$

Prefix $c_0[\mathbf{n}_0]$ denotes an output on c_0, and $d_0(x_0)$ an input on d_0. For now, let $\mathbf{m}$ and $\mathbf{n}$ denote data. Process close_i closes the channels used by A_i: the details of this closure are irrelevant here (however, they are as in processes Q and R in Example 2). Process Q_i uses the message received from A_i, in internal computation. The construct $(\boldsymbol{\nu} ab)$ creates two channel endpoints a and b and binds them together. The system *Sched* is deadlock-free because $A_1, ..., A_{n-1}$ each wait for a message from the previous A_i before sending, and A_0 sends the initial message.

Sched is not typable in the original type systems by Caires-Pfenning and Wadler. To do that, it would be necessary to break A_0 into two parallel agents $A'_0 \triangleq c_0[\mathbf{n}_0].\mathsf{close}_{c_0}$ and $A''_0 \triangleq d_0(x_0).a_0[\mathbf{m}_0].\mathsf{close}_{d_0,a_0}$. This changes the design of the system, yielding a different one. Moreover, if the scheduler continues into a second round of communication, this redesign is not possible because of the potential dependency from the input on d_0 to the next output on c_0. However, *Sched* is typable in PCP; we will show the type assignment at the end of Sect. 2.

There is a natural question at this point: *given that the cyclic scheduler is deadlock-free, is it possible to encode its semantics in* CP, *thus eliminating the need for* PCP? It is possible to define a centralised agent A that communicates with all the collectors P_i, resulting in a system that is semantically equivalent to our *Sched.* However, such an encoding has a global character, and changes the structure of the overall system from distributed to centralised. In programming terms, it corresponds to changing the software design, as we pointed out in Example 1, and ultimately the software architecture, which is not always desirable or even feasible. The aim of PCP is to generalise CP so that deadlock-free processes can be constructed with their natural structure. We would want any encoding of PCP into CP to be structure-preserving, which would mean translating the Cycle rule (given in Fig. 2) homomorphically; this is clearly impossible.

Contributions and Structure of the Paper. In Sect. 2 we define priority-based linear logic (PLL), which extends classical linear logic (CLL) with priorities attached to propositions. These priorities are based on Kobayashi's annotations for deadlock freedom [32]. By following the propositions-as-types paradigm, we define a term assignment for PLL proofs, resulting in priority-based classical processes (PCP), which extends Wadler's CP [41] with MIX and CYCLE rules (Fig. 2). In Sect. 3 we define an operational semantics for PCP. In Sect. 4 we prove CYCLE-elimination (Theorem 1) for PLL, analogous to the standard CUT-elimination theorem for CLL. Consequently, the results for PCP are subject reduction (Theorem 2), top-level deadlock-freedom (Theorem 3), and full deadlock-freedom for closed processes (Theorem 4). In Sect. 5 we discuss related work and conclude the paper.

2 PCP: Classical Processes with MIX and CYCLE

Priority-based CP (PCP) follows the style of Wadler's Classical Processes (CP) [41], with details inspired by Carbone *et al.* [14] and Caires and Pérez [11].

Types. We start with types, which are based on CLL propositions. Let A, B range over types, given in Definition 1. Let $\mathsf{o}, \kappa \in \mathbb{N} \cup \{\omega\}$ range over *priorities*, which are used to annotate types. Let ω be a special element such that $\mathsf{o} < \omega$ for all $\mathsf{o} \in \mathbb{N}$. Often, we will omit ω. We will explain priorities later in this section.

Definition 1 (Types). *Types (A, B) are given by:*

$$A, B ::= \bot^{\mathsf{o}} \mid \mathbf{1}^{\mathsf{o}} \mid A \otimes^{\mathsf{o}} B \mid A \parr^{\mathsf{o}} B \mid \oplus^{\mathsf{o}}\{l_i : A_i\}_{i \in I} \mid \&^{\mathsf{o}}\{l_i : A_i\}_{i \in I} \mid ?^{\mathsf{o}} A \mid !^{\mathsf{o}} A$$

$\bot^{\mathsf{o}}$ and $\mathbf{1}^{\mathsf{o}}$ are associated with channel endpoints that are ready to be closed. $A \otimes^{\mathsf{o}} B$ (respectively, $A \parr^{\mathsf{o}} B$) is associated with a channel endpoint that first outputs (respectively, inputs) a channel of type A and then proceeds as B. $\oplus^{\mathsf{o}}\{l_i : A_i\}_{i \in I}$ is associated with a channel endpoint over which we can select a label from $\{l_i\}_{i \in I}$, and proceed as A_i. Dually, $\&^{\mathsf{o}}\{l_i : A_i\}_{i \in I}$ is associated with a channel endpoint that can offer a set of labelled types. $?^{\mathsf{o}} A$ types a collection of clients requesting A. Dually, $!^{\mathsf{o}} A$ types a server repeatedly accepting A.

Duality on types is total and is given in Definition 2. It preserves priorities of types.

Definition 2 (Duality). *The* duality *function* $(\cdot)^{\perp}$ *on types is given by:*

$$\begin{array}{rlrl}
(A \parr^{\mathsf{o}} B)^{\perp} &= A^{\perp} \otimes^{\mathsf{o}} B^{\perp} & (\bot^{\mathsf{o}})^{\perp} &= \mathbf{1}^{\mathsf{o}} \\
(A \otimes^{\mathsf{o}} B)^{\perp} &= A^{\perp} \parr^{\mathsf{o}} B^{\perp} & (\mathbf{1}^{\mathsf{o}})^{\perp} &= \bot^{\mathsf{o}} \\
(\&^{\mathsf{o}}\{l_i : A_i\}_{i \in I})^{\perp} &= \oplus^{\mathsf{o}}\{l_i : A_i^{\perp}\}_{i \in I} & ?^{\mathsf{o}} A^{\perp} &= !^{\mathsf{o}} A^{\perp} \\
(\oplus^{\mathsf{o}}\{l_i : A_i\}_{i \in I})^{\perp} &= \&^{\mathsf{o}}\{l_i : A_i^{\perp}\}_{i \in I} & !^{\mathsf{o}} A^{\perp} &= ?^{\mathsf{o}} A^{\perp}
\end{array}$$

Processes. Let P, Q range over processes, given in Definition 3. Let x, y range over channel endpoints, and $\mathbf{m}, \mathbf{n}$ over channel endpoints of type either $\bot^{\mathsf{o}}$ or $\mathbf{1}^{\mathsf{o}}$.

Definition 3 (Processes). *Processes (P, Q) are given by:*

$$\begin{array}{llll} P, Q ::= x[y].P & (output) & \mathbf{0} & (inaction) \\ \quad x(y).P & (input) & P \mid Q & (composition) \\ \quad x \triangleleft l_j.P & (selection) & (\boldsymbol{\nu} x^A y)P & (sessionrestriction) \\ \quad x \triangleright \{l_i : P_i\}_{i \in I} & (branching) & x[\,].\mathbf{0} & (emptyoutput) \\ \quad x \rightarrow y^A & (forwarding) & x().P & (emptyinput) \end{array}$$

Process $x[y].P$ (respectively, $x(y).P$) outputs (respectively, inputs) y on channel endpoint x, and proceeds as P. Process $x \triangleleft l_j.P$ uses x to select l_j from a labelled choice process, typically being $x \triangleright \{l_i : P_i\}_{i \in I}$, and triggers P_j; labels indexed by the finite set I are pairwise distinct. Process $x \rightarrow y^A$ forwards communications from x to y, the latter having type A. Processes also include the inaction process $\mathbf{0}$, the parallel composition of P and Q, denoted $P \mid Q$, and the double restriction constructor $(\boldsymbol{\nu} x^A y)P$: the intention is that x and y denote dual session channel endpoints in P, and A is the type of x. Processes $x[\,].\mathbf{0}$ and $x().P$ are the empty output and empty input, respectively. They denote the closure of a session from the viewpoint of each of the two communicating participants.

Notions of bound/free names in processes are standard; we write $\mathtt{fn}(P)$ to denote the set of free names of P. Also, we write $P\{x/z\}$ to denote the (capture-avoiding) substitution of x for the free occurrences of z in P. Finally, we let $\tilde{x}$, which is different from x, denote a sequence $x_1, \ldots, x_n$ for $n > 0$.

Typing Rules. Typing contexts, ranged over by Γ, Δ, Θ, are sets of typing assumptions $x : A$. We write Γ, Δ for union, requiring the contexts to be disjoint. A typing judgement $P \vdash \Gamma$ means "process P is well typed using context Γ".

Before presenting the typing rules, we need some auxiliary definitions. Our priorities are based on the annotations used by Kobayashi [32], but simplified to single priorities *à la* Padovani [37]. They obey the following laws:

(i) An action of priority o must be prefixed only by actions of priorities *strictly smaller than* o.
(ii) Communication requires *equal priorities* for the complementary actions.

Definition 4 (Priority). *The* priority *function* $\mathsf{pr}(\cdot)$ *on types is given by:*

$$\begin{array}{rcl} \mathsf{pr}(A \mathbin{\invamp}^{\mathsf{o}} B) = \mathsf{pr}(A \otimes^{\mathsf{o}} B) = \mathsf{o} & & \mathsf{pr}(\bot^{\mathsf{o}}) = \mathsf{pr}(\mathbf{1}^{\mathsf{o}}) = \mathsf{o} \\ \mathsf{pr}(\oplus^{\mathsf{o}}\{l_i : A_i\}_{i \in I}) = \mathsf{pr}(\&^{\mathsf{o}}\{l_i : A_i\}_{i \in I}) = \mathsf{o} & & \mathsf{pr}(\,?^{\mathsf{o}} A) = \mathsf{pr}(\,!^{\mathsf{o}} A) = \mathsf{o} \end{array}$$

Definition 5 (Lift). *Let $t \in \mathbb{N}$. The* lift *operator* $\uparrow^t(\cdot)$ *on types is given by:*

$$\begin{array}{ll} \uparrow^t(A \mathbin{\invamp}^{\mathsf{o}} B) = (\uparrow^t A) \mathbin{\invamp}^{(\mathsf{o}+t)} (\uparrow^t B) & \uparrow^t \bot^{\mathsf{o}} = \mathbf{1}^{(\mathsf{o}+t)} \\ \uparrow^t(A \otimes^{\mathsf{o}} B) = (\uparrow^t A) \otimes^{(\mathsf{o}+t)} (\uparrow^t B) & \uparrow^t \mathbf{1}^{\mathsf{o}} = \bot^{(\mathsf{o}+t)} \\ \uparrow^t(\&^{\mathsf{o}}\{l_i : A_i\}_{i \in I}) = \&^{(\mathsf{o}+t)}\{l_i : \uparrow^t A_i\}_{i \in I} & \uparrow^t(\,?^{\mathsf{o}} A) = \,?^{(\mathsf{o}+t)}(\uparrow^t A) \\ \uparrow^t(\oplus^{\mathsf{o}}\{l_i : A_i\}_{i \in I}) = \oplus^{(\mathsf{o}+t)}\{l_i : \uparrow^t A_i\}_{i \in I} & \uparrow^t(\,!^{\mathsf{o}} A) = \,!^{(\mathsf{o}+t)}(\uparrow^t A) \end{array}$$

We assume $\omega + t = \omega$ for all $t \in \mathbb{N}$.
The operator $\uparrow^t$ is extended component-wise to typing contexts: $\uparrow^t \Gamma$.

$$\frac{}{x \to y^A \vdash x : A^\perp, y : A}\ \textsc{Ax} \qquad \frac{P \vdash \Gamma \quad Q \vdash \Delta}{P \mid Q \vdash \Gamma, \Delta}\ \textsc{Mix} \qquad \frac{P \vdash \Gamma, x : A, y : A^\perp}{(\boldsymbol{\nu} x^A y)P \vdash \Gamma}\ \textsc{Cycle}$$

$$\frac{}{\mathbf{0} \vdash \emptyset}\ \emptyset \qquad \frac{}{x[].\mathbf{0} \vdash x : \mathbf{1}^{\mathsf{o}}}\ \mathbf{1} \qquad \frac{P \vdash \Gamma \quad \mathsf{o} < \mathsf{pr}(\Gamma)}{x().P \vdash x : \bot^{\mathsf{o}}, \Gamma}\ \bot$$

$$\frac{P \vdash \Gamma, y : A, x : B \quad \mathsf{o} < \mathsf{pr}(\Gamma)}{x(y).P \vdash \Gamma, x : A \mathbin{⅋^{\mathsf{o}}} B}\ ⅋ \qquad \frac{P \vdash \Gamma, y : A, x : B \quad \mathsf{o} < \mathsf{pr}(\Gamma)}{x[y].P \vdash \Gamma, x : A \otimes^{\mathsf{o}} B}\ \otimes$$

$$\frac{\forall i \in I.(P_i \vdash \Gamma, x : A_i) \quad \mathsf{o} < \mathsf{pr}(\Gamma)}{x \rhd \{l_i : P_i\}_{i \in I} \vdash \Gamma, x : \&^{\mathsf{o}}\{l_i : A_i\}_{i \in I}}\ \& \qquad \frac{P \vdash \Gamma, x : A_j \quad j \in I \quad \mathsf{o} < \mathsf{pr}(\Gamma)}{x \lhd l_j.P \vdash \Gamma, x : \oplus^{\mathsf{o}}\{l_i : A_i\}_{i \in I}}\ \oplus$$

$$\frac{P \vdash ?\Gamma, y : A \quad \mathsf{o} < \mathsf{pr}(?\Gamma)}{!x(y).P \vdash ?\Gamma, x : !^{\mathsf{o}} A}\ ! \qquad \frac{P \vdash \Gamma, y : A \quad \mathsf{o} < \mathsf{pr}(\Gamma)}{?x[y].P \vdash \Gamma, x : ?^{\mathsf{o}} A}\ ?$$

$$\frac{P \vdash \Gamma}{P \vdash \Gamma, x : ?^{\mathsf{o}} A}\ \mathrm{W} \qquad \frac{P \vdash \Gamma, y : ?^{\kappa} A, z : ?^{\kappa'} A \quad \mathsf{o} \le \kappa \quad \mathsf{o} \le \kappa' \quad \mathsf{o} < \mathsf{pr}(\Gamma)}{P\{x/y, x/z\} \vdash \Gamma, x : ?^{\mathsf{o}} A}\ \mathrm{C}$$

Fig. 2. Typing rules for PCP.

The typing rules are given in Fig. 2. Ax states that the forwarding process $x \to y^A$ is well typed if x and y have dual types, respectively $A^\perp$ and A. Mix types the parallel composition of two processes P and Q in the union of their disjoint typing contexts. Cycle is our key typing rule; it states that the restriction process is well typed, if the endpoints x and y have dual types, respectively A and $A^\perp$. By Definition 2, A and $A^\perp$ also have the same priorities, enforcing law (ii) above. In classical logic this rule would be unsound, but in PLL it allows deadlock-free cycles. Rule $\emptyset$ states that inaction is well typed in the empty context. Rules $\mathbf{1}$ and $\bot$ type channel closure actions from the viewpoint of each participant. Rule ⅋ (respectively $\otimes$) types an input process $x(y).P$ (respectively, output process $x[y].P$), with y bound and x of type $A \mathbin{⅋^{\mathsf{o}}} B$ (respectively, $A \otimes^{\mathsf{o}} B$). The priority o is strictly smaller than any priorities in the continuation process P, enforcing law (i) above. This is captured by $\mathsf{o} < \mathsf{pr}(\Gamma)$ in the premises of both rules, abbreviating "for all $z \in \mathtt{dom}(\Gamma), \mathsf{o} < \mathsf{pr}(\Gamma(z))$". Rules & and $\oplus$ type external and internal choice, respectively, and follow the previous two rules. Rule ! types a server and states that if P communicates along y following protocol A, then $!x(y).P$ communicates along x following protocol $!^{\mathsf{o}} A$. The three remaining rules type different numbers of clients. Rule ? is for a single client: if P communicates along y following A, then $?x[y].P$ communicates along x following $?^{\mathsf{o}} A$. Rule W is for no client: if P does not communicate along any channel following A, then it may be regarded as communicating along x following $?^{\mathsf{o}} A$, for some priority o. Rule C is for multiple clients: if P communicates along y following $?^{\kappa} A$, and z following protocol $?^{\kappa'} A$, then $P\{x/y, x/z\}$ communicates along a single channel x following $?^{\mathsf{o}} A$, where $\mathsf{o} \leqslant \kappa$ and $\mathsf{o} \leqslant \kappa'$. The last two conditions are necessary to deal with some cases in the proof of Cycle-elimination (Theorem 1).

Lifting preserves typability, by an easy induction on typing derivations.

Lemma 1. *If* $P \vdash \Gamma$ *then* $P \vdash \uparrow^t \Gamma$.

We will use this result in the form of an admissible rule: $\dfrac{P \vdash \Gamma}{P \vdash \uparrow^t \Gamma}\ \uparrow^t$

The Design of PCP. We have included Mix and Cycle, which allow derivation of both the standard Cut and the Multicut by Abramsky *et al.* [2].

$$\left.\dfrac{\dfrac{\vdash \Gamma, A_1, \ldots, A_n \quad \vdash \Delta, A_1^\perp, \ldots, A_n^\perp}{\vdash \Gamma, \Delta, A_1, \ldots, A_n, A_1^\perp, \ldots, A_n^\perp}\ \textsc{Mix}}{\vdash \Gamma, \Delta}\ \textsc{Cycle}^n\right\}\textsc{Multicut}$$

Conversely, Mix is the nullary case of Multicut, and Cycle can be derived from Ax and Multicut:

$$\left.\dfrac{\vdash \Gamma, A, A^\perp \quad \dfrac{}{\vdash A^\perp, A}\ \textsc{Ax}}{\vdash \Gamma}\ \textsc{Multicut}\right\}\textsc{Cycle}$$

Having included Mix, we choose Cycle instead of Multicut, as Cycle is more primitive.

In the presence of Mix and Cycle, there is an isomorphism between $A \otimes B$ and $A \parr B$ in CLL. Both $A \otimes B \multimap A \parr B$ and $A \parr B \multimap A \otimes B$, are derivable, where $C \multimap D \triangleq C^\perp \parr D$ in CLL. Equivalently, both $(A^\perp \parr B^\perp) \parr (A \parr B)$ and $(A^\perp \otimes B^\perp) \parr (A \otimes B)$ are derivable. For simplicity, let $\mathsf{pr}(A) = \mathsf{pr}(B) = \omega$; by duality also $\mathsf{pr}(A^\perp) = \mathsf{pr}(B^\perp) = \omega$.

$$\dfrac{\dfrac{\dfrac{\dfrac{\dfrac{}{\vdash A^\perp, A} \quad \dfrac{}{\vdash B^\perp, B}}{\vdash A^\perp, B^\perp, A, B}\ \textsc{Mix} \quad \mathsf{o}_1 < \omega}{\vdash A^\perp \parr^{\mathsf{o}_1} B^\perp, A, B}\ \parr \quad \mathsf{o}_2 < \mathsf{o}_1}{\vdash A^\perp \parr^{\mathsf{o}_1} B^\perp, A \parr^{\mathsf{o}_2} B}\ \parr}{\vdash (A^\perp \parr^{\mathsf{o}_1} B^\perp) \parr^{\mathsf{o}} (A \parr^{\mathsf{o}_2} B)}\ \parr$$

$$\dfrac{\dfrac{\dfrac{\dfrac{\dfrac{\dfrac{}{\vdash A^\perp, A} \quad \dfrac{}{\vdash B^\perp, B}}{\vdash A^\perp, B^\perp, A, B}\ \textsc{Mix} \quad \mathsf{o}_1 < \omega}{\vdash A^\perp \otimes^{\mathsf{o}_1} B^\perp, A, B}\ \otimes \quad \dfrac{\dfrac{\dfrac{}{\vdash A^\perp, A} \quad \dfrac{}{\vdash B^\perp, B}}{\vdash A^\perp, B^\perp, A, B}\ \textsc{Mix} \quad \mathsf{o}_2 < \omega}{\vdash A^\perp, B^\perp, A \otimes^{\mathsf{o}_2} B}\ \otimes}{\vdash A^\perp \otimes^{\mathsf{o}_1} B^\perp, A \otimes^{\mathsf{o}_2} B, A^\perp, A, B^\perp, B}\ \textsc{Mix}}{\vdash A^\perp \otimes^{\mathsf{o}_1} B^\perp, A \otimes^{\mathsf{o}_2} B}\ \textsc{Cycle}^2}{\vdash (A^\perp \otimes^{\mathsf{o}_1} B^\perp) \parr^{\mathsf{o}} (A \otimes^{\mathsf{o}_2} B)}\ \parr$$

The above derivations *without* priorities show the isomorphism between $A \otimes B$ and $A \parr B$ in CLL, which does not hold in our PLL, in particular as $\mathsf{o}_1 \neq \mathsf{o}_2$. The distinction between $\otimes$ and $\parr$, preserves the distinction between output and input in the term assignment. However, to simplify derivations, both typing rules (Fig. 2) have the same form. The usual tensor rule, where there are two separate derivations in the premise rather than just one, is derivable by using Mix.

Our type system performs priority-checking. Priorities can be inferred, as in Kobayashi's type system [32] and the tool TyPiCal [28]. We have opted for priority checking over priority inference, as the presentation is more elegant.

The following two examples illustrate the use of priorities. We first establish the structure of the typing derivation, then calculate the priorities. We conclude the section by showing the typing for the cyclic scheduler from Sect. 1.

Example 2 (Cyclic process: deadlock-free). Consider the following process

$$P \triangleq (\boldsymbol{\nu} x_1 y_1)(\boldsymbol{\nu} x_2 y_2)\big[x_1(v).x_2(w).R \mid y_1[\mathbf{n}].y_2[\mathbf{n}'].Q\big]$$

where $R \triangleq x_1().v().x_2().w().\mathbf{0}$ and $Q \triangleq y_1[].\mathbf{0} \mid \mathbf{n}[].\mathbf{0} \mid y_2[].\mathbf{0} \mid \mathbf{n}'[].\mathbf{0}$. First, we show the typing derivation for the left-hand side of the parallel, $x_1(v).x_2(w).R$:

$$\dfrac{\dfrac{\dfrac{\dfrac{}{\mathbf{0} \vdash \emptyset}\;\emptyset \qquad \kappa_4 < \kappa_3 < \kappa_2 < \kappa_1}{R \vdash x_1 \colon \bot^{\kappa_4}\; v \colon \bot^{\kappa_3}, x_2 \colon \bot^{\kappa_2}, w \colon \bot^{\kappa_1}}\;\bot^4 \qquad o_1 < \kappa_4}{x_2(w).R \vdash x_1 \colon \bot^{\kappa_4}, v \colon \bot^{\kappa_3}, x_2 \colon \bot^{\kappa_1} \parr^{o_1} \bot^{\kappa_2}}\;\parr \qquad o_2 < o_1}{x_1(v).x_2(w).R \vdash x_2 \colon \bot^{\kappa_1} \parr^{o_1} \bot^{\kappa_2}, x_1 \colon \bot^{\kappa_3} \parr^{o_2} \bot^{\kappa_4}}\;\parr \tag{1}$$

Now, the typing derivation for the right-hand side of the parallel, $y_1[\mathbf{n}].y_2[\mathbf{n}'].Q$, and recall that $\kappa_4 < \kappa_3 < \kappa_2 < \kappa_1$:

$$\dfrac{\dfrac{\dfrac{\dfrac{}{y_1[].\mathbf{0} \vdash y_1 : \mathbf{1}^{\kappa_4}}\;\mathbf{1} \quad \dfrac{}{\mathbf{n}[].\mathbf{0} \vdash \mathbf{n} \colon \mathbf{1}^{\kappa_3}}\;\mathbf{1} \quad \dfrac{}{y_2[].\mathbf{0} \vdash y_1 : \mathbf{1}^{\kappa_2}}\;\mathbf{1} \quad \dfrac{}{\mathbf{n}'[].\mathbf{0} \vdash \mathbf{n}' \colon \mathbf{1}^{\kappa_1}}\;\mathbf{1}}{y_1[].\mathbf{0} \mid \mathbf{n}[].\mathbf{0} \mid y_2[].\mathbf{0} \mid \mathbf{n}'[].\mathbf{0} \vdash y_1 \colon \mathbf{1}^{\kappa_4}, \mathbf{n} \colon \mathbf{1}^{\kappa_3}, y_2 \colon \mathbf{1}^{\kappa_2}, \mathbf{n}' \colon \mathbf{1}^{\kappa_1}}\;\textsc{Mix}^3 \qquad o_3 < \kappa_4}{y_2[\mathbf{n}'].Q \vdash y_1 \colon \mathbf{1}^{\kappa_4}, \mathbf{n} \colon \mathbf{1}^{\kappa_3}, y_2 \colon \mathbf{1}^{\kappa_1} \otimes^{o_3} \mathbf{1}^{\kappa_2}}\;\otimes \qquad o_4 < o_3}{y_1[\mathbf{n}].y_2[\mathbf{n}'].Q \vdash y_2 \colon \mathbf{1}^{\kappa_1} \otimes^{o_3} \mathbf{1}^{\kappa_2}, y_1 \colon \mathbf{1}^{\kappa_3} \otimes^{o_4} \mathbf{1}^{\kappa_4}}\;\otimes \tag{2}$$

Finally, the typing derivation for process P is as follows:

$$\dfrac{\dfrac{\dfrac{(1) \qquad\qquad (2)}{\begin{array}{l} x_1(v).x_2(w).R \mid y_1[\mathbf{n}].y_2[\mathbf{n}'].Q \vdash \\ \quad x_2 \colon \bot^{\kappa_1} \parr^{o_1} \bot^{\kappa_2}, x_1 \colon \bot^{\kappa_3} \parr^{o_2} \bot^{\kappa_4}, y_2 \colon \mathbf{1}^{\kappa_1} \otimes^{o_3} \mathbf{1}^{\kappa_2}, y_1 \colon \mathbf{1}^{\kappa_3} \otimes^{o_4} \mathbf{1}^{\kappa_4} \end{array}}\;\textsc{Mix} \qquad o_1 = o_3}{\begin{array}{l} (\boldsymbol{\nu} x_2 y_2)\big[x_1(v).x_2(w).R \mid y_1[\mathbf{n}].y_2[\mathbf{n}'].Q\big] \vdash \\ \quad x_1 \colon \bot^{\kappa_3} \parr^{o_2} \bot^{\kappa_4}, y_1 \colon \mathbf{1}^{\kappa_3} \otimes^{o_4} \mathbf{1}^{\kappa_4} \end{array}}\;\textsc{Cycle} \qquad o_2 = o_4}{(\boldsymbol{\nu} x_1 y_1)(\boldsymbol{\nu} x_2 y_2)\big[x_1(v).x_2(w).R \mid y_1[\mathbf{n}].y_2[\mathbf{n}'].Q\big] \vdash \emptyset}\;\textsc{Cycle}$$

The system of equations

$$o_2 < o_1 \qquad o_4 < o_3 \qquad o_1 = o_3 \qquad o_2 = o_4$$

can be solved by the assignment $o_1 = o_3 = 1$ and $o_2 = o_4 = 0$.

Example 3 (Cyclic process: deadlocked!). Now consider the process

$$P' = (\boldsymbol{\nu} x_1 y_1)(\boldsymbol{\nu} x_2 y_2)\big[x_1(v).x_2(w).R \mid y_2[\mathbf{n}'].y_1[\mathbf{n}].Q\big]$$

where $R = x_1().v().x_2().w().\mathbf{0}$ and $Q = y_1[].\mathbf{0} \mid \mathbf{n}[].\mathbf{0} \mid y_2[].\mathbf{0} \mid \mathbf{n}'[].\mathbf{0}$. Notice that the order of actions on channels y_1 and y_2 is now swapped, thus causing a deadlock! If we tried to construct a typing derivation for process P', we would have for the right-hand side of the parallel the following:

$$\dfrac{\dfrac{\dfrac{\dfrac{}{y_1[].\mathbf{0} \vdash y_1 : \mathbf{1}^{\kappa_4}}\ \mathbf{1} \quad \dfrac{}{\mathbf{n}[].\mathbf{0} \vdash \mathbf{n} : \mathbf{1}^{\kappa_3}}\ \mathbf{1} \quad \dfrac{}{y_2[].\mathbf{0} \vdash y_1 : \mathbf{1}^{\kappa_2}}\ \mathbf{1} \quad \dfrac{}{\mathbf{n}'[].\mathbf{0} \vdash \mathbf{n}' : \mathbf{1}^{\kappa_1}}\ \mathbf{1}}{y_1[].\mathbf{0} \mid \mathbf{n}[].\mathbf{0} \mid y_2[].\mathbf{0} \mid \mathbf{n}'[].\mathbf{0} \vdash y_1 : \mathbf{1}^{\kappa_4}, \mathbf{n} : \mathbf{1}^{\kappa_3}, y_2 : \mathbf{1}^{\kappa_2}, \mathbf{n}' : \mathbf{1}^{\kappa_1} \qquad \mathsf{o}_4 < \kappa_4}\ \textsc{Mix}^3}{y_1[\mathbf{n}].Q \vdash \mathbf{n}' : \mathbf{1}^{\kappa_1}, y_2 : \mathbf{1}^{\kappa_2}, y_1 : \mathbf{1}^{\kappa_3} \otimes^{\mathsf{o}_4} \mathbf{1}^{\kappa_4} \qquad \mathsf{o}_3 < \mathsf{o}_4}\ \otimes}{y_2[\mathbf{n}'].y_1[\mathbf{n}].Q \vdash y_1 : \mathbf{1}^{\kappa_3} \otimes^{\mathsf{o}_4} \mathbf{1}^{\kappa_4}, y_2 : \mathbf{1}^{\kappa_1} \otimes^{\mathsf{o}_3} \mathbf{1}^{\kappa_2}}\ \otimes$$

Then, the system of equations

$$\mathsf{o}_2 < \mathsf{o}_1 \qquad \mathsf{o}_3 < \mathsf{o}_4 \qquad \mathsf{o}_1 = \mathsf{o}_3 \qquad \mathsf{o}_2 = \mathsf{o}_4$$

has no solution because it requires $\mathsf{o}_2 < \mathsf{o}_3$ and $\mathsf{o}_3 < \mathsf{o}_2$, which is impossible.

Example 1 continued (Cyclic Scheduler)

$$\begin{array}{rll} Sched & \triangleq ...(\boldsymbol{\nu} a_i b_i)...(\boldsymbol{\nu} c_i d_{(i+1) \bmod n})(A_0 \mid A_1 \mid ... \mid A_{n-1} \mid P_0 \mid P_1 \mid ... \mid P_{n-1}) & \\ A_0 & \triangleq c_0[\mathbf{n}_0].d_0(x_0).a_0[\mathbf{m}_0].\mathsf{close}_0 & \\ A_i & \triangleq d_i(x_i).a_i[\mathbf{m}_i].c_i[\mathbf{n}_i].\mathsf{close}_i & i \in \{1, ..., n-1\} \\ P_i & \triangleq b_i(y_i).Q_i & i \in \{0, ..., n-1\} \end{array}$$

By applying the typing rules in Fig. 2 we can derive $Sched \vdash \emptyset$, since it is a closed process, and assign the following types and priorities:

$$\begin{array}{llll} c_0 : \mathbf{1} \otimes^0 \mathbf{1} & d_0 : \bot \,⅋^{2(n-1)} \bot & a_0 : \mathbf{1} \otimes^{2(n-1)+1} \mathbf{1} & \text{for } A_0 \\ d_i : \bot \,⅋^{2i-2} \bot & a_i : \mathbf{1} \otimes^{2i-1} \mathbf{1} & c_i : \mathbf{1} \otimes^{2i} \mathbf{1} & \text{for } A_i,\ 0 < i < n \\ b_0 : \bot \,⅋^{2(n-1)+1} \bot & b_i : \bot \,⅋^{2i-1} \bot & & \text{for } P_0 \text{ and } P_i,\ 0 < i < n \end{array}$$

The priorities of types $\bot$ and $\mathbf{1}$ could be easily assigned as Example 2. As the priority of d_{i+1} is $2(i+1) - 2 = 2i$, we can connect it to a_i with a CYCLE.

3 Operational Semantics of PCP

In this section we define structural equivalence, the principal β-reduction rules and commuting conversions. The detailed derivations can be found in [18].

We define structural equivalence to be the smallest congruence relation satisfying the following axioms. SC-AX-SWP allows swapping channels in the forwarding process. SC-AX-CYCLE states that cycle applied to a forwarding process is equivalent to inaction. This allows elimination of unnecessary cycles. Axioms SC-MIX-NIL, SC-MIX-COMM and SC-MIX-ASC state that parallel composition uses the inaction as the neutral element and is commutative and associative. SC-CYCLE-EXT is the standard scope extrusion rule. SC-CYCLE-SWP allows swapping channels and SC-CYCLE-COMM states the commutativity of restriction[1].

[1] Note that associativity of restriction is derived from SC-MIX-COMM and SC-CYCLE-COMM.

$$\begin{array}{ll}
\textsc{SC-Ax-Swp} & x \to y^{A} \vdash x{:}A^{\perp}, y{:}A \;\equiv\; y \to x^{A^{\perp}} \vdash x{:}A^{\perp}, y{:}A \\
\textsc{SC-Ax-Cycle} & (\boldsymbol{\nu} x^{A^{\perp}} y)\, x \to y^{A} \vdash \emptyset \;\equiv\; \mathbf{0} \vdash \emptyset \\
\textsc{SC-Mix-Nil} & \mathbf{0} \mid P \vdash \Gamma \;\equiv\; P \vdash \Gamma \\
\textsc{SC-Mix-Comm} & P \mid Q \vdash \Gamma, \Delta \;\equiv\; Q \mid P \vdash \Gamma, \Delta \\
\textsc{SC-Mix-Asc} & P \mid (Q \mid R) \vdash \Gamma, \Delta, \Theta \;\equiv\; (P \mid Q) \mid R \vdash \Gamma, \Delta, \Theta \\
\textsc{SC-Cycle-Ext} & (\boldsymbol{\nu} x^{A} y)(P \mid Q) \vdash \Gamma, \Delta \;\equiv\; P \mid (\boldsymbol{\nu} x^{A} y) Q \vdash \Gamma, \Delta \quad x, y \notin \mathtt{fn}(P) \\
\textsc{SC-Cycle-Swp} & (\boldsymbol{\nu} x^{A} y) P \vdash \Gamma \;\equiv\; (\boldsymbol{\nu} y^{A^{\perp}} x) P \vdash \Gamma \\
\textsc{SC-Cycle-Comm} & (\boldsymbol{\nu} x^{A} y)(\boldsymbol{\nu} z^{B} w) P \vdash \Gamma \;\equiv\; (\boldsymbol{\nu} z^{B} w)(\boldsymbol{\nu} x^{A} y) P \vdash \Gamma
\end{array}$$

The core of the operational semantics consists of β-reductions. In π-calculus terms these are communication steps; in logical terms they are Cycle-elimination steps. $\beta_{\otimes ⅋}$ is given in Fig. 3 to illustrate priorities. It simplifies a cycle connecting x of type $A \otimes^{\circ} B$ and y of type $A ⅋^{\circ} B$, which corresponds to communication between an output on x and an input on y, respectively. Both actions have priority o, which is strictly smaller than any priorities in their typing contexts, respecting the fact that they are top-level prefixes. The remaining β-reductions are summarised below. $\beta_{\textsc{AxCycle}}$ simplifies a Cycle involving an axiom. $\beta_{\mathbf{1}\perp}$ closes and eliminates channels. $\beta_{\oplus \&}$, similarly to $\beta_{\otimes ⅋}$, simplifies a communication between a selection and a branching. $\beta_{!?}$ simplifies a cycle between one server of type $!^{\circ} A$ and one client of type $?^{\circ} A$. The last two rules differ in the number of clients involved: rule $\beta_{!\mathrm{W}}$ considers no clients, whether $\beta_{!\mathrm{C}}$ considers multiple clients.

$$\begin{array}{rl}
\beta_{\textsc{AxCycle}} & (\boldsymbol{\nu} y^{A} z)(x \to y^{A} \mid P) \vdash \Gamma, x{:}A^{\perp} \;\longrightarrow\; P\{x/z\} \vdash \Gamma, x{:}A^{\perp} \\
\beta_{\mathbf{1}\perp} & (\boldsymbol{\nu} x^{A} y)(x[\,].\mathbf{0} \mid y().P) \vdash \Gamma \;\longrightarrow\; P \vdash \Gamma \\
\beta_{\oplus \&} & (\boldsymbol{\nu} x^{\oplus^{\circ}\{l_i : B_i\}_{i \in I}} y)\big(x \triangleleft l_j.P \mid y \triangleright \{l_i : Q_i\}_{i \in I}\big) \vdash \Gamma, \Delta \longrightarrow \\
 & \qquad (\boldsymbol{\nu} x^{B_j} y)\big(P \mid Q_j\big) \vdash \Gamma, \Delta \\
\beta_{!?} & (\boldsymbol{\nu} x^{!^{\circ} A} y)\big(!x(v).P \mid ?y[w].Q\big) \vdash ?\Gamma, \Delta \;\longrightarrow\; (\boldsymbol{\nu} v^{A} w)\big(P \mid Q\big) \vdash ?\Gamma, \Delta \\
\beta_{!\mathrm{W}} & (\boldsymbol{\nu} x^{!^{\circ} A} y)\big(!x(v).P \mid Q\big) \vdash ?\Gamma, \Delta \;\longrightarrow\; Q \vdash ?\Gamma, \Delta \\
\beta_{!\mathrm{C}} & (\boldsymbol{\nu} x^{!^{\circ} A} y)\big(!x(v).P \mid Q\{y/y', y/y''\}\big) \vdash ?\Gamma, \Delta \;\longrightarrow \\
 & (\boldsymbol{\nu} x'^{\,!^{\circ} A} y')(!x'(v').P' \mid (\boldsymbol{\nu} x''^{\,!^{\circ} A} y'')(!x''(v'').P'' \mid Q)) \vdash ?\Gamma, \Delta
\end{array}$$

$$\dfrac{\dfrac{\dfrac{\mathsf{o} < \mathsf{pr}(\Gamma) \quad P \vdash \Gamma, v{:}A, x{:}B}{x[v].P \vdash \Gamma, x{:}A \otimes^{\circ} B}\otimes \qquad \dfrac{\mathsf{o} < \mathsf{pr}(\Delta) \quad Q \vdash \Delta, w{:}A^{\perp}, y{:}B^{\perp}}{y(w).Q \vdash \Delta, y{:}A^{\perp} ⅋^{\circ} B^{\perp}}⅋}{x[v].P \mid y(w).Q \vdash \Gamma, \Delta, x{:}A \otimes^{\circ} B, y{:}A^{\perp} ⅋^{\circ} B^{\perp}}\textsc{Mix}}{(\boldsymbol{\nu} x^{A \otimes^{\circ} B} y)\big(x[v].P \mid y(w).Q\big) \vdash \Gamma, \Delta}\textsc{Cycle}$$

$$\longrightarrow \quad \dfrac{\dfrac{P \vdash \Gamma, v{:}A, x{:}B \qquad Q \vdash \Delta, w{:}A^{\perp}, y{:}B^{\perp}}{P \mid Q \vdash \Gamma, \Delta, v{:}A, x : B, w{:}A^{\perp}, y : B^{\perp}}\textsc{Mix}}{(\boldsymbol{\nu} v^{A} w)(\boldsymbol{\nu} x^{B} y)\big(P \mid Q\big) \vdash \Gamma, \Delta}\textsc{Cycle}^{2}$$

Fig. 3. β-reduction for $\otimes$ and ⅋.

Commuting conversions, following [12,41], allow communication prefixes to be moved to the conclusion of a typing derivation, corresponding to pulling them out of the scope of Cycle rules. In order to account for the sequence of Cycles, here we use $\widetilde{\cdot}$. Due to this movement, if a prefix on a channel endpoint x with priority o is pulled out at top level, then to preserve priority conditions in the typing rules in Fig. 2, it is necessary to increase priorities of all actions after the prefix on x. This increase is achieved by using $\uparrow^{\mathsf{o}+1}(\cdot)$ in the typing contexts.

$$
\begin{array}{ll}
\kappa_{\bot} & (\boldsymbol{\nu}\widetilde{x^{A}y})(x().P \mid Q) \vdash \Gamma, \Delta, x{:}\,\bot^{\mathsf{o}} \longrightarrow \\
& \qquad x().[(\boldsymbol{\nu}\widetilde{x^{A}y})(P \mid Q)] \vdash \uparrow^{\mathsf{o}+1}\Gamma, \uparrow^{\mathsf{o}+1}\Delta, x{:}\,\bot^{\mathsf{o}} \\
\kappa_{\otimes} & (\boldsymbol{\nu}\widetilde{x^{A}y})(x[v].P \mid Q) \vdash \Gamma, \Delta, x{:}A \otimes^{\mathsf{o}} B \longrightarrow \\
& x[v].\big[(\boldsymbol{\nu}\widetilde{x^{A}y})(P \mid Q)\big] \vdash (\uparrow^{\mathsf{o}+1}\Gamma),\ (\uparrow^{\mathsf{o}+1}\Delta),\ x{:}(\uparrow^{\mathsf{o}+1}A) \otimes^{\mathsf{o}} (\uparrow^{\mathsf{o}+1}B) \\
\kappa_{⅋} & (\boldsymbol{\nu}\widetilde{x^{A}y})(x(w).P \mid Q) \vdash \Gamma, \Delta, x{:}A ⅋^{\mathsf{o}} B \longrightarrow \\
& x(w).\big[(\boldsymbol{\nu}\widetilde{x^{A}y})(P \mid Q)\big] \vdash (\uparrow^{\mathsf{o}+1}\Gamma),\ (\uparrow^{\mathsf{o}+1}\Delta),\ x{:}(\uparrow^{\mathsf{o}+1}A) ⅋^{\mathsf{o}} (\uparrow^{\mathsf{o}+1}B) \\
\kappa_{\oplus} & (\boldsymbol{\nu}\widetilde{x^{A}y})(x \triangleleft l_j.P \mid Q) \vdash \Gamma, \Delta, x{:}\oplus^{\mathsf{o}}\{l_i : B_i\}_{i\in I} \longrightarrow \\
& x \triangleleft l_j.\big[(\boldsymbol{\nu}\widetilde{x^{A}y})(P \mid Q)\big] \vdash (\uparrow^{\mathsf{o}+1}\Gamma),\ (\uparrow^{\mathsf{o}+1}\Delta),\ x{:}\oplus^{\mathsf{o}}\{l_i : \uparrow^{\mathsf{o}+1}B_i\}_{i\in I} \\
\kappa_{\&} & (\boldsymbol{\nu}\widetilde{x^{A}y})(x \triangleright \{l_i : P_i\}_{i\in I} \mid Q) \vdash \Gamma, \Delta, x{:}\&^{\mathsf{o}}\{l_i : B_i\}_{i\in I} \longrightarrow \\
& x \triangleright \{l_i : (\boldsymbol{\nu}\widetilde{x^{A}y})(P_i \mid Q)\}_{i\in I} \vdash (\uparrow^{\mathsf{o}+1}\Gamma),\ (\uparrow^{\mathsf{o}+1}\Delta),\ x{:}\&^{\mathsf{o}}\{l_i : \uparrow^{\mathsf{o}+1}B_i\}_{i\in I} \\
\kappa_{?} & (\boldsymbol{\nu}\widetilde{x^{A}y})(?x[w].P \mid Q) \vdash \Gamma,\ \Delta,\ x{:}\ ?^{\mathsf{o}}A \longrightarrow \\
& \qquad ?x[w].\big[(\boldsymbol{\nu}\widetilde{x^{A}y})(P \mid Q)\big] \vdash (\uparrow^{\mathsf{o}+1}\Gamma),\ (\uparrow^{\mathsf{o}+1}\Delta),\ x{:}\ ?^{\mathsf{o}}(\uparrow^{\mathsf{o}+1}A) \\
\kappa_{!} & (\boldsymbol{\nu}\widetilde{x^{?^{\mathsf{o}}A}y})(!x(v).P \mid Q) \vdash ?\Gamma,\ \Delta,\ x{:}\ !^{\mathsf{o}}A \longrightarrow \\
& \qquad !x(v).\big[(\boldsymbol{\nu}\widetilde{x^{?^{\mathsf{o}}A}y})(P \mid Q)\big] \vdash (\uparrow^{\mathsf{o}+1}\Gamma),\ (\uparrow^{\mathsf{o}+1}\Delta),\ x{:}\ !^{\mathsf{o}}(\uparrow^{\mathsf{o}+1}A)
\end{array}
$$

Finally, we give the following additional reduction rules: closure under structural equivalence, and two congruence rules, for restriction and for parallel.

$$
\begin{array}{ll}
\textsc{Close-Equiv} & P \equiv Q \quad Q \longrightarrow R \quad R \equiv S \ \text{ implies } \ P \longrightarrow S \\
\textsc{Cong-Cycle} & P \longrightarrow Q \ \text{ implies } \ (\boldsymbol{\nu}x^{A}y)P \longrightarrow (\boldsymbol{\nu}x^{A}y)Q \\
\textsc{Cong-Mix} & P \longrightarrow Q \ \text{ implies } \ P \mid R \longrightarrow Q \mid R
\end{array}
$$

4 Results for PLL and PCP

4.1 Cycle-Elimination for PLL

We start with results for Cycle-elimination for PLL; thus here we refer to A, B as propositions, rather than types. The detailed proofs can be found in [18].

Definition 6. *The* degree *function* $\partial(\cdot)$ *on propositions is defined by:*

- $\partial(\mathbf{1}^{\mathsf{o}}) = \partial(\bot^{\mathsf{o}}) = 1$
- $\partial(A \otimes^{\mathsf{o}} B) = \partial(A ⅋^{\mathsf{o}} B) = \partial(A) + \partial(B) + 1$
- $\partial(\&^{\mathsf{o}}\{l_i : A_i\}_{i\in I}) = \partial(\oplus^{\mathsf{o}}\{l_i : A_i\}_{i\in I}) = \sum_{i\in I}\{\partial(A_i)\} + 1$
- $\partial(\,?^{\mathsf{o}}A) = \partial(\,!^{\mathsf{o}}A) = \partial(A) + 1.$

Definition 7. *A* Maxicut *is a maximal sequence of* Mix *and* Cycle *rules, ending with a* Cycle *rule.*

Maximality means that the rules applied immediately before a MAXICUT are any rules in Fig. 2, other than MIX or CYCLE. The order in which MIX and CYCLE rules are applied within a MAXICUT is irrelevant. However, Proposition 1, which follows directly from structural equivalence (Sect. 3), allows us to simplify a MAXICUT.

Proposition 1 (Canonical MAXICUT). *Given an arbitrary* MAXICUT, *it is always possible to obtain from it a* canonical MAXICUT *consisting of a sequence of only* MIX *rules followed by a sequence of only* CYCLE *rules.*

Definition 8. *A* single-MIX MAXICUT *contains only one* MIX *rule.*
$A_1, \ldots, A_n, A$ *are* MAXICUT propositions *if they are eliminated by a* MAXICUT.
The degree of a sequence of CYCLES *is the sum of the degrees of the eliminated propositions.*
The degree of a MAXICUT *is the sum of the degrees of the* CYCLES *in it.*
The degree of a proof π, $d(\pi)$, *is the* sup *of the degrees of its* MAXICUTS, *implying* $d(\pi) = 0$ *if and only if proof* π *has no* CYCLES.
The height of a proof π, $h(\pi)$, *is the height of its tree, and it is defined as* $h(\pi) = \sup\big(h(\pi_i)\big)_{i \in I} + 1$, *where* $\{\pi_i\}_{i \in I}$ *are the subproofs of* π.

MAXICUT has some similarities with the derived MULTICUT: it generalises MULTICUT in the number of MIXES, and a single-MIX MAXICUT is an occurrence of MULTICUT.

The core of CYCLE-elimination for our PLL, as for CUT-elimination for CLL [10,25], is the Principal Lemma (Lemma 3), which eliminates a CYCLE by either (i) replacing it with another CYCLE on simpler propositions, or (ii) pushing it further up the proof tree. Item (i) corresponds to (the logical part of) β-reductions (Sect. 3); and (ii) corresponds to (the logical part of) commuting conversions (Sect. 3).

Exceptionally, $\beta_{!\mathrm{C}}$ reduces the original proof in a way that neither (i) nor (ii) are respected. In order to cope with this case, we introduce Lemma 2, which is inspired by Lemma B.1.3 in Bräuner [10], and adapted to our PLL. Lemma 2 allows us to reduce the degree of a proof ending with a single-MIX MAXICUT and having the same degree as the whole proof, and where the last rule applied on the left hand-side immediate subproof is !. Let $[n]$ denote the set $\{1, \ldots, n\}$.

Lemma 2 (Inspired by B.1.3 in Bräuner [10]). *Let* τ *be a proof of the following form, ending with a single-*MIX MAXICUT*:*

$$
\dfrac{\dfrac{\dfrac{\begin{array}{c}\pi\\ \vdots\\ \mathsf{o} < \mathsf{pr}(?\Gamma)\\ \forall i \in [n] : \mathsf{o} < \mathsf{o}_i\\ \vdash ?\Gamma,\ ?^{\mathsf{o}_1} A_1, \ldots, ?^{\mathsf{o}_n} A_n, A\end{array}}{\vdash ?\Gamma,\ ?^{\mathsf{o}_1} A_1, \ldots, ?^{\mathsf{o}_n} A_n,\ !^{\mathsf{o}} A}\ ! \qquad \dfrac{\begin{array}{c}\pi'\\ \vdots\\ \mathsf{o} < \mathsf{pr}(\Delta)\\ \forall i \in [n] : \mathsf{o} < \mathsf{o}_i \quad \forall j \in [k] : \mathsf{o} \leqslant \kappa_j\\ \vdash \Delta,\ !^{\mathsf{o}_1} A_1^{\perp}, \ldots, !^{\mathsf{o}_n} A_n^{\perp}, (?^{\kappa_j} A^{\perp})_{j \in [k]}\end{array}}{\vdash \Delta,\ !^{\mathsf{o}_1} A_1^{\perp}, \ldots, !^{\mathsf{o}_n} A_n^{\perp},\ ?^{\mathsf{o}} A^{\perp}}\ \mathrm{C}^{k-1}}{\vdash ?\Gamma, \Delta,\ ?^{\mathsf{o}_1} A_1, \ldots, ?^{\mathsf{o}_n} A_n,\ !^{\mathsf{o}} A,\ !^{\mathsf{o}_1} A_1^{\perp}, \ldots, !^{\mathsf{o}_n} A_n^{\perp},\ ?^{\mathsf{o}} A^{\perp}}\ \textsc{Mix}}{\vdash ?\Gamma, \Delta}\ \textsc{Cycle}
$$

where $d(\pi) < d(\tau)$ and $d(\pi') < d(\tau)$. Then, there is a proof τ' of $\vdash ?\Gamma, \Delta$ such that $d(\tau') < d(\tau)$.

Proof. Induction on $h(\pi')$, with a case-analysis on the last rule applied in π'. □

Lemma 3 (The Principal Lemma). *Let τ be a proof of $\vdash \Gamma$, ending with a canonical* MAXICUT*:*

$$\dfrac{\dfrac{\pi_1 \ldots \pi_m}{\vdash \Gamma, A_1, ..., A_n, A, A_1^\perp, ..., A_n^\perp, A^\perp}\ \text{MIX}}{\vdash \Gamma}\ \text{CYCLE}$$

such that for all $i \in [m]$, $d(\pi_i) < d(\tau)$. Then there is a proof τ' of $\vdash \uparrow^t \Gamma$, for some $t \geqslant 0$, such that $d(\tau') < d(\tau)$.

Proof. The proof is by induction on $\sum_{i\in[m]} h(\pi_i)$. Let r_i be the last rule applied in π_i, for $i \in [m]$ and let C_{r_i} be the proposition introduced by r_i. Consider the proposition with the *smallest* priority. If the proposition is not unique, just pick one. Let this proposition be C_{r_k}. Then, π_k is the following proof: $\dfrac{\cdots}{\vdash \Gamma', C_{r_k}}\ r_k$ We proceed by cases on π_k.

– r_k is $\otimes$ on one of the MAXICUT propositions $A_1, \ldots, A_n, A$. Without loss of generality, suppose r_k is applied on A, meaning $A = E \otimes^{\mathsf{o}} F$ for some E and F and $\mathsf{o} \geqslant 0$. By $\otimes$ rule in Fig. 2, $\mathsf{o} < \mathsf{pr}(\Gamma')$. Since A is a MAXICUT proposition, by Definition 2, $A^\perp = E^\perp \parr^{\mathsf{o}} F^\perp$. Since $\mathsf{o} < \mathsf{pr}(\Gamma')$ and $\mathsf{pr}(A^\perp) = \mathsf{o}$, it must be that $A^\perp$ is in another proof, say π_h: $\dfrac{\cdots}{\vdash \Gamma'', E^\perp \parr^{\mathsf{o}} F^\perp}\ r_h$

Consider the case where r_h is a multiplicative, additive, exponential or $\perp$ rule in Fig. 2. Suppose r_h is applied on C_{r_h} which is not $A^\perp$. All the mentioned rules require $\mathsf{pr}(C_{r_h}) < \mathsf{pr}(\Gamma'', E^\perp \parr^{\mathsf{o}} F^\perp \setminus C_{r_h})$, implying $\mathsf{pr}(C_{r_h}) < \mathsf{pr}(E^\perp \parr^{\mathsf{o}} F^\perp) = \mathsf{pr}(E \otimes^{\mathsf{o}} F) = \mathsf{o}$. This contradicts the fact that o is the smallest priority. Hence, r_h must be a $\parr$ introducing $A^\perp$.

We construct proof τ_A ending with a single-MIX MAXICUT applied on *at least* A:

$$\dfrac{\dfrac{\dfrac{\dfrac{\pi_\otimes}{\vdash \Gamma', E, F \quad \mathsf{o} < \mathsf{pr}(\Gamma')}}{\vdash \Gamma', E \otimes^{\mathsf{o}} F}\ \otimes \qquad \dfrac{\dfrac{\pi_\parr}{\vdash \Gamma'', E^\perp, F^\perp \quad \mathsf{o} < \mathsf{pr}(\Gamma'')}}{\vdash \Gamma'', E^\perp \parr^{\mathsf{o}} F^\perp}\ \parr}{\vdash \Gamma', \Gamma'', E \otimes^{\mathsf{o}} F, E^\perp \parr^{\mathsf{o}} F^\perp}\ \text{MIX}}{\vdash \Gamma'''}\ \text{CYCLE}$$

Then, by structural equivalence, we can rewrite τ in terms of τ_A. By applying $\beta_{\otimes\parr}$ on τ_A (only considering the logical part), we obtain a proof τ'_A such that $d(\tau'_A) < d(\tau_A) \leq d(\tau)$, because $\partial(E)+\partial(F) < \partial(E \otimes^{\mathsf{o}} F)$. We can then construct τ' by substituting τ'_A for τ_A in τ, which concludes this case.

– r_k is ! on one of the MAXICUT propositions $A_1, \ldots, A_n, A$. Without loss of generality, suppose r_k introduces A, implying that $A = !^{\mathsf{o}} A'$ for some A' and $\mathsf{o} \geqslant 0$. Then π_k is the following proof:

$$\dfrac{\begin{array}{c}\pi_! \\ \vdots \\ \vdash ?\Theta, A' \quad \mathsf{o} < \mathsf{pr}(?\Theta)\end{array}}{\vdash ?\Theta, !^{\mathsf{o}} A'}\ !$$

where $\Gamma' = ?\Theta$. Since A is a MAXICUT proposition, by duality $A^{\perp} = ?^{\mathsf{o}} A'^{\perp}$. Since $\mathsf{o} < \mathsf{pr}(\Gamma')$ and $\mathsf{pr}(A^{\perp}) = \mathsf{o}$, it must be that $A^{\perp}$ is in another proof. Let it be π_h for $h \in [m]$ and $h \neq k$. Then we apply Lemma 2 to π_k and π_h, obtaining a proof which we use to construct τ', as we did in the previous case. □

Lemma 4. *Given a proof τ of $\vdash \Gamma$, such that $d(\tau) > 0$, then for some $t \geqslant 0$ there is a proof τ' of $\vdash \uparrow^t \Gamma$ such that $d(\tau') < d(\tau)$.*

Proof. By induction on $h(\tau)$. We have the following cases.

– If τ ends in a MAXICUT whose degree is *the same as* the degree of τ:

$$\dfrac{\dfrac{\pi_1 \ldots \pi_m}{\vdash \Gamma, A_1, ..., A_n, A, A_1^{\perp}, ..., A_n^{\perp}, A^{\perp}}\ \text{MIX}^m}{\vdash \Gamma}\ \text{CYCLE}^{n+1}$$

we can apply the induction hypothesis to the subproofs of τ right before the last MIX preceding the sequence of CYCLE. This allows us to reduce their degrees to become smaller than $d(\tau)$. Then we use Lemma 3.

– Otherwise, by using the inductive hypothesis on the immediate subproofs to reduce their degree, we also reduce the degree of the whole proof. □

Theorem 1 (CYCLE-Elimination). *Given any proof of $\vdash \Gamma$, we can construct a CYCLE-free proof of $\vdash \uparrow^t \Gamma$, for some $t \geqslant 0$.*

Proof. Iteration on Lemma 4. □

CYCLE-elimination increases the priorities of the propositions in Γ. This is solely due to the (logical part of) our commuting conversions in Sect. 3.

4.2 Deadlock-Freedom for PCP

Theorem 2 (Subject Reduction). *If $P \vdash \Gamma$ and $P \longrightarrow Q$, then $Q \vdash \uparrow^t \Gamma$, for some $t \geqslant 0$.*

Proof. Follows from the β-reductions and commuting conversions in Sect. 3. □

Definition 9. *A process is a CYCLE if it is of the form $(\boldsymbol{\nu} x^A y)P$.*

Theorem 3 (Top-Level Deadlock-Freedom). *If $P \vdash \Gamma$ and P is a* Cycle, *then there is some Q such that $P \longrightarrow^* Q$ and Q is not a* Cycle.

Proof. The interpretation of Lemma 3 for PCP is that either (i) a top-level communication occurs, corresponding to a β-reduction, or (ii) commuting conversions are used to push Cycle further inwards in a process. Consequently, iterating Lemma 3 results in eliminating top-level Cycles. □

Eliminating all Cycles, as specified by Theorem 1, would correspond to a semantics in which reduction occurs under prefixes, as discussed by Wadler [41]. In order to achieve this, we would need to introduce additional congruence rules, such as:

$$\frac{P \longrightarrow Q}{x(y).P \longrightarrow x(y).Q}$$

and similarly for other actions. Reductions of this kind are not present in the π-calculus, and we also omit them in our framework.

However, we can eliminate all Cycles in a proof of $\vdash \emptyset$, corresponding to full deadlock-freedom for closed processes. Kobayashi's type system [32] satisfies the same property.

Theorem 4 (Deadlock-Freedom for Closed Processes). *If $P \vdash \emptyset$, then either $P \equiv \mathbf{0}$ or there is Q such that $P \longrightarrow Q$.*

Proof. This follows from Theorems 2 and 3, because if $Q \vdash \emptyset$ and Q is not a Cycle then Q must be a parallel composition of $\mathbf{0}$ processes. □

5 Related Work and Conclusion

Cycle and Multicut rules were explored by Abramsky *et al.* [2–4] in the context of $*$-autonomous categories. That work is not directly comparable with ours, as it only presented a typed semantics for CCS-like processes and did not give a type system for a language or a term assignment for a logical system. Atkey *et al.* [5] added a Multicut rule to CP, producing an isomorphism between $\otimes$ and $\invamp$, but they did not consider deadlock-freedom.

In Kobayashi's original type-theoretic approach to deadlock-freedom [29], priorities were abstract tags from a partially ordered set. In later work abstract tags were simplified to natural numbers, and priorities were replaced by pairs of obligations and capabilities [30,32]. The latter change allows more processes to be typed, at the expense of a more complex type system. Padovani [36] adapted Kobayashi's approach to session types, and later on he simplified it to a single priority for linear π-calculus [37]. Then, the single priority technique can be transferred to session types by the encoding of session types into linear types [16,17,19,33]. For simplicity, we have opted for single priorities, as Padovani [37].

The first work on progress for session types, by Dezani-Ciancaglini *et al.* [15,22], guaranteed the property by allowing only one active session at a time. Later work [21] introduced a partial order on channels in Kobayashi-style [29].

Bettini *et al.* [9] applied similar ideas to multiparty session types. The main difference with our work is that we associate priorities with individual communication operations, rather than with entire channels. Carbone *et al.* [13] proved that progress is a compositional form of lock-freedom and introduced a new technique for progress in session types by adopting Kobayashi's type system and the encoding of session types [19]. Vieira and Vasconcelos [40] used single priorities and an abstract partial order in session types to guarantee deadlock-freedom.

The linear logic approach to deadlock-free session types started with Caires and Pfenning [12], based on dual intuitionistic linear logic, and was later formulated for classical linear logic by Wadler [41]. All subsequent work on linear logic and session types enforces deadlock-freedom by forbidding cyclic connections. In their original work, Caires and Pfenning commented that it would be interesting to compare process typability in their system with other approaches including Kobayashi's and Dezani-Ciancaglini's. However, we are aware of only one comparative study of the expressivity of type systems for deadlock-freedom, by Dardha and Pérez [20]. They compared Kobayashi-style typing and CLL typing, and proved that CLL corresponds to Kobayashi's system with the restriction that only single cuts, not multicuts, are allowed.

In this paper, we have presented a new logic, priority-based linear logic (PLL), and a term assignment system, priority-based CP (PCP), that increase the expressivity of deadlock-free session type systems, by combining Caires and Pfenning's linear logic-based approach and Kobayashi's priority-based type system. The novel feature of PLL and PCP is CYCLE, which allows cyclic process structures to be formed if they do not violate ordering conditions on the priorities of prefixes. Following the propositions-as-types paradigm, we prove a CYCLE-elimination theorem analogous to the standard CUT-elimination theorem. As a result of this theorem, we obtain deadlock-freedom for a class of π-calculus processes which is larger than the class typed by Caires and Pfenning. In particular, these are processes that typically share more than one channel in parallel.

There are two main directions for future work. First, develop a type system for a functional language, priority-based GV, and translate it into PCP, along the lines of Lindley and Morris' [34] translation of GV [41] into CP. Second, extend PCP to allow recursion and sharing [6], in order to support more general concurrent programming, while maintaining deadlock-freedom, as well as termination, or typed behavioural equivalence.

Acknowledgements. We are grateful for suggestions and feedback from the anonymous reviewers and colleagues: Wen Kokke, Sam Lindley, Roly Perera, Frank Pfenning, Carsten Schürmann and Philip Wadler.

References

1. Abramsky, S.: Proofs as processes. Theor. Comput. Sci. **135**(1), 5–9 (1994)
2. Abramsky, S., Gay, S.J., Nagarajan, R.: Interaction categories and the foundations of typed concurrent programming. In: Broy, M. (ed.) Proceedings of the NATO Advanced Study Institute on Deductive Program Design, pp. 35–113 (1996)

3. Abramsky, S., Gay, S., Nagarajan, R.: A type-theoretic approach to deadlock-freedom of asynchronous systems. In: Abadi, M., Ito, T. (eds.) TACS 1997. LNCS, vol. 1281, pp. 295–320. Springer, Heidelberg (1997). https://doi.org/10.1007/BFb0014557
4. Abramsky, S., Gay, S.J., Nagarajan, R.: A specification structure for deadlock-freedom of synchronous processes. Theor. Comput. Sci. **222**(1–2), 1–53 (1999)
5. Atkey, R., Lindley, S., Morris, J.G.: Conflation confers concurrency. In: Lindley, S., McBride, C., Trinder, P., Sannella, D. (eds.) A List of Successes That Can Change the World. LNCS, vol. 9600, pp. 32–55. Springer, Cham (2016). https://doi.org/10.1007/978-3-319-30936-1_2
6. Balzer, S., Pfenning, F.: Manifest sharing with session types. In: Proceedings of the ACM on Programming Languages, vol. 1(ICFP), pp. 37:1–37:29 (2017)
7. Barber, A.: Dual intuitionistic linear logic. Technical report ECS-LFCS-96-347, University of Edinburgh (1996). www.lfcs.inf.ed.ac.uk/reports/96/ECS-LFCS-96-347
8. Bellin, G., Scott, P.J.: On the pi-calculus and linear logic. Theor. Comput. Sci. **135**(1), 11–65 (1994)
9. Bettini, L., Coppo, M., D'Antoni, L., De Luca, M., Dezani-Ciancaglini, M., Yoshida, N.: Global progress in dynamically interleaved multiparty sessions. In: van Breugel, F., Chechik, M. (eds.) CONCUR 2008. LNCS, vol. 5201, pp. 418–433. Springer, Heidelberg (2008). https://doi.org/10.1007/978-3-540-85361-9_33
10. Bräuner, T.: Introduction to linear logic. Technical report BRICS LS-96-6, Basic Research Institute in Computer Science, University of Aarhus (1996)
11. Caires, L., Pérez, J.A.: Linearity, control effects, and behavioral types. In: Yang, H. (ed.) ESOP 2017. LNCS, vol. 10201, pp. 229–259. Springer, Heidelberg (2017). https://doi.org/10.1007/978-3-662-54434-1_9
12. Caires, L., Pfenning, F.: Session types as intuitionistic linear propositions. In: Gastin, P., Laroussinie, F. (eds.) CONCUR 2010. LNCS, vol. 6269, pp. 222–236. Springer, Heidelberg (2010). https://doi.org/10.1007/978-3-642-15375-4_16
13. Carbone, M., Dardha, O., Montesi, F.: Progress as compositional lock-freedom. In: Kühn, E., Pugliese, R. (eds.) COORDINATION 2014. LNCS, vol. 8459, pp. 49–64. Springer, Heidelberg (2014). https://doi.org/10.1007/978-3-662-43376-8_4
14. Carbone, M., Lindley, S., Montesi, F., Schürmann, C., Wadler, P.: Coherence generalises duality: a logical explanation of multiparty session types. In: CONCUR. LIPIcs, vol. 59, pp. 33:1–33:15. Schloss Dagstuhl–Leibniz-Zentrum für Informatik (2016)
15. Coppo, M., Dezani-Ciancaglini, M., Yoshida, N.: Asynchronous session types and progress for object oriented languages. In: Bonsangue, M.M., Johnsen, E.B. (eds.) FMOODS 2007. LNCS, vol. 4468, pp. 1–31. Springer, Heidelberg (2007). https://doi.org/10.1007/978-3-540-72952-5_1
16. Dardha, O.: Recursive session types revisited. In: BEAT. EPTCS, vol. 162, pp. 27–34 (2014)
17. Dardha, O.: Type Systems for Distributed Programs: Components and Sessions. Atlantis Studies in Computing, vol. 7. Atlantis Press, Paris (2016). https://doi.org/10.2991/978-94-6239-204-5
18. Dardha, O., Gay, S.J.: A new linear logic for deadlock-free session typed processes. In: 21st International Conference on Foundations of Software Science and Computation Structures, FoSSaCS 2018 (Extended Version). http://www.dcs.gla.ac.uk/~ornela/publications/DG18-Extended.pdf
19. Dardha, O., Giachino, E., Sangiorgi, D.: Session types revisited. In: PPDP, pp. 139–150. ACM (2012)

20. Dardha, O., Pérez, J.A.: Comparing deadlock-free session typed processes. In: EXPRESS/SOS. EPTCS, vol. 190, pp. 1–15 (2015)
21. Dezani-Ciancaglini, M., de'Liguoro, U., Yoshida, N.: On progress for structured communications. In: Barthe, G., Fournet, C. (eds.) TGC 2007. LNCS, vol. 4912, pp. 257–275. Springer, Heidelberg (2008). https://doi.org/10.1007/978-3-540-78663-4_18
22. Dezani-Ciancaglini, M., Mostrous, D., Yoshida, N., Drossopoulou, S.: Session types for object-oriented languages. In: Thomas, D. (ed.) ECOOP 2006. LNCS, vol. 4067, pp. 328–352. Springer, Heidelberg (2006). https://doi.org/10.1007/11785477_20
23. Gay, S.J., Vasconcelos, V.T.: Linear type theory for asynchronous session types. J. Funct. Program. **20**(1), 19–50 (2010)
24. Girard, J.: Linear logic. Theor. Comput. Sci. **50**, 1–102 (1987)
25. Girard, J.-Y., Taylor, P., Lafont, Y.: Proofs and Types. Cambridge University Press, New York (1989)
26. Honda, K.: Types for dyadic interaction. In: Best, E. (ed.) CONCUR 1993. LNCS, vol. 715, pp. 509–523. Springer, Heidelberg (1993). https://doi.org/10.1007/3-540-57208-2_35
27. Honda, K., Vasconcelos, V.T., Kubo, M.: Language primitives and type discipline for structured communication-based programming. In: Hankin, C. (ed.) ESOP 1998. LNCS, vol. 1381, pp. 122–138. Springer, Heidelberg (1998). https://doi.org/10.1007/BFb0053567
28. Kobayashi, N.: TyPiCal: type-based static analyzer for the pi-calculus. www-kb.is.s.u-tokyo.ac.jp/~koba/typical
29. Kobayashi, N.: A partially deadlock-free typed process calculus. ACM Trans. Program. Lang. Syst. **20**(2), 436–482 (1998)
30. Kobayashi, N.: A type system for lock-free processes. Inf. Comput. **177**(2), 122–159 (2002)
31. Kobayashi, N.: Type systems for concurrent programs. In: Aichernig, B.K., Maibaum, T. (eds.) Formal Methods at the Crossroads. From Panacea to Foundational Support. LNCS, vol. 2757, pp. 439–453. Springer, Heidelberg (2003). https://doi.org/10.1007/978-3-540-40007-3_26
32. Kobayashi, N.: A new type system for deadlock-free processes. In: Baier, C., Hermanns, H. (eds.) CONCUR 2006. LNCS, vol. 4137, pp. 233–247. Springer, Heidelberg (2006). https://doi.org/10.1007/11817949_16
33. Kobayashi, N.: Type systems for concurrent programs. Extended version of [31], Tohoku University (2007)
34. Lindley, S., Morris, J.G.: A semantics for propositions as sessions. In: Vitek, J. (ed.) ESOP 2015. LNCS, vol. 9032, pp. 560–584. Springer, Heidelberg (2015). https://doi.org/10.1007/978-3-662-46669-8_23
35. Milner, R.: Communication and Concurrency. Prentice Hall, Upper Saddle River (1989)
36. Padovani, L.: From lock freedom to progress using session types. In: PLACES. EPTCS, vol. 137, pp. 3–19 (2013)
37. Padovani, L.: Deadlock and lock freedom in the linear π-Calculus. In: CSL-LICS, pp. 72:1–72:10. ACM (2014)
38. Takeuchi, K., Honda, K., Kubo, M.: An interaction-based language and its typing system. In: Halatsis, C., Maritsas, D., Philokyprou, G., Theodoridis, S. (eds.) PARLE 1994. LNCS, vol. 817, pp. 398–413. Springer, Heidelberg (1994). https://doi.org/10.1007/3-540-58184-7_118
39. Toninho, B., Caires, L., Pfenning, F.: Dependent session types via intuitionistic linear type theory. In: PPDP, pp. 161–172. ACM (2011)

40. Torres Vieira, H., Thudichum Vasconcelos, V.: Typing progress in communication-centred systems. In: De Nicola, R., Julien, C. (eds.) COORDINATION 2013. LNCS, vol. 7890, pp. 236–250. Springer, Heidelberg (2013). https://doi.org/10.1007/978-3-642-38493-6_17
41. Wadler, P.: Propositions as sessions. In: ICFP, pp. 273–286. ACM (2012)
42. Wadler, P.: Propositions as types. Commun. ACM **58**(12), 75–84 (2015)

2

A Framework for Parameterized Monitorability

Luca Aceto[1,2], Antonis Achilleos[2(✉)], Adrian Francalanza[3], and Anna Ingólfsdóttir[2]

[1] Gran Sasso Science Institute, L'Aquila, Italy
[2] School of Computer Science, Reykjavik University, Reykjavik, Iceland
{luca,antonios,annai}@ru.is
[3] Department of Computer Science, ICT, University of Malta, Msida, Malta
adrian.francalanza@um.edu.mt

Abstract. We introduce a general framework for Runtime Verification, parameterized with respect to a set of conditions. These conditions are encoded in the trace generated by a monitored process, which a monitor can observe. We present this parameterized framework in its general form and prove that it corresponds to a fragment of HML with recursion, extended with these conditions. We then show how this framework can be applied to a number of instantiations of the set of conditions.

1 Introduction

Runtime Verification (RV) is a lightweight verification technique that checks whether a system satisfies a correctness property by analysing the *current execution* of the system [20,29], expressed as a trace of execution events. Using the additional information obtained at runtime, the technique can often mitigate state explosion problems typically associated with more traditional verification techniques. At the same time, limiting the verification analysis to the current execution trace hinders the expressiveness of RV when compared to more exhaustive approaches. In fact, there are correctness properties that cannot be satisfactorily verified at runtime (*e.g.* the finiteness of the trace considered up to the current execution point prohibits the verification of liveness properties). Because of this reason, RV is often used as part of a multi-pronged approach towards ensuring system correctness [5,6,8,14,15,25], *complementing* other verification techniques such as model checking, testing and type checking.

In order to attain an effective verification strategy consisting of multiple verification techniques that include RV, it is crucial to understand the expressive power of each technique: one can then determine how to best decompose the verification burden into subtasks that can then be assigned to the most appropriate verification technique. *Monitorability* concerns itself with identifying the properties that are analysable by RV. In [21,22] (and subsequently in [2]), the problem of monitorability was studied for properties expressed in a variant of the modal μ-calculus [26] called μHML [28]. The choice of the logic was motivated by the fact that it can embed widely used logics such as CTL and LTL, and by the fact that it is agnostic of the underlying verification method used—this leads to better separation of concerns and guarantees a good level of generality for the results obtained. The main result in [2,21,22] is the identification of a monitorable syntactic subset of the logic μHML (*i.e.*, a set of logical formulas for which monitors carrying out the necessary runtime analysis exist) that is shown to be maximally expressive (*i.e.*, any property that is monitorable in the logic may be expressed in terms of this syntactic subset). We are unaware of other maximality results of this kind in the context of RV.

In this work we strive towards extending the monitorability limits identified in [2,21,22] for μHML. Particularly, for any logic or specification language, monitorability is a function of the underlying monitoring setup. In [2,21,22], the framework assumes a *classical* monitoring setup, whereby a (single) monitor incrementally analyses an ordered trace of events describing the computation steps that were executed by the system. A key observation made by this paper is that, in general, execution traces need *not* be limited to the reporting of events *that happened.* For instance, they may describe events that *could not have happened* at specific points in the execution of a system. Alternatively, they may also include descriptions for depth-bounded trees of computations that *were possible* at specific points in an execution. We conjecture that there are instances where this additional information can be feasibly encoded in a trace, either dynamically or by way of a pre-processing phase (based, *e.g.*, on the examination of logs of previous system executions, or on the full static checking of sub-components making up the system). More importantly, this additional information could, in principle, permit the verification of more properties at runtime.

The contribution of this paper is a study of how the aforementioned augmented monitoring setups may affect the monitorability of μHML, potentially extending the maximality limits identified in [2,21,22]. More concretely:

1. We show how these aspects can be expressed and studied in a general monitoring framework with (abstract) conditions, Theorems 3 and 4 *resp.* in Sects. 3 and 5.
2. We instantiate the general framework with trace conditions that describe the inability to perform actions, amounting to refusals [31], Propositions 1 and 5.
3. We also instantiate the framework with conditions describing finite execution graphs, amounting to the recursion-free fragment of the logic [24], Propositions 2 and 3.
4. Finally, we instantiate the framework with trace conditions that record information from previous monitored runs of the system, Proposition 4. This, in turn, leads us to a notion of alternating monitoring that allows monitors to aggregate information over monitored runs. We show that this extends the monitorable fragment of our logic in a natural and significant way.

The remainder of the paper is structured as follows. After outlining the necessary preliminaries in Sect. 2, we develop our parameterized monitoring framework with conditions in Sect. 3 for a monitoring setup that allows monitors to observe both silent and external actions of systems. The two condition instantiations for this strong setting are presented in Sect. 4. In Sect. 5 we extend the parameterized monitoring framework with conditions to a weak monitoring setup that abstracts from internal moves, followed by two instantiations similar to those presented in Sect. 4. Section 6 concludes by discussing related and future work.

2 Background

Labelled Transition Systems. We assume a set of *external* actions $\textsc{Act}$ and a distinguished *silent* action τ. We let α range over $\textsc{Act}$ and μ over $\textsc{Act} \cup \{\tau\}$. A *Labelled Transition System* (LTS) on $\textsc{Act}$ is a triple

$$L = \langle P, \textsc{Act}, \rightarrow_L \rangle,$$

where P is a nonempty set of system states referred to as *processes* $p, q, \ldots$, and $\rightarrow_L \subseteq P \times (\textsc{Act} \cup \{\tau\}) \times P$ is a transition relation. We write $p \xrightarrow{\mu}_L q$ instead of $(p, \mu, q) \in \rightarrow_L$. By $p \xrightarrow{\mu}_L$ we mean that there is some q such that $p \xrightarrow{\mu}_L q$. We use $p \overset{\mu}{\Rightarrow}_L q$ to mean that, in L, p can derive q using a single μ action and any number of silent actions, *i.e.*, $p(\xrightarrow{\tau}_L)^* \xrightarrow{\mu}_L (\xrightarrow{\tau}_L)^* q$. We distinguish between (general) traces $s = \mu_1\mu_2 \ldots \mu_r \in (\textsc{Act} \cup \{\tau\})^*$ and *external traces* $t = \alpha_1\alpha_2 \ldots \alpha_r \in \textsc{Act}^*$. For a general trace $s = \mu_1\mu_2 \ldots \mu_r \in (\textsc{Act} \cup \{\tau\})^*$, $p \xrightarrow{s}_L q$ means $p \xrightarrow{\mu_1}_L \xrightarrow{\mu_2}_L \ldots \xrightarrow{\mu_r}_L q$; and for an external trace $t = \alpha_1\alpha_2 \ldots \alpha_r \in \textsc{Act}^*$, $p \overset{t}{\Rightarrow}_L q$ means $p \overset{\alpha_1}{\Longrightarrow}_L \overset{\alpha_2}{\Longrightarrow}_L \ldots \overset{\alpha_r}{\Longrightarrow}_L q$ when $r \geq 1$ and $p(\xrightarrow{\tau})^* q$ when $t = \varepsilon$ is the empty trace. We occasionally omit the subscript L when it is clear from the context.

Example 1. The (standard) regular fragment of CCS [30] with grammar:

$$p, q \in \textsc{Proc} ::= \mathsf{nil} \quad | \ \mu.p \quad | \ p + q \quad | \ \mathsf{rec}\ x.p \quad | \ x,$$

where $x, y, z, \ldots$ are from some countably infinite set of variables $\textsc{Var}$, and the transition relation defined as:

$$\textsc{Act}\frac{}{\mu.p \xrightarrow{\mu} p} \qquad \textsc{Rec}\frac{p[\mathsf{rec}\ x.p/x] \xrightarrow{\mu} q}{\mathtt{rec}x.p \xrightarrow{\mu} q} \qquad \textsc{SelL}\frac{p \xrightarrow{\mu} p'}{p + q \xrightarrow{\mu} p'} \qquad \textsc{SelR}\frac{q \xrightarrow{\mu} q'}{p + q \xrightarrow{\mu} q'}$$

constitutes the LTS $\langle \textsc{Proc}, \textsc{Act}, \rightarrow \rangle$. We often use the CCS notation above to describe processes. ■

Specification Logic. Properties about the behaviour of processes may be specified via the logic μHML [4,28], a reformulation of the modal μ-calculus [26].

Definition 1. μHML *formulae on* Act *are defined by the grammar:*

$$\begin{array}{lllll} \varphi,\psi \in \mu\text{HML} ::= \mathsf{tt} & \mid \mathsf{ff} & \mid \varphi \wedge \psi & \mid \varphi \vee \psi & \\ \quad \mid \langle\mu\rangle\varphi & \mid [\mu]\varphi & \mid \mathsf{min}\ X.\varphi & \mid \mathsf{max}\ X.\varphi & \mid X \end{array}$$

where $X, Y, Z, \ldots$ *come from a countably infinite set of logical variables* LVar. *For a given LTS* $L = \langle P, \text{Act}, \rightarrow\rangle$, *an environment* ρ *is a function* $\rho : \text{LVar} \rightarrow 2^P$. *Given an environment* ρ, $X \in \text{LVar}$, *and* $S \subseteq P$, $\rho[x \mapsto S]$ *denotes the environment where* $\rho[X \mapsto S](X) = S$ *and* $\rho[X \mapsto S](Y) = \rho(Y)$, *for all* $Y \neq X$. *The semantics of a* μHML *formula* φ *over an LTS* L *relative to an environment* ρ, *denoted as* $[\![\varphi, \rho]\!]_L$, *is defined as follows:*

$$[\![\mathsf{tt}, \rho]\!]_L = P \qquad [\![\mathsf{ff}, \rho]\!]_L = \emptyset \qquad [\![X, \rho]\!]_L = \rho(X)$$

$$[\![\varphi_1 \wedge \varphi_2, \rho]\!]_L = [\![\varphi_1, \rho]\!]_L \cap [\![\varphi_2, \rho]\!]_L \qquad [\![\varphi_1 \vee \varphi_2, \rho]\!]_L = [\![\varphi_1, \rho]\!]_L \cup [\![\varphi_2, \rho]\!]_L$$

$$[\![[\mu]\varphi, \rho]\!]_L = \left\{p \mid \forall q.\ p \xrightarrow{\mu} q \text{ implies } q \in [\![\varphi, \rho]\!]_L\right\}$$

$$[\![\langle\mu\rangle\varphi, \rho]\!]_L = \left\{p \mid \exists q.\ p \xrightarrow{\mu} q \text{ and } q \in [\![\varphi, \rho]\!]_L\right\}$$

$$[\![\mathsf{min}\ X.\varphi, \rho]\!]_L = \bigcap \{S \mid S \supseteq [\![\varphi, \rho[X \mapsto S]]\!]_L\}$$

$$[\![\mathsf{max}\ X.\varphi, \rho]\!]_L = \bigcup \{S \mid S \subseteq [\![\varphi, \rho[X \mapsto S]]\!]_L\}$$

Formulas φ *and* ψ *are equivalent, denoted as* $\varphi \equiv \psi$, *when* $[\![\varphi, \rho]\!]_L = [\![\psi, \rho]\!]_L$ *for every environment* ρ *and LTS* L. *We often consider closed formulae and simply write* $[\![\varphi]\!]_L$ *for* $[\![\varphi, \rho]\!]_L$ *when the semantics of* φ *is independent of* ρ. ■

The logic μHML is very expressive. It is also agnostic of the technique to be employed for verification. The property of monitorability, however, fundamentally relies on the monitoring setup considered.

Monitoring Systems. A *monitoring setup* on Act is a triple $\langle M, I, L\rangle$, where L is a system LTS on Act, M is a monitor LTS on Act, and I is the instrumentation describing how to compose L and M into an LTS, denoted by $I(M, L)$, on Act. We call the pair (M, I) a *monitoring system* on Act. For $M = \langle \text{Mon}, \text{Act}, \rightarrow_M\rangle$, Mon is set of monitor states (ranged over by m) and $\rightarrow_M$ is the *monitor semantics* described in terms of the behavioural state transitions a monitor takes when it analyses trace events $\mu \in \text{Act} \cup \{\tau\}$. The states of the composite LTS $I(M, L)$ are written as $m \triangleleft p$, where m is a monitor state and p is a system state; the monitored-system transition relation is denoted here by $\rightarrow_{I(M,L)}$. We present our results with a focus on *rejection* monitors, *i.e.*, monitors with a designated rejection state no, and hence safety fragments of the logic μHML. However, our results and arguments apply dually to acceptance monitors (with a designated acceptance state yes) and co-safety properties; see [21,22] for details.

Definition 2. *Fix a monitoring setup $\langle M, I, L\rangle$ on* $\textsc{Act}$ *and let m be a monitor state of M and φ a closed formula of μHML on* $\textsc{Act}$*. We say that m (M, I)*-rejects *(or simply* rejects*, if M, I are evident) a process p in L, written as $\mathbf{rej}_{\langle M,I,L\rangle}(m, p)$, when there are a process q in L and a trace $s \in (\textsc{Act} \cup \{\tau\})^*$ such that $m \triangleleft p \xrightarrow{s}_{I(M,L)} \mathsf{no} \triangleleft q$. We say that m (M, I)*-monitors for *φ on L whenever*

$$for\ each\ process\ p\ of\ L, \mathbf{rej}_{\langle M,I,L\rangle}(m, p)\ if\ and\ only\ if\ p \notin [\![\varphi]\!]_L.$$

(Subscripts are omitted when they are clear from the context.) Finally, m (M, I)-monitors for *φ when m (M, I)-monitors for φ on L for every LTS L on* $\textsc{Act}$*. The monitoring system (M, I) is often omitted when evident.* ■

We define monitorability for μHML in terms of monitoring systems (M, I).

Definition 3. *Fix a monitoring system (M, I) and a fragment Λ of μHML. We say that (M, I) rejection-monitors for Λ whenever:*

- *For all closed $\varphi \in \Lambda$, there exists an m from M that (M, I)-monitors for φ.*
- *For all m of M, there exists a closed $\varphi \in \Lambda$ that is (M, I)-monitored by m.* ■

We note that if a monitoring system and a fragment Λ of μHML satisfy the conditions of Definition 3, then Λ is the largest fragment of μHML that is monitored by the monitoring system. Stated otherwise, any other logic fragment Λ' that satisfies the conditions of Definition 3 must be equally expressive to Λ, *i.e.*, $\forall \varphi' \in \Lambda' \cdot \exists \varphi \in \Lambda \cdot \varphi \equiv \varphi'$ and vice versa. Definition 3 can be dually given for acceptance-monitorability, when considering acceptance monitors. We next review two monitoring systems that respectively rejection-monitor for two different fragments of μHML. We omit the corresponding monitoring systems for acceptance-monitors, that monitor for the dual fragments of μHML.

The Basic Monitoring Setup. The following monitoring system, presented in [2], does *not* distinguish between silent actions and external actions.

Definition 4. *A* basic *monitor on* $\textsc{Act}$ *is defined by the grammar:*

$$m, n \in \textsc{Mon}_b ::= \mathsf{end} \quad | \ \mathsf{no} \quad | \ \mu.m \quad | \ m + n \quad | \ \mathsf{rec}\ x.m \quad | \ x,$$

where x comes from a countably infinite set of monitor variables. Constant no *denotes the* rejection verdict *state whereas* end *denotes the* inconclusive verdict *state. The basic monitor LTS M_b is the one whose states are the closed monitors of $\textsc{Mon}_b$ and whose transition relation is defined by the (standard) rules in Table 1 (we elide the symmetric rule for $m + n$).* ■

Note that by rule mVrd in Table 1, verdicts are irrevocable and monitors can only describe suffix-closed behaviour.

Table 1. Behaviour and instrumentation rules for monitored systems ($v \in \{\mathsf{end}, \mathsf{no}\}$).

Monitor semantics			
$\textsc{mRec}\,\dfrac{m[\mathsf{rec}\,x.m/x] \xrightarrow{\mu} m'}{\mathsf{rec}\,x.m \xrightarrow{\mu} m'}$	$\textsc{mSel}\,\dfrac{m \xrightarrow{\mu} m'}{m+n \xrightarrow{\mu} m'}$	$\textsc{mAct}\,\dfrac{}{\mu.m \xrightarrow{\mu} m}$	$\textsc{mVrd}\,\dfrac{}{v \xrightarrow{\mu} v}$
Instrumentation semantics			
$\textsc{iMon}\,\dfrac{p \xrightarrow{\mu}_L q \quad m \xrightarrow{\mu}_M n}{m \triangleleft p \xrightarrow{\mu}_{I(M,L)} n \triangleleft q}$	$\textsc{iTer}\,\dfrac{p \xrightarrow{\mu}_L q \quad m \xrightarrow{\mu}_M}{m \triangleleft p \xrightarrow{\mu}_{I(M,L)} \mathsf{end} \triangleleft q}$	$\textsc{iAbs}\,\dfrac{p \xrightarrow{\tau}_L q}{m \triangleleft p \xrightarrow{\tau}_{I(M,L)} m \triangleleft q}$	

Definition 5. *Given a system LTS L and a monitor LTS M that agree on* Act, *the* basic *instrumentation LTS, denoted by $I_b(M, L)$, is defined by the rules* iMon *and* iTer *in Table 1. (We do* not *consider rule* iAbs *for now.)* ■

Instrumentation often relegates monitors to a passive role, whereby a monitored system transitions only when the system itself can. In rule iMon, when the system produces a trace event μ that the monitor is able to analyse (and transition from m to n), the constituent components of a monitored system $m \triangleleft p$ move in lockstep. Conversely, when the system produces an event μ that the monitor is *unable* to analyse, the monitored system still executes, according to iTer, but the monitor transitions to the inconclusive state, where it remains for the rest of the computation.

We refer to the pair (M_b, I_b) from Definitions 4 and 5 as the *basic monitoring system*. For each system LTS L that agrees with the full monitoring system on Act, we can show a correspondence between the respective monitoring setup $\langle M_b, I_b, L\rangle$ and the following syntactic subset of μHML.

Definition 6. *The* safety μHML *is defined by the grammar:*

$$\theta, \chi \in \text{sHML} ::= \mathsf{tt} \quad | \; \mathsf{ff} \quad | \; [\mu]\theta \quad | \; \theta \wedge \chi \quad | \; \mathsf{max}\, X.\theta \quad | \; X \quad ■$$

Theorem 1 ([2])**.** *The* basic *monitoring system (M_b, I_b) monitors for the logical fragment* sHML. □

The proof of Theorem 1 relies on a monitor synthesis and a formula synthesis function. The monitor synthesis function, $(\!|-|\!) : \text{sHML} \to \textsc{Mon}_b$, is defined on the structure of the input formula and assumes a bijective mapping between formula variables and monitor recursion variables:

$$(\!|\mathsf{tt}|\!) = \mathsf{end} \qquad (\!|\mathsf{ff}|\!) = \mathsf{no} \qquad (\!|X|\!) = x$$

$$(\!|[\mu]\psi|\!) = \begin{cases} \mathsf{end} & \text{if } (\!|\psi|\!) = \mathsf{end} \\ \mu.(\!|\psi|\!) & \text{otherwise} \end{cases} \qquad (\!|\mathsf{max}\, X.\psi|\!) = \begin{cases} \mathsf{end} & \text{if } (\!|\psi|\!) = \mathsf{end} \\ \mathsf{rec}\, x.(\!|\psi|\!) & \text{otherwise} \end{cases}$$

$$(\!|\psi_1 \wedge \psi_2|\!) = \begin{cases} (\!|\psi_1|\!) & \text{if } (\!|\psi_2|\!) = \mathsf{end} \\ (\!|\psi_2|\!) & \text{if } (\!|\psi_1|\!) = \mathsf{end} \\ (\!|\psi_1|\!) + (\!|\psi_2|\!) & \text{otherwise} \end{cases}$$

The case analyses in the above synthesis procedure handle some of the redundancies that may be present in formula specifications. For instance, it turns out that $\mathsf{max}\ X.[\mu]\mathsf{tt} \equiv \mathsf{tt}$ and, accordingly, $(\!|\mathsf{max}\ X.[\mu]\mathsf{tt}|\!) = (\!|\mathsf{tt}|\!) = \mathsf{end}$. The formula synthesis function is defined analogously (see [2, 22] for more details).

Monitoring for External Actions. The results obtained in [21, 22] can be expressed and recovered within our more general framework. We can express a weak version of the modalities employed in [3, 21, 22] as follows:

$$[[\mu]]\varphi \equiv \mathsf{max}\ X.([\tau]X \wedge [\mu]\mathsf{max}\ Y.(\varphi \wedge [\tau]Y)) \quad \text{and}$$
$$\langle\langle\mu\rangle\rangle\varphi \equiv \mathsf{min}\ X.(\langle\tau\rangle X \vee \langle\mu\rangle\mathsf{min}\ Y.(\varphi \vee \langle\tau\rangle Y)).$$

Definition 7. Weak safety μHML, *presented in [21, 22], is defined by the grammar:*

$$\pi, \kappa \in \text{WsHML} ::= \mathit{tt} \quad |\ \mathit{ff} \quad |\ [[\alpha]]\pi \quad |\ \pi \wedge \kappa \quad |\ \mathsf{max}\ X.\pi \quad |\ X. \quad ■$$

Definition 8. *The set* MON_e *of external monitors on* ACT *contains all the basic monitors that do not use the silent action* τ. *The corresponding external monitor LTS* M_e, *is defined similarly to* M_b, *but with the closed monitors in* MON_e *as its states.* External instrumentation, *denoted by* I_e, *is defined by the* three *rules* iMON, iTER *and* iABS *in Table 1, where in the case of* iMON *and* iTER, *action* μ *is substituted by the external action* α. *We refer to the pair* (M_e, I_e) *as the* external monitoring system, *amounting to the setup in [21, 22].* ■

Theorem 2 ([22]). *The* external *monitoring system* (M_e, I_e) *rejection-monitors for the logical fragment* WsHML. □

3 Monitors that Detect Conditions

Given a set of processes P, a pair (C, r) is a condition framework when C is a non-empty set of *conditions* and $r : C \to 2^P$ is a valuation function. We assume a fixed condition framework (C, r) and we extend the syntax and semantics of μHML so that for every condition $c \in C$, both c and $\neg c$ are formulas and for every LTS L on set of processes P, $[\![c]\!] = r(c)$ and $[\![\neg c]\!] = P \setminus r(c)$. We call the extended logic $\mu\text{HML}^{(C,r)}$. Since, in all the instances we consider, r is easily inferred from C, it is often omitted and we simply write C instead of (C, r) and $\mu\text{HML}^{(C,r)}$ as μHML^{C}. We say that process p satisfies c when $p \in [\![c]\!]$. We assume that C is closed under negation, meaning that for every $c \in C$, there is some $c' \in C$, such that $[\![c']\!] = [\![\neg c]\!]$. Conditions represent certain properties of processes that the instrumentation is able to report.

We extend the syntax of monitors, so that if m is a monitor and c a condition, then $c.m$ is a monitor. The idea is that if $c.m$ detects that the process satisfies c, then it can transition to m.

Definition 9. *A* basic C-monitor *on* $\textsc{Act}$ *is defined by the grammar:*

$$m, n \in \textsc{Mon}_b^C ::= \textit{end} \quad | \ \textit{no} \quad | \ \mu.m \quad | \ c.m \quad | \ m+n \quad | \ \textit{rec}\ x.m \quad | \ x,$$

where x comes from a countably infinite set of monitor variables and $c \in C$. Basic C-monitor behaviour is defined as in Table 1, but allowing μ to range over $\textsc{Act} \cup C \cup \{\tau\}$. *We call the resulting monitor LTS M_b^C.* ■

A monitor detects the satisfaction of condition c when the monitored system has transitioned to a process that satisfies c. To express this intuition, we add rule $\textsc{iCon}$ to the instrumentation rules of Table 1:

$$\textsc{iCon}\ \frac{p \in [\![c]\!] \ \text{ and } \ m \xrightarrow{c}_M n}{m \triangleleft p \ \xrightarrow{\tau}_{I(M,L)} \ n \triangleleft p}.$$

We call the resulting instrumentation I_b^C. We observe that the resulting monitor setup is transparent with respect to external actions: an external trace of the monitored system results in exactly the same external trace of the instrumentation LTS. However, the general traces are not preserved, as the rule $\textsc{iCon}$ may introduce additional silent transitions for the instrumentation trace. However, we argue that this is an expected consequence of the instrumentation verifying the conditions of C. C-monitors monitor for sHML^C:

Definition 10. *The strong safety fragment of μHML^C is defined as:*

$$\varphi, \psi \in \text{sHML}^C ::= \textit{tt} \quad | \ \textit{ff} \quad | \ [\mu]\varphi \quad | \ \neg c \vee \varphi \quad | \ \varphi \wedge \psi \quad | \ \textit{max}\ X.\varphi \quad | \ X,$$

where $c \in C$. We note that $\neg c \vee \varphi$ can be viewed as an implication $c \rightarrow \varphi$ asserting that if c holds, then φ must also hold. ■

It is immediate to see that sHML^C is a fragment of μHML^C and when $C \subseteq \mu\text{HML}$, it is also a fragment of μHML. Finally, if C is closed under negation, then $\neg c \vee \varphi$ can be rewritten as $c' \vee \varphi$, where $[\![c']\!] = [\![\neg c]\!]$, and in the following we often take advantage of this equivalence to simplify the syntax of sHML^C.

Theorem 3. *The monitoring system (M_b^C, I_b^C) monitors for* sHML^C. □

We note that Theorem 3 implies that sHML^C is the largest monitorable fragment of μHML^C, relative to C.

4 Instantiations

We consider two possible instantiations for parameter C in the framework presented in Sect. 3. Since each of these instantiations consists of a fragment from the logic μHML itself, they both show how monitorability for μHML can be extended when using certain augmented traces.

4.1 The Inability to Perform an Action

The monitoring framework of [2,22] (used also in other works such as [18,19]), is based on the idea that, while a system is executing, it performs discrete computational steps called events (actions) that are recorded and relayed to the monitor for analysis. Based on the analysed events, the monitor then transitions from state to state. One may however also consider instrumentations that record a system's *inability* to perform a certain action. Examples of this arise naturally in situations where actions are requested unsuccessfully by an external entity on a system, or whenever the instrumentation is able to report system stability (*i.e.*, the inability of performing internal actions). For instance, such observations were considered in [1,31], in the context of testing preorders.

In our setting, a process is unable to perform action μ exactly when it satisfies $[\mu]\mathsf{ff}$. For monitors that are able to detect the inability or failure of a process to perform actions, we set $F_{\text{ACT}} = \{[\mu]\mathsf{ff} \mid \mu \in \text{ACT} \cup \{\tau\}\}$ as the set of conditions. By Theorem 3, the resulting maximal monitorable fragment of μHML is given by the grammar:

$$\begin{array}{llll} \varphi, \psi \in \text{sHML}^{F_{\text{ACT}}} ::= \mathsf{tt} & \mid \mathsf{ff} & \mid [\mu]\varphi & \mid \langle\mu\rangle\mathsf{tt} \vee \varphi \\ \qquad \mid \varphi \wedge \psi & \mid \mathsf{max}\ X.\varphi & \mid X. & \end{array}$$

We note the fact that μHML is closed under negation, where $\neg[\mu]\mathsf{ff} = \langle\mu\rangle\mathsf{tt}$.

Proposition 1. *The monitoring system* $(M_b^{F_{\text{ACT}}}, I_b^{F_{\text{ACT}}})$ *monitors for the logical fragment* $\text{sHML}^{F_{\text{ACT}}}$. □

A special case of interest are monitors that can detect process stability, *i.e.*, processes satisfying $[\tau]\mathsf{ff}$. Such monitors monitor for $\text{sHML}^{\{[\tau]\mathsf{ff}\}}$, namely sHML from Definition 6 extended with formulas of the form $\langle\tau\rangle\mathsf{tt} \vee \varphi$.

4.2 Depth-Bounded Static Analysis

In multi-pronged approaches using a combination of verification techniques, one could statically verify parts of a program (from specific execution points) with respect to certain behavioural properties using techniques such as Bounded Model Checking [11] and Partial Model Checking [7]. Typical examples arise in component-based software using modules, objects or agents that can be verified in isolation. This pre-computed verification can then be recorded as annotations to a component and subsequently reported by the instrumentation as part of the execution trace. This strategy would certainly be feasible for depth-bounded static analysis for which the original logic HML [24]—the recursion-free fragment of μHML given below—is an ideal fit.

$$\eta, \chi \in \text{HML} ::= \mathsf{tt} \quad \mid \mathsf{ff} \quad \mid \eta \wedge \chi \quad \mid \eta \vee \chi \quad \mid [\mu]\eta \quad \mid \langle\mu\rangle\eta.$$

Again, HML is closed under negation [4]. If we allow monitors to detect the satisfaction of these kinds of conditions, then, according to Theorem 3, the maximal fragment of μHML that we can monitor for, with HML as a condition framework, is $\mathrm{sHML}^{\mathrm{HML}}$, defined by the following grammar:

$$\varphi, \psi ::= \mathsf{tt} \quad | \ \mathsf{ff} \quad | \ [\mu]\varphi \quad | \ \eta \vee \varphi \quad | \ \varphi \wedge \psi \quad | \ \mathsf{max}\ X.\varphi \quad | \ X,$$

where $\eta \in$ HML. Another way to describe $\mathrm{sHML}^{\mathrm{HML}}$ is as the μHML fragment that includes all formulas whereby for every subformula of the form $\varphi \vee \psi$, at most *one* of the constituent subformulas φ, ψ uses recursion.

Proposition 2. *The monitoring system* $(M_b^{\mathrm{HML}}, I_b^{\mathrm{HML}})$ *monitors for the logical fragment* $\mathrm{sHML}^{\mathrm{HML}}$. □

Instead of HML, we can alternatively use a fragment HML^d of HML that only allows formulas with nesting depth for the modalities of at most d. Since the complexity of checking HML formulas is directly dependent on this modal depth, there are cases where the overheads of checking such formulas are deemed to be low enough to be adequately checked for at runtime instead of checking for them statically.

5 Extending External Monitorability

We explore the impact of considering traces that encode conditions from Sect. 3 on the monitorability of the weak version of the logic used in [21,22]:

$$\begin{aligned} \varphi, \psi \in \mathrm{W}\mu\mathrm{HML} ::= \ & \mathtt{tt} \quad && | \ \mathtt{ff} \quad && | \ \varphi \wedge \psi \quad && | \ \varphi \vee \psi \\ | \ & \langle\langle \alpha \rangle\rangle \varphi && | \ [[\alpha]]\varphi && | \ \mathsf{min}\ X.\varphi && | \ \mathsf{max}\ X.\varphi \quad | \ X. \end{aligned}$$

This version of the logic abstracts away from internal moves performed by the system—note that the weak modality formulas are restricted to external actions α as opposed to the general ones, μ. The semantics follows that presented in Sect. 2, but can alternatively be given a more direct inductive definition, *e.g.*

$$[\![[[\alpha]]\varphi, \rho]\!] = \{p \mid \forall q.\ p \overset{\alpha}{\Rightarrow} q \text{ implies } q \in [\![\varphi, \rho]\!]\}.$$

The main aim of this section is to extend the maximally-expressive monitorable subset of μHML that was identified in [21,22] using the framework developed in Sect. 3.

5.1 External Monitoring with Conditions

We define the external monitoring system with conditions similarly to Sect. 3. The syntax of Definition 8 is extended so that, for any instance of C, if m is a monitor and c a condition from C, then $c.m$ is a monitor.

Definition 11. *An* external C-monitor *on* Act *is defined by the grammar:*

$$m, n \in \text{Mon}_e^C ::= \textsf{end} \quad | \ \textsf{no} \quad | \ \alpha.m \quad | \ c.m \quad | \ m + n \quad | \ \textsf{rec}\ x.m \quad | \ x,$$

where $c \in C$. *C-monitor behaviour is defined as in Table 1, but extending rule* mAct *to condition prefixes that generate condition actions (i.e., μ ranges over* $\text{Act} \cup C$*). We call the resulting monitor LTS* M_e^C.

For the instrumentation relation called I_e^C*, we consider the rules* iMon, iTer *from Table 1 for external actions α instead of the general action μ, rule* iAbs *from the same table, and rule* iCon *from Sect. 3.* ■

Note that the monitoring system (M_e^C, I_e^C) may be used to detect τ-transitions *implicitly*—we conjecture that this cannot be avoided in general. Consider two conflicting conditions c_1 and c_2, *i.e.*, $[\![c_1]\!] \cap [\![c_2]\!] = \emptyset$. Definition 11 permits monitors of the form $c_1.c_2.m$ that encode the fact that state m can only be reached when the system under scrutiny performs a non-empty sequence of τ-moves to transition from a state satisfying c_1 to another state satisfying c_2. This, in some sense, is also related to obscure silent action monitoring studied in [2].

We identify the grammar for the maximally-expressive monitorable syntactic subset of the logic WμHML. It uses the formula $[[\varepsilon]]\varphi$ defined as:

$$[[\varepsilon]]\varphi \equiv \textsf{max}\ X.(\varphi \wedge [\tau]X)$$

The modality $[[\varepsilon]]\varphi$ quantifies universally over the set of processes that can be reached from a given one via any number of silent steps. Together with its dual $\langle\langle\varepsilon\rangle\rangle\varphi$ modality, $[[\varepsilon]]\varphi$ is used in the modal characterisation of weak bisimilarity [30,34], in which τ transitions from one process may be matched by a (possibly empty) sequence of τ transitions from another.

Definition 12. *The weak safety fragment of* WμHML *with C is defined as:*

$$\begin{aligned} \varphi, \psi \in \text{WsHML}^C ::= \ & \textsf{tt} \quad && | \ \textsf{ff} && | \ [[\alpha]]\varphi && | \ [[\varepsilon]](\neg c \vee \varphi) \\ | \ & \varphi \wedge \psi && | \ \textsf{max}\ X.\varphi && | \ X, && \end{aligned}$$

where $c \in C$. ■

Theorem 4. *The monitoring system* (M_e^C, I_e^C) *monitors for* WsHML^C. □

We highlight the need to insulate the appearance of the implication $\neg c \vee \varphi$ from internal system behaviour by using the modality $[[\varepsilon]]$ in Definition 12. For conditions that are invariant under τ-transitions, this modality is not required but it cannot be eliminated otherwise; we revisit this point in Example 2.

5.2 Instantiating External Monitors with Conditions

We consider three different instantiations to our parametric external monitoring system of Sect. 5.1.

Recursion-Free Formulas. The weak version of HML, denoted by wHML, is the recursion-free fragment of WμHML. Similarly to what was argued earlier in Sect. 4.2, it is an appropriate set of conditions to instantiate set C in WsHML^C, and the maximal monitorable fragment of WμHML with conditions from wHML is WsHML$^{w\text{HML}}$, defined by the following grammar, where $\eta \in w$HML:

$$\varphi, \psi ::= \mathsf{tt} \quad | \ \mathsf{ff} \quad | \ [[\alpha]]\varphi \quad | \ [[\varepsilon]](\eta \vee \varphi) \quad | \ \varphi \wedge \psi \quad | \ \mathsf{max}\ X.\varphi \quad | \ X.$$

Proposition 3. *The monitoring system* $(M_e^{w\text{HML}}, I_e^{w\text{HML}})$ *monitors for the logical fragment* WsHML$^{w\text{HML}}$. □

An important observation (that is perhaps surprising) is that WsHML$^{w\text{HML}}$ is *not* a fragment of WμHML, as the following example demonstrates.

Example 2. Although for any (closed) WsHML formula φ we have the logical equivalence $[[\varepsilon]]\varphi \equiv \varphi$ (notice that the monitor for φ that is guaranteed by Theorem 2 also monitors for $[[\varepsilon]]\varphi$), this logical equivalence does not hold for a formula φ from WμHML. Consider the formula φ_ϵ below that may be expressed using a formula from WsHML$^{w\text{HML}}$:

$$\varphi_\epsilon = [[\varepsilon]]\langle\langle\alpha\rangle\rangle\mathsf{tt} \equiv [[\varepsilon]](\langle\langle\alpha\rangle\rangle\mathsf{tt} \vee \mathsf{ff}) \in \text{WsHML}^{w\text{HML}}.$$

Formula φ_ϵ is not equivalent to $\langle\langle\alpha\rangle\rangle\mathsf{tt}$ (*e.g.* the process $\alpha.\mathsf{nil} + \tau.\mathsf{nil}$ satisfies $\langle\langle\alpha\rangle\rangle\mathsf{tt}$, but not φ_ϵ) meaning that $[[\varepsilon]]$ plays a discerning role in the context of WμHML. Furthermore, φ_ϵ holds for process $\tau.\alpha.\mathsf{nil}$, but not for $\alpha.\mathsf{nil}+\tau.\mathsf{nil}$, even though these two processes cannot be distinguished by *any* WμHML formula. In fact, it turns out that they are bisimilar with respect to *weak external transitions* and this bisimulation characterises the satisfaction of WμHML formulas [24]. Thus, there is no formula in WμHML that is equivalent to φ_ϵ. ■

Previous Runs and Alternating Monitoring. A monitoring system could reuse information from previous system runs, perhaps recorded as execution logs, and whenever (sub)traces can be associated with specific states of the system, these can also be used as an instantiation for our parametric framework. More concretely, in [21,22] it is shown that traces can be used to characterise the violation of WsHML formulas, or the satisfaction of formulas from the dual fragment, WcHML, defined below.

Definition 13. *The* co-safety WμHML *is defined by the grammar:*

$$\pi, \kappa \in \text{WcHML} ::= \mathit{tt} \quad | \ \mathit{ff} \quad | \ \langle\langle\alpha\rangle\rangle\theta \quad | \ \theta \vee \chi \quad | \ \mathit{min}\ X.\theta \quad | \ X \ \blacksquare$$

The witnessed rejection and acceptance traces can in turn be used as part of an augmented trace for an instantiation for C to obtain the monitorable dual logics WsHML^{WcHML} and WcHML^{WsHML} that alternate between rejection monitoring and acceptance monitoring. The logic $\mathrm{WsHML}^{\mathrm{WcHML}}$ is defined by the following grammar, where $\theta \in \mathrm{WsHML}$:

$$\varphi, \psi ::= \mathsf{tt} \quad | \; \mathsf{ff} \quad | \; [[\alpha]]\varphi \quad | \; [[\varepsilon]](\theta \vee \varphi) \quad | \; \varphi \wedge \psi \quad | \; \mathsf{max}\, X.\varphi \quad | \; X;$$

and $\mathrm{WcHML}^{\mathrm{WsHML}}$ is defined by the following grammar, where $\chi \in \mathrm{WcHML}$:

$$\pi, \kappa ::= \mathsf{tt} \quad | \; \mathsf{ff} \quad | \; \langle\langle\alpha\rangle\rangle\pi \quad | \; \langle\langle\varepsilon\rangle\rangle(\chi \wedge \pi) \quad | \; \pi \vee \kappa \quad | \; \mathsf{min}\, X.\varphi \quad | \; X.$$

Proposition 4. *The monitoring system* $(M_e^{\mathrm{WcHML}}, I_e^{\mathrm{WcHML}})$ *rejection-monitors for the logical fragment* $\mathrm{WsHML}^{\mathrm{WcHML}}$. □

One should observe that in this case, $\mathrm{WsHML}^{\mathrm{WcHML}}$ *is* a fragment of WμHML, in contrast to the previous instantiation $\mathrm{WsHML}^{w\mathrm{HML}}$ from Sect. 5.2.

Lemma 1. *For every* $[[\varepsilon]](\eta \vee \varphi) \in \mathrm{WsHML}^{\mathrm{WcHML}}$ *(where* $\eta \in \mathrm{WsHML}$*), we have* $[[\varepsilon]](\eta \vee \varphi) \equiv \eta \vee \varphi$. □

Corollary 1. *For every formula in* $\mathrm{WsHML}^{\mathrm{WcHML}}$*, there is a logically equivalent formula in* WμHML. □

This entails that $\mathrm{WsHML}^{\mathrm{WcHML}}$ can be reformulated using the following, simpler, grammar (here $\eta \in \mathrm{WsHML}$) which is clearly a fragment of WμHML:

$$\varphi, \psi ::= \mathsf{tt} \quad | \; \mathsf{ff} \quad | \; [[\alpha]]\varphi \quad | \; \eta \vee \varphi \quad | \; \varphi \wedge \psi \quad | \; \mathsf{max}\, X.\varphi \quad | \; X.$$

If the monitoring system can use such information from previous runs, there is no reason to limit this information to just one previous run. If the instrumentation mechanism can record up to i prior runs, the monitorable logic may be described as WsHML^{i+1}, defined inductively in the following way:

- $\mathrm{WsHML}^1 = \mathrm{WsHML}$ and $\mathrm{WcHML}^1 = \mathrm{WcHML}$; and
- $\mathrm{WsHML}^{i+1} = \mathrm{WsHML}^{\mathrm{WcHML}^i}$ and $\mathrm{WcHML}^{i+1} = \mathrm{WcHML}^{\mathrm{WsHML}^i}$.

Whenever this setup can be extended to unlimited prior runs, the resulting rejection-monitorable fragment would be $\mathrm{WsHML}^\omega = \bigcup_i \mathrm{WsHML}^i$, which is also described by the following grammar:

$$\varphi, \psi ::= \mathsf{tt} \quad | \; \mathsf{ff} \quad | \; [[\alpha]]\varphi \quad | \; \varphi \vee \psi \quad | \; \varphi \wedge \psi \quad | \; \mathsf{max}\, X.\varphi \quad | \; X.$$

WsHML^ω is a non-trivial extension of WsHML *which is still within* WμHML.

Failure to Execute an Action and Refusals. In Subsect. 4.1, we instantiated the condition set C as the set of formulas from μHML that assert the inability of a process to perform an action. These formulas are of the form $[\alpha]\mathsf{ff}$. We recast this approach in the setting of weak monitorability. In this setting where the monitoring system and the specification formulas ignore any silent transitions, the inability of a process to perform an α-transition acquires a different meaning from the one used for the basic system. In particular, we consider a stronger version of these conditions that incorporates stability; this makes them invariant over τ-transitions. We say that p *refuses* α when $p \not\xrightarrow{\tau}$ and $p \not\xrightarrow{\alpha}$. In [31], a very similar notion is used for refusal testing (see also [1]). Thus, much in line with [31], we use the following definition.

Definition 14. *A process p of an LTS L* refuses *action $\alpha \in$ ACT and write p **ref** α when $p \not\xrightarrow{\tau}_L$ and $p \not\xrightarrow{\alpha}_L$. The set of conditions that corresponds to refusals is thus $R_{\text{ACT}} = \{[\tau]ff \wedge [\alpha]ff \mid \alpha \in \text{ACT}\}$.* ■

According to Theorem 4, the largest fragment of μHML that we can monitor for, using monitors that can detect refusals, is $\text{WsHML}^{R_{\text{ACT}}}$, given by the following grammar:

$$\begin{aligned}\varphi, \psi ::= \;& \mathsf{tt} && \mid \mathsf{ff} && \mid [[\alpha]]\varphi && \mid [[\varepsilon]](\langle\tau\rangle\mathsf{tt} \vee \langle\alpha\rangle\mathsf{tt} \vee \varphi)\\ \mid\;& \varphi \wedge \psi && \mid \mathsf{max}\ X.\varphi && \mid X.\end{aligned}$$

Again, $\langle\tau\rangle\mathsf{tt} \vee \langle\alpha\rangle\mathsf{tt} \vee \varphi$ is best read as the implication $([\tau]\mathsf{ff} \wedge [\alpha]\mathsf{ff}) \to \varphi$: if the process is stable and cannot perform an α-transition, then φ must hold.

Proposition 5. *The monitoring system $(M_e^{R_{\text{ACT}}}, I_e^{R_{\text{ACT}}})$ monitors for the logical fragment $\text{WsHML}^{R_{\text{ACT}}}$.* □

Example 3. Consider the formula

$$\varphi_s = [[\varepsilon]](\langle\tau\rangle\mathsf{tt} \vee \langle\alpha\rangle\mathsf{tt} \vee [[\beta]]\mathsf{ff}) \in \text{WsHML}^{R_{\text{ACT}}}.$$

Formula φ_s claims that at every stable state that the system can reach, if action α is impossible, then action β should also be impossible. We can see that φ_s is true for $\tau.\mathsf{nil} + \beta.\mathsf{nil}$, but not for $\beta.\mathsf{nil}$. However, the two processes cannot be distinguished by WμHML, as they have the same weak external transitions. Therefore, $\text{WsHML}^{R_{\text{ACT}}}$ is not a fragment of WμHML—but, as we have seen, it is a fragment of μHML. Here we have a part of the formula that clearly is not part of WμHML. That is $\langle\tau\rangle\mathsf{tt}$, which asserts that the process can perform a silent transition. ■

Example 4. Let us consider an LTS L_0 of stable processes—that is, L_0 is an LTS without any silent transitions. L_0 offers a simplified setting to cast our observations. In this case, the $[[\varepsilon]]$, $[\tau]$, and $\langle\tau\rangle$ modalities can be eliminated from our formulas, and weak modalities are equivalent to strong modalities. This allows us to simplify the grammar for $\text{WsHML}^{F_{\text{ACT}}}$ as follows:

$$\begin{aligned}\varphi, \psi ::= \;& \mathsf{tt} && \mid \mathsf{ff} && \mid [\alpha]\varphi && \mid \langle\alpha\rangle\mathsf{tt} \vee \varphi\\ \mid\;& \varphi \wedge \psi && \mid \mathsf{max}\ X.\varphi && \mid X.\end{aligned}$$

Perhaps unsurprisingly, this grammar yields the same formulas as the restriction of grammar of Subsect. 4.1 on external actions. An instance of a specification that can be formalized in this fragment is the following. Consider a simple server-client system, where the client can request a resource, which is represented by action `rq`, and the server may give a positive response, represented by action `rs`, after which it needs to allocate said resource to the client, represented by action `al`. A reasonable specification for the server is that if it is impossible at the moment to provide a resource, then it should not give a positive response to the client. In the above simplification of $\mathrm{WsHML}^{F_{\mathrm{ACT}}}$, this specification can be formalized as $[\mathtt{rq}](\langle\mathtt{al}\rangle\mathsf{tt} \vee [\mathtt{rs}]\mathsf{ff})$. If the LTS includes silent transitions, the corresponding specification would be written as

$$\varphi_r = [\mathtt{rq}][[\varepsilon]](\langle\tau\rangle\mathsf{tt} \vee \langle\mathtt{al}\rangle\mathsf{tt} \vee [[\mathtt{rs}]]\mathsf{ff}).$$

In other words, after a request, if the server cannot provide a resource and it is stable—so, there is no possibility that after some time the resource will be available—then the server should not give a positive response to the client. ■

6 Conclusions

In order to devise effective verification strategies that straddle between the pre- and post-deployment phases of software production, one needs to understand better the monitorability aspects of the correctness properties that are to be verified. We have presented a general framework that allows us to determine maximal monitorable fragments of an expressive logic that is agnostic of the verification technique employed, namely μHML. By way of a number of instantiations, we also show how the framework can be used to reason about the monitorability induced by various forms of augmented traces. Our next immediate concern is to validate the proposed instantiations empirically by constructing monitoring systems and tools that are based on these results, as we did already for the original monitorability results of [21, 22] in [9, 10, 12].

Related Work. Monitorability for μHML was first examined in [21, 22]. This work introduced the external monitoring system and identified WsHML as the largest monitorable fragment of μHML, with respect to that system. The ensuring work in [2] focused on monitoring setups that can distinguish silent actions to a varying degree, and introduced the basic monitoring system, showing analogous monitorability results for μHML.

Monitorability has also been examined for languages defined over traces, such as LTL. Pnueli and Zaks in [32] define a notion of monitorability over traces, although they do not attempt maximal monitorability results. Diekert and Leuckert revisited monitorability from a topological perspective in [16]. Falcone *et al.* in [17] extended the work in [32] to incorporate enforcement and introduced a notion of monitorability on traces that is parameterized with respect to a truth domain that corresponds to our separation to acceptance- and rejection-monitorable properties. In [13], the authors use a monitoring system that can generate derivations of satisfied formulas from a fragment of LTL. However, they do not argue that this fragment is somehow maximal. There is a significant body of work on synthesizing monitors from LTL formulas, *e.g.* [13,23,33,35], and it would be worth investigating whether our general techniques for monitor synthesis can be applied effectively in these cases.

Phillips introduced *refusal testing* in [31] as a way to extend the capabilities of testing (see [18] for a discussion on how our monitoring setup relates to testing preorders). The meaning of refusals in [31] is very close to the one in Definition 14 and it is interesting to note how Phillips' use of tests for refusal formulas is similar to our monitoring mechanisms for refusals. Abramsky [1] uses refusals in the context of a much more powerful testing machinery, in order to identify the kind of testing power that is required for distinguishing non-bisimilar processes.

The decomposition of the verification burden across verification techniques, or across iterations of alternating monitoring runs as presented in Sect. 5, can be seen as a method for *quotienting*. In [7] Andersen studies quotienting of the specification logics discussed in this paper to reduce the state-space during model checking and thus increase its efficiency (see also [27] for a more recent treatment). The techniques used rely heavily on the model's concurrency constructs and may produce formulas that are larger in size than the original, but which can be checked against a smaller component of the model. In multi-pronged approaches to verification one would expect to encounter similar difficulties occasionally.

References

1. Abramsky, S.: Observation equivalence as a testing equivalence. Theor. Comput. Sci. **53**(2–3), 225–241 (1987)
2. Aceto, L., Achilleos, A., Francalanza, A., Ingólfsdóttir, A.: Monitoring for silent actions. In: 37th IARCS Annual Conference on Foundations of Software Technology and Theoretical Computer Science, FSTTCS 2017 (2017, to appear)
3. Aceto, L., Achilleos, A., Francalanza, A., Ingólfsdóttir, A., Kjartansson, S.Ö.: Determinizing monitors for HML with recursion. CoRR abs/1611.10212 (2016)
4. Aceto, L., Ingólfsdóttir, A., Larsen, K.G., Srba, J.: Reactive Systems: Modelling, Specification and Verification. Cambridge University Press, New York (2007)
5. Ahrendt, W., Chimento, J.M., Pace, G.J., Schneider, G.: A specification language for static and runtime verification of data and control properties. In: Bjørner, N., de Boer, F. (eds.) FM 2015. LNCS, vol. 9109, pp. 108–125. Springer, Cham (2015). https://doi.org/10.1007/978-3-319-19249-9_8
6. Aktug, I., Naliuka, K.: ConSpec - a formal language for policy specification. Sci. Comput. Programm. **74**(1–2), 2–12 (2008)
7. Andersen, H.R.: Partial model checking (extended). In: Proceedings of Tenth Annual IEEE Symposium on Logic in Computer Science, pp. 398–407. IEEE (1995)
8. Artho, C., Barringer, H., Goldberg, A., Havelund, K., Khurshid, S., Lowry, M.R., Pasareanu, C.S., Rosu, G., Sen, K., Visser, W., Washington, R.: Combining test case generation and runtime verification. Theor. Comput. Sci. **336**(2–3), 209–234 (2005)
9. Attard, D.P., Francalanza, A.: A monitoring tool for a branching-time logic. In: Falcone, Y., Sánchez, C. (eds.) RV 2016. LNCS, vol. 10012, pp. 473–481. Springer, Cham (2016). https://doi.org/10.1007/978-3-319-46982-9_31

10. Attard, D.P., Francalanza, A.: Trace partitioning and local monitoring for asynchronous components. In: Cimatti, A., Sirjani, M. (eds.) SEFM 2017. LNCS, vol. 10469, pp. 219–235. Springer, Cham (2017). https://doi.org/10.1007/978-3-319-66197-1_14
11. Biere, A., Cimatti, A., Clarke, E., Zhu, Y.: Symbolic model checking without BDDs. In: Cleaveland, W.R. (ed.) TACAS 1999. LNCS, vol. 1579, pp. 193–207. Springer, Heidelberg (1999). https://doi.org/10.1007/3-540-49059-0_14
12. Cassar, I., Francalanza, A.: On implementing a monitor-oriented programming framework for actor systems. In: Ábrahám, E., Huisman, M. (eds.) IFM 2016. LNCS, vol. 9681, pp. 176–192. Springer, Cham (2016). https://doi.org/10.1007/978-3-319-33693-0_12
13. Cini, C., Francalanza, A.: An LTL proof system for runtime verification. In: Baier, C., Tinelli, C. (eds.) TACAS 2015. LNCS, vol. 9035, pp. 581–595. Springer, Heidelberg (2015). https://doi.org/10.1007/978-3-662-46681-0_54
14. Decker, N., Leucker, M., Thoma, D.: jUnit^{RV}–adding runtime verification to jUnit. In: Brat, G., Rungta, N., Venet, A. (eds.) NFM 2013. LNCS, vol. 7871, pp. 459–464. Springer, Heidelberg (2013). https://doi.org/10.1007/978-3-642-38088-4_34
15. Desai, A., Dreossi, T., Seshia, S.A.: Combining model checking and runtime verification for safe robotics. In: Lahiri, S., Reger, G. (eds.) RV 2017. LNCS, vol. 10548, pp. 172–189. Springer, Cham (2017). https://doi.org/10.1007/978-3-319-67531-2_11
16. Diekert, V., Leucker, M.: Topology, monitorable properties and runtime verification. Theor. Comput. Sci. **537**, 29–41 (2014)
17. Falcone, Y., Fernandez, J.C., Mounier, L.: What can you verify and enforce at runtime? Int. J. Softw. Tools Technol. Trans. **14**(3), 349–382 (2012)
18. Francalanza, A.: A theory of monitors. In: Jacobs, B., Löding, C. (eds.) FoSSaCS 2016. LNCS, vol. 9634, pp. 145–161. Springer, Heidelberg (2016). https://doi.org/10.1007/978-3-662-49630-5_9
19. Francalanza, A.: Consistently-detecting monitors. In: Meyer, R., Nestmann, U. (eds.) 28th International Conference on Concurrency Theory (CONCUR 2017). LIPIcs, vol. 85, pp. 8:1–8:19. Schloss Dagstuhl, Dagstuhl (2017)
20. Francalanza, A., Aceto, L., Achilleos, A., Attard, D.P., Cassar, I., Della Monica, D., Ingólfsdóttir, A.: A foundation for runtime monitoring. In: Lahiri, S., Reger, G. (eds.) RV 2017. LNCS, vol. 10548, pp. 8–29. Springer, Cham (2017). https://doi.org/10.1007/978-3-319-67531-2_2
21. Francalanza, A., Aceto, L., Ingolfsdottir, A.: On verifying Hennessy-Milner logic with recursion at runtime. In: Bartocci, E., Majumdar, R. (eds.) RV 2015. LNCS, vol. 9333, pp. 71–86. Springer, Cham (2015). https://doi.org/10.1007/978-3-319-23820-3_5
22. Francalanza, A., Aceto, L., Ingolfsdottir, A.: Monitorability for the Hennessy-Milner logic with recursion. Formal Meth. Syst. Des. (FMSD) **51**(1), 87–116 (2017)
23. Geilen, M.: On the construction of monitors for temporal logic properties. Electron. Notes Theor. Comput. Sci. **55**(2), 181–199 (2001)
24. Hennessy, M., Milner, R.: Algebraic laws for nondeterminism and concurrency. J. ACM **32**(1), 137–161 (1985)
25. Kejstová, K., Ročkai, P., Barnat, J.: From model checking to runtime verification and back. In: Lahiri, S., Reger, G. (eds.) RV 2017. LNCS, vol. 10548, pp. 225–240. Springer, Cham (2017). https://doi.org/10.1007/978-3-319-67531-2_14
26. Kozen, D.: Results on the propositional μ-calculus. Theor. Comput. Sci. **27**(3), 333–354 (1983)

27. Lang, F., Mateescu, R.: Partial model checking using networks of labelled transition systems and boolean equation systems. Log. Meth. Comput. Sci. **9**(4), 1–32 (2013)
28. Larsen, K.G.: Proof systems for satisfiability in Hennessy-Milner logic with recursion. Theor. Comput. Sci. **72**(2), 265–288 (1990)
29. Leucker, M., Schallhart, C.: A brief account of runtime verification. J. Log. Algebraic Program. **78**(5), 293–303 (2009)
30. Milner, R.: Communication and Concurrency. Prentice-Hall Inc, Upper Saddle River (1989)
31. Phillips, I.: Refusal testing. Theor. Comput. Sci. **50**(3), 241–284 (1987)
32. Pnueli, A., Zaks, A.: PSL model checking and run-time verification via testers. In: Misra, J., Nipkow, T., Sekerinski, E. (eds.) FM 2006. LNCS, vol. 4085, pp. 573–586. Springer, Heidelberg (2006). https://doi.org/10.1007/11813040_38
33. Sen, K., Roşu, G., Agha, G.: Generating optimal linear temporal logic monitors by coinduction. In: Saraswat, V.A. (ed.) ASIAN 2003. LNCS, vol. 2896, pp. 260–275. Springer, Heidelberg (2003). https://doi.org/10.1007/978-3-540-40965-6_17
34. Stirling, C.: Modal and Temporal Properties of Processes. Springer, New York (2001)
35. Vardi, M.Y.: An automata-theoretic approach to linear temporal logic. In: Moller, F., Birtwistle, G. (eds.) Logics for Concurrency. LNCS, vol. 1043, pp. 238–266. Springer, Heidelberg (1996). https://doi.org/10.1007/3-540-60915-6_6

3

From Symmetric Pattern-Matching to Quantum Control

Amr Sabry[1], Benoît Valiron[2(✉)] and Juliana Kaizer Vizzotto[3]

[1] Indiana University, Bloomington, IN, USA
sabry@indiana.edu
[2] LRI, CentraleSupélec, Université Paris-Saclay, Orsay, France
benoit.valiron@lri.fr
[3] Universidade Federal de Santa Maria, Santa Maria, Brazil
juvizzotto@inf.ufsm.br

Abstract. One perspective on quantum algorithms is that they are classical algorithms having access to a special kind of memory with exotic properties. This perspective suggests that, even in the case of quantum algorithms, the control flow notions of sequencing, conditionals, loops, and recursion are entirely classical. There is however, another notion of control flow, that is itself quantum. The notion of quantum conditional expression is reasonably well-understood: the execution of the two expressions becomes itself a superposition of executions. The quantum counterpart of loops and recursion is however not believed to be meaningful in its most general form.

In this paper, we argue that, under the right circumstances, a reasonable notion of quantum loops and recursion is possible. To this aim, we first propose a classical, typed, reversible language with lists and fixpoints. We then extend this language to the *closed* quantum domain (without measurements) by allowing linear combinations of terms and restricting fixpoints to structurally recursive fixpoints whose termination proofs match the proofs of convergence of sequences in infinite-dimensional Hilbert spaces. We additionally give an operational semantics for the quantum language in the spirit of algebraic lambda-calculi and illustrate its expressiveness by modeling several common unitary operations.

1 Introduction

The control flow of a program describes how its elementary operations are organized along the execution. Usual primitive control mechanisms are sequences, tests, iteration and recursion. Elementary operations placed in sequence are executed in order. Tests allow conditionally executing a group of operations and changing the course of the execution of the program. Finally, iteration gives the possibility to iterate a process an arbitrary number of times and recursion generalizes iteration to automatically manage the history of the operations performed during iteration. The structure of control flow for conventional (classical) computation is well-understood. In the case of *quantum* computation, control flow is still subject to debate. This paper proposes a working notion of quantum control in closed quantum systems, shedding new light on the problem, and clarifying several of the previous concerns.

Quantum Computation. A good starting point for understanding quantum computation is to consider classical circuits over *bits* but replacing the bits with *qubits*, which are intuitively superpositions of bits weighed by complex number amplitudes. Computationally, a qubit is an abstract data type governed by the laws of quantum physics, whose values are normalized vectors of complex numbers in the Hilbert space $\mathbb{C}^2$ (modulo a global phase). By choosing an orthonormal basis, say the classical bits `tt` and `ff`, a qubit can be regarded as a complex linear combination, $\alpha\ \mathtt{tt} + \beta\ \mathtt{ff}$, where α and β are complex numbers such that $|\alpha|^2 + |\beta|^2 = 1$. This generalizes naturally to multiple qubits: the state of a system of n qubits is a vector in the Hilbert space $(\mathbb{C}^2)^{\otimes n}$.

The operations one can perform on a quantum memory are of two kinds: quantum gates and measurements. Quantum gates are unitary operations that are "purely quantum" in the sense that they modify the quantum memory without giving any feedback to the outside world: the quantum memory is viewed as a *closed system.* A customary graphical representation for these operations is the *quantum circuit*, akin to conventional boolean circuits: wires represent qubits while boxes represents operations to perform on them. One of the peculiar aspects of quantum computation is that the state of a qubit is non-duplicable [1], a result known as the *no-cloning theorem.* A corollary is that a quantum circuit is a very simple kind of circuit: wires neither split nor merge.

Measurement is a fundamentally different kind of operation: it queries the state of the quantum memory and returns a classical result. Measuring the state of a quantum bit is a probabilistic and destructive operation: it produces a classical answer with a probability that depends on the amplitudes α, β in the state of the qubit while projecting this state onto `tt` or `ff`, based on the result.

For a more detailed introduction to quantum computation, we refer the reader to recent textbooks (e.g., [2]).

Control Flow in Quantum Computation. In the context of quantum programming languages, there is a well-understood notion of control flow: the so-called *classical control flow.* A quantum program can be seen as the construction, manipulation and evaluation of quantum circuits [3,4]. In this setting, circuits are simply considered as special kinds of data without much computational content, and programs are ruled by regular classical control.

One can however consider the circuit being manipulated as a program in its own right: a particular sequence of execution on the quantum memory is then seen as a closed system. One can then try to derive a notion of *quantum control* [5], with "quantum tests" and "quantum loops". Quantum tests are a bit tricky to perform [5,6] but they essentially correspond to well-understood controlled operations. The situation with quantum loops is more subtle [6,7]. First, a hypothetical quantum loop *must* terminate. Indeed, a non-terminating quantum loop would entail an infinite quantum circuit, and this concept has so far no meaning. Second, the interaction of quantum loops with measurement is problematic: it is known that the canonical model of *open* quantum computation based on superoperators [8,9] is incompatible with such quantum control [6]. Finally, the mathematical operator corresponding to a quantum loop would need to act on an infinite-dimensional Hilbert space and the question of mixing programming languages with infinitary Hilbert spaces is still an unresolved issue.

Our Contribution. In this paper, we offer a novel solution to the question of quantum control: we define a purely quantum language, inspired by Theseus [10], featuring tests and fixpoints in the presence of lists. More precisely, we propose (1) a typed, reversible language, extensible to linear combinations of terms, with a reduction strategy akin to algebraic lambda-calculi [11–13]; (2) a model for the language based on unitary operators over infinite-dimensional Hilbert spaces, simplifying the Fock space model of Ying [7]. This model captures lists, tests, and structurally recursive fixpoints. We therefore settle two longstanding issues. (1) We offer a solution to the problem of quantum loops, with the use of *terminating, structurally recursive, purely quantum* fixpoints. We dodge previously noted concerns (e.g., [6]) by staying in the closed quantum setting and answer the problem of the external system of quantum "coins" [7] with the use of lists. (2) By using a linear language based on patterns and clauses, we give an extensible framework for reconciling algebraic calculi with quantum computation [11,12,16].

In the remainder of the paper, we first introduce the key idea underlying our classical reversible language in a simple first-order setting. We then generalize the setting to allow second-order functions, recursive types (e.g., lists), and fixpoints. After illustrating the expressiveness of this classical language, we adapt it to the quantum domain and give a semantics to the resulting quantum language in infinite-dimensional Hilbert spaces. Technical material that would interrupt the flow or that is somewhat complementary has been relegated to an extended version of the paper [17].

2 Pattern-Matching Isomorphisms

The most elementary control structure in a programming language is the ability to conditionally execute one of several possible code fragments. Expressing such an abstraction using predicates and nested **if**-expressions makes it difficult for both humans and compilers to reason about the control flow structure. Instead, in modern functional languages, this control flow paradigm is elegantly expressed using *pattern-matching*. This approach yields code that is not only more concise and readable but also enables the compiler to easily verify two crucial properties:

(i) non-overlapping patterns and (ii) exhaustive coverage of a datatype using a collection of patterns. Indeed most compilers for functional languages perform these checks, warning the user when they are violated. At a more fundamental level, e.g., in type theories and proof assistants, these properties are actually necessary for correct reasoning about programs. Our first insight, explained in this section, is that these properties, perhaps surprisingly, are sufficient to produce a simple and intuitive first-order reversible programming language.

```
f :: Either Int Int -> a
f (Left 0)     = undefined
f (Left (n+1)) = undefined
f (Right n)    = undefined
```

Fig. 1. A skeleton

```
g :: (Bool,Int) -> a
g (False,n)   = undefined
g (True,0)    = undefined
g (True,n+1)  = undefined
```

Fig. 2. Another skeleton

```
h :: Either Int Int <-> (Bool,Int)
h (Left 0)     = (True,0)
h (Left (n+1)) = (False,n)
h (Right n)    = (True,n+1)
```

Fig. 3. An isomorphism

2.1 An Example

We start with a small illustrative example, written in a Haskell-like syntax. Figure 1 gives the skeleton of a function `f` that accepts a value of type `Either Int Int`; the patterns on the left-hand side exhaustively cover every possible incoming value and are non-overlapping. Similarly, Fig. 2 gives the skeleton for a function `g` that accepts a value of type `(Bool,Int)`; again the patterns on the left-hand side exhaustively cover every possible incoming value and are non-overlapping. Now we claim that since the types `Either Int Int` and `(Bool,Int)` are isomorphic, we can combine the patterns of `f` and `g` into *symmetric pattern-matching clauses* to produce a reversible function between the types `Either Int Int` and `(Bool,Int)`. Figure 3 gives one such function; there, we suggestively use `<->` to indicate that the function can be executed in either direction. This reversible function is obtained by simply combining the non-overlapping exhaustive patterns on the two sides of a clause. In order to be well-formed in either direction, these clauses are subject to the constraint that each variable occurring on one side must occur exactly once on the other side (and with the same type). Thus it is acceptable to swap the second and third right-hand sides of `h` but not the first and second ones.

2.2 Terms and Types

We present a formalization of the ideas presented above using a simple typed first-order reversible language. The language is two-layered. The first layer contains values, which also play the role of patterns. These values are constructed from variables ranged over x and the introduction forms for the finite types a, b constructed from the unit type and sums and products of types. The second layer contains collections of pattern-matching clauses that denote isomorphisms of type $a \leftrightarrow b$. Computations are chained applications of isomorphisms to values:

$$\begin{array}{llcl}
\text{(Value types)} & a, b & ::= & \mathbb{1} \mid a \oplus b \mid a \otimes b \\
\text{(Iso types)} & T & ::= & a \leftrightarrow b \\
\\
\text{(Values)} & v & ::= & () \mid x \mid \texttt{inj}_l\ v \mid \texttt{inj}_r\ v \mid \langle v_1, v_2 \rangle \\
\text{(Isos)} & \omega & ::= & \{ \mid v_1 \leftrightarrow v_1' \mid v_2 \leftrightarrow v_2' \ \ldots \} \\
\text{(Terms)} & t & ::= & v \mid \omega\, t
\end{array}$$

The typing rules are defined using two judgments: $\Delta \vdash_v v : a$ for typing values (or *patterns*) and terms; and $\vdash_\omega \omega : a \leftrightarrow b$ for typing collections of pattern-matching clauses denoting an isomorphism. As it is customary, we write $a_1 \otimes a_2 \otimes \cdots \otimes a_n$ for $((a_1 \otimes a_2) \otimes \cdots \otimes a_n)$, and similarly $\langle x_1, x_2, \ldots, x_n \rangle$ for $\langle\langle x_1, x_2\rangle, \ldots, x_n\rangle$.

The typing rules for values are the expected ones. The only subtlety is the fact that they are linear: because values act as patterns, we forbid the repetition of variables. A typing context Δ is a set of typed variables $x_1 : a_1, \ldots, x_n : a_n$. A value typing judgment is valid if it can be derived from the following rules:

$$\frac{}{\vdash_v () : \mathbb{1}}, \qquad \frac{}{x : a \vdash_v x : a}, \qquad \frac{\Delta_1 \vdash_v v_1 : a \quad \Delta_2 \vdash_v v_2 : b}{\Delta_1, \Delta_2 \vdash_v \langle v_1, v_2 \rangle : a \otimes b}.$$

$$\frac{\Delta \vdash_v v : a}{\Delta \vdash_v \texttt{inj}_l\ v : a \oplus b}, \qquad \frac{\Delta \vdash_v v : b}{\Delta \vdash_v \texttt{inj}_r\ v : a \oplus b},$$

The typing rule for term construction is simple and forces the term to be closed:

$$\frac{\vdash_v t : a \quad \vdash_\omega \omega : a \leftrightarrow b}{\vdash_v \omega\ t : b}$$

The most interesting type rule is the one for isomorphisms. We present the rule and then explain it in detail:

$$\frac{\begin{array}{llll} \Delta_1 \vdash_v v_1 : a & \Delta_n \vdash_v v_n : a & \forall i \neq j, v_i \bot v_j & \dim(a) = n \\ \Delta_1 \vdash_v v_1' : b \quad \cdots & \Delta_n \vdash_v v_n' : b & \forall i \neq j, v_i' \bot v_j' & \dim(b) = n \end{array}}{\vdash_\omega \{ \mid v_1 \leftrightarrow v_1' \mid v_2 \leftrightarrow v_2' \ \ldots \} : a \leftrightarrow b}, \tag{1}$$

The rule relies on two auxiliary conditions as motivated in the beginning of the section. These conditions are (i) the orthogonality judgment $v \bot v'$ that formalizes that patterns must be *non-overlapping* and (ii) the condition $\dim(a) = n$ which formalizes that patterns are *exhaustive*. The rules for deriving orthogonality of values or patterns are:

$$\frac{}{\texttt{inj}_l\ v_1 \bot \texttt{inj}_r\ v_2} \qquad \frac{}{\texttt{inj}_r\ v_1 \bot \texttt{inj}_l\ v_2}$$

$$\frac{v_1 \bot v_2}{\texttt{inj}_l\ v_1 \bot \texttt{inj}_l\ v_2} \qquad \frac{v_1 \bot v_2}{\texttt{inj}_r\ v_1 \bot \texttt{inj}_r\ v_2} \qquad \frac{v_1 \bot v_2}{\langle v, v_1 \rangle \bot \langle v', v_2 \rangle} \qquad \frac{v_1 \bot v_2}{\langle v_1, v \rangle \bot \langle v_2, v' \rangle}$$

The idea is simply that the left and right injections are disjoint subspaces of values. To characterize that a set of patterns is exhaustive, we associate a *dimension* with each type. For finite types, this is just the number of elements in the type and is inductively defined as follows: $\dim(\mathbb{1}) = 1$; $\dim(a \oplus b) = \dim(a) + \dim(b)$;

and $\dim(a \otimes b) = \dim(a) \cdot \dim(b)$. For a given type a, if a set of non-overlapping clauses has cardinality $\dim(a)$, it is exhaustive. Conversely, any set of exhaustive clauses for a type a either has cardinality $\dim(a)$ or can be extended to an equivalent exhaustive set of clauses of cardinality $\dim(a)$.

2.3 Semantics

We equip our language with a simple operational semantics on terms, using the natural notion of matching. To formally define it, we first introduce the notion of variable assignation, or valuation, which is a partial map from a finite set of variables (the support) to a set of values. We denote the matching of a value w against a pattern v and its associated valuation σ as $\sigma[v] = w$ and define it as follows:

$$\frac{}{\sigma[()] = ()} \qquad \frac{\sigma = \{x \mapsto v\}}{\sigma[x] = v} \qquad \frac{\sigma[v] = w}{\sigma[\mathtt{inj}_l\ v] = \mathtt{inj}_l\ w} \qquad \frac{\sigma[v] = w}{\sigma[\mathtt{inj}_r\ v] = \mathtt{inj}_r\ w}$$

$$\frac{\sigma_2[v_1] = w_1 \quad \sigma_1[v_2] = w_2 \quad \mathrm{supp}(\sigma_1) \cap \mathrm{supp}(\sigma_2) = \emptyset \quad \sigma = \sigma_1 \cup \sigma_2}{\sigma[\langle v_1, v_2 \rangle] = \langle w_1, w_2 \rangle}$$

If σ is a valuation whose support contains the variables of v, we write $\sigma(v)$ for the value where the variables of v have been replaced with the corresponding values in σ.

Given these definitions, we can define the reduction relation on terms. The redex $\{ \mid v_1 \leftrightarrow v'_1 \mid v_2 \leftrightarrow v'_2 \ \ldots\ \} v$ reduces to $\sigma(v'_i)$ whenever $\sigma[v_i] = v'_i$. Because of the conditions on patterns, a matching pattern exists by exhaustivity of coverage, and this pattern is unique by the non-overlapping condition. Congruence holds: $\omega\, t \to \omega\, t'$ whenever $t \to t'$. As usual, we write $s \to t$ to say that s rewrites in one step to t and $s \to^* t$ to say that s rewrites to t in 0 or more steps.

Because of the conditions set on patterns, the rewrite system is deterministic. More interestingly, we can swap the two sides of all pattern-matching clauses in an isomorphism ω to get ω^{-1}. The execution of ω^{-1} is the reverse execution of ω in the sense that $\omega^{-1}(\omega\ t) \to^* t$ and $\omega(\omega^{-1}\ t') \to^* t'$.

3 Second-Order Functions, Lists, and Recursion

The first-order reversible language from the previous section embodies symmetric-pattern matching clauses as its core notion of control. Its expressiveness is limited, however. We now show that it is possible to extend it to have more in common with a conventional functional language. To that end, we extend the language with the ability to parametrically manipulate isomorphisms, with a recursive type (lists), and with recursion.

3.1 Terms and Types

Formally, the language is now defined as follows.

$$\begin{array}{lrcl}
\text{(Val \& term types)} & a, b & ::= & \mathbb{1} \mid a \oplus b \mid a \otimes b \mid [a] \\
\text{(Iso types)} & T & ::= & a \leftrightarrow b \mid (a \leftrightarrow b) \to T \\
\\
\text{(Values)} & v & ::= & () \mid x \mid \mathtt{inj}_l\, v \mid \mathtt{inj}_r\, v \mid \langle v_1, v_2 \rangle \\
\text{(Products)} & p & ::= & () \mid x \mid \langle p_1, p_2 \rangle \\
\text{(Extended Values)} & e & ::= & v \mid \mathtt{let}\, p_1 = \omega\ p_2\ \mathtt{in}\ e \\
\text{(Isos)} & \omega & ::= & \{ \mid v_1 \leftrightarrow e_1 \mid v_2 \leftrightarrow e_2 \ \dots \} \mid \lambda f.\omega \mid \\
& & & \mu f.\omega \mid f \mid \omega_1\, \omega_2 \\
\text{(Terms)} & t & ::= & () \mid x \mid \mathtt{inj}_l\, t \mid \mathtt{inj}_r\, t \mid \langle t_1, t_2 \rangle \mid \\
& & & \omega\ t \mid \mathtt{let}\, p = t_1\ \mathtt{in}\ t_2
\end{array}$$

We use variables f to span a set of iso-variables and variables x to span a set of term-variables. We extend the layer of isos so that it can be parameterized by a fixed number of other isos, i.e., we now allow higher-order manipulation of isos using $\lambda f.\omega$, iso-variables, and applications. Isos can now be used inside the definition of other isos with a let-notation. These let-constructs are however restricted to products of term-variables: they essentially serve as syntactic sugar for composition of isos. An extended value is then a value where some of its free variables are substituted with the result of the application of one or several isos. Given an extended value e, we define its *bottom value*, denoted with $\mathrm{Val}(e)$ as the value "at the end" of the let-chain: $\mathrm{Val}(v) = v$, and $\mathrm{Val}(\mathtt{let}\, p = \omega p\ \mathtt{in}\ e) = \mathrm{Val}(e)$. The orthogonality of extended values is simply the orthogonality of their bottom value.

As usual, the type of lists $[a]$ of elements of type a is a recursive type and is equivalent to $\mathbb{1} \oplus (a \times [a])$. We build the value $[]$ (empty list) as $\mathtt{inj}_l\, ()$ and the term $t_1 : t_2$ (cons of t_1 and t_2) as $\mathtt{inj}_r\, \langle t_1, t_2 \rangle$. In addition, to take full advantage of recursive datatypes, it is natural to consider recursion. Modulo a termination guarantee it is possible to add a fixpoint to the language: we extend isos with the fixpoint constructor $\mu f.\omega$. Some reversible languages allow infinite loops and must work with partial isomorphisms instead. Since we plan on using our language as a foundation for a quantum language we insist of termination.

Since the language features two kinds of variables, there are typing contexts (written Δ) consisting of base-level typed variables of the form $x : a$, and typing context (written Ψ) consisting of typed iso-variables of the form $f : T$. As terms and values contain both base-level and iso-variables, one needs two typing contexts. Typing judgments are therefore written respectively as $\Delta; \Psi \vdash_v t : a$. The updated rules for $(\vdash_v)$ are found in Table 1. As the only possible free variables in isos are iso-variables, their typing judgments only need one context and are written as $\Psi \vdash_\omega \omega : T$.

The rules for typing derivations of isos are in Table 2. It is worthwhile mentioning that isos are treated in a usual, non-linear way: this is the purpose of the typing context separation. The intuition is that an iso is the description of a closed computation with respect to inputs: remark that isos cannot accept

Table 1. Typing rules for terms and values

$$\frac{}{\emptyset; \Psi \vdash_v () : \mathbb{1}} \qquad \frac{}{x : a; \Psi \vdash_v x : a}$$

$$\frac{\Delta; \Psi \vdash_v t : a}{\Delta; \Psi \vdash_v \mathtt{inj}_l\, t : a \oplus b} \quad \frac{\Delta; \Psi \vdash_v t : b}{\Delta; \Psi \vdash_v \mathtt{inj}_r\, t : a \oplus b} \quad \frac{\Delta_1; \Psi \vdash_v t_1 : a \quad \Delta_2; \Psi \vdash_v t_2 : b}{\Delta_1, \Delta_2; \Psi \vdash_v \langle t_1, t_2 \rangle : a \otimes b}$$

$$\frac{\Psi \vdash_\omega \omega : a \leftrightarrow b \quad \Delta; \Psi \vdash_v t : a}{\Delta; \Psi \vdash_v \omega\, t : b} \qquad \frac{\Delta; \Psi \vdash_v t_1 : a \otimes b \quad \Delta, x : a, y : b; \Psi \vdash_v t_2 : c}{\Delta; \Psi \vdash_v \mathtt{let}\, \langle x, y \rangle = t_1\, \mathtt{in}\, t_2 : c}$$

Table 2. Typing rules for isos

$$\frac{\begin{array}{lll} \Delta_1; \Psi \vdash_v v_1 : a & \ldots \quad \Delta_n; \Psi \vdash_v v_n : a & \mathrm{OD}_a\{v_1, \ldots, v_n\} \\ \Delta_1; \Psi \vdash_v e_1 : b & \ldots \quad \Delta_n; \Psi \vdash_v e_n : b & \mathrm{OD}_b^{ext}\{e_1, \ldots, e_n\} \end{array}}{\Psi \vdash_\omega \{ \mid v_1 \leftrightarrow e_1 \mid v_2 \leftrightarrow e_2 \ \ldots \} : a \leftrightarrow b.}$$

$$\frac{\Psi, f : a \leftrightarrow b \vdash_\omega \omega : T}{\Psi \vdash_\omega \lambda f.\omega : (a \leftrightarrow b) \to T} \qquad \frac{}{\Psi, f : T \vdash_\omega f : T}$$

$$\frac{\Psi \vdash_\omega \omega_1 : (a \leftrightarrow b) \to T \quad \Psi \vdash_\omega \omega_2 : a \leftrightarrow b}{\Psi \vdash_\omega \omega_1 \omega_2 : T}$$

$$\frac{\begin{array}{c} \Psi, f : a \leftrightarrow b \vdash_\omega \omega : (a_1 \leftrightarrow b_1) \to \cdots \to (a_n \leftrightarrow b_n) \to (a \leftrightarrow b) \\ \mu f.\omega \text{ terminates in any finite context} \end{array}}{\Psi \vdash_\omega \mu f.\omega : (a_1 \leftrightarrow b_1) \to \cdots \to (a_n \leftrightarrow b_n) \to (a \leftrightarrow b)}$$

value-types. As computations, they can be erased or duplicated without issues. On the other hand, value-types still need to be treated linearly.

In the typing rule for recursion, the condition "$\mu f.\omega$ terminates in any finite context" formally refers to the following requirement. A well-typed fixpoint $\mu f.\omega$ of type $\Psi \vdash_\omega \mu f.\omega : (a_1 \leftrightarrow b_1) \to \cdots \to (a_n \leftrightarrow b_n) \to (a \leftrightarrow b)$ is *terminating in a 0-context* if for all closed isos $\omega_i : a_i \leftrightarrow b_i$ not using fixpoints and for every closed value v of type a, the term $((\mu f.\omega)\omega_1 \ldots \omega_n)v$ terminates. We say that the fixpoint is *terminating in an* $(n+1)$*-context* if for all closed isos $\omega_i : a_i \leftrightarrow b_i$ terminating in n-contexts, and for every closed value v of type a, the term $((\mu f.\omega)\omega_1 \ldots \omega_n)v$ terminates. Finally, we say that the fixpoint is *terminating in any finitary context* if for all n it is terminating in any n-context.

With the addition of lists, the non-overlapping and exhaustivity conditions need to be modified. The main problem is that we can no longer define the dimension of types using natural numbers: $[a]$ is in essence an infinite sum, and would have an "infinite" dimension. Instead, we combine the two conditions into the concept of *orthogonal decomposition*. Formally, given a type a, we say that a set S of patterns is an *orthogonal decomposition*, written $\mathrm{OD}_a(S)$, when these patterns are pairwise orthogonal and when they cover the whole type. We

Table 3. Reduction rules

$$\frac{t_1 \to t_2}{C[t_1] \to C[t_2]}\ \text{Cong} \qquad \frac{\sigma[p] = v_1}{\texttt{let}\, p = v_1\ \texttt{in}\ t_2 \to \sigma(t_2)}\ \text{LetE}$$

$$\frac{\sigma[v_i] = v}{\{\ |\ v_1 \leftrightarrow t_1\ |\ \dots\ |\ v_n \leftrightarrow t_n\ \}\ v \to \sigma(t_i)}\ \text{IsoApp} \qquad \frac{}{(\lambda f.\omega)\ \omega_2 \to \omega[\omega_2/f]}\ \text{HIsoApp}$$

$$\frac{\Psi, f : a \leftrightarrow b \vdash_\omega \omega : (a_1 \leftrightarrow b_1) \to \cdots \to (a_n \leftrightarrow b_n) \to (a \leftrightarrow b)}{\mu f.\omega \to \lambda f_1 \dots f_n.(\omega[((\mu f.\omega) f_1 \dots f_n)/f]) f_1 \dots f_n}\ \text{IsoRec}$$

formally define $\mathrm{OD}_a(S)$ as follows. For all types a, $\mathrm{OD}_a\{x\}$ is valid. For the unit type, $\mathrm{OD}_{\mathbb{1}}\{()\}$ is valid. If $\mathrm{OD}_a(S)$ and $\mathrm{OD}_b(T)$, then

$$\begin{aligned} &\mathrm{OD}_{a\oplus b}(\{\texttt{inj}_l\ v \mid v \in S\} \cup \{\texttt{inj}_r\ v \mid v \in T\}) \\ \text{and}\quad &\mathrm{OD}_{a\otimes b}\{\langle v_1, v_2\rangle \mid v_1 \in S,\ v_2 \in T,\ \mathrm{FV}(v_1) \cap \mathrm{FV}(v_2) = \emptyset\}, \end{aligned}$$

where $\mathrm{FV}(t)$ stands for the set of free value-variables in t. We then extend the notion of orthogonal decomposition to extended values as follows. If S is a set of extended values, $\mathrm{OD}_a^{ext}(S)$ is true whenever $\mathrm{OD}_a\{\mathrm{Val}(e) \mid e \in S\}$. With this new characterization, the typing rule of iso in Eq. 1 still holds, and then can be re-written using this notion of orthogonal decomposition as shown in Table 2.

3.2 Semantics

In Table 3 we present the reduction rules for the reversible language. We assume that the reduction relation applies to well-typed terms. In the rules, the notation $C[-]$ stands for an *applicative context*, and is defined as: $C[-] ::= [-] \mid \texttt{inj}_l\ C[-] \mid \texttt{inj}_r\ C[-] \mid (C[-])\omega \mid \{\cdots\}\ (C[-]) \mid \texttt{let}\, p = C[-]\ \texttt{in}\ t_2 \mid \langle C[-], v\rangle \mid \langle v, C[-]\rangle$.

The inversion of isos is still possible but more subtle than in the first-order case. We define an inversion operation $(-)^{-1}$ on iso types with, $(a \leftrightarrow b)^{-1} := (b \leftrightarrow a)$, $((a \leftrightarrow b) \to T)^{-1} := ((b \leftrightarrow a) \to (T^{-1}))$. Inversion of isos is defined as follows. For fixpoints, $(\mu f.\omega)^{-1} = \mu f.(\omega{-}1)$. For variables, $(f)^{-1} := f$. For applications, $(\omega_1\ \omega_2)^{-1} := (\omega_1)^{-1}\ (\omega_2)^{-1}$. For abstraction, $(\lambda f.\omega)^{-1} := \lambda f.(\omega^{-1})$. Finally, clauses are inverted as follows:

$$\begin{pmatrix} v_1 \leftrightarrow \texttt{let}\, p_1 = \omega_1\, p_1'\ \texttt{in} \\ \cdots \\ \texttt{let}\, p_n = \omega_n\, p_n'\ \texttt{in}\ v_1' \end{pmatrix}^{-1} := \begin{pmatrix} v_1' \leftrightarrow \texttt{let}\, p_n' = \omega_n^{-1}\, p_n\ \texttt{in} \\ \cdots \\ \texttt{let}\, p_1' = \omega_1^{-1}\, p_1\ \texttt{in}\ v_1 \end{pmatrix}.$$

Note that $(-)^{-1}$ only inverts first-order arrows $(\leftrightarrow)$, not second-order arrows $(\to)$. This is reflected by the fact that iso-variable are non-linear while value-variables are. This is due to the clear separation of the two layers of the language.

The rewriting system satisfies the usual properties for well-typed terms: it is terminating, well-typed closed terms have a unique normal value-form, and it preserves typing.

Theorem 1. *The inversion operation is well-typed, in the sense that if* $f_1 : a_1 \leftrightarrow b_1, \ldots, f_n : a_n \leftrightarrow b_n \vdash_\omega \omega : T$ *then we also have* $f_1 : b_1 \leftrightarrow a_1, \ldots, f_n : b_n \leftrightarrow a_n \vdash_\omega \omega^{-1} : T^{-1}$. □

Thanks to the fact that the language is terminating, we also recover the operational result of Sect. 2.3.

Theorem 2. *Consider a well-typed, closed iso* $\vdash_\omega \omega : a \leftrightarrow b$, *and suppose that* $\vdash_v v : a$ *and that* $\vdash_v w : b$, *then* $\omega^{-1}(\omega\ v) \to^* v$ *and* $\omega(\omega^{-1}\ w) \to^* w$. □

4 Examples

In the previous sections, we developed a novel classical reversible language with a familiar syntax based on pattern-matching. The language includes a limited notion of higher-order functions and (terminating) recursive functions. We illustrate the expressiveness of the language with a few examples and motivate the changes and extensions needed to adapt the language to the quantum domain.

We encode booleans as follows: $\mathbb{B} = \mathbb{1} \oplus \mathbb{1}$, $\mathtt{tt} = \mathtt{inj}_l\ ()$, and $\mathtt{ff} = \mathtt{inj}_r\ ()$. One of the easiest function to define is $\mathtt{not} : \mathbb{B} \leftrightarrow \mathbb{B}$ which flips a boolean. The controlled-not gate which flips the second bit when the first is true can also be expressed:

$$\mathtt{not} : \mathbb{B} \leftrightarrow \mathbb{B} = \begin{pmatrix} \mathtt{ff} & \leftrightarrow & \mathtt{tt} \\ \mathtt{tt} & \leftrightarrow & \mathtt{ff} \end{pmatrix}, \quad \mathtt{cnot} : \mathbb{B} \otimes \mathbb{B} \leftrightarrow \mathbb{B} \otimes \mathbb{B} = \begin{pmatrix} \langle \mathtt{ff}, x \rangle & \leftrightarrow & \langle \mathtt{ff}, x \rangle \\ \langle \mathtt{tt}, \mathtt{ff} \rangle & \leftrightarrow & \langle \mathtt{tt}, \mathtt{tt} \rangle \\ \langle \mathtt{tt}, \mathtt{tt} \rangle & \leftrightarrow & \langle \mathtt{tt}, \mathtt{ff} \rangle \end{pmatrix}.$$

All the patterns in the previous two functions are orthogonal decompositions which guarantee reversibility as desired.

By using the abstraction facilities in the language, we can define higher-order operations that build complex reversible functions from simpler ones. For example, we can define a conditional expression parameterized by the functions used in the two branches:

$$\begin{array}{l} \mathtt{if} : (a \leftrightarrow b) \to (a \leftrightarrow b) \to (\mathbb{B} \otimes a \leftrightarrow \mathbb{B} \otimes b) \\ \mathtt{if} = \lambda g.\lambda h. \begin{pmatrix} \langle \mathtt{tt}, x \rangle & \leftrightarrow & \mathtt{let}\ y = g\ x\ \mathtt{in}\ \langle \mathtt{tt}, y \rangle \\ \langle \mathtt{ff}, x \rangle & \leftrightarrow & \mathtt{let}\ y = h\ x\ \mathtt{in}\ \langle \mathtt{ff}, y \rangle \end{pmatrix} \end{array}$$

Using `if` and the obvious definition for the identity function `id`, we can define $\mathtt{ctrl} :: (a \leftrightarrow a) \to (\mathbb{B} \otimes a \leftrightarrow \mathbb{B} \otimes a)$ as $\mathtt{ctrl}\ f = \mathtt{if}\ f\ \mathtt{id}$ and recover an alternative definition of `cnot` as `ctrl not`. We can then define the controlled-controlled-not gate (aka the Toffoli gate) by writing `ctrl cnot`. We can even iterate this construction using fixpoints to produce an n-controlled-not function that takes a list of n control bits and a target bit and flips the target bit iff all the control bits are `tt`:

$$\texttt{cnot*} : ([\mathbb{B}] \otimes \mathbb{B}) \leftrightarrow ([\mathbb{B}] \otimes \mathbb{B})$$

$$\texttt{cnot*} = \mu f. \begin{pmatrix} \langle [], tb \rangle \leftrightarrow \texttt{let}\, tb' = \texttt{not}\ tb\ \texttt{in}\ \langle [], tb' \rangle \\ \langle \texttt{ff} : cbs, tb \rangle \leftrightarrow \langle \texttt{ff} : cbs, tb \rangle \\ \langle \texttt{tt} : cbs, tb \rangle \leftrightarrow \texttt{let}\ \langle cbs', tb' \rangle = f\ \langle cbs, tb \rangle\ \texttt{in}\ \langle \texttt{tt} : cbs', tb' \rangle \end{pmatrix}$$

The language is also expressible enough to write conventional recursive (and higher-order) programs. We illustrate this expressiveness using the usual `map` operation and an accumulating variant `mapAccu`:

$$\texttt{map} : (a \leftrightarrow b) \to ([a] \leftrightarrow [b]) \qquad \lambda g.\mu f. \begin{pmatrix} [] & \leftrightarrow & [] \\ h : t & \leftrightarrow & \texttt{let}\, x = g\ h\ \texttt{in} \\ & & \texttt{let}\, y = f\ t\ \texttt{in}\ x : y \end{pmatrix},$$

$$\texttt{mapAccu} : (a \otimes b \leftrightarrow a \otimes c) \to (a \otimes [b] \leftrightarrow a \otimes [c]) \qquad \lambda g.\mu f. \begin{pmatrix} \langle x, [] \rangle & \leftrightarrow & \langle x, [] \rangle \\ \langle x, (h : t) \rangle & \leftrightarrow & \texttt{let}\ \langle y, h' \rangle = g\ \langle x, h \rangle\ \texttt{in} \\ & & \texttt{let}\ \langle z, t' \rangle = f\ \langle y, t \rangle\ \texttt{in} \\ & & \langle z, (h' : t') \rangle \end{pmatrix}.$$

The three examples `cnot*`, `map` and `mapAccu` uses fixpoints which are clearly terminating in any finite context. Indeed, the functions are structurally recursive. A formal definition of this notion for the reversible language is as follows.

$$\begin{array}{c|ccc} & v_1 & v_2 & v_3 \\ \hline v_1' & 1 & 0 & 0 \\ v_2' & 0 & 1 & 0 \\ v_3' & 0 & 0 & 1 \end{array}$$

Fig. 4. Classical iso

$$\begin{array}{c|ccc} & v_1 & v_2 & v_3 \\ \hline v_1' & a_{11} & a_{12} & a_{13} \\ v_2' & a_{21} & a_{22} & a_{23} \\ v_3' & a_{31} & a_{32} & a_{33} \end{array}$$

Fig. 5. Quantum iso

$$\begin{array}{c|cc} & \langle \texttt{tt}, x \rangle & \langle \texttt{ff}, x \rangle \\ \hline \langle \texttt{tt}, x \rangle & \frac{1}{\sqrt{2}}\texttt{Had} & \frac{1}{\sqrt{2}}\texttt{Id} \\ \langle \texttt{ff}, x \rangle & \frac{1}{\sqrt{2}}\texttt{Had} & \frac{-1}{\sqrt{2}}\texttt{Id} \end{array}$$

Fig. 6. Semantics of `Gate`

Definition 1. Define a *structurally recursive type* as a type of the form $[a] \otimes b_1 \otimes \ldots \otimes b_n$. Let $\omega = \{v_i \leftrightarrow e_i \mid i \in I\}$ be an iso such that $f : a \leftrightarrow b \vdash_\omega \omega : a \leftrightarrow c$ where a is a structurally recursive type. We say that $\mu f.\omega$ is *structurally recursive* provided that for each $i \in I$, the value v_i is either of the form $\langle [], p_1, \ldots p_n \rangle$ or of the form $\langle h : t, p_1, \ldots p_n \rangle$. In the former case, e_i does not contain f as a free variable. In the latter case, e_i is of the form $C[f\,\langle t, p_1', \ldots, p_n' \rangle]$ where C is a context of the form $C[-] ::= [-] \mid \texttt{let}\, p = C[-]\ \texttt{in}\ t \mid \texttt{let}\, p = t\ \texttt{in}\ C[-]$.

This definition will be critical for quantum loops in the next section.

5 From Reversible Isos to Quantum Control

In the language presented so far, an iso $\omega : a \leftrightarrow b$ describes a bijection between the set $\mathcal{B}_a$ of closed values of type a and the set $\mathcal{B}_b$ of closed values of type b. If one regards $\mathcal{B}_a$ and $\mathcal{B}_b$ as the basis elements of some vector space $[\![a]\!]$ and $[\![b]\!]$, the iso ω becomes a 0/1 matrix.

As an example, consider an iso ω defined using three clauses of the form $\{ \mid v_1 \leftrightarrow v_1' \mid v_2 \leftrightarrow v_2' \mid v_3 \leftrightarrow v_3' \}$. From the exhaustivity and non-overlapping conditions derives the fact that the space $[\![a]\!]$ can be split into the direct sum of the three subspaces $[\![a]\!]_{v_i}$ $(i = 1, 2, 3)$ generated by v_i. Similarly, $[\![b]\!]$ is split into the direct sum of the subspaces $[\![b]\!]_{v'_i}$ generated by v'_i. One can therefore represent ω as the matrix $[\![\omega]\!]$ in Fig. 4: The "1" in each column v_i indicates to which subspace $[\![b]\!]_{v'_j}$ an element of $[\![a]\!]_{v_i}$ is sent to.

In Sect. 2.2 we discussed the fact that $v_i \bot v_j$ when $i \neq j$. This notation hints at the fact that $[\![a]\!]$ and $[\![b]\!]$ could be seen as Hilbert spaces and the mapping $[\![\omega]\!]$ as a unitary map from $[\![a]\!]$ to $[\![b]\!]$. The purpose of this section is to extend and formalize precisely the correspondence between isos and unitary maps.

The definition of clauses is extended following this idea of seeing isos as unitaries, and not only bijections on basis elements of the input space. We therefore essentially propose to generalize the clauses to complex, linear combinations of values on the right-hand-side, such as shown on the left, with the side conditions on that the matrix of Fig. 5 is unitary. We define in Sect. 5.1 how this extends to second-order.

$$\left\{\begin{array}{l} \mid v_1 \leftrightarrow a_{11}v'_1 + a_{21}v'_2 + a_{31}v'_3 \\ \mid v_2 \leftrightarrow a_{12}v'_1 + a_{22}v'_2 + a_{23}v'_3 \\ \mid v_3 \leftrightarrow a_{31}v'_1 + a_{32}v'_2 + a_{33}v'_3 \end{array}\right\}$$

5.1 Extending the Language to Linear Combinations of Terms

The quantum unitary language extends the reversible language from the previous section by closing extended values and terms under complex, finite linear combinations. For example, if v_1 and v_2 are values and α and β are complex numbers, $\alpha \cdot v_1 + \beta \cdot v_2$ is now an extended value.

Several approaches exist for performing such an extension. One can update the reduction strategy to be able to reduce these sums and scalar multiplications to normal forms [12,18], or one can instead consider terms modulo the usual algebraic equalities [13,18]: this is the strategy we follow for this paper.

When extending a language to linear combination of terms in a naive way, this added structure might generate inconsistencies in the presence of unconstrained fixpoints [12,13,18]. The weak condition on termination we imposed on fixpoints in the classical language was enough to guarantee reversibility. With the presence of linear combinations, we want the much stronger guarantee of unitarity. For this reason, we instead impose fixpoints to be *structurally recursive*.

The quantum unitary language is defined by allowing sums of terms and values and multiplications by complex numbers: if t and t' are terms, so is $\alpha \cdot t + t'$. Terms and values are taken modulo the equational theory of modules. We furthermore consider the value and term constructs $\langle -, - \rangle$, $\texttt{let}\, p = -\ \texttt{in}\ -$, $\texttt{inj}_l\,(-)$, $\texttt{inj}_r\,(-)$ distributive over sum and scalar multiplication. We do *not* however take iso-constructions as distributive over sum and scalar multiplication: $\{\ \mid\ v_1 \leftrightarrow \alpha v_2 + \beta v_3\ \}$ is *not* the same thing as $\alpha\{\ \mid\ v_1 \leftrightarrow v_2\ \} + \beta\{\ \mid\ v_1 \leftrightarrow v_3\ \}$. This is in the spirit of Lineal [11,12].

The typing rules for terms and extended values are updated as follows. We only allow linear combinations of terms and values of the same type and of the same free variables. Fixpoints are now required to be *structurally recursive*, as introduced in Definition 1. Finally, an iso is now not only performing an "identity" as in Fig. 4 but a true unitary operation:

$$\frac{\begin{array}{lll} \Delta_1; \Psi \vdash_v v_1 : a & \dots & \Delta_n; \Psi \vdash_v v_n : a \\ \Delta_1; \Psi \vdash_v e_1 : b & \dots & \Delta_n; \Psi \vdash_v e_n : b \\ \mathrm{OD}_a\{v_1, \dots, v_n\} & & \mathrm{OD}_b^{ext}\{e_1, \dots, e_n\} \end{array} \quad \begin{pmatrix} a_{11} & \cdots & a_{1n} \\ \vdots & & \vdots \\ a_{n1} & \cdots & a_{nn} \end{pmatrix} \text{ is unitary}}{\Psi \vdash_\omega \left\{ \begin{array}{lcl} v_1 & \leftrightarrow & a_{11} \cdot e_1 + \cdots + a_{1n} \cdot e_n \\ & \dots & \\ v_n & \leftrightarrow & a_{n1} \cdot e_1 + \cdots + a_{nn} \cdot e_n \end{array} \right\} : a \leftrightarrow b.}$$

The reduction relation is updated in a way that it remains deterministic in this extended setting. It is split into two parts: the reduction of pure terms, i.e. non-extended terms or values, and linear combinations thereof. Pure terms and values reduce using the reduction rules found in Table 3. We do not extend applicative contexts to linear combinations. For linear combinations of pure terms, we simply ask that *all* pure terms that are not normal forms in the combination are reduced. This makes the extended reduction relation deterministic.

Example 1. This allows one to define an iso behaving as the Hadamard gate, or a slightly more complex iso conditionally applying another iso, whose behavior as a matrix is shown in Fig. 6.

$$\begin{array}{ll} \mathtt{Had} : \mathbb{B} \leftrightarrow \mathbb{B} & \mathtt{Gate} : \mathbb{B} \otimes \mathbb{B} \leftrightarrow \mathbb{B} \otimes \mathbb{B} \\ \begin{pmatrix} \mathtt{tt} & \leftrightarrow & \frac{1}{\sqrt{2}}\mathtt{tt} + \frac{1}{\sqrt{2}}\mathtt{ff} \\ \mathtt{ff} & \leftrightarrow & \frac{1}{\sqrt{2}}\mathtt{tt} - \frac{1}{\sqrt{2}}\mathtt{ff} \end{pmatrix}, & \begin{pmatrix} \langle \mathtt{tt}, x \rangle & \leftrightarrow & \mathtt{let}\, y = \mathtt{Had}\, x \ \mathtt{in} \ \frac{1}{\sqrt{2}}\langle \mathtt{tt}, y \rangle + \frac{1}{\sqrt{2}}\langle \mathtt{ff}, y \rangle \\ \langle \mathtt{ff}, x \rangle & \leftrightarrow & \mathtt{let}\, y = \mathtt{Id}\, x \ \mathtt{in} \ \frac{1}{\sqrt{2}}\langle \mathtt{tt}, y \rangle - \frac{1}{\sqrt{2}}\langle \mathtt{ff}, y \rangle \end{pmatrix}. \end{array}$$

With this extension to linear combinations of terms, one can characterize normal forms as follows.

Lemma 1 (Structure of the Normal Forms). *Let ω be such that $\vdash_\omega \omega : a \leftrightarrow b$. For all closed values v of type a, the term $\omega\, v$ rewrites to a normal form $\sum_{i=1}^{N} \alpha_i \cdot w_i$ where $N < \infty$, each w_i is a closed value of type b and $\sum_i |\alpha_i| = 1$.*

Proof. The fact that $\omega\, v$ converges to a normal form is a corollary of the fact that we impose structural recursion on fixpoints. The property of the structure of the normal form is then proven by induction on the maximal number of steps it takes to reach it. It uses the restriction on the introduction of sums in the typing rule for clauses in isos and the determinism of the reduction. □

In the classical setting, isos describe bijections between sets of closed values: it was proven by considering the behavior of an iso against its inverse. In the presence of linear combinations of terms, we claim that isos describe more than bijections: they describe unitary maps. In the next section, we discuss how types can be understood as Hilbert spaces (Sect. 5.2) and isos as unitary maps (Sects. 5.3 and 5.4).

5.2 Modeling Types as Hilbert Spaces

By allowing complex linear combinations of terms, closed normal forms of finite types such as $\mathbb{B}$ or $\mathbb{B} \otimes \mathbb{B}$ can be regarded as complex vector spaces with basis consisting of closed values. For example, $\mathbb{B}$ is associated with $[\![\mathbb{B}]\!] = \{\alpha \cdot \mathtt{tt} + \beta \cdot \mathtt{ff} \mid \alpha, \beta \in \mathbb{C}\} \equiv \mathbb{C}^2$. We can consider this space as a complex Hilbert space where the scalar product is defined on basis elements in the obvious way: $\langle v|v\rangle = 1$ and $\langle v|w\rangle = 0$ if $v \neq w$. The map Had of Example 1 is then effectively a unitary map on the space $[\![\mathbb{B}]\!]$.

The problem comes from lists: the type $[\mathbb{1}]$ is inhabited by an infinite number of closed values: $[]$, $[()]$, $[(), ()]$, $[(), (), ()]$,... To account for this case, we need to consider infinitely dimensional complex Hilbert spaces. In general, a complex Hilbert space [19] is a complex vector space endowed with a scalar product that is complete with respect the distance induced by the scalar product. The completeness requirement implies for example that the infinite linear combination $[] + \frac{1}{2} \cdot [()] + \frac{1}{4}[(), ()] + \frac{1}{8}[(), (), ()] + \cdots$ needs to be an element of $[\![[\mathbb{B}]]\!]$. To account for these limit elements, we propose to use the standard [19] Hilbert space ℓ^2 of infinite sequences.

Definition 2. Let a be a value type. As before, we write $\mathcal{B}_a$ for the set of closed values of type a, that is, $\mathcal{B}_a = \{v \mid \vdash_v v : a\}$. The *span of* a is defined as the Hilbert space $[\![a]\!] = \ell^2(\mathcal{B}_a)$ consisting of sequences $(\phi_v)_{v \in \mathcal{B}_a}$ of complex numbers indexed by $\mathcal{B}_a$ such that $\sum_{v \in \mathcal{B}_a} |\phi_v|^2 < \infty$. The scalar product on this space is defined as $\langle (\phi_v)_{v \in \mathcal{B}_a} | (\psi_v)_{v \in \mathcal{B}_a} \rangle = \sum_{v \in \mathcal{B}_a} \overline{\phi_v} \psi_v$.

We shall use the following conventions. A closed value v of $[\![a]\!]$ is identified with the sequence $(\delta_{v,v'})_{v' \in \mathcal{B}_a}$ where $\delta_{v,v} = 1$ and $\delta_{v,v'} = 0$ if $v \neq v'$. An element $(\phi_v)_{v \in \mathcal{B}_a}$ of $[\![a]\!]$ is also written as the infinite, formal sum $\sum_{v \in \mathcal{B}_a} \phi_v \cdot v$.

5.3 Modeling Isos as Bounded Linear Maps

We can now define what is the linear map associated to an iso.

Definition 3. For each closed iso $\vdash_\omega \omega : a \leftrightarrow b$ we define $[\![\omega]\!]$ as the linear map from $[\![a]\!]$ to $[\![b]\!]$ sending the closed value $v : a$ to the normal form of $\omega\, v : b$ under the rewrite system.

In general, the fact that $[\![\omega]\!]$ is well-defined is not trivial. If it is formally stated in Theorem 3, we can first try to understand what could go wrong. The problem comes from the fact that the space $[\![a]\!]$ is not finite in general. Consider the iso `map Had` $: [\mathbb{B}] \leftrightarrow [\mathbb{B}]$. Any closed value $v : [\mathbb{B}]$ is a list and the term (`map Had`) v rewrites to a normal form consisting of a linear combination of lists. Denote the linear combination associated to v with L_v. An element of $[\![[\mathbb{B}]]\!]$ is a sequence $\phi = (\phi_v)_{v \in \mathcal{B}_{[\mathbb{B}]}}$. From Definition 3, the map $[\![\omega]\!]$ sends the element $\phi \in [\![[\mathbb{B}]]\!]$ to $\sum_{v \in \mathcal{B}_{[\mathbb{B}]}} \phi_v \cdot L_v$. This is an infinite sum of sums of complex numbers: we need to make sure that it is well-defined: this is the purpose of the next result. Because of the constraints on the language, we can even show that it is a *bounded* linear map.

In the case of the map `map Had`, we can understand why it works as follows. The space $[\![[\mathbb{B}]]\!]$ can be decomposed as the direct sum $\sum_{i=0}^{\infty} E_i$, where E_i is generated with all the lists in $\mathbb{B}$ of size i. The map `map Had` is acting locally on each finitely-dimensional subspace E_i. It is therefore well-defined. Because of the unitarity constraint on the linear combinations appearing in `Had`, the operation performed by `map Had` sends elements of norm 1 to elements of norm 1. This idea can be formalized and yield the following theorem.

Theorem 3. *For each closed iso* $\vdash_\omega \omega : a \leftrightarrow b$ *the linear map* $[\![\omega]\!] : [\![a]\!] \to [\![b]\!]$ *is well-defined and bounded.* □

5.4 Modeling Isos as Unitary Maps

In this section, we show that not only closed isos can be modeled as bounded linear maps, but that these linear maps are in fact unitary maps. The problem comes from fixpoints. We first consider the case of isos written without fixpoints, and then the case with fixpoints.

Without recursion. The case without recursion is relatively easy to treat, as the linear map modeling the iso can be compositionally constructed out of elementary unitary maps.

Theorem 4. *Given a closed iso* $\vdash_\omega \omega : a \leftrightarrow b$ *defined without the use of recursion, the linear map* $[\![\pi]\!] : [\![a]\!] \to [\![b]\!]$ *is unitary.* □

The proof of the theorem relies on the fact that to each closed iso $\vdash_\omega \omega : a \leftrightarrow b$ one can associate an operationally equivalent iso $\vdash_\omega \omega' : a \leftrightarrow b$ that does not use iso-variables nor lambda-abstractions. We can define a notion of *depth* of an iso as the number of nested isos. The proof is done by induction on this depth of the iso ω: it is possible to construct a unitary map for ω using the unitary maps for each ω_{ij} as elementary building blocks.

As an illustration, the semantics of `Gate` of Example 1 is given in Fig. 6.

Isos with structural recursion. When considering fixpoints, we cannot rely anymore on this finite compositional construction: the space $[\![a]\!]$ cannot anymore be regarded as a *finite* sum of subspaces described by each clause.

We therefore need to rely on the formal definition of unitary maps in general, infinite Hilbert spaces. On top of being bounded linear, a map $[\![\omega]\!] : [\![a]\!] \to [\![b]\!]$ is unitary if (1) it preserves the scalar product: $\langle [\![\omega]\!](e) | [\![\omega]\!](f)\rangle = \langle e|f\rangle$ for all e and f in $[\![a]\!]$ and (2) it is surjective.

Theorem 5. *Given a closed iso* $\vdash_\omega \omega : a \leftrightarrow b$ *that can use structural recursion, the linear map* $[\![\pi]\!] : [\![a]\!] \to [\![b]\!]$ *is unitary.* □

The proof uses the idea highlighted in Sect. 5.4: for a structurally recursive iso of type $[a] \otimes b \leftrightarrow c$, the Hilbert space $[\![[a] \otimes b]\!]$ can be split into a canonical decomposition $E_0 \oplus E_1 \oplus E_2 \oplus \cdots$, where E_i contains only the values of the form $\langle [x_1 \ldots x_i], y\rangle$, containing the lists of size i. On each E_i, the iso is equivalent to an iso without structural recursion.

6 Conclusion

In this paper, we proposed a reversible language amenable to quantum superpositions of values. The language features a weak form of higher-order that is nonetheless expressible enough to get interesting maps such as generalized Toffoli operators. We sketched how this language effectively encodes bijections in the classical case and unitary operations in the quantum case. It would be interesting to see how this relates to join inverse categories [14, 15].

In the vectorial extension of the language we have the same control as in the classical, reversible language. Tests are captured by clauses, and naturally yield quantum tests: this is similar to what can be found in QML [5, 6], yet more general since the QML approach is restricted to `if-then-else` constructs. The novel aspect of quantum control that we are able to capture here is a notion of *quantum loops*. These loops were believed to be hard, if not impossible. What makes it work in our approach is the fact that we are firmly within a closed quantum system, without measurements. This makes it possible to only consider unitary maps and frees us from the Löwer order on positive matrices [6]. As we restrict fixpoints to structural recursion, valid isos are regular enough to capture unitarity. Ying [7] also proposes a framework for quantum while-loops that is similar in spirit to our approach at the level of denotations: in his approach the control part of the loops is modeled using an external systems of "coins" which, in our case, correspond to conventional lists. Reducing the manipulation of this external coin system to iteration on lists allowed us to give a simple operational semantics for the language.

References

1. Wootters, W.K., Zurek, W.H.: A single quantum cannot be cloned. Nature **299**, 802–803 (1982)
2. Nielsen, M.A., Chuang, I.L.: Quantum Computation and Quantum Information. Cambridge University Press, Cambridge (2002)
3. Green, A.S., Lumsdaine, P.L., Ross, N.J., Selinger, P., Valiron, B.: Quipper: a scalable quantum programming language. In: Proceedings of PLDI 2013, pp. 333–342 (2013)
4. Paykin, J., Rand, R., Zdancewic, S.: QWIRE: A core language for quantum circuits. In: Proceedings of POPL 2017, pp. 846–858 (2017)
5. Altenkirch, T., Grattage, J.: A functional quantum programming language. In: Proceedings of LICS 2005, pp. 249–258 (2005)
6. Badescu, C., Panangaden, P.: Quantum alternation: Prospects and problems. In: Proceedings 12th International Workshop on Quantum Physics and Logic, QPL 2015, Oxford, UK, 15–17 July 2015, pp. 33–42 (2015)
7. Ying, M.: Foundations of Quantum Programming. Morgan Kaufmann, Cambridge (2016)
8. Selinger, P.: Towards a quantum programming language. Math. Struct. Comput. Sci. **14**(4), 527–586 (2004)
9. Vizzotto, J.K., Altenkirch, T., Sabry, A.: Structuring quantum effects: superoperators as arrows. Math. Struct. Comput. Sci. **16**(3), 453–468 (2006)

10. James, R.P., Sabry, A.: Theseus: a high-level language for reversible computation. In: Reversible Computation, Booklet of work-in-progress and short reports (2016)
11. Arrighi, P., Díaz-Caro, A., Valiron, B.: The vectorial λ-calculus. Inf. Comput. **254**(1), 105–139 (2017)
12. Arrighi, P., Dowek, G.: Lineal: a linear-algebraic lambda-calculus. Log. Methods Comput. Sci. **13**(1) (2013). https://doi.org/10.23638/LMCS-13(1:8)2017
13. Vaux, L.: The algebraic lambda calculus. Math. Struct. Comput. Sci. **19**(5), 1029–1059 (2009)
14. Glück, R., Kaarsgaard, R.: A categorical foundation for structured reversible flowchart languages: soundness and adequacy. arXiv:1710.03666 [cs.PL] (2017)
15. Kaarsgaard, R., Axelsen, H.B., Glück, R.: Join inverse categories and reversible recursion. J. Log. Algebraic Methods Program. **87**, 33–50 (2017)
16. van Tonder, A.: A lambda calculus for quantum computation. SIAM J. Comput. **33**(5), 1109–1135 (2004)
17. Sabry, A., Valiron, B., Vizzotto, J.K.: From symmetric pattern-matching to quantum control (extended version). In: FOSSACS 2018 (2018, to appear)
18. Assaf, A., Díaz-Caro, A., Perdrix, S., Tasson, C., Valiron, B.: Call-by-value, call-by-name and the vectorial behaviour of the algebraic λ-calculus. Log. Methods Comput. Sci. **10**(4:8) (2014)
19. Young, N.: An Introduction to Hilbert Space. Cambridge University Press, New York (1988)

4

Comparator Automata in Quantitative Verification

Suguman Bansal(✉), Swarat Chaudhuri(✉) and Moshe Y. Vardi(✉)

Rice University, Houston, TX 77005, USA
{suguman,swarat}@rice.edu, vardi@cs.rice.edu

Abstract. The notion of comparison between system runs is fundamental in formal verification. This concept is implicitly present in the verification of qualitative systems, and is more pronounced in the verification of quantitative systems. In this work, we identify a novel mode of comparison in quantitative systems: the online comparison of the aggregate values of two sequences of quantitative weights. This notion is embodied by *comparator automata* (*comparators*, in short), a new class of automata that read two infinite sequences of weights synchronously and relate their aggregate values.

We show that comparators that are finite-state and accept by the Büchi condition lead to generic algorithms for a number of well-studied problems, including the quantitative inclusion and winning strategies in quantitative graph games with incomplete information, as well as related non-decision problems, such as obtaining a finite representation of all counterexamples in the quantitative inclusion problem.

We study comparators for two aggregate functions: discounted-sum and limit-average. We prove that the discounted-sum comparator is ω-regular for all integral discount factors. Not every aggregate function, however, has an ω-regular comparator. Specifically, we show that the language of sequence-pairs for which limit-average aggregates exist is neither ω-regular nor ω-context-free. Given this result, we introduce the notion of *prefix-average* as a relaxation of limit-average aggregation, and show that it admits ω-context-free comparators.

1 Introduction

Many classic questions in formal methods can be seen as involving *comparisons* between different system runs or inputs. Consider the problem of verifying if a system S satisfies a linear-time temporal property P. Traditionally, this problem is phrased language-theoretically: S and P are interpreted as sets of (infinite) words, and S is determined to satisfy P if $S \subseteq P$. The problem, however, can also be framed in terms of a *comparison* between words in S and P. Suppose a word w is assigned a weight of 1 if it belongs to the language of the system or property, and 0 otherwise. Then determining if $S \subseteq P$ amounts to checking whether the weight of every word in S is less than or equal to its weight in P [5].

The need for such a formulation is clearer in quantitative systems, in which every run of a word is associated with a sequence of (rational-valued) weights. The weight of a run is given by *aggregate function* $f : \mathbb{Q}^\omega \to \mathbb{R}$, which returns the real-valued *aggregate value* of the run's weight sequence. The weight of a word is given by the supremum or infimum of the weight of all its runs. Common examples of aggregate functions include discounted-sum and limit-average.

In a well-studied class of problems involving quantitative systems, the objective is to check if the aggregate value of words of a system exceed a constant threshold value [14–16]. This is a natural generalization of emptiness problems in qualitative systems. Known solutions to the problem involve arithmetic reasoning via linear programming and graph algorithms such as negative-weight cycle detection, computation of maximum weight of cycles etc. [4, 18].

A more general notion of comparison relates aggregate values of two weight sequences. Such a notion arises in the *quantitative inclusion problem* for weighted automata [1], where the goal is to determine whether the weight of words in one weighted automaton is less than that in another. Here it is necessary to compare the aggregate value along runs between the two automata. Approaches based on arithmetic reasoning do not, however, generalize to solving such problems. In fact, the known solution to discounted-sum inclusion with integer discount-factor combines linear programming with a *specialized* subset-construction-based determinization step, rendering an EXPTIME algorithm [4, 6]. Yet, this approach does not match the PSPACE lower bound for discounted-sum inclusion.

In this paper, we present an automata-theoretic formulation of this form of comparison between weighted sequences. Specifically, we introduce *comparator automata* (*comparators*, in short), a class of automata that read pairs of infinite weight sequences synchronously, and compare their aggregate values in an online manner. While comparisons between weight sequences happen implicitly in prior approaches to quantitative systems, comparator automata make these comparisons explicit. We show that this has many benefits, including generic algorithms for a large class of quantitative reasoning problems, as well as a direct solution to the problem of discounted-sum inclusion that also closes its complexity gap.

A *comparator for aggregate function* f is an automaton that accepts a pair (A, B) of sequences of bounded rational numbers iff $f(A)\ R\ f(B)$, where R is an inequality relation ($>$, $<$, $\geq$, $\leq$) or the equality relation. A comparator could be finite-state or (pushdown) infinite-state. This paper studies such comparators.

A comparator is *ω-regular* if it is finite-state and accepts by the Büchi condition. We show that ω-regular comparators lead to generic algorithms for a number of well-studied problems including the quantitative inclusion problem, and in showing existence of winning strategies in incomplete-information quantitative games. Our algorithm yields PSPACE-completeness of quantitative inclusion when the ω-regular comparator is provided. The same algorithm extends to obtaining finite-state representations of counterexample words in inclusion.

Next, we show that the discounted-sum aggregation function admits an ω-regular comparator when the discount-factor $d > 1$ is an integer. Using properties of ω-regular comparators, we conclude that the discounted-sum inclusion is PSPACE-complete, hence resolving the complexity gap. Furthermore, we prove that the discounted-sum comparator for $1 < d < 2$ cannot be ω-regular. We suspect this result extends to non-integer discount-factors as well.

Finally, we investigate the limit-average comparator. Since limit-average is only defined for sequences in which the average of prefixes converge, limit-average comparison is not well-defined. We show that even a Büchi pushdown automaton cannot separate sequences for which limit-average exists from those for which it does not. Hence, we introduce the novel notion of *prefix-average comparison* as a relaxation of limit-average comparison. We show that the prefix-average comparator admits a comparator that is ω-context-free, i.e., given by a Büchi pushdown automaton, and we discuss the utility of this characterization.

This paper is organized as follows: Preliminaries are given in Sect. 2. Comparator automata is formally defined in Sect. 3. Generic algorithms for ω-regular comparators are discussed in Sects. 3.1 and 3.2. The construction and properties of discounted-sum comparator, and limit-average and prefix-average comparator are given in Sects. 4 and 5, respectively. We conclude with future directions in Sect. 6.

Related Work. The notion of comparison has been widely studied in quantitative settings. Here we mention only a few of them. Such aggregate-function based notions appear in weighted automata [1,17], quantitative games including mean-payoff and energy games [16], discounted-payoff games [3,4], in systems regulating cost, memory consumption, power consumption, verification of quantitative temporal properties [14,15], and others. Common solution approaches include graph algorithms such as weight of cycles or presence of cycle [18], linear-programming-based approaches, fixed-point-based approaches [8], and the like. The choice of approach for a problem typically depends on the underlying aggregate function. In contrast, in this work we present an automata-theoretic approach that unifies solution approaches to problems on different aggregate functions. We identify a class of aggregate functions, ones that have an ω-regular comparator, and present generic algorithms for some of these problems.

While work on finite-representations of counterexamples and witnesses in the qualitative setting is known [5], we are not aware of such work in the quantitative verification domain. This work can be interpreted as automata-theoretic arithmetic, which has been explored in regular real analysis [12].

2 Preliminaries

Definition 1 (Büchi automata [21]**).** *A (finite-state)* Büchi automaton *is a tuple* $\mathcal{A} = (S, \Sigma, \delta, Init, \mathcal{F})$*, where* S *is a finite set of* states, Σ *is a finite* input alphabet, $\delta \subseteq (S \times \Sigma \times S)$ *is the* transition relation, $Init \subseteq S$ *is the set of* initial states, *and* $\mathcal{F} \subseteq S$ *is the set of* accepting states.

A Büchi automaton is *deterministic* if for all states s and inputs a, $|\{s'|(s,a,s') \in \delta \text{ for some } s'\}| \leq 1$ and $|Init| = 1$. Otherwise, it is *nondeterministic*. For a word $w = w_0 w_1 \cdots \in \Sigma^\omega$, a *run* ρ of w is a sequence of states $s_0 s_1 \ldots$ s.t. $s_0 \in Init$, and $\tau_i = (s_i, w_i, s_{i+1}) \in \delta$ for all i. Let $inf(\rho)$ denote the set of states that occur infinitely often in run ρ. A run ρ is an *accepting run* if $inf(\rho) \cap \mathcal{F} \neq \emptyset$. A word w is an accepting word if it has an accepting run. Büchi automata are known to be closed under set-theoretic union, intersection, and complementation [21]. Languages accepted by these automata are called *ω-regular languages.*

Definition 2 (Weighted ω-automaton [10,20]**).** *A* weighted ω-automaton *over infinite words is a tuple $\mathcal{A} = (\mathcal{M}, \gamma)$, where $\mathcal{M} = (S, \Sigma, \delta, Init, S)$ is a Büchi automaton, and $\gamma : \delta \rightarrow \mathbb{Q}$ is a* weight function.

Words and *runs* in weighted ω-automata are defined as they are in Büchi automata. Note that all states are accepting states in this definition. The *weight sequence* of run $\rho = s_0 s_1 \ldots$ of word $w = w_0 w_1 \ldots$ is given by $wt_\rho = n_0 n_1 n_2 \ldots$ where $n_i = \gamma(s_i, w_i, s_{i+1})$ for all i. The *weight of a run* ρ is given by $f(wt_\rho)$, where $f : \mathbb{Q}^\omega \rightarrow \mathbb{R}$ is an *aggregate function.* We use $f(\rho)$ to denote $f(wt_\rho)$.

Here the *weight of a word* $w \in \Sigma^\omega$ in weighted ω-automata is defined as $wt_\mathcal{A}(w) = sup\{f(\rho)|\rho \text{ is a run of } w \text{ in } \mathcal{A}\}$. It can also be defined as the infimum of the weight of all its runs. By convention, if word $w \notin \mathcal{A}$, $wt_\mathcal{A}(w) = 0$ [10].

Definition 3 (Quantitative inclusion). *Given two weighted ω-automata P and Q with aggregate function f, the* quantitative-inclusion problem, *denoted by $P \subseteq_f Q$, asks whether for all words $w \in \Sigma^\omega$, $wt_P(w) \leq wt_Q(w)$.*

Quantitative inclusion is PSPACE-complete for limsup and liminf [10], and undecidable for limit-average [16]. For discounted-sum with integer discount-factor it is in EXPTIME [6,10], and decidability is unknown for rational discount-factors

Definition 4 (Incomplete-information quantitative games). *An* incomplete-information quantitative game *is a tuple $\mathcal{G} = (S, s_\mathcal{I}, O, \Sigma, \delta, \gamma, f)$, where S, O, Σ are sets of* states, observations, *and* actions, *respectively, $s_\mathcal{I} \in S$ is the* initial state, *$\delta \subseteq S \times \Sigma \times S$ is the* transition relation, *$\gamma : S \rightarrow \mathbb{N} \times \mathbb{N}$ is the* weight function, *and $f : \mathbb{N}^\omega \rightarrow \mathbb{R}$ is the* aggregate function.

The transition relation δ is *complete*, i.e., for all states p and actions a, there exists a state q s.t. $(p, a, q) \in \delta$. A *play* ρ is a sequence $s_0 a_0 s_1 a_1 \ldots$, where $\tau_i = (s_i, a_i, s_{i+1}) \in \delta$. The *observation of state* s is denoted by $O(s) \in O$. The *observed play* o_ρ of ρ is the sequence $o_0 a_0 o_1 a a_1 \ldots$, where $o_i = O(s_i)$. Player P_0 has incomplete information about the game $\mathcal{G}$; it only perceives the observation play o_ρ. Player P_1 receives full information and witnesses play ρ. Plays begin in the initial state $s_0 = s_\mathcal{I}$. For $i \geq 0$, Player P_0 selects action a_i. Next, player P_1 selects the state s_{i+1}, such that $(s_i, a_i, s_{i+1}) \in \delta$. The *weight of state* s is the pair of payoffs $\gamma(s) = (\gamma(s)_0, \gamma(s)_1)$. The *weight sequence* wt_i of player P_i along ρ is given by $\gamma(s_0)_i \gamma(s_1)_i \ldots$, and its payoff from ρ is given by $f(wt_i)$ for aggregate function f, denoted by $f(\rho_i)$, for simplicity. A play on which a player receives a greater payoff is said to be a *winning play* for the player. A strategy for player P_0 is given by a function $\alpha : O^* \to \Sigma$ since it only sees observations. Player P_0 follows strategy α if for all i, $a_i = \alpha(o_0 \dots o_i)$. A strategy α is said to be a *winning strategy* for player P_0 if all plays following α are winning plays for P_0.

Definition 5 (Büchi pushdown automata [13]**).** *A* Büchi pushdown automaton (Büchi PDA) *is a tuple* $\mathcal{A} = (S, \Sigma, \Gamma, \delta, Init, Z_0, \mathcal{F})$*, where* S*,* Σ*,* Γ*, and* $\mathcal{F}$ *are finite sets of* states, input alphabet, pushdown alphabet *and* accepting states, *respectively.* $\delta \subseteq (S \times \Gamma \times (\Sigma \cup \{\epsilon\}) \times S \times \Gamma)$ *is the* transition relation, $Init \subseteq S$ *is a set of* initial states, $Z_0 \in \Gamma$ *is the* start symbol.

A *run* ρ on a word $w = w_0 w_1 \dots \in \Sigma^\omega$ of a Büchi PDA $\mathcal{A}$ is a sequence of configurations $(s_0, \gamma_0), (s_1, \gamma_1) \dots$ satisfying (1) $s_0 \in Init$, $\gamma_0 = Z_0$, and (2) $(s_i, \gamma_i, w_i, s_{i+1}, \gamma_{i+1}) \in \delta$ for all i. Büchi PDA consists of a *stack*, elements of which are the tokens Γ, and initial element Z_0. Transitions *push* or *pop* token(s) to/from the top of the stack. Let $inf(\rho)$ be the set of states that occur infinitely often in state sequence $s_0 s_1 \dots$ of run ρ. A run ρ is an *accepting run* in Büchi PDA if $inf(\rho) \cap \mathcal{F} \neq \emptyset$. A word w is an *accepting word* if it has an accepting run. Languages accepted by Büchi PDA are called *ω-context-free languages* (ω-CFL).

We introduce some notation. For an infinite sequence $A = (a_0, a_1, \dots)$, $A[i]$ denotes its i-th element. Abusing notation, we write $w \in \mathcal{A}$ and $\rho \in \mathcal{A}$ if w and ρ are an accepting word and an accepting run of $\mathcal{A}$ respectively.

For missing proofs and constructions, refer to the supplementary material.

3 Comparator Automata

Comparator automata (often abbreviated as *comparators*) are a class of automata that can read pairs of weight sequences synchronously and establish an equality or inequality relationship between these sequences. Formally, we define:

Definition 6 (Comparator automata). *Let* Σ *be a finite set of rational numbers, and* $f : \mathbb{Q}^\omega \to \mathbb{R}$ *denote an aggregate function. A* comparator automaton for aggregate function f *is an automaton over the alphabet* $\Sigma \times \Sigma$ *that accepts a pair* (A, B) *of (infinite) weight sequences iff* $f(A)$ R $f(B)$*, where* R *is an inequality or the equality relation.*

From now on, unless mentioned otherwise, we assume that all weight sequences are bounded, natural number sequences. The boundedness assumption is justified since the set of weights forming the alphabet of a comparator is bounded. For all aggregate functions considered in this paper, the result of comparison of weight sequences is preserved by a uniform linear transformation that converts rational-valued weights into natural numbers; justifying the natural number assumption.

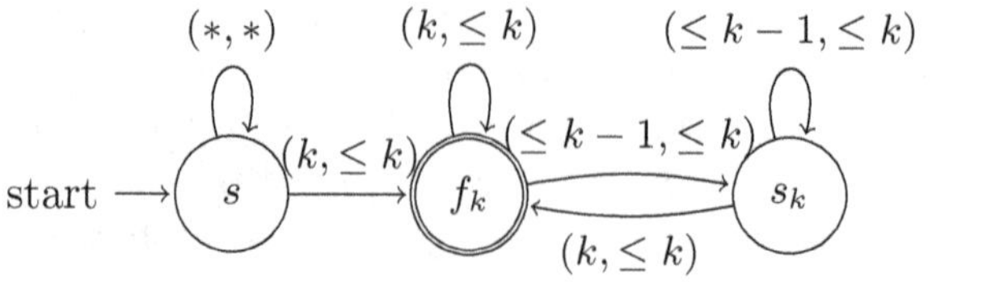

Fig. 1. State f_k is an accepting state. Automaton $\mathcal{A}_k$ accepts (A, B) iff $\mathsf{LimSup(A)} = k$, $\mathsf{LimSup(B)} \leq k$. $*$ denotes $\{0, 1 \ldots \mu\}$, $\leq m$ denotes $\{0, 1 \ldots, m\}$

We explain comparators through an example. The *limit supremum* (limsup, in short) of a bounded, integer sequence A, denoted by $\mathsf{LimSup(A)}$, is the largest integer that appears infinitely often in A. The *limsup comparator* is a Büchi automaton that accepts the pair (A, B) of sequences iff $\mathsf{LimSup(A)} \geq \mathsf{LimSup(B)}$.

The working of the limsup comparator is based on non-deterministically guessing the limsup of sequences A and B, and then verifying that $\mathsf{LimSup(A)} \geq \mathsf{LimSup(B)}$. Büchi automaton $\mathcal{A}_k$ (Fig. 1) illustrates the basic building block of the limsup comparator. Automaton $\mathcal{A}_k$ accepts pair (A, B) of number sequences iff $\mathsf{LimSup(A)} = k$, and $\mathsf{LimSup(B)} \leq k$, for integer k. To see why this is true, first note that all incoming edges to accepting state f_k occur on alphabet $(k, \leq k)$ while all transitions between states f_k and s_k occur on alphabet $(\leq k, \leq k)$, where $\leq k$ denotes the set $\{0, 1, \ldots k\}$. So, the integer k must appear infinitely often in A and all elements occurring infinitely often in A and B are less than or equal to k. Together these ensure that $\mathsf{LimSup(A)} = k$, and $\mathsf{LimSup(B)} \leq k$. The union of such automata $\mathcal{A}_k$ for $k \in \{0, 1, \ldots \mu\}$ for upper bound μ, results in the limsup comparator. The *limit infimum* (liminf, in short) of an integer sequence is the smallest integer that appears infinitely often in it; its comparator is similar.

When the comparator for an aggregate function is a Büchi automaton, we call it an *ω-regular comparator*. Likewise, when the comparator for an aggregate function is a Büchi pushdown automaton, we call it an *ω-context-free comparator*. As seen here, the limsup and liminf comparators are ω-regular. Later, we see that discounted-sum comparator and prefix-average comparator are ω-regular and ω-context-free respectively (Sects. 4 and 5). We call an aggregate function *ω-regular* when it has an ω-regular comparator for at least one inequality relation. Due to closure properties of Büchi automata, comparators for all inequality and equality relations of an ω-regular aggregate function are also ω-regular.

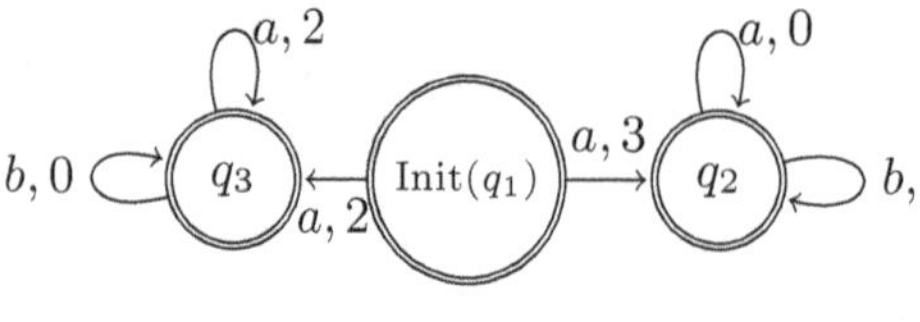

Fig. 2. Weighted automaton P

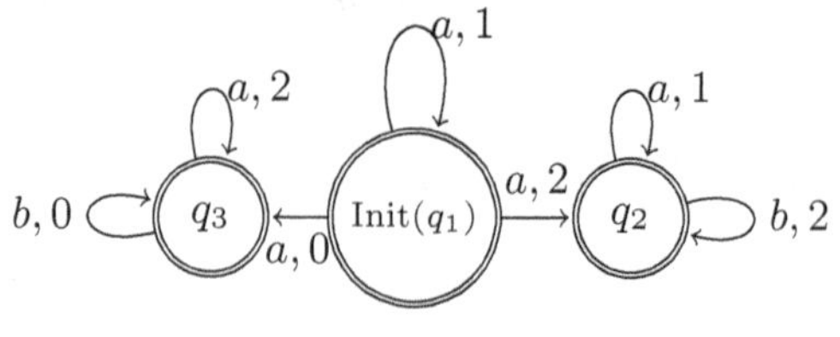

Fig. 3. Weighted automaton Q

Motivating Example. Let weighted ω-automata P and Q be as illustrated in Figs. 2 and 3. The word $w = a(ab)^\omega$ has two runs $\rho_1^P = q_1(q_2)^\omega$, $\rho_2^P = q_1(q_3)^\omega$

Algorithm 1. InclusionReg($P, Q, \mathcal{A}_f$), Is $P \subseteq_f Q$?

1: **Input:** Weighted automata P, Q, and ω-regular comparator $\mathcal{A}_f$ (Inequality $\leq$)
2: **Output:** True if $P \subseteq_f Q$, False otherwise
3: $\hat{P} \leftarrow$ AugmentWtAndLabel(P)
4: $\hat{Q} \leftarrow$ AugmentWtAndLabel(Q)
5: $\hat{P} \times \hat{Q} \leftarrow$ MakeProduct($\hat{P}, \hat{Q}$)
6: $\mathit{DimProof} \leftarrow$ Intersect($\hat{P} \times \hat{Q}, \mathcal{A}_{\succeq}$)
7: $\mathit{Dim} \leftarrow$ FirstProject($\mathit{DimProof}$)
8: **return** $\hat{P} \equiv \mathit{Dim}$

in P, and four runs $\rho_1^Q = q_1(q_2)^\omega$, $\rho_2^Q = q_1(q_3)^\omega$, $\rho_3^Q = q_1q_1(q_2)^\omega$ $\rho_4^Q = q_1q_1(q_3)^\omega$ in Q. Their weight-sequences are $wt_1^P = 3, (0,1)^\omega$, $wt_2^P = 2, (2,0)^\omega$ in P, and $wt_1^Q = (2,1)^\omega$, $wt_2^Q = (0,2)^\omega$, $wt_3^Q = 1, 2, (2,1)^\omega$, $wt_4^Q = 1, 0, (0,2)^\omega$ in Q.

To determine if w has greater weight in P or in Q, compare aggregate value of weight-sequences of runs in P and Q. Take the comparator for aggregate function f that accepts a pair (A, B) of weight-sequence iff $f(A) \leq f(B)$. For $wt_P(w) \leq wt_Q(w)$, for every run ρ_i^P in P, there exists a run ρ_j^Q in Q s.t. (ρ_i^P, ρ_j^Q) is accepted by the comparator. This forms the basis for quantitative inclusion.

3.1 Quantitative Inclusion

InclusionReg (Algorithm 1) is an algorithm for quantitative inclusion for ω-regular aggregate functions. For weighted ω-automata P, Q, and ω-regular comparator $\mathcal{A}_f$, InclusionReg returns True iff $P \subseteq_f Q$. We assume $P \subseteq Q$ (qualitative inclusion) to avoid trivial corner cases.

Key Ideas. $P \subseteq_f Q$ holds if for every run ρ_P in P on word w, there exists a run ρ_Q in Q on the same word w such that $f(\rho_P) \leq f(\rho_Q)$. We refer to such runs of P by *diminished run*. Hence, $P \subseteq_f Q$ iff all runs of P are diminished.

InclusionReg constructs Büchi automaton Dim that consists of exactly the diminished runs of P. It returns True iff Dim contains all runs of P. To obtain Dim, it constructs Büchi automaton $\mathit{DimProof}$ that accepts word (ρ_P, ρ_Q) iff ρ_P and ρ_Q are runs of the same word in P and Q respectively, and $f(\rho_P) \leq f(\rho_Q)$. The ω-regular comparator for inequality $\leq$ for function f ensures $f(\rho_P) \leq f(\rho_Q)$. The projection of $\mathit{DimProof}$ on runs of P results in Dim.

Algorithm Details. InclusionReg has three steps: (a). UniqueId (Lines 3–4): Enables unique identification of runs in P and Q through *labels*. (b). Compare (Lines 5–7): Compares weight of runs in P with weight of runs in Q, and constructs Dim. (c). DimEnsure (Line 8): Ensures if all runs of P are diminished.

1. UniqueId: AugmentWtAndLabel transforms weighted ω-automaton $\mathcal{A}$ into Büchi automaton $\hat{\mathcal{A}}$ by converting transition $\tau = (s, a, t)$ with weight $\gamma(\tau)$ in $\mathcal{A}$ to transition $\hat{\tau} = (s, (a, \gamma(\tau), l), t)$ in $\hat{\mathcal{A}}$, where l is a unique label assigned to transition τ. The word $\hat{\rho} = (a_0, n_0, l_0)(a_1, n_1, l_1) \cdots \in \hat{A}$ iff run $\rho \in \mathcal{A}$ on word $a_0a_1\ldots$ with weight sequence $n_0n_1\ldots$. Labels ensure bijection between

runs in $\mathcal{A}$ and words in $\hat{A}$. Words of $\hat{A}$ have a single run in $\hat{A}$.
Hence, transformation of weighted ω-automata P and Q to Büchi automata $\hat{P}$ and $\hat{Q}$ enables disambiguation between runs of P and Q (Line 3–4).

2. Compare: The output of this step is the Büchi automaton *Dim*, that contains the word $\hat{\rho} \in \hat{P}$ iff ρ is a diminished run in P (Lines 5–7).
MakeProduct($\hat{P}, \hat{Q}$) constructs $\hat{P} \times \hat{Q}$ s.t. word $(\hat{\rho_P}, \hat{\rho_Q}) \in \hat{P} \times \hat{Q}$ iff ρ_P and ρ_Q are runs of the same word in P and Q respectively (Line 5). Concretely, for transition $\hat{\tau_\mathcal{A}} = (s_\mathcal{A}, (a, n_\mathcal{A}, l_\mathcal{A}), t_\mathcal{A})$ in automaton $\mathcal{A}$, where $\mathcal{A} \in \{\hat{P}, \hat{Q}\}$, transition $\hat{\tau_P} \times \hat{\tau_Q} = ((s_P, s_Q), (a, n_P, l_P, n_Q, l_Q), (t_P, t_Q))$ is in $\hat{P} \times \hat{Q}$.
Intersect intersects the weight components of $\hat{P} \times \hat{Q}$ with comparator $\mathcal{A}_f$ (Line 6). The resulting automaton *DimProof* accepts word $(\hat{\rho_P}, \hat{\rho_Q})$ iff $f(\rho_P) \leq f(\rho_Q)$, and ρ_P and ρ_Q are runs on the same word in P and Q respectively. The projection of *DimProof* on the words of $\hat{P}$ returns *Dim* which contains the word $\hat{\rho_P}$ iff ρ_P is a diminished run in P (Line 7).
3. DimEnsure: $P \subseteq_f Q$ iff $\hat{P} \equiv Dim$ (qualitative equivalence) since $\hat{P}$ consists of all runs of P and *Dim* consists of all diminished runs of P (Line 8).

Lemma 1. *Given weighted ω-automata P and Q with an ω-regular aggregate function f.* InclusionReg$(P, Q, \mathcal{A}_f)$ *returns* True *iff $P \subseteq_f Q$.*

Further, InclusionReg is adapted for quantitative *strict*-inclusion $P \subset_f Q$ i.e. for all words w, $wt_P(w) < wt_Q(w)$ by taking the ω-regular comparator $\mathcal{A}_f$ that accepts (A, B) iff $f(A) < f(B)$. Similarly for quantitative equivalence $P \equiv_f Q$.

Complexity Analysis. All operations in InclusionReg until Line 7 are polytime operations in the size of weighted ω-automata P, Q and comparator $\mathcal{A}_f$. Hence, *Dim* is polynomial in size of P, Q and $\mathcal{A}_f$. Line 8 solves a PSPACE-complete problem. Therefore, the quantitative inclusion for ω-regular aggregate function f is in PSPACE in size of the inputs P, Q, and $\mathcal{A}_f$.

The PSPACE-hardness of the quantitative inclusion is established via reduction from the *qualitative* inclusion problem, which is PSPACE-complete. The formal reduction is as follows: Let P and Q be Büchi automata (with all states as accepting states). Reduce P, Q to weighted automata $\overline{P}$, $\overline{Q}$ by assigning a weight of 1 to each transition. Since all runs in $\overline{P}$, $\overline{Q}$ have the same weight sequence, weight of all words in $\overline{P}$ and $\overline{Q}$ is the same for any function f. It is easy to see $P \subseteq Q$ (qualitative inclusion) iff $\overline{P} \subseteq_f \overline{Q}$ (quantitative inclusion).

Theorem 1. *Let P and Q be weighted ω-automata and $\mathcal{A}_f$ be an ω-regular comparator. The complexity of the quantitative inclusion problem, quantitative strict-inclusion problem, and quantitative equivalence problem for ω-regular aggregate function f is* PSPACE*-complete.*

Theorem 1 extends to weighted ω-automata when weight of words is the *infimum* of weight of runs. The key idea for $P \subseteq_f Q$ here is to ensure that for every run ρ_Q in Q there exists a run on the same word in ρ_P in P s.t. $f(\rho_P) \leq f(\rho_Q)$.

Representation of Counterexamples. When $P \nsubseteq_f Q$, there exists word(s) $w \in \Sigma^*$ s.t $wt_P(w) > wt_Q(w)$. Such a word w is said to be a *counterexample* *word*. Previously, finite-state representations of counterexamples have been useful in verification and synthesis in qualitative systems [5], and could be useful in quantitative settings as well. However, we are not aware of procedures for such representations in the quantitative settings. Here we show that a trivial extension of InclusionReg yields Büchi automata-representations for all counterexamples of the quantitative inclusion problem for ω-regular functions.

For word w to be a counterexample, it must contain a run in P that is not diminished. Clearly, all non-diminished runs of P are members of $\hat{P} \setminus Dim$. The counterexamples words can be obtained from $\hat{P} \setminus Dim$ by modifying its alphabet to the alphabet of P by dropping transition weights and their unique labels.

Theorem 2. *All counterexamples of the quantitative inclusion problem for an ω-regular aggregate function can be expressed by a Büchi automaton.*

3.2 Incomplete-Information Quantitative Games

Given an incomplete-information quantitative game $\mathcal{G} = (S, s_{\mathcal{I}}, O, \Sigma, \delta, \gamma, f)$, our objective is to determine if player P_0 has a winning strategy $\alpha : O^* \rightarrow \Sigma$ for ω-regular aggregate function f. We assume we are given the ω-regular comparator $\mathcal{A}_f$ for function f. Note that a function $A^* \rightarrow B$ can be treated like a B-labeled A-tree, and vice-versa. Hence, we proceed by finding a Σ-labeled O-tree – the *winning strategy tree*. Every branch of a winning strategy-tree is an observed play o_ρ of $\mathcal{G}$ for which every actual play ρ is a winning play for P_0.

We first consider all *game trees* of $\mathcal{G}$ by interpreting $\mathcal{G}$ as a tree-automaton over Σ-labeled S-trees. Nodes $n \in S^*$ of the game-tree correspond to states in S and labeled by actions in Σ taken by player P_0. Thus, the *root node* ε corresponds to $s_{\mathcal{I}}$, and a node $s_{i_0}, \dots, s_{i_k}$ corresponds to the state s_{i_k} reached via $s_{\mathcal{I}}, s_{i_0}, \dots, s_{i_{k-1}}$. Consider now a node x corresponding to state s and labeled by an action σ. Then x has children $xs_1, \dots xs_n$, for every $s_i \in S$. If $s_i \in \delta(s, \sigma)$, then we call xs_i a *valid* child, otherwise we call it an *invalid* child. Branches that contain invalid children correspond to invalid plays.

A game-tree τ is a *winning tree* for player P_0 if every branch of τ is either a winning play for P_0 or an invalid play of $\mathcal{G}$. One can check, using an automata, if a play is invalid by the presence of invalid children. Furthermore, the winning condition for P_0 can be expressed by the ω-regular comparator $\mathcal{A}_f$ that accepts (A, B) iff $f(A) > f(B)$. To use the comparator $\mathcal{A}_f$, it is determinized to parity automaton D_f. Thus, a product of game $\mathcal{G}$ with D_f is a deterministic parity tree-automaton accepting precisely winning-trees for player P_0.

Winning trees for player P_0 are Σ-labeled S-trees. We need to convert them to Σ-labeled O-trees. Recall that every state has a unique observation. We can simulate these Σ-labeled S-trees on strategy trees using the technique of *thinning* states S to observations O [19]. The resulting alternating parity tree automaton $\mathcal{M}$ will accept a Σ-labeled O-tree τ_o iff for all actual game-tree τ of τ_o, τ is a winning-tree for P_0 with respect to the strategy τ_o. The problem of existence of winning-strategy for P_0 is then reduced to non-emptiness checking of $\mathcal{M}$.

Theorem 3. *Given an incomplete-information quantitative game $\mathcal{G}$ and ω-regular comparator $\mathcal{A}_f$ for the aggregate function f, the complexity of determining whether P_0 has a winning strategy is exponential in $|\mathcal{G}| \cdot |D_f|$, where $|D_f| = |\mathcal{A}_f|^{O(|\mathcal{A}_f|)}$.*

Since, D_f is the deterministic parity automaton equivalent to $\mathcal{A}_f, |D_f| = |\mathcal{A}_f|^{O(|\mathcal{A}_f|)}$. The thinning operation is linear in size of $|\mathcal{G} \times D_f|$, therefore $|\mathcal{M}| = |\mathcal{G}| \cdot |D_f|$. Non-emptiness checking of alternating parity tree automata is exponential. Therefore, our procedure is doubly exponential in size of the comparator and exponential in size of the game. The question of tighter bounds is open.

4 Discounted-Sum Comparator

The discounted-sum of an infinite sequence A with discount-factor $d > 1$, denoted by $DS(A, d)$, is defined as $\Sigma_{i=0}^{\infty} A[i]/d^i$. The discounted-sum comparator (DS-comparator, in short) for discount-factor d, denoted by $\mathcal{A}_{\succ_{DS(d)}}$, accepts a pair (A, B) of weight sequences iff $DS(A, d) < DS(B, d)$. We investigate properties of the DS-comparator, and show that the DS-comparator is ω-regular for all integral discount-factors d, and cannot be ω-regular when $1 < d < 2$.

Theorem 4. *DS-comparator for rational discount-factor $1 < d < 2$ is not ω-regular.*

For discounted-sum automaton $\mathcal{A}$ with discount factor d, the *cut-point language* of $\mathcal{A}$ w.r.t. $r \in \mathbb{R}$ is defined as $L^{\geq r} = \{w \in L(\mathcal{A}) | DS(w, d) \geq r\}$. It is known that the cut-point language $L^{\geq 1}$ with discount-factor $1 < d < 2$ is not ω-regular [9]. One can show that if DS-comparator for discount-factor $1 < d < 2$ were ω-regular, then cut-point language $L^{\geq 1}$ is also ω-regular; thus proving Theorem 4.

We provide the construction of DS-comparator with integer discount-factor.

Key Ideas. The core intuition is that sequences bounded by μ can be converted to their value in base d via a finite-state transducer. Lexicographic comparison of the resulting sequences renders the desired result. Conversion of sequences to base d requires a certain amount of *book-keeping* by the transducer. Here we describe a direct method for book-keeping and lexicographic comparison.

For natural-number sequence A and integer discount-factor $d > 1$, $DS(A, d)$ can be interpreted as a value in base d i.e. $DS(A, d) = A[0] + \frac{A[1]}{d} + \frac{A[2]}{d^2} + \cdots = (A[0].A[1]A[2]\ldots)_d$ [12]. Unlike comparison of numbers in base d, the lexicographically larger sequence may not be larger in value. This occurs because (i) The elements of weight sequences may be larger in value than base d, and (ii) Every value has multiple infinite-sequence representations.

To overcome these challenges, we resort to arithmetic techniques in base d. Note that $DS(B, d) > DS(A, d)$ iff there exists a sequence C such that $DS(B, d) = DS(A, d) + DS(C, d)$, and $DS(C, d) > 0$. Therefore, to compare the discounted-sum of A and B, we obtain a sequence C. Arithmetic in base d also results in sequence X of carry elements. Then, we see:

Lemma 2. *Let A, B, C, X be number sequences, $d > 1$ be a positive integer such that following equations holds true:*

1. *When $i = 0$, $A[0] + C[0] + X[0] = B[0]$*
2. *When $i \geq 1$, $A[i] + C[i] + X[i] = B[i] + d \cdot X[i-1]$*

Then $DS(B, d) = DS(A, d) + DS(C, d)$.

Hence, to determine $DS(B, d) - DS(A, d)$, systematically guess sequences C and X using the equations, element-by-element beginning with the 0-th index and moving rightwards. There are two crucial observations here: (i) Computation of i-th element of C and X only depends on i-th and $(i-1)$-th elements of A and B. Therefore guessing $C[i]$ and $X[i]$ requires *finite memory* only. (ii) C refers to a representation of value $DS(B, d) - DS(A, d)$ in base d, and X is the carry-sequence. Hence if A and B are bounded-integer sequences, not only are X and C bounded sequences, they can be constructed from a *fixed finite set of integers*:

Lemma 3. *Let $d > 1$ be an integer discount-factor. Let A and B be nonnegative integer sequences bounded by μ s.t. $DS(A, d) < DS(B, d)$. Let C and X be as constructed in Lemma 2. There exists at least one pair of integer-sequences C and X that satisfy the following two equations*

1. *For all $i \geq 0$, $0 \leq C[i] \leq \mu \cdot \frac{d}{d-1}$. and*
2. *For all $i \geq 0$, $0 \leq |X[i]| \leq 1 + \frac{\mu}{d-1}$*

In Büchi automaton $\mathcal{A}_{\succ_{DS(d)}}$ (i) states are represented by (x, c) where x and c range over all possible elements of X and C, which are finite, (ii) a special start state s, (iii) transitions from the start state $(s, (a, b), (x, c))$ satisfy $a + c + x = b$ to replicate Eq. 1 (Lemma 2) at the 0-th index, (iv) all other transitions $((x_1, c_1), (a, b), (x_2, c_2))$ satisfy $a + c_2 + x_2 = b + d \cdot x_1$ to replicate Eq. 2 (Lemma 2) at indexes $i > 0$, and (v) all (x, c) states are accepting. Lemma 2 ensures that $\mathcal{A}_{\succ_{DS(d)}}$ accepts (A, B) iff $DS(B, d) = DS(A, d) + DS(C, d)$.

However, $\mathcal{A}_{\succ_{DS(d)}}$ is yet to guarantee $DS(C, d) > 0$. For this, we include non-accepting states $(x, \bot)$, where x ranges over all possible (finite) elements of X. Transitions into and out of states $(x, \bot)$ satisfy Eqs. 1 or 2 (depending on whether transition is from start state s) where $\bot$ is treated as $c = 0$. Transition from $(x, \bot)$-states to (x, c)-states occurs only if $c > 0$. Hence, any valid execution of (A, B) will be an accepting run only if the execution witnesses a non-zero value of c. Since C is a non-negative sequence, this ensures $DS(C, d) > 0$.

Construction. Let $\mu_C = \mu \cdot \frac{d}{d-1}$ and $\mu_X = 1 + \frac{\mu}{d-1}$. $\mathcal{A}_{\succ_{DS(d)}} = (S, \Sigma, \delta_d, Init, \mathcal{F})$

- $S = Init \cup \mathcal{F} \cup S_\bot$ where
  $Init = \{s\}$, $\mathcal{F} = \{(x, c) | |x| \leq \mu_X, 0 \leq c \leq \mu_C\}$, and
  $S_\bot = \{(x, \bot) | |x| \leq \mu_X\}$ where $\bot$ is a special character, and $c \in \mathbb{N}$, $x \in \mathbb{Z}$.
- $\Sigma = \{(a, b) : 0 \leq a, b \leq \mu\}$ where a and b are integers.
- $\delta_d \subset S \times \Sigma \times S$ is defined as follows:
  1. Transitions from start state s:
     i $(s, (a, b), (x, c))$ for all $(x, c) \in \mathcal{F}$ s.t. $a + x + c = b$ and $c \neq 0$

ii $(s, (a, b), (x, \bot))$ for all $(x, \bot) \in S_\bot$ s.t. $a + x = b$

2. Transitions within $S_\bot$: $((x, \bot), (a, b), (x', \bot))$ for all $(x, \bot)$, $(x', \bot) \in S_\bot$, if $a + x' = b + d \cdot x$
3. Transitions within $\mathcal{F}$: $((x, c), (a, b), (x', c'))$ for all (x, c), $(x', c') \in \mathcal{F}$ where $c' < d$, if $a + x' + c' = b + d \cdot x$
4. Transition between $S_\bot$ and $\mathcal{F}$: $((x, \bot), (a, b), (x', c'))$ for all $(x, \bot) \in S_\bot$, $(x', c') \in \mathcal{F}$ where $0 < c' < d$, if $a + x' + c' = b + d \cdot x$

Theorem 5. *The DS-comparator with maximum bound μ, is ω-regular for integer discount-factors $d > 1$. Size of the discounted-sum comparator is $\mathcal{O}(\frac{\mu^2}{d})$.*

DS-comparator with non-strict inequality $\leq$ and equality $=$ follow similarly. Consequently, properties of ω-regular comparators hold for DS-comparator with integer discount-factor. Specifically, DS-inclusion is PSPACE-complete in size of the input weighted automata and DS-comparator. Since, size of DS-comparator is polynomial w.r.t. to upper bound μ (in unary), DS-inclusion is PSPACE in size of input weighted automata and μ. Not only does this bound improve upon the previously known upper bound of EXPTIME but it also closes the gap between upper and lower bounds for DS-inclusion.

Corollary 1. *Given weighted automata P and Q, maximum weight on their transitions μ in unary form and integer discount-factor $d > 1$, the DS-inclusion, DS-strict-inclusion, and DS-equivalence problems are* PSPACE*-complete.*

As mentioned earlier, the known upper bound for discounted-sum inclusion with integer discount-factor is exponential [6,10]. This bound is based on an exponential determinization construction (subset construction) combined with arithmetical reasoning. We observe that the determinization construction can be performed on-the-fly in PSPACE. To perform, however, the arithmetical reasoning on-the-fly in PSPACE would require essentially using the same bit-level ((x, c)-state) techniques that we have used to construct DS-comparator automata.

5 Limit-Average Comparator

The limit-average of an infinite sequence M is the point of convergence of the average of prefixes of M. Let $\mathsf{Sum}(M[0, n-1])$ denote the sum of the n-length prefix of sequence M. The *limit-average infimum*, denoted by $\mathsf{LimInfAvg}(M)$, is defined as $\lim\inf_{n\to\infty} \frac{1}{n} \cdot \mathsf{Sum}(M[0, n-1])$. Similarly, the *limit-average supremum*, denoted by $\mathsf{LimSupAvg}(M)$, is defined as $\lim\sup_{n\to\infty} \frac{1}{n} \cdot \mathsf{Sum}(M[0, n-1])$. The limit-average of sequence M, denoted by $\mathsf{LimAvg}(M)$, is defined *only if* the limit-average infimum and limit-average supremum coincide, and then $\mathsf{LimAvg}(M) = \mathsf{LimInfAvg}(M)$ ($= \mathsf{LimSupAvg}(M)$). Note that while limit-average infimum and supremum exist for all bounded sequences, the limit-average may not.

In existing work, limit-average is defined as the limit-average infimum (or limit-average supremum) to ensure that limit-average exists for all sequences [7,10,11,22]. While this definition is justified in context of the application, it may lead to a misleading comparison in some cases. For example, consider sequence A s.t. $\mathsf{LimSupAvg}(A) = 2$ and $\mathsf{LimInfAvg}(A) = 0$, and sequence B s.t. $\mathsf{LimAvg}(B) = 1$. Clearly, limit-average of A does not exist. Suppose, $\mathsf{LimAvg}(A) = \mathsf{LimInfAvg}(A) = 0$, then $\mathsf{LimAvg}(A) < \mathsf{LimAvg}(B)$, deluding that average of prefixes of A are always less than those of B in the limit. This is untrue since $\mathsf{LimSupAvg}(A) = 2$.

Such inaccuracies in limit-average comparison may occur when the limit-average of at least one sequence does not exist. However, it is not easy to distinguish sequences for which limit-average exists from those for which it doesn't.

We define *prefix-average comparison* as a relaxation of limit-average comparison. Prefix-average comparison coincides with limit-average comparison when limit-average exists for both sequences. Otherwise, it determines whether eventually the average of prefixes of one sequence are greater than those of the other. This comparison does not require the limit-average to exist to return intuitive results. Further, we show that the *prefix-average comparator* is ω-context-free.

5.1 Limit-Average Language and Comparison

Let $\Sigma = \{0, 1, \ldots, \mu\}$ be a finite alphabet with $\mu > 0$. The *limit-average language* $\mathcal{L}_{LA}$ contains the sequence (word) $A \in \Sigma^\omega$ iff its limit-average exists. Suppose $\mathcal{L}_{LA}$ were ω-regular, then $\mathcal{L}_{LA} = \bigcup_{i=0}^{n} U_i \cdot V_i^\omega$, where $U_i, V_i \subseteq \Sigma^*$ are regular languages over *finite* words. The limit-average of sequences is determined by its behavior in the limit, so limit-average of sequences in V_i^ω exists. Additionally, the average of all (finite) words in V_i must be the same. If this were not the case, then two words in V_i with unequal averages l_1 and l_2, can generate a word $w \in V_i^\omega$ s.t the average of its prefixes oscillates between l_1 and l_2. This cannot occur, since limit-average of w exists. Let the average of sequences in V_i be a_i, then limit-average of sequences in V_i^ω and $U_i \cdot V_i^\omega$ is also a_i. This is contradictory since there are sequences with limit-average different from the a_i (see appendix). Similarly, since every ω-CFL is represented by $\bigcup_{i=1}^{n} U_i \cdot V_i^\omega$ for CFLs U_i, V_i over finite words [13], a similar argument proves that $\mathcal{L}_{LA}$ is not ω-context-free.

Quantifiers $\exists^\infty i$ and $\exists^f i$ denote the existence of *infinitely* many and *only finitely* many indices i, respectively.

Theorem 6. *$\mathcal{L}_{LA}$ is neither an ω-regular nor an ω-context-free language.*

In the next section, we will define *prefix-average comparison* as a relaxation of limit-average comparison. To show how prefix-average comparison relates to limit-average comparison, we will require the following two lemmas:

Lemma 4. *Let A and B be sequences s.t. their limit average exists. If $\exists^\infty i, \mathsf{Sum}(A[0, i-1]) \geq \mathsf{Sum}(B[0, i-1])$ then $\mathsf{LimAvg}(A) \geq \mathsf{LimAvg}(B)$.*

Lemma 5. *Let A, B be sequences s.t their limit-average exists. If $\mathsf{LimAvg}(A) > \mathsf{LimAvg}(B)$ then $\exists^f i, \mathsf{Sum}(B[0, i-1]) \geq \mathsf{Sum}(A[0, i-1])$ and $\exists^\infty i, \mathsf{Sum}(A[0, i-1]) > \mathsf{Sum}(B[0, i-1])$.*

5.2 Prefix-Average Comparison and Comparator

The previous section relates limit-average comparison with the sums of equal length prefixes of the sequences (Lemmas 4 and 5). The comparison criteria is based on the number of times sum of prefix of one sequence is greater than the other, which does not rely on the existence of limit-average. Unfortunately, this criteria cannot be used for limit-average comparison since it is incomplete (Lemma 5). Specifically, for sequences A and B with equal limit-average it is possible that $\exists^\infty i, \mathsf{Sum}(A[0, n-1]) > \mathsf{Sum}(B[0, n-1])$ and $\exists^\infty i, \mathsf{Sum}(B[0, n-1]) > \mathsf{Sum}(A[0, n-1])$. Instead, we use this criteria to define *prefix-average comparison*. In this section, we define prefix-average comparison and explain how it relaxes limit-average comparison. Lastly, we construct the prefix-average comparator, and prove that it is not ω-regular but is ω-context-free.

Definition 7 (Prefix-average comparison). *Let A and B be number sequences. We say* $\mathsf{PrefixAvg}(A) \geq \mathsf{PrefixAvg}(B)$ *if* $\exists^f i, \mathsf{Sum}(B[0, i-1]) \geq \mathsf{Sum}(A[0, i-1])$ *and* $\exists^\infty i, \mathsf{Sum}(A[0, i-1]) > \mathsf{Sum}(B[0, i-1])$.

Intuitively, prefix-average comparison states that $\mathsf{PrefixAvg}(A) \geq \mathsf{PrefixAvg}(B)$ if eventually the sum of prefixes of A are always greater than those of B. We use $\geq$ since the average of prefixes may be equal when the difference between the sum is small. It coincides with limit-average comparison when the limit-average exists for both sequences. Definition 7 and Lemmas 4, 5 relate limit-average comparison and prefix-average comparison:

Corollary 2. *When limit-average of A and B exists, then*

- $\mathsf{PrefixAvg}(A) \geq \mathsf{PrefixAvg}(B) \implies \mathsf{LimAvg}(A) \geq \mathsf{LimAvg}(B)$.
- $\mathsf{LimAvg}(A) > \mathsf{LimAvg}(B) \implies \mathsf{PrefixAvg}(A) \geq \mathsf{PrefixAvg}(B)$.

Therefore, limit-average comparison and prefix-average comparison return the same result on sequences for which limit-average exists. In addition, prefix-average returns intuitive results when even when limit-average may not exist. For example, suppose limit-average of A and B do not exist, but $\mathsf{LimInfAvg}(A) > \mathsf{LimSupAvg}(B)$, then $\mathsf{PrefixAvg}(A) \geq \mathsf{PrefixAvg}(B)$. Therefore, prefix-average comparison relaxes limit-average comparison.

The rest of this section describes *prefix-average comparator* $\mathcal{A}_{\succeq_{PA(\cdot)}}$, an automaton that accepts the pair (A, B) of sequences iff $\mathsf{PrefixAvg}(A) \geq \mathsf{PrefixAvg}(B)$.

Lemma 6 ***(Pumping Lemma for ω-regular language [2]).*** *Let L be an ω-regular language. There exists $p \in \mathbb{N}$ such that, for each $w = u_1 w_1 u_2 w_2 \cdots \in L$ such that $|w_i| \geq p$ for all i, there are sequences of finite words $(x_i)_{i \in \mathbb{N}}$, $(y_i)_{i \in \mathbb{N}}$, $(z_i)_{i \in \mathbb{N}}$ s.t., for all i, $w_i = x_i y_i z_i$, $|x_i y_i| \leq p$ and $|y_i| > 0$ and for every sequence of pumping factors $(j_i)_{i \in \mathbb{N}} \in \mathbb{N}$, the pumped word $u_1 x_1 y_1^{j_1} z_1 u_2 x_2 y_2^{j_2} z_2 \cdots \in L$.*

Theorem 7. *The prefix-average comparator is not ω-regular.*

Proof (Proof Sketch). We use Lemma 6 to prove that $\mathcal{A}_{\succeq_{PA(\cdot)}}$ is not ω-regular. Suppose $\mathcal{A}_{\succeq_{PA(\cdot)}}$ were ω-regular. For $p > 0 \in \mathbb{N}$, let $w = (A, B) = ((0,1)^p(1,0)^{2p})^\omega$. The segment $(0,1)^*$ can be pumped s.t the resulting word is no longer in $\mathcal{L}_{\succeq_{PA(\cdot)}}$.

Concretely, $A = (0^p1^{2p})^\omega$, $B = (1^p0^{2p})^\omega$, $\mathsf{LimAvg}(A) = \frac{2}{3}$, $\mathsf{LimAvg}(B) = \frac{1}{3}$. So, $w = (A, B) \in \mathcal{A}_{\succeq_{PA(\cdot)}}$. Select as factor w_i (from Lemma 6) the sequence $(0,1)^p$. Pump each y_i enough times so that the resulting word is $\hat{w} = (\hat{A}, \hat{B}) = ((0,1)^{m_i}(1,0)^{2p})^\omega$ where $m_i > 4p$. It is easy to show that $\hat{w} = (\hat{A}, \hat{B}) \notin \mathcal{L}_{\succeq_{PA(\cdot)}}$.

We discuss key ideas and sketch the construction of the prefix average comparator. The term *prefix-sum difference at i* indicates $\mathsf{Sum}(A[0, i-1]) - \mathsf{Sum}(B[0, i-1])$, i.e. the difference between sum of i-length prefix of A and B.

Key Ideas. For sequences A and B to satisfy $\mathsf{PrefixAvg}(A) \geq \mathsf{PrefixAvg}(B)$, $\exists^f i, \mathsf{Sum}(B[0, i-1]) \geq \mathsf{Sum}(A[0, i-1])$ and $\exists^\infty i, \mathsf{Sum}(A[0, i-1]) > \mathsf{Sum}(B[0, i-1])$. This occurs iff there exists an index N s.t. for all indices $i > N$, $\mathsf{Sum}(A[0, i-1]) - \mathsf{Sum}(B[0, i-1]) > 0$. While reading a word, the prefix-sum difference is maintained by states and the stack of ω-PDA: states maintain whether it is negative or positive, while number of tokens in the stack equals its absolute value. The automaton non-deterministically guesses the aforementioned index N, beyond which the automaton ensure that prefix-sum difference remains positive.

Construction Sketch. The push-down comparator $\mathcal{A}_{\succeq_{PA(\cdot)}}$ consists of three states: (i) State s_P and (ii) State s_N that indicate that the prefix-sum difference is greater than zero and or not respectively, (iii) accepting state s_F. An execution of (A, B) begins in state s_N with an empty stack. On reading letter (a, b), the stack pops or pushes $|(a-b)|$ tokens from the stack depending on the current state of the execution. From state s_P, the stack pushes tokens if $(a-b) > 0$, and pops otherwise. The opposite occurs in state s_N. State transition between s_N and s_P occurs only if the stack action is to pop but the stack consists of $k < |a-b|$ tokens. In this case, stack is emptied, state transition is performed and $|a-b| - k$ tokens are pushed into the stack. For an execution of (A, B) to be an accepting run, the automaton non-deterministically transitions into state s_F. State s_F acts similar to state s_P except that execution is terminated if there aren't enough tokens to pop out of the stack. $\mathcal{A}_{\succeq_{PA(\cdot)}}$ accepts by accepting state.

To see why the construction is correct, it is sufficient to prove that at each index i, the number of tokens in the stack is equal to $|\mathsf{Sum}(A[0, i-1]) - \mathsf{Sum}(B[0, i-1])|$. Furthermore, in state s_N, $\mathsf{Sum}(A[0, i-1]) - \mathsf{Sum}(B[0, i-1]) \leq 0$, and in state s_P and s_F, $\mathsf{Sum}(A[0, i-1]) - \mathsf{Sum}(B[0, i-1]) > 0$. Next, the index at which the automaton transitions to the accepting state s_F coincides with index N. The execution is accepted if it has an infinite execution in state s_F, which allows transitions only if $\mathsf{Sum}(A[0, i-1]) - \mathsf{Sum}(B[0, i-1]) > 0$.

Theorem 8. *The prefix-average comparator is an ω-CFL.*

While ω-CFL can be easily expressed, they do not possess closure properties, and problems on ω-CFL are easily undecidable. Hence, the application of ω-context-free comparator will require further investigation.

6 Conclusion

In this paper, we identified a novel mode for comparison in quantitative systems: the online comparison of aggregate values of sequences of quantitative weights. This notion is embodied by comparators automata that read two infinite sequences of weights synchronously and relate their aggregate values. We showed that ω-regular comparators not only yield generic algorithms for problems including quantitative inclusion and winning strategies in incomplete-information quantitative games, they also result in algorithmic advances. We show that the discounted-sum inclusion problem is PSAPCE-complete for integer discount-factor, hence closing a complexity gap. We also studied the discounted-sum and prefix-average comparator, which are ω-regular and ω-context-free, respectively.

We believe comparators, especially ω-regular comparators, can be of significant utility in verification and synthesis of quantitative systems, as demonstrated by the existence of finite-representation of counterexamples of the quantitative inclusion problem. Another potential application is computing equilibria in quantitative games. Applications of the prefix-average comparator, in general ω-context-free comparators, is open to further investigation. Another direction to pursue is to study aggregate functions in more detail, and develop a clearer understanding of when aggregate functions are ω-regular.

Acknowledgements. We thank the anonymous reviewers for their comments. We thank K. Chatterjee, L. Doyen, G. A. Perez and J. F. Raskin for corrections to earlier drafts, and their contributions to this paper. We thank P. Ganty and R. Majumdar for preliminary discussions on the limit-average comparator. This work was partially supported by NSF Grant No. 1704883, "Formal Analysis and Synthesis of Multiagent Systems with Incentives".

References

1. Almagor, S., Boker, U., Kupferman, O.: What's decidable about weighted automata? In: Bultan, T., Hsiung, P.-A. (eds.) ATVA 2011. LNCS, vol. 6996, pp. 482–491. Springer, Heidelberg (2011). https://doi.org/10.1007/978-3-642-24372-1_37
2. Alur, R., Degorre, A., Maler, O., Weiss, G.: On omega-languages defined by mean-payoff conditions. In: de Alfaro, L. (ed.) FoSSaCS 2009. LNCS, vol. 5504, pp. 333–347. Springer, Heidelberg (2009). https://doi.org/10.1007/978-3-642-00596-1_24
3. Andersen, G., Conitzer, V.: Fast equilibrium computation for infinitely repeated games. In: Proceedings of AAAI, pp. 53–59 (2013)
4. Andersson, D.: An improved algorithm for discounted payoff games. In: ESSLLI Student Session, pp. 91–98 (2006)
5. Baier, C., Katoen, J.-P., et al.: Principles of Model Checking. MIT Press, Cambridge (2008)
6. Boker, U., Henzinger, T.A.: Exact and approximate determinization of discounted-sum automata. LMCS **10**(1) (2014)
7. Brim, L., Chaloupka, J., Doyen, L., Gentilini, R., Raskin, J.-F.: Faster algorithms for mean-payoff games. Formal Methods Syst. Des. **38**(2), 97–118 (2011)

8. Chatterjee, K., Doyen, L.: Energy parity games. In: Abramsky, S., Gavoille, C., Kirchner, C., Meyer auf der Heide, F., Spirakis, P.G. (eds.) ICALP 2010, Part II. LNCS, vol. 6199, pp. 599–610. Springer, Heidelberg (2010). https://doi.org/10.1007/978-3-642-14162-1_50
9. Chatterjee, K., Doyen, L., Henzinger, T.A.: Expressiveness and closure properties for quantitative languages. In: Proceedings of LICS, pp. 199–208. IEEE (2009)
10. Chatterjee, K., Doyen, L., Henzinger, T.A.: Quantitative languages. Trans. Comput. Log. **11**(4), 23 (2010)
11. Chatterjee, K., Henzinger, T.A., Jurdzinski, M.: Mean-payoff parity games. In: Proceedings of LICS, pp. 178–187. IEEE (2005)
12. Chaudhuri, S., Sankaranarayanan, S., Vardi, M.Y.: Regular real analysis. In: Proceedings of LICS, pp. 509–518 (2013)
13. Cohen, R.S., Gold, A.Y.: Theory of ω-languages: characterizations of ω-context-free languages. J. Comput. Syst. Sci. **15**(2), 169–184 (1977)
14. de Alfaro, L., Faella, M., Henzinger, T.A., Majumdar, R., Stoelinga, M.: Model checking discounted temporal properties. In: Jensen, K., Podelski, A. (eds.) TACAS 2004. LNCS, vol. 2988, pp. 77–92. Springer, Heidelberg (2004). https://doi.org/10.1007/978-3-540-24730-2_6
15. de Alfaro, L., Faella, M., Stoelinga, M.: Linear and branching metrics for quantitative transition systems. In: Díaz, J., Karhumäki, J., Lepistö, A., Sannella, D. (eds.) ICALP 2004. LNCS, vol. 3142, pp. 97–109. Springer, Heidelberg (2004). https://doi.org/10.1007/978-3-540-27836-8_11
16. Degorre, A., Doyen, L., Gentilini, R., Raskin, J.-F., Toruńczyk, S.: Energy and mean-payoff games with imperfect information. In: Dawar, A., Veith, H. (eds.) CSL 2010. LNCS, vol. 6247, pp. 260–274. Springer, Heidelberg (2010). https://doi.org/10.1007/978-3-642-15205-4_22
17. Droste, M., Kuich, W., Vogler, H.: Handbook of Weighted Automata. Springer, Heidelberg (2009). https://doi.org/10.1007/978-3-642-01492-5
18. Karp, R.M.: A characterization of the minimum cycle mean in a digraph. Discret. Math. **23**(3), 309–311 (1978)
19. Kupferman, O., Vardi, M.Y.: Synthesis with incomplete informatio. In: Barringer, H., Fisher, M., Gabbay, D., Gough, G. (eds.) Advances in Temporal Logic, pp. 109–127. Springer, Dordrecht (2000). https://doi.org/10.1007/978-94-015-9586-5_6
20. Mohri, M.: Weighted automata algorithms. In: Mohri, M. (ed.) Handbook of Weighted Automata, pp. 213–254. Springer, Heidelberg (2009). https://doi.org/10.1007/978-3-642-01492-5_6
21. Grädel, E., Thomas, W., Wilke, T. (eds.): Automata Logics, and Infinite Games: A Guide to Current Research. LNCS, vol. 2500. Springer, Heidelberg (2002). https://doi.org/10.1007/3-540-36387-4
22. Zwick, U., Paterson, M.: The complexity of mean payoff games on graphs. Theor. Comput. Sci. **158**(1), 343–359 (1996)

5

Non-angelic Concurrent Game Semantics

Simon Castellan[1(✉)], Pierre Clairambault[2], Jonathan Hayman[3], and Glynn Winskel[3]

[1] Imperial College London, London, UK
simon@phis.me
[2] Univ Lyon, CNRS, ENS de Lyon, UCB Lyon 1, LIP, Lyon, France
[3] Computer Laboratory, University of Cambridge, Cambridge, UK

Abstract. The *hiding* operation, crucial in the compositional aspect of game semantics, removes computation paths not leading to observable results. Accordingly, games models are usually biased towards *angelic* non-determinism: diverging branches are forgotten.

We present here new categories of games, not suffering from this bias. In our first category, we achieve this by avoiding hiding altogether; instead morphisms are *uncovered* strategies (with neutral events) up to *weak bisimulation*. Then, we show that by hiding only certain events dubbed *inessential* we can consider strategies up to *isomorphism*, and still get a category – this partial hiding remains sound up to weak bisimulation, so we get a concrete representations of programs (as in standard concurrent games) while avoiding the angelic bias. These techniques are illustrated with an interpretation of affine nondeterministic PCF which is adequate for weak bisimulation; and may, must and fair convergences.

1 Introduction

Game semantics represents programs as strategies for two player games determined by the types. Traditionally, a strategy is simply a collection of execution traces, each presented as a play (a structured sequence of events) on the corresponding game. Beyond giving a compositional framework for the formal semantics of programming languages, game semantics proved exceptionally versatile, providing very precise (often fully abstract) models of a variety of languages and programming features. One of its rightly celebrated achievements is the realisation that combinations of certain effects, such as various notions of state or control, could be characterised via corresponding conditions on strategies (innocence, well bracketing, ...) in a single unifying framework. This led Abramsky to propose the *semantic cube* programme [1], aiming to extend this success to further programming features: concurrency, non-determinism, probabilities, etc...

However, this elegant picture soon showed some limitations. While indeed the basic category of games was successfully extended to deal with concurrency [10,13], non-determinism [11], and probabilities [9] among others, these extensions (although fully abstract) are often incompatible with each other, and really, incompatible as well with the central condition of innocence. Hence a semantic hypercube encompassing all these effects remained out of reach. It is only recently that some new progress has been made with the discovery that some of these effects could be reconciled in a more refined, more intensional games framework. For instance, in [6,16] innocence is reconciled with non-determinism, and in [15] with probabilities. In [7], innocence is reconciled with concurrency.

But something is still missing: the works above dealing with non-deterministic innocence consider only *may-convergence*; they ignore execution branches leading to divergence. To some extent this seems to be a fundamental limitation of the game semantics methodology: at the heart of the composition of strategies lies the *hiding* operation that removes unobservable events. Diverging paths, by nature non-observable, are forgotten by hiding. Some models of must-testing do exist for particular languages, notably McCusker and Harmer's model for non-deterministic Idealized Algol [11]; the model works by annotating strategies with *stopping traces*, recording where the program may diverge. But this approach again mixes poorly with other constructions (notably innocence), and more importantly, is tied to may and must equivalences. It is not clear how it could be extended to support richer notions of convergence, such as *fair-testing* [2].

Our aim is to present a basis for non-deterministic game semantics which, besides being compatible with innocence, concurrency, *etc.*, is not biased towards may-testing; it is *non-angelic*. It should not be biased towards must-testing either; it should in fact be *agnostic* with respect to the testing equivalence, and support them all. Clearly, for this purpose it is paramount to remember the non-deterministic branching information; indeed in the absence of that information, notions such as *fair-testing* are lost. In fact, there has been a lot of activity in the past five years or so around games model that *do* observe the branching information. It is a feature of Hirschowitz's work presenting strategies as presheaves or sheaves on certain categories of cospans [12]; of Tsukada and Ong's work on nondeterministic innocence via sheaves [16]; and of our own line of work presenting strategies as certain event structures [5,7,14].

But observing branching information is not sufficient. Of the works mentioned above, those of Tsukada and Ong and our own previous work are still angelic, because they rely on hiding for composition. On the other hand, Hirschowitz's work gets close to achieving our goals; by refraining from hiding altogether, his model constructs an agnostic and precise representation of the operational behaviour of programs, on which he then considers fair-testing. But by not considering hiding he departs from the previous work and methods of game semantics, and from the methodology of denotational semantics. In contrast, we would like an agnostic games model that still has the categorical structure of traditional semantics. A games model with partial hiding was also recently introduced by Yamada [18], albeit for a different purpose: he uses partial hiding to represent normalization steps, whereas we use it to represent fine-grained nondeterminism.

Contributions. In this paper, we present the first category of games and strategies equipped to handle non-determinism, but agnostic with respect to the notion of convergence (including fair convergence). We showcase our model by interpreting $\mathbf{APCF}_{+}$, an affine variant of non-deterministic PCF: it is the simplest language featuring the phenomena of interest. We show adequacy with respect to may, must and fair convergences. The reader will find in the first author's PhD thesis [3] corresponding results for full non-deterministic PCF (with detailed proofs), and an interpretation of a higher-order language with shared memory concurrency. In [3], the model is proved compatible with our earlier notions of innocence, by establishing a result of full abstraction for may equivalence, for nondeterministic PCF. We have yet to prove full abstraction in the fair and must cases; finite definability does not suffice anymore.

Outline. We begin Sect. 2 by introducing $\mathbf{APCF}_+$. To set the stage, we describe an angelic interpretation of $\mathbf{APCF}_+$ in the category **CG** built in [14] with strategies up to isomorphism, and hint at our two new interpretations. In Sect. 3, starting from the observation that the cause of "angelism" is hiding, we omit it altogether, constructing an *uncovered* variant of our concurrent games, similar to that of Hirschowitz. Despite not hiding, when restricting the location of non-deterministic choices to internal events, we can still obtain a category up to *weak bisimulation*. But weak bisimulation is not perfect: it does not preserve must-testing, and is not easily computed. So in Sect. 4, we reinstate some hiding: we show that by hiding all synchronised events except some dubbed *essential*, we arrive at the best of both worlds. We get an agnostic category of games and strategies *up to isomorphism*, and we prove our adequacy results.

2 Three Interpretations of Affine Nondeterministic PCF

2.1 Syntax of $\mathbf{APCF}_+$

The language $\mathbf{APCF}_+$ extends affine PCF with a nondeterministic boolean choice, `choice`. Its types are $A, B ::= \mathbb{B} \mid A \multimap B$, where $A \multimap B$ represents affine functions from A to B. The following grammar describes terms of $\mathbf{APCF}_+$:

$$M, N ::= x \mid M\,N \mid \lambda x.\,M \mid \mathtt{tt} \mid \mathtt{ff} \mid \mathtt{if}\ M\,N_1\,N_2 \mid \mathtt{choice} \mid \bot$$

Typing rules are standard, we show application and conditionals. As usual, a conditional eliminating to arbitrary types can be defined as syntactic sugar.

$$\frac{\Gamma \vdash M : A \multimap B \qquad \Delta \vdash N : A}{\Gamma, \Delta \vdash M\,N : B} \qquad \frac{\Gamma \vdash M : \mathbb{B} \qquad \Delta \vdash N_1 : \mathbb{B} \qquad \Delta \vdash N_2 : \mathbb{B}}{\Gamma, \Delta \vdash \mathtt{if}\ M\,N_1\,N_2 : \mathbb{B}}$$

The first rule is *multiplicative*: Γ and Δ are disjoint. The operational semantics is that of PCF extended with the (only) two nondeterministic rules $\mathtt{choice} \to \mathtt{tt}$ and $\mathtt{choice} \to \mathtt{ff}$.

2.2 Game Semantics and Event Structures

Game semantics interprets an open program by a strategy, recording the behaviour of the program (Player) against the context (Opponent) in a 2-player game. Usually, the executions recorded are represented as *plays*, *i.e.* linear sequences of computational events called *moves*; a strategy being then a set of such plays. For instance, the nondeterministic boolean would be represented as the (even-prefix closure of the) set of plays $\{q^- \cdot \mathtt{tt}^+, q^- \cdot \mathtt{ff}^+\}$ on the game for booleans. In the play $q^- \cdot \mathtt{tt}^+$, the context starts the computation by asking the value of the program (q^-) and the program replies ($\mathtt{tt}^+$). Polarity indicates the origin (Program (+) or Opponent/Environment (−)) of the event.

Being based on sequences of moves, traditional game semantics handles concurrency via interleavings [10]. In contrast, in concurrent games [14], plays are generalised to partial orders which can express concurrency as a primitive. For instance, the execution of a parallel implementation of and against the context (tt, tt) gives the following partial order:

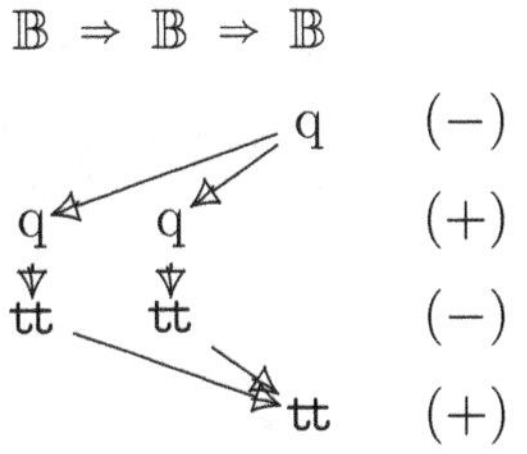

In this picture, the usual chronological linear order is replaced by an explicit partial order representing **causality**. Moves are concurrent when they are incomparable (as the two Player questions here). Following the longstanding convention in game semantics, we show which component of the type a computational event corresponds to by displaying it under the corresponding occurrence of a ground type. For instance in this diagram, Opponent first triggers the computation by asking the output value, and then and concurrently evaluates his two arguments. The arguments having evaluated to tt, and can finally answer Opponent's initial question and provide the output value.

In [7], we have shown how deterministic pure functional parallel programs can be interpreted (in a *fully abstract* way) using such representations.

Partial-Orders and Non-determinism. To represent nondeterminism in this partial order setting, one possibility is to use sets of partial orders [4]. This representation suffers however from two drawbacks: firstly it forgets the point of non-deterministic branching; secondly, one cannot talk of an *occurrence* of a move independently of an execution. Those issues are solved by moving to *event structures* [17], where the nondeterministic boolean can be represented as:

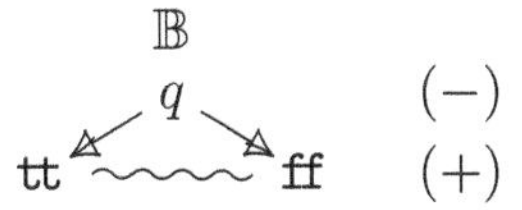

The wiggly line ($\sim\!\sim$) indicates *conflict*: the boolean values cannot coexist in an execution. Together this forms an *event structure*, defined formally later.

2.3 Interpretations of $\mathbf{APCF}_+$ with Event Structures

Let us introduce informally our interpretations by showing which event structures they associate to certain terms of $\mathbf{APCF}_+$.

Angelic Covered Interpretation. Traditional game semantics interpretations of nondeterminism are angelic (with exceptions, see *e.g.* [11]); they only describe what terms may do, and forget where they might get stuck. The interpretation of $M = (\lambda b.\ \texttt{if}\ b\,\texttt{tt}\,\bot)\ \texttt{choice}$ for instance, in usual game semantics is the same as that of $\texttt{tt}$. This is due to the nature of composition which tends to forget paths that do not lead to a value. Consider the strategy for the function $\lambda b.\ \texttt{if}\ b\,\texttt{tt}\,\bot$:

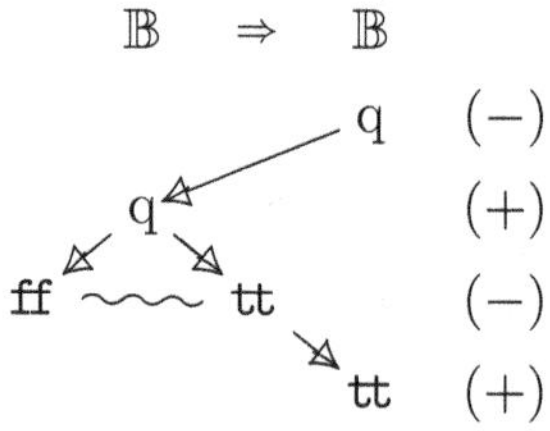

The interpretation of M arises as the *composition* of this strategy with the nondeterministic boolean. Composition is defined in two steps: interaction (Fig. 1a) and then hiding (Fig. 1b). Hiding removes intermediate behaviour which does not correspond to visible actions in the output type of the composition.

Hiding is crucial in order for composition to satisfy basic categorical properties (without it, the identity candidate, copycat, is not even idempotent). Strategies on event structures are usually considered *up to isomorphism*, which is the strongest equivalence relation that makes sense. Without hiding, there is no hope to recover categorical laws up to isomorphism. However, it turns out that, treating events in the middle as τ-transitions ($*$ in Fig. 1a), weak bisimulation equates enough strategies to get a category. Following these ideas, a category of *uncovered* strategies up to *weak bisimilarity* is built in Sect. 3.

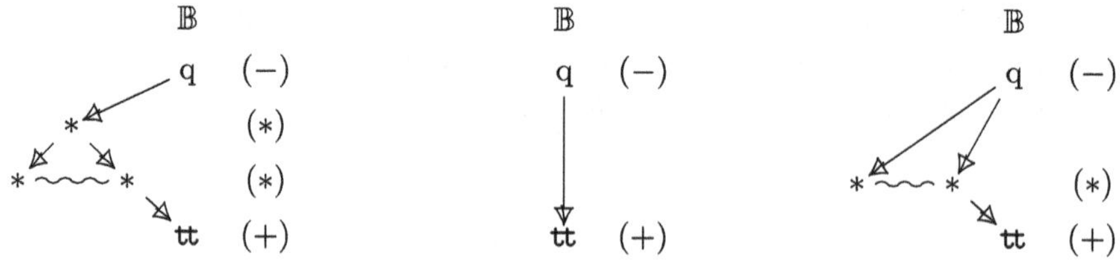

(a) Interp. before hiding (b) Interp. after hiding (c) Interp. with partial hiding

Fig. 1. Three interpretations of $(\lambda b.\ \texttt{if}\ b\,\texttt{tt}\,\bot)\ \texttt{choice}$

Interpretation with Partial Hiding. However, considering uncovered strategies up to weak bisimulation blurs their concrete nature; *causal information* is lost, for instance. Moreover checking for weak bisimilarity is computationally expensive, and because of the absence of hiding, a term evaluating to **skip** may yield a very large representative. However, there is a way to cut down the strategies to reach a compromise between hiding *no* internal events, or hiding *all* of them and collapsing to an angelic interpretation.

In our games based on event structures, having a non-ambiguous notion of an occurrence of event allows us to give a simple definition of the internal events we need to retain (Definition 9). Hiding other internal events yields a strategy still weakly bisimilar to the original (uncovered) strategy, while allowing us to get a category *up to isomorphism*. The interpretation of M in this setting appears in Fig. 1c. As before, only the events under the result type (not labelled $*$) are now *visible*, *i.e.* observable by a context. But the events corresponding to the argument evaluation are only partially hidden; those remaining are considered *internal*, treated like *τ-transitions*. Because of their presence, the partial hiding performed loses no information (*w.r.t.* the uncovered interpretation) up to weak bisimilarity. But we have hidden enough so that the required categorical laws between strategies hold *w.r.t.* isomorphism. The model is more precise and concrete than that of weak bisimilarity, preserves causal information and preserves must-convergence (unlike weak bisimilarity).

Following these ideas, a category of partially covered strategies up to iso (the target of our adequacy results) is constructed in Sect. 4.

3 Uncovered Strategies up to Weak Bisimulation

We now construct a category of "uncovered strategies", up to weak bisimulation. Uncovered strategies are very close to the *partial strategies* of [8], but [8] focused on connections with operational semantics rather than categorical structure.

3.1 Preliminaries on Event Structures

Definition 1. *An* **event structure** *is a triple* $(E, \leq_E, \mathrm{Con}_E)$ *where* $(E, \leq_E)$ *is a partial-order and* Con_E *is a non-empty collection of finite subsets of* E *called* consistent sets *subject to the following axioms:*

- *If* $e \in E$, *the set* $[e] = \{e' \in E \mid e' \leq e\}$ *is finite,*
- *For all* $e \in E$, *the set* $\{e\}$ *is consistent,*
- *For all* $Y \in \mathrm{Con}_E$, *for all* $X \subseteq Y$, *then* $X \in \mathrm{Con}_E$.
- *If* $X \in \mathrm{Con}_E$ *and* $e \leq e' \in X$ *then* $X \cup \{e\}$ *is consistent.*

A down-closed subset of events whose finite subsets are all consistent is called a **configuration**. The set of finite configurations of E is denoted $\mathscr{C}(E)$. If $x \in \mathscr{C}(E)$ and $e \notin x$, we write $x \overset{e}{\longrightarrow\!\!\!\!\subset} x'$ when $x' = x \cup \{e\} \in \mathscr{C}(E)$; this is the **covering relation** between configurations, and we say that e gives an **extension** of x.

Two extensions e and e' of x are **compatible** when $x \cup \{e, e'\} \in \mathscr{C}(E)$, **incompatible** otherwise. In the latter case, we have a **minimal conflict** between e and e' **in context** x (written $e \rightsquigarrow_x e'$).

These event structures are based on *consistent sets* rather than the more commonly-encountered binary *conflict* relation. Consistent sets are more general, and more handy mathematically, but throughout this paper, event structures concretely represented in diagrams will only use *binary conflict*, *i.e.* the relation $e \rightsquigarrow_x e'$ does not depend on x, meaning $e \rightsquigarrow_y e'$ whenever y extends with e, and with e' – in which case we only write $e \rightsquigarrow e'$. Then consistent sets can be recovered as those finite $X \subseteq E$ such that $\neg(e \rightsquigarrow e')$ for all $e, e' \in X$. Our diagrams display the relation $\rightsquigarrow$, along with the *Hasse diagram* of $\leq_E$, called **immediate causality** and denoted by $\rightarrowtriangle_E$. All the diagrams above denote event structures. The missing ingredient in making the diagrams formal is the *names* accompanying the events $(\mathbf{q}, \mathtt{tt}, \mathtt{ff}, \dots)$. These will arise as annotations by events from *games*, themselves event structures, representing the types.

The **parallel composition** $E_0 \parallel E_1$ of event structures E_0 and E_1 has for *events* $(\{0\} \times E_0) \cup (\{1\} \times E_1)$. The *causal order* is given by $(i, e) \leq_{E_0 \parallel E_1} (j, e')$ when $i = j$ and $e \leq_{E_i} e'$, and *consistent sets* by those finite subsets of $E_0 \parallel E_1$ that project to consistent sets in both E_0 and E_1.

A **(partial) map of event structures** $f : A \rightharpoonup B$ is a (partial) function on events which *(1)* maps any finite configuration of A to a configuration of B, and *(2)* is locally injective: for $a, a' \in x \in \mathscr{C}(A)$ and $fa = fa'$ (both defined) then $a = a'$. We write $\mathscr{E}$ for the category of event structures and total maps and $\mathscr{E}_\perp$ for the category of event structures and partial maps.

An **event structure with partial polarities** is an event structure A with a map $pol : A \rightarrow \{-, +, *\}$ (where events are labelled "negative", "positive", or "internal" respectively). It is a **game** when no events are internal. The dual $A^\perp$ of a game A is obtained by reversing polarities. Parallel composition naturally extends to games. If x and y are configurations of an event structure with partial polarities we use $x \subseteq^p y$ where $p \in \{-, +, *\}$ for $x \subseteq y$ & $pol(y \setminus x) \subseteq \{p\}$.

Given an event structure E and a subset $V \subseteq E$ of events, there is an event structure $E \downarrow V$ whose events are V and causality and consistency are inherited from E. This construction is called the **projection** of E to V and is used in [14] to perform hiding during composition.

3.2 Definition of Uncovered Pre-strategies

As in [14], we first introduce *pre-strategies* and their composition, and then consider *strategies*, those pre-strategies well-behaved with respect to copycat.

Uncovered Pre-strategies. An **uncovered pre-strategy** on a game A is a partial map of event structures $\sigma : S \rightharpoonup A$. Events in the domain of σ are called **visible** or **external**, and events outside **invisible** or **internal**. Via σ, visible events inherit polarities from A.

Uncovered pre-strategies are drawn just like the usual strategies of [14]: the event structure S has its events drawn as their labelling in A if defined or $*$ if undefined. The drawing of Fig. 1a is an example of an uncovered pre-strategy. From an (uncovered) pre-strategy, one can get a pre-strategy in the sense of [14]: for $\sigma : S \rightharpoonup A$, define $S_\downarrow = S \downarrow \mathrm{dom}(\sigma)$ where $\mathrm{dom}(\sigma)$ is the domain of σ. By restriction σ yields $\sigma_\downarrow : S_\downarrow \to A$, called a **covered pre-strategy**. A configuration x of S can be decomposed as the disjoint union $x_\downarrow \cup x_*$ where $x_\downarrow$ is a configuration of $S_\downarrow$ and x_* a set of internal events of S.

A pre-strategy **from a game** A **to a game** B is a (uncovered) pre-strategy on $A^\perp \parallel B$. An important pre-strategy from a game A to itself is the **copycat pre-strategy**. In $A^\perp \parallel A$, each move of A appears twice with dual polarity. The copycat pre-strategy æ_A simply waits for the negative occurrence of a move a before playing the positive occurrence. See [5] for a formal definition.

Isomorphism of strategies [14] can be extended to uncovered pre-strategies:

Definition 2. *Pre-strategies $\sigma : S \rightharpoonup A, \tau : T \rightharpoonup A$ are* ***isomorphic*** *(written $\sigma \cong \tau$) if there is an iso $\varphi : S \cong T$ s.t. $\tau \circ \varphi = \sigma$ (equality of partial maps).*

Interaction of Pre-strategies. Recall that in the covered case, composition is performed first by interaction, then hiding; where interaction of pre-strategies is described as their pullback in the category of *total maps* [14]. Even though $\mathscr{E}_\perp$ has pullbacks, those pullbacks are inadequate to describe interaction. In [8], uncovered strategies are seen as total maps $\sigma : S \to A \parallel N$, and their interaction as a pullback involving these. This method has its awkwardness so, instead, here we give a direct universal construction of interaction, replacing pullbacks.

We start with the simpler case of a **closed** interaction of a pre-strategy $\sigma : S \rightharpoonup A$ against a counter pre-strategy $\tau : T \rightharpoonup A^\perp$. As in [5] we first describe the expected *states* of the closed interaction in terms of *secured bijections*, from which we construct an event structure; before characterising the whole construction via a universal property.

Definition 3 (Secured bijection). *Let $\mathbf{q}, \mathbf{q}'$ be partial orders and $\varphi : \mathbf{q} \simeq \mathbf{q}'$ be a bijection between the carrier sets (non necessarily order-preserving). It is* ***secured*** *when the following relation $\lhd_\varphi$ on the graph of φ is acyclic:*

$$(s, \varphi(s)) \lhd_\varphi (s', \varphi(s')) \textit{ iff } s \rightarrowtriangle_{\mathbf{q}} s' \vee \varphi(s) \rightarrowtriangle_{\mathbf{q}'} \varphi(s') \tag{1}$$

If so, the resulting partial order $(\lhd_\varphi)^*$ is written $\leq_\varphi$.

Let $\sigma : S \rightharpoonup A$ and $\tau : T \rightharpoonup A$ be partial maps of event structures (we dropped polarities, as the construction is completely independent of them). A pair $(x, y) \in \mathscr{C}(S) \times \mathscr{C}(T)$ such that $\sigma_\downarrow x = \tau_\downarrow y \in \mathscr{C}(A)$, induces a bijection $\varphi_{x,y} : x \parallel y_* \simeq x_* \parallel y$ defined by local injectivity of σ and τ:

$$\begin{aligned} \varphi_{x,y}(0, s) &= (0, s) & (s \in x_*) \\ \varphi_{x,y}(0, s) &= (1, \tau^{-1}(\sigma s)) & (s \in x_\downarrow) \\ \varphi_{x,y}(1, t) &= (1, t) \end{aligned}$$

The configurations x and y have a partial order inherited from S and T. Viewing y_* and x_* as discrete orders (the ordering relation is the equality), $\varphi_{x,y}$

is a bijection between carrier sets of partial orders. An **interaction state** of σ and τ is $(x, y) \in \mathscr{C}(S) \times \mathscr{C}(T)$ with $\sigma_{\downarrow} x = \tau_{\downarrow} y$ for which $\varphi_{x,y}$ is secured. As a result (the graph of) $\varphi_{x,y}$ is naturally partial ordered. Write $\mathscr{S}_{\sigma,\tau}$ for the set of interaction states of σ and τ. As usual [5], we can recover an event structure:

Definition 4 (Closed interaction of uncovered pre-strategies). *Let A be an event structure, and $\sigma : S \rightharpoonup A$ and $\tau : T \rightharpoonup A$ be partial maps of event structures. The following data defines an event structure $S \wedge T$:*

- events: *those interaction states (x, y) such that $\varphi_{x,y}$ has a top element,*
- causality: $(x, y) \leq_{S \wedge T} (x', y')$ *iff* $x \subseteq x'$ *and* $y \subseteq y'$*,*
- consistency: *a finite set of interaction states $X \subseteq S \wedge T$ is consistent iff its union $\bigcup X$ is an interaction state in $\mathscr{S}_{\sigma,\tau}$.*

This event structure comes with partial maps $\Pi_1 : S \wedge T \rightharpoonup S$ and $\Pi_2 : S \wedge T \rightharpoonup T$, analogous to the usual projections of a pullback: for $(x, y) \in S \wedge T$, $\Pi_1(x, y)$ is defined to $s \in S$ whenever the top-element of $\varphi_{x,y}$ is $((0, s), w_2)$ for some $w_2 \in x_* \parallel y$. The map Π_1 is undefined only on events of $S \wedge T$ corresponding to internal events of T (*i.e.* (x, y) with top element of $\varphi_{x,y}$ of the form $((1, t), (1, t))$). The map Π_2 is defined symmetrically, and undefined on events corresponding to internal events of S. We write $\sigma \wedge \tau$ for $\sigma \circ \Pi_1 = \tau \circ \Pi_2 : S \wedge T \rightharpoonup A$.

Lemma 1. *Let $\sigma : S \rightharpoonup A$ and $\tau : T \rightharpoonup A$ be partial maps. Let $(X, f : X \rightharpoonup S, g : X \rightharpoonup T)$ be a triple such that the following outer square commutes:*

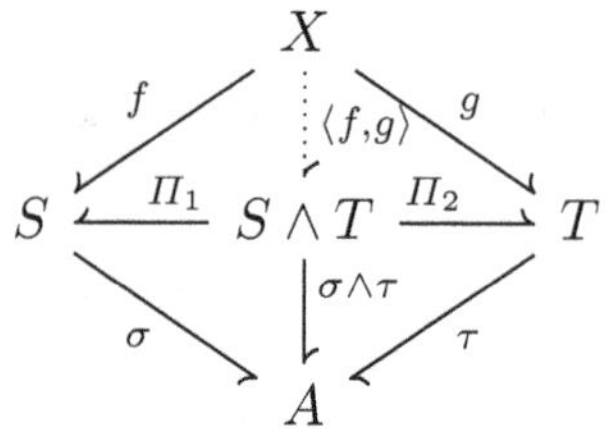

If for all $p \in X$ with $f\,p$ and $g\,p$ defined, $\sigma(f\,p) = \tau(g\,p)$ is defined, then there exists a unique $\langle f, g\rangle : X \rightharpoonup S \wedge T$ making the two upper triangles commute.

From this closed interaction, we define the open interaction as in [14]. Given two pre-strategies $\sigma : S \to A^{\perp} \parallel B$ and $\tau : T \to B^{\perp} \parallel C$, their interaction

$$\tau \circledast \sigma : (S \parallel C) \wedge (A \parallel T) \rightharpoonup A^{\perp} \parallel C$$

is defined as the composite partial map $(S \parallel C) \wedge (A \parallel T) \rightharpoonup A \parallel B \parallel C \rightharpoonup A \parallel C$, where the "pullback" is first computed ignoring polarities – the codomain of the resulting partial map is $A^{\perp} \parallel C$, once we reinstate polarities.

Weak Bisimulation. To compare uncovered pre-strategies, we cannot use isomorphisms as in [14], since as hinted earlier, $\text{\ae}_A \circledast \sigma$ comprises synchronised events not corresponding to those in σ. To solve this, we introduce weak bisimulation between uncovered strategies:

Definition 5. *Let $\sigma : S \rightharpoonup A$ and $\tau : T \rightharpoonup A$ be uncovered pre-strategies. A weak bisimulation between σ and τ is a relation $\mathscr{R} \subseteq \mathscr{C}(S) \times \mathscr{C}(T)$ containing $(\emptyset, \emptyset)$, such that for all $x \mathscr{R} y$, we have:*

- *If $x \overset{s}{\longrightarrow\!\!\subset} x'$ such that s is visible, then there exists $y \subseteq^* y' \overset{t}{\longrightarrow\!\!\subset} y''$ with $\sigma s = \tau t$ and $x' \mathscr{R} y''$ (and the symmetric condition for τ)*
- *If $x \overset{s}{\longrightarrow\!\!\subset} x'$ such that s is internal, then there exists $y \subseteq^* y'$ such that $x' \mathscr{R} y'$ (and the symmetric condition for τ)*

Two uncovered pre-strategies σ, τ are weakly bisimilar (written $\sigma \simeq \tau$) when there is a weak bisimulation between them.

Associativity of interaction (up to isomorphism, hence up to weak bisimulation) follows directly from Lemma 1. Moreover, it is straightforward to check that weak bisimulation is a congruence (*i.e.* compatible with composition).

Composition of Covered Strategies. From interaction, we can easily define the composition of covered strategies. If $\sigma : S \to A^\perp \parallel B$ and $\tau : T \to B^\perp \parallel C$ are covered pre-strategies, their composition (in the sense of [14]) $\tau \odot \sigma$ is defined as $(\tau \circledast \sigma)_\downarrow$. The operation $\downarrow$ is well-behaved with respect to interaction:

Lemma 2. *For σ, τ composable pre-strategies, $(\tau \circledast \sigma)_\downarrow \cong \tau_\downarrow \odot \sigma_\downarrow$.*

3.3 A Compact-Closed Category of Uncovered Strategies

Although we have a notion of morphism (pre-strategies) between games and an associative composition, we do not have a category up to weak bisimulation yet. Unlike in [14], races in a game may cause copycat on this game to not be idempotent (see [3] for a counterexample), which is necessary for it to be an identity. To ensure that, we restrict ourselves to **race-free** games: those such that whenever a configuration x can be extended by a_1, a_2 of distinct polarities, the union $x \cup \{a_1, a_2\}$ is consistent. From now on, games are assumed race-free.

Lemma 3. *For a race-free game A, $\text{\ae}_A \circledast \text{\ae}_A \simeq \text{\ae}_A$.*

Proof. It will follow from the forthcoming Lemma 4.

Uncovered Strategies. Finally, we characterise the pre-strategies invariant under composition with copycat. The two ingredients of [5,14], receptivity and courtesy (called *innocence* in [14]) are needed, but this is not enough: we need another condition as witnessed by the following example.

Consider the strategy $\sigma : \oplus_1 \sim\!\sim \oplus_2$ on the game $A = \oplus_1 \oplus_2$ playing non-deterministically one of the two moves. Then the interaction $\mathrm{c\!\!c}_A \circledast \sigma$ is:

$$\begin{array}{ccc} A^* & & A \\ & & \\ *_1 & \longrightarrow\!\!\!\!\triangleright & \oplus_1 \\ \wr & & \\ *_2 & \longrightarrow\!\!\!\!\triangleright & \oplus_2 \end{array}$$

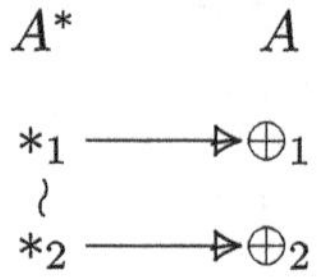

It is not weakly bisimilar to σ: $\mathrm{c\!\!c}_A \circledast \sigma$ can do $*_1$, an internal transition, to which σ can only respond by not doing anything. Then σ can still do $\oplus_1$ and $\oplus_2$ whereas $\mathrm{c\!\!c}_A \circledast \sigma$ cannot: it is committed to doing $\oplus_1$. To solve this problem, we need to force strategies to decide their nondeterministic choices *secretly*, by means of internal events – so σ will not be a valid uncovered strategy, but $\mathrm{c\!\!c}_A \circledast \sigma$ will. Indeed, $\mathrm{c\!\!c}_A \circledast (\mathrm{c\!\!c}_A \circledast \sigma)$ below is indeed weakly bisimilar to $\mathrm{c\!\!c}_A \circledast \sigma$.

$$\begin{array}{ccccc} A^* & & A^* & & A \\ & & & & \\ *_1 & \longrightarrow\!\!\!\!\triangleright & *_1 & \longrightarrow\!\!\!\!\triangleright & \oplus_1 \\ \wr & & & & \\ *_2 & \longrightarrow\!\!\!\!\triangleright & *_2 & \longrightarrow\!\!\!\!\triangleright & \oplus_2 \end{array}$$

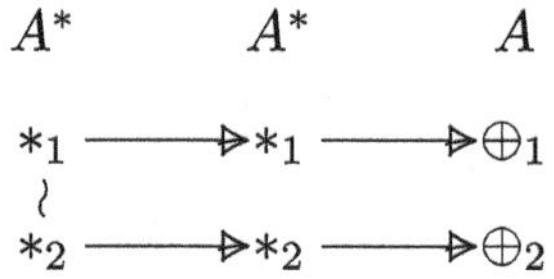

Definition 6. *An (uncovered) strategy is a pre-strategy $\sigma : S \rightharpoonup A$ satisfying:*

- receptivity: *if $x \in \mathscr{C}(S)$ is such that $\sigma x \overset{a}{\longrightarrow\!\!\!\subset}$ with $a \in A$ negative, then there exists a unique $x \overset{s}{\longrightarrow\!\!\!\subset}$ with $\sigma s = a$.*
- courtesy: *if $s \rightarrowtriangle s'$ and s is positive or s' is negative, then $\sigma s \rightarrowtriangle \sigma s'$.*
- secrecy: *if $x \in \mathscr{C}(S)$ extends with s_1, s_2 but $x \cup \{s_1, s_2\} \notin \mathscr{C}(S)$, then s_1 and s_2 are either both negative, or both internal.*

Receptivity and courtesy are stated exactly as in [14]. As a result, hiding the internal events of an uncovered strategy yields a strategy $\sigma_\downarrow$ in the sense of [14].

For any game A, $\mathrm{c\!\!c}_A$ is an uncovered strategy: it satisfies secrecy as its only minimal conflicts are inherited from the game and are between negative events.

The Category $\mathbf{CG}_\circledast$. Our definition of uncovered strategy does imply that copycat is neutral for composition.

Lemma 4. *Let $\sigma : S \rightharpoonup A$ be an uncovered strategy. Then $\mathrm{c\!\!c}_A \circledast \sigma \simeq \sigma$.*

The result follows immediately:

Theorem 1. *Race-free games and uncovered strategies up to weak bisimulation form a compact-closed category $\mathbf{CG}_\circledast$.*

3.4 Interpretation of Affine Nondeterministic PCF

From now on, strategies are by default considered uncovered. We sketch the interpretation of $\mathbf{APCF}_+$ inside $\mathbf{CG}_\circledast$. As a compact-closed category, $\mathbf{CG}_\circledast$ supports an interpretation of the linear λ-calculus. However, the empty game 1 is not terminal, as there are no natural transformation $\epsilon_A : A \to 1$ in $\mathbf{CG}_\circledast$.

The negative category $\mathbf{CG}_\circledast^-$. We solve this issue as in [4], by looking at negative strategies and negative games.

Definition 7. *An event structure with partial polarities is **negative** when all its minimal events are negative.*

A strategy $\sigma : S \rightharpoonup A$ is negative when S is. Copycat on a negative game is negative, and negative strategies are stable under composition:

Lemma 5. *There is a subcategory $\mathbf{CG}_\circledast^-$ of $\mathbf{CG}_\circledast$ consisting in negative race-free games and negative strategies. It inherits a monoidal structure from $\mathbf{CG}$ in which the unit (the empty game) is terminal.*

Moreover, $\mathbf{CG}_\circledast^-$ has products. The **product** $A \& B$ of two games A and B, has events, causality, polarities as for $A \parallel B$, but consistent sets restricted to those of the form $\{0\} \times X$ or $\{1\} \times X$ with X consistent in A or B. The **projections** are $\varpi_A : \mathbb{CC}_A \to (A \& B)^\perp \parallel A$, and $\varpi_B : \mathbb{CC}_B \to (A \& B)^\perp \parallel B$.

Finally, the **pairing** of negative strategies $\sigma : S \rightharpoonup A^\perp \parallel B$ and $\tau : T \rightharpoonup A^\perp \parallel C$ is the obvious map $\langle \sigma, \tau \rangle : S \& T \rightharpoonup A^\perp \parallel B \& C$, and the laws for the cartesian product are direct verifications.

We also need a construction to interpret the function space. However, for A and B negative, $A^\perp \parallel B$ is not usually negative. To circumvent this, we introduce a negative variant $A \multimap B$, the linear arrow. To simplify the presentation, we only define it in a special case. A game is **well-opened** when it has at most one initial event. When B is well-opened, we define $A \multimap B$ to be 1 if $B = 1$; and otherwise $A^\perp \parallel B$ with the exception that every move in A depends on the single minimal move in B. As a result $\multimap$ preserves negativity. We get:

Lemma 6. *If B is well-opened, $A \multimap B$ is well-opened and is an exponential object of A and B.*

In other words, well-opened games are an exponential ideal in $\mathbf{CG}_\circledast^-$. We interpret types of $\mathbf{APCF}_+$ inside well-opened games of $\mathbf{CG}_\circledast^-$:

$$[\![\mathbf{com}]\!] = \begin{array}{c} \mathbf{run}^- \\ \downarrow \\ \mathbf{done}^+ \end{array} \qquad [\![\mathbb{B}]\!] = \begin{array}{c} q^- \\ \swarrow \quad \searrow \\ \mathbf{tt}^+ \sim\!\!\sim \mathbf{ff}^+ \end{array} \qquad [\![A \multimap B]\!] = [\![A]\!] \multimap [\![B]\!]$$

Interpretation of Terms. Interpretation of the affine λ-calculus in $\mathbf{CG}_\circledast^\circledast$ follows standard methods. First, the primitives $\mathbf{tt}, \mathbf{ff}, \perp, \mathbf{if}$ are interpreted as:

$$[\![\mathbf{tt}]\!] : \mathbb{B} \qquad \mathbf{ff} : \mathbb{B} \qquad [\![\perp]\!] : \mathbb{B} \qquad \mathbf{if} : \quad \mathbb{B} \multimap (\mathbb{B} \& \mathbb{B}) \multimap \mathbb{B}$$

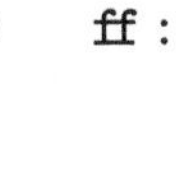

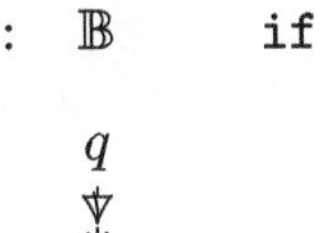

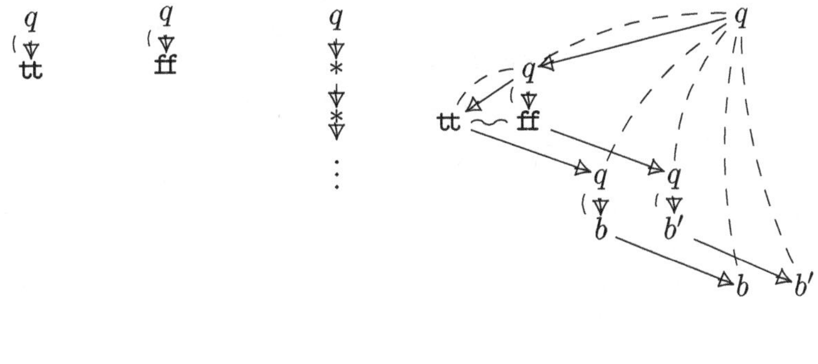

A non-standard point is the interpretation of $\bot$: usually interpreted in game semantics by the minimal strategy simply playing q (as will be done in the next section), our interpretation here reflects the fact that $\bot$ represents an infinite computation that never returns. Conditionals are implemented as usual:

$$[\![\texttt{if}\ M\,N\,N']\!]_{\circledast} = \texttt{if}\ \circledast\ ([\![M]\!]_{\circledast} \parallel \langle [\![N]\!]_{\circledast}, [\![N']\!]_{\circledast}\rangle).$$

Soundness and Adequacy. We now prove adequacy for various notions of convergence. First, we build an uncovered strategy from the operational semantics.

Definition 8 (The operational tree). *Let M be a closed term of type $\mathbb{B}$. We define the pre-strategy $\mathfrak{t}(M)$ on $\mathbb{B}$ as follows:*

Events: *An initial event $\bot$ plus one event per derivation $M \rightarrow^* M'$.*
Causality: *$\bot$ is below other events, and derivations are ordered by prefix*
Consistency: *A set of events is consistent when its events are comparable.*
Labelling: *$\bot$ has label q, a derivation $M \rightarrow^* b$ where $b \in \{\texttt{tt}, \texttt{ff}\}$ is labelled by b. Other derivations are internal.*

As a result, $\mathfrak{t}(M)$ is a tree. Our main result of adequacy can now be stated:

Theorem 2. *For a term $\vdash M : \mathbb{B}$, $\mathfrak{t}(\texttt{if}\ M\,\texttt{tt}\,\texttt{ff})$ and $[\![M]\!]_{\circledast}$ are weakly bisimilar.*

We need to consider $\mathfrak{t}(\texttt{if}\ M\,\texttt{tt}\,\texttt{ff})$ and not simply $\mathfrak{t}(M)$ to ensure secrecy. From this theorem, adequacy results for may and fair convergences arise:

Corollary 1. *For any term $\vdash M : \mathbb{B}$, we have:*

May: *$M \rightarrow^* \texttt{tt}$ if and only if $[\![M]\!]_{\circledast}$ contains a positive move*
Fair: *For all $M \rightarrow^* M'$, M' can converge, if and only if all finite configurations of $[\![M']\!]_{\circledast}$ can be extended to contain a positive move.*

However, we cannot conclude adequacy for must equivalence from Theorem 2. Indeed, must convergence is not generally stable under weak bisimilarity: for instance, (the strategies representing) $\texttt{tt}$ and $Y\ (\lambda x.\ \texttt{if}\ \texttt{choice}\ \texttt{tt}\ x)$ are weakly bisimilar but the latter is not must convergent. To address this in the next section we will refine the interpretation to obtain a closer connection with syntax.

4 Essential Events

The model presented in the previous section is very operational; configurations of $[\![M]\!]_{\circledast}$ can be seen as derivations for an operational semantics. The price, however, is that besides the fact that the interpretation grows dramatically in size, we can only get a category up to weak bisimulation, which can be too coarse (for instance for must convergence). We would like to remove all events that are not relevant to the behaviour of terms up to weak bisimulation. In other words, we want a notion of *essential internal events* that *(1)* suffices to recover all behaviour with respect to weak bisimulation, but which *(2)* is not an obstacle to getting a category up to isomorphism (which amounts to $\text{æ}_A \circ \sigma \cong \sigma$).

4.1 Definition of Essential Events

As shown before, the loss of behaviours when hiding is due to the disappearance of events participating in a conflict. A neutral event may not have visible consequences but still be relevant if in a minimal conflict; such events are *essential.*

Definition 9. *Let $\sigma : S \rightharpoonup A$ be an uncovered pre-strategy. An* **essential event** *of S is an event s which is either visible, or (internal and) involved in a minimal conflict (that is such that we have $s \rightsquigarrow_x s'$ for some s', x).*

Write E_S for the set of essential events of σ. Any pre-strategy $\sigma : S \rightharpoonup A$ induces another pre-strategy $\mathscr{E}(\sigma) : \mathscr{E}(S) = S \downarrow E_S \rightharpoonup A$ called **the essential part** of σ. The following proves that our definition satisfies *(1)*: no behaviour is lost.

Lemma 7. *An uncovered pre-strategy $\sigma : S \rightharpoonup A$ is weakly bisimilar to $\mathscr{E}(\sigma)$.*

This induces a new notion of (associative) composition only keeping the essential events. For $\sigma : A^\perp \parallel B$ and $\tau : B^\perp \parallel C$, let $\tau \circledcirc \sigma = \mathscr{E}(\tau \circledast \sigma)$. We observe that $\mathscr{E}(\tau \circledast \sigma) \cong \mathscr{E}(\tau) \circledcirc \mathscr{E}(\sigma)$.

Which pre-strategies compose well with copycat with this new composition?

4.2 Essential Strategies

We now can state property *(2)*: the events added by composition with copycat are inessential, hence hidden during composition:

Theorem 3. *Let $\sigma : S \rightharpoonup A$ be an uncovered strategy. Then $\text{æ}_A \circledcirc \sigma \cong \mathscr{E}(\sigma)$.*

This prompts the following definition. An uncovered pre-strategy σ is **essential** when it is a strategy, and if, equivalently: *(1)* all its events are essential, *(2)* $\sigma \cong \mathscr{E}(\sigma)$. We obtain a characterisation of strategies in the spirit of [14]:

Theorem 4. *A pre-strategy $\sigma : S \rightharpoonup A$ is essential if and only if $\text{æ}_A \circledcirc \sigma \cong \sigma$.*

As a result, we get:

Theorem 5. *Race-free games, and essential strategies up to isomorphism form a compact-closed category $\boldsymbol{CG}_\circledcirc$.*

Relationship Between CG and $\mathbf{CG}_\circledcirc$. Covered strategies can be made into a compact-closed category [5,14]. Remember that the composition of $\sigma : S \to A^\perp \parallel B$ and $\tau : T \to B^\perp \parallel C$ in **CG** is defined as $\tau \odot \sigma = (\tau \circledast \sigma)_\downarrow$.

Lemma 8. *The operation $\sigma \mapsto \sigma_\downarrow$ extends to an identity-on-object functor $\boldsymbol{CG}_\circledcirc \to \boldsymbol{CG}$.*

In the other direction, a strategy $\sigma : A$ might not be an essential strategy; in fact it might not even be an uncovered strategy, as it may fail secrecy. Sending σ to $\text{æ}_A \circledcirc \sigma$ delegates the non-deterministic choices to internal events and yields an essential strategy, but this operation is not functorial.

Relationship Between $\mathbf{CG}_{\circledcirc}$ and $\mathbf{CG}_{\circledast}$. The forgetful operation mapping an essential strategy σ to itself, seen as an uncovered strategy, defines a functor $\mathbf{CG}_{\circledcirc} \to \mathbf{CG}_{\circledast}$. Indeed, if two essential strategies are isomorphic, they are also weakly bisimilar. Moreover, we have that $\tau \circledast \sigma \simeq \mathscr{E}(\tau \circledast \sigma) = \tau \circledcirc \sigma$. However the operation $\mathscr{E}(\cdot)$ does not extend to a functor in the other direction even though $\mathscr{E}(\tau) \circledcirc \mathscr{E}(\sigma) \cong \mathscr{E}(\tau \circledast \sigma)$, as it is defined only on concrete representatives, not on equivalence classes for weak bisimilarity.

4.3 Interpretation of $\mathbf{APCF}_+$

We now show that this new category also supports a sound and adequate interpretation of $\mathbf{APCF}_+$ for various testing equivalences, including must. As before, we need to construct the category of negative games and strategies.

Lemma 9. *There is a cartesian symmetric monoidal category $\boldsymbol{CG}^-_{\circledcirc}$ of negative race-free games and negative essential strategies up to isomorphism. Well-opened negative race-free games form an exponential ideal of $\boldsymbol{CG}^-_{\circledcirc}$.*

We keep the same interpretation of types of affine nondeterministic PCF. Moreover, the strategy `if` is essential. As a result, we let:

$$[\![\bot]\!]_{\circledcirc} = q : \mathbb{B} \qquad [\![\texttt{if}\ M\,N\,N']\!]_{\circledcirc} = \texttt{if} \circledcirc ([\![M]\!]_{\circledcirc} \parallel \langle [\![N]\!]_{\circledcirc}, [\![N']\!]_{\circledcirc} \rangle)$$

Using $\mathscr{E}(\sigma \circledast \tau) = \mathscr{E}(\sigma) \circledcirc \mathscr{E}(\tau)$, one can prove by induction that for any term M we have $[\![M]\!]_{\circledcirc} = \mathscr{E}([\![M]\!]_{\circledast})$. Furthermore, this interpretation permits a stronger link between the operational and the denotational semantics:

Theorem 6. *For all terms $\vdash M : \mathbb{B}$, $\mathscr{E}(\mathsf{t}(M)) \cong [\![M]\!]_{\circledcirc}$.*

Theorem 6 implies Theorem 2. It also implies adequacy for must:

Corollary 2. *The interpretation $[\![\cdot]\!]_{\circledcirc}$ is adequate for may, and fair, and must: $\vdash M : \mathbb{B}$ has no infinite derivations if and only if all (possibly infinite) maximal configurations of $[\![M]\!]_{\circledcirc}$ have a positive event.*

This result also implies that $[\![\cdot]\!]_{\circledast}$ is adequate for must.

5 Conclusion

We have described an extension of the games of [14] to uncovered strategies, composed without hiding. It has strong connections with operational semantics, as the interpretations of terms of base type match their tree of reductions. It also forms a compact-closed category up to weak bisimulation, and is adequate for the denotational semantics of programming languages. Identifying the *inessential* events as those responsible for the non-neutrality of copycat, we remove them to yield a compact closed category up to isomorphism. Doing so we obtain our sought-after setting for the denotational semantics of programming languages, one *agnostic w.r.t.* the chosen testing equivalence. The work blends well with the technology of [7] (symmetry, concurrent innocence) dealing with non-affine languages and characterising strategies corresponding to pure programs; these developments appear in the first author's PhD thesis [3].

Acknowledgements. We gratefully acknowledge the support of the ERC Advanced Grant ECSYM, EPSRC grants EP/K034413/1 and EP/K011715/1, and LABEX MILYON (ANR-10-LABX-0070) of Université de Lyon, within the program "Investissements d'Avenir" (ANR-11-IDEX-0007) operated by the ANR.

References

1. Abramsky, S.: Game semantics for programming languages. In: Prívara, I., Ružička, P. (eds.) MFCS 1997. LNCS, vol. 1295, pp. 1–4. Springer, Heidelberg (1997). https://doi.org/10.1007/BFb0029944
2. Brinksma, E., Rensink, A., Vogler, W.: Fair testing. In: Lee, I., Smolka, S.A. (eds.) CONCUR 1995. LNCS, vol. 962, pp. 313–327. Springer, Heidelberg (1995). https://doi.org/10.1007/3-540-60218-6_23
3. Castellan, S.: Concurrent structures in game semantics. Ph.D. thesis, ENS Lyon, France (2017)
4. Castellan, S., Clairambault, P.: Causality vs. interleaving in game semantics. In: CONCUR 2016 - Concurrency Theory (2016)
5. Castellan, S., Clairambault, P., Rideau, S., Winskel, G.: Games and strategies as event structures. Log. Methods Comput. Sci. **13** (2017)
6. Castellan, S., Clairambault, P., Winskel, G.: Symmetry in concurrent games. In: Henzinger, T.A., Miller, D. (eds.) CSL-LICS 2014, Vienna, Austria, July 14–18, 2014, p. 28. ACM (2014)
7. Castellan, S., Clairambault, P., Winskel, G.: The parallel intensionally fully abstract games model of PCF. In: LICS 2015. IEEE Computer Society (2015)
8. Castellan, S., Hayman, J., Lasson, M., Winskel, G.: Strategies as concurrent processes. Electr. Notes Theor. Comput. Sci. **308**, 87–107 (2014)
9. Danos, V., Harmer, R.: Probabilistic game semantics. In: 15th Annual IEEE Symposium on Logic in Computer Science, Santa Barbara, California, USA, 26–29 June 2000, pp. 204–213 (2000)
10. Ghica, D.R., Murawski, A.S.: Angelic semantics of fine-grained concurrency. Ann. Pure Appl. Log. **151**(2–3), 89–114 (2008)
11. Harmer, R., McCusker, G.: A fully abstract game semantics for finite nondeterminism. In: 14th Annual IEEE Symposium on Logic in Computer Science, Trento, Italy, 2–5 July 1999, pp. 422–430 (1999)
12. Hirschowitz, T.: Full abstraction for fair testing in CCS. In: Heckel, R., Milius, S. (eds.) CALCO 2013. LNCS, vol. 8089, pp. 175–190. Springer, Heidelberg (2013). https://doi.org/10.1007/978-3-642-40206-7_14
13. Laird, J.: A game semantics of idealized CSP. Electr. Notes Theor. Comput. Sci. **45**, 232–257 (2001)
14. Rideau, S., Winskel, G.: Concurrent strategies. In: LICS, pp. 409–418. IEEE Computer Society (2011)
15. Tsukada, T., Luke Ong, C.-H.: Innocent strategies are sheaves over plays - deterministic, non-deterministic and probabilistic innocence. CoRR, abs/1409.2764 (2014)
16. Tsukada, T., Luke Ong, C.-H.: Nondeterminism in game semantics via sheaves. In: 30th Annual ACM/IEEE Symposium on Logic in Computer Science, LICS 2015, Kyoto, Japan, 6–10 July 2015, pp. 220–231 (2015)

17. Winskel, G.: Event structures. In: Brauer, W., Reisig, W., Rozenberg, G. (eds.) ACPN 1986. LNCS, vol. 255, pp. 325–392. Springer, Heidelberg (1987). https://doi.org/10.1007/3-540-17906-2_31
18. Yamada, N., Abramsky, S.: Dynamic games and strategies. CoRR, abs/1601.04147 (2016)

6

Realizability Interpretation and Normalization of Typed Call-by-Need λ-calculus with Control

Étienne Miquey[1,2(✉)] and Hugo Herbelin[2]

[1] Équipe Gallinette, Inria, LS2N (CNRS), Université de Nantes, Nantes, France
etienne.miquey@inria.fr

[2] Équipe πr^2, Inria, IRIF (CNRS), Université Paris-Diderot, Paris, France
herbelin@inria.fr

Abstract. We define a variant of Krivine realizability where realizers are pairs of a term and a substitution. This variant allows us to prove the normalization of a simply-typed call-by-need λ-calculus with control due to Ariola *et al.* Indeed, in such call-by-need calculus, substitutions have to be delayed until knowing if an argument is really needed. We then extend the proof to a call-by-need λ-calculus equipped with a type system equivalent to classical second-order predicate logic, representing one step towards proving the normalization of the call-by-need classical second-order arithmetic introduced by the second author to provide a proof-as-program interpretation of the axiom of dependent choice.

1 Introduction

1.1 Realizability-Based Normalization

Normalization by realizability is a standard technique to prove the normalization of typed λ-calculi. Originally introduced by Tait [36] to prove the normalization of System T, it was extended by Girard to prove the normalization of System F [11]. This kind of techniques, also called normalization by reducibility or normalization by logical relations, works by interpreting each type by a set of typed or untyped terms seen as realizers of the type, then showing that the way these sets of realizers are built preserve properties such as normalization. Over the years, multiple uses and generalization of this method have been done, for a more detailed account of which we refer the reader to the work of Gallier [9].

Realizability techniques were adapted to the normalization of various calculi for classical logic (see e.g. [3,32]). A specific framework tailored to the study of realizability for classical logic has been designed by Krivine [19] on top of a λ-calculus with control whose reduction is defined in terms of an abstract machine. In such a machinery, terms are evaluated in front of stacks; and control (thus classical logic) is made available through the possibility of saving and restoring stacks. During the last twenty years, Krivine's classical realizability turned out to be fruitful both from the point of view of logic, leading to the construction of new models of set theory, and generalizing in particular the technique of Cohen's forcing [20–22]; and on its computational facet, providing alternative tools to the analysis of the computational content of classical programs[1].

Noteworthily, Krivine realizability is one of the approaches contributing to advocating the motto that through the Curry-Howard correspondence, with new programming instructions come new reasoning principles[2]. Our original motivation for the present work is actually in line with this idea, in the sense that our long-term purpose is to give a realizability interpretation to dPA$^\omega$, a call-by-need calculus defined by the second author [15]. In this calculus, the lazy evaluation is indeed a fundamental ingredient in order to obtain an executable proof term for the axiom of dependent choice.

1.2 Contributions of the Paper

In order to address the normalization of typed call-by-need λ-calculus, we design a variant of Krivine's classical realizability, where the realizers are closures (a term with a substitution for its free variables). The call-by-need λ-calculus with control that we consider is the $\overline{\lambda}_{[lv\tau\star]}$-calculus. This calculus, that was defined by Ariola *et al.* [2], is syntactically described in an extension with explicit substitutions of the $\lambda\mu\tilde{\mu}$-calculus [6,14,29]. The syntax of the $\lambda\mu\tilde{\mu}$-calculus itself refines the syntax of the λ-calculus by syntactically distinguishing between *terms* and *evaluation contexts*. It also contains *commands* which combine terms and evaluation contexts so that they can interact together. Thinking of evaluation contexts as stacks and commands as states, the $\lambda\mu\tilde{\mu}$-calculus can also be seen as a syntax for abstract machines. As for a proof-as-program point of view, the $\lambda\mu\tilde{\mu}$-calculus and its variants can be seen as a term syntax for proofs of Gentzen's sequent calculus. In particular, the $\lambda\mu\tilde{\mu}$-calculus contains control operators which give a computational interpretation to classical logic.

We give a proof of normalization first for the simply-typed $\overline{\lambda}_{[lv\tau\star]}$-calculus[3], then for a type system with first-order and second-order quantification. While we only apply our technique to the normalization of the $\overline{\lambda}_{[lv\tau\star]}$-calculus, our interpretation incidentally suggests a way to adapt Krivine realizability to other call-by-need settings. This paves the way to the computational interpretation of classical proofs using lazy evaluation or shared memory cells, including the case of the call-by-need second order arithmetic dPA$^\omega$ [15].

---

[1] See for instance [27] about witness extraction or [12,13] about specification problems.

[2] For instance, one way to realize the axiom of dependent choice in classical realizability is by means of an extra instruction `quote` [18].

[3] Even though it has not been done formally, the normalization of the $\overline{\lambda}_{lv}$-calculus presented in [2] should also be derivable from Polonowski's proof of strong normalization of the non-deterministic $\lambda\mu\tilde{\mu}$-calculus [35]. The $\overline{\lambda}_{lv}$-calculus (a big-step variant of the $\overline{\lambda}_{[lv\tau\star]}$-calculus introduced in Ariola *et al.*) is indeed a particular evaluation strategy for the $\lambda\mu\tilde{\mu}$-calculus, so that the strong normalization of the non-deterministic variant of the latter should imply the normalization of the former as a particular case.

2 The $\overline{\lambda}_{[lv\tau\star]}$-calculus

2.1 The Call-by-Need Evaluation Strategy

The call-by-need evaluation strategy of the λ-calculus evaluates arguments of functions only when needed, and, when needed, shares their evaluations across all places where the argument is required. The call-by-need evaluation is at the heart of a functional programming language such as Haskell. It has in common with the call-by-value evaluation strategy that all places where a same argument is used share the same value. Nevertheless, it observationally behaves like the call-by-name evaluation strategy (for the pure λ-calculus), in the sense that a given computation eventually evaluates to a value if and only if it evaluates to the same value (up to inner reduction) along the call-by-name evaluation. In particular, in a setting with non-terminating computations, it is not observationally equivalent to the call-by-value evaluation. Indeed, if the evaluation of a useless argument loops in the call-by-value evaluation, the whole computation loops, which is not the case of call-by-name and call-by-need evaluations.

These three evaluation strategies can be turned into equational theories. For call-by-name and call-by-value, this was done by Plotkin through continuation-passing-style (CPS) semantics characterizing these theories [34]. For the call-by-need evaluation strategy, a specific equational theory reflecting the intensional behavior of the strategy into a semantics was proposed independently by Ariola and Felleisen [1], and by Maraist et al. [26]. A continuation-passing-style semantics was proposed in the 90s by Okasaki et al. [30]. However, this semantics does not ensure normalization of simply-typed call-by-need evaluation, as shown in [2], thus failing to ensure a property which holds in the simply-typed call-by-name and call-by-value cases.

Continuation-passing-style semantics *de facto* gives a semantics to the extension of λ-calculus with control operators[4]. In particular, even though call-by-name and call-by-need are observationally equivalent on pure λ-calculus, their different intentional behaviors induce different CPS semantics, leading to different observational behaviors when control operators are considered. On the other hand, the semantics of calculi with control can also be reconstructed from an analysis of the duality between programs and their evaluation contexts, and the duality between the `let` construct (which binds programs) and a control operator such as Parigot's μ (which binds evaluation contexts). Such an analysis can be done in the context of the $\lambda\mu\tilde{\mu}$-calculus [6,14].

In the call-by-name and call-by-value cases, the approach based on $\lambda\mu\tilde{\mu}$-calculus leads to continuation-passing style semantics similar to the ones given by Plotkin or, in the call-by-name case, also to the one by Lafont et al. [23]. As for call-by-need, in [2] is defined the $\overline{\lambda}_{lv}$-calculus, a call-by-need version of the $\lambda\mu\tilde{\mu}$-calculus. A continuation-passing style semantics is then defined via a calculus called $\overline{\lambda}_{[lv\tau\star]}$ [2]. This semantics, which is different from Okasaki, Lee and Tarditi's one [30], is the object of study in this paper.

[4] That is to say with operators such as Scheme's `callcc`, Felleisen's $\mathcal{C}$, $\mathcal{K}$, or $\mathcal{A}$ operators [8], Parigot's μ and [ ] operators [31], Crolard's `catch` and `throw` operators [5].

2.2 Explicit Environments

While the results presented in this paper could be directly expressed using the $\overline{\lambda}_{lv}$-calculus, the realizability interpretation naturally arises from the decomposition of this calculus into a different calculus with an explicit *environment*, the $\overline{\lambda}_{[lv\tau\star]}$-calculus [2]. Indeed, as we shall see in the sequel, the decomposition highlights different syntactic categories that are deeply involved in the type system and in the definition of the realizability interpretation.

The $\overline{\lambda}_{[lv\tau\star]}$-calculus is a reformulation of the $\overline{\lambda}_{lv}$-calculus with explicit environments, called *stores* and denoted by τ. Stores consists of a list of bindings of the form $[x := t]$, where x is a term variable and t a term, and of bindings of the form $[\alpha := e]$ where α is a context variable and e a context. For instance, in the closure $c\tau[x := t]\tau'$, the variable x is bound to t in c and τ'. Besides, the term t might be an unevaluated term (*i.e.* lazily stored), so that if x is eagerly demanded at some point during the execution of this closure, t will be reduced in order to obtain a value. In the case where t indeed produces a value V, the store will be updated with the binding $[x := V]$. However, a binding of this form (with a value) is fixed for the rest of the execution. As such, our so-called stores somewhat behave like lazy explicit substitutions or mutable environments.

To draw the comparison between our structures and the usual notions of stores and environments, two things should be observed. First, the usual notion of store refers to a structure of list that is fully mutable, in the sense that the cells can be updated at any time and thus values might be replaced. Second, the usual notion of environment designates a structure in which variables are bounded to closures made of a term and an environment. In particular, terms and environments are duplicated, *i.e.* sharing is not allowed. Such a structure resemble to a tree whose nodes are decorated by terms, as opposed to a machinery allowing sharing (like ours) whose underlying structure is broadly a directed acyclic graph. See for instance [24] for a Krivine abstract machine with sharing.

2.3 Syntax and Reduction Rules

The lazy evaluation of terms allows for the following reduction rule: us to reduce a command $\langle \mu\alpha.c \| \tilde{\mu}x.c' \rangle$ to the command c' together with the binding $[x := \mu\alpha.c]$.

$$\langle \mu\alpha.c \| \tilde{\mu}x.c' \rangle \rightarrow c'[x := \mu\alpha.c]$$

In this case, the term $\mu\alpha.c$ is left unevaluated ("frozen") in the store, until possibly reaching a command in which the variable x is needed. When evaluation reaches a command of the form $\langle x \| F \rangle \tau[x := \mu\alpha.c]\tau'$, the binding is opened and the term is evaluated in front of the context $\tilde{\mu}[x].\langle x \| F \rangle \tau'$:

$$\langle x \| F \rangle \tau[x := \mu\alpha.c]\tau' \rightarrow \langle \mu\alpha.c \| \tilde{\mu}[x].\langle x \| F \rangle \tau' \rangle \tau$$

The reader can think of the previous rule as the "defrosting" operation of the frozen term $\mu\alpha.c$: this term is evaluated in the prefix of the store τ which predates it, in front of the context $\tilde{\mu}[x].\langle x \| F \rangle \tau'$ where the $\tilde{\mu}[x]$ binder is waiting for a value.

Strong values	$v ::= \lambda x.t \mid \mathbf{k}$	
Weak values	$V ::= v \mid x$	
Terms	$t, u ::= V \mid \mu\alpha.c$	
Forcing contexts	$F ::= t \cdot E \mid \boldsymbol{\kappa}$	
Catchable contexts	$E ::= F \mid \alpha \mid \tilde{\mu}[x].\langle x\|F\rangle\tau$	
Evaluation contexts	$e ::= E \mid \tilde{\mu}x.c$	
Stores	$\tau ::= \varepsilon \mid \tau[x := t] \mid \tau[\alpha := E]$	
Commands	$c ::= \langle t\|e\rangle$	
Closures	$l ::= c\tau$	

(Beta)	$\langle \lambda x.t\|u \cdot E\rangle\tau$	$\to$	$\langle u\|\tilde{\mu}x.\langle t\|E\rangle\rangle\tau$
(Let)	$\langle t\|\tilde{\mu}x.c\rangle\tau$	$\to$	$c\tau[x := t]$
(Catch)	$\langle \mu\alpha.c\|E\rangle\tau$	$\to$	$c\tau[\alpha := E]$
(Lookup$_\alpha$)	$\langle V\|\alpha\rangle\tau[\alpha := E]\tau'$	$\to$	$\langle V\|E\rangle\tau[\alpha := E]\tau'$
(Lookup$_x$)	$\langle x\|F\rangle\tau[x := t]\tau'$	$\to$	$\langle t\|\tilde{\mu}[x].\langle x\|F\rangle\tau'\rangle\tau$
(Restore)	$\langle V\|\tilde{\mu}[x].\langle x\|F\rangle\tau'\rangle\tau$	$\to$	$\langle V\|F\rangle\tau[x := V]\tau'$

Fig. 1. Syntax and reduction rules of the $\overline{\lambda}_{[lv\tau\star]}$-calculus

This context keeps trace of the part of the store τ' that was originally located after the binding $[x := ...]$. This way, if a value V is indeed furnished for the binder $\tilde{\mu}[x]$, the original command $\langle x\|F\rangle$ is evaluated in the updated full store:

$$\langle V\|\tilde{\mu}[x].\langle x\|F\rangle\tau'\rangle\tau \to \langle V\|F\rangle\tau[x := V]\tau'$$

The brackets in $\tilde{\mu}[x].c$ are used to express the fact that the variable x is forced at top-level (unlike contexts of the shape $\tilde{\mu}x.C[\langle x\|F\rangle]$ in the $\overline{\lambda}_{lv}$-calculus). The reduction system resembles the one of an abstract machine. Especially, it allows us to keep the standard redex at the top of a command and avoids searching through the meta-context for work to be done.

Note that our approach slightly differ from [2] since we split values into two categories: strong values (v) and weak values (V). The strong values correspond to values strictly speaking. The weak values include the variables which force the evaluation of terms to which they refer into shared strong value. Their evaluation may require capturing a continuation. The syntax of the language, which includes constants $\mathbf{k}$ and co-constants $\boldsymbol{\kappa}$, is given in Fig. 1. As for the reduction $\to$, we define it as the compatible reflexive transitive closure of the rules given in Fig. 1.

The different syntactic categories can be understood as the different levels of alternation in a context-free abstract machine (see [2]): the priority is first given to contexts at level e (lazy storage of terms), then to terms at level t (evaluation of $\mu\alpha$ into values), then back to contexts at level E and so on until level v. These different categories are directly reflected in the definition of the abstract machine defined in [2], and will thus be involved in the definition of our realizability interpretation. We chose to highlight this by distinguishing different types of sequents already in the typing rules that we shall now present.

$$\frac{(\mathbf{k}:X)\in\mathcal{S}}{\Gamma\vdash_v \mathbf{k}:X}\,(\mathbf{k}) \qquad \frac{\Gamma,x:A\vdash_t t:B}{\Gamma\vdash_v \lambda x.t:A\to B}\,(\to_r) \qquad \frac{(x:A)\in\Gamma}{\Gamma\vdash_V x:A}\,(x) \qquad \frac{\Gamma\vdash_v v:A}{\Gamma\vdash_V v:A}\,(\uparrow^V)$$

$$\frac{(\boldsymbol{\kappa}:A)\in\mathcal{S}}{\Gamma\vdash_F \boldsymbol{\kappa}:A^\perp}\,(\boldsymbol{\kappa}) \qquad \frac{\Gamma\vdash_t t:A \quad \Gamma\vdash_E E:B^\perp}{\Gamma\vdash_F t\cdot E:(A\to B)^\perp}\,(\to_l) \qquad \frac{(\alpha:A)\in\Gamma}{\Gamma\vdash_E \alpha:A^\perp}\,(\alpha)$$

$$\frac{\Gamma\vdash_F F:A^\perp}{\Gamma\vdash_E F:A^\perp}\,(\uparrow^E) \qquad \frac{\Gamma\vdash_V V:A}{\Gamma\vdash_t V:A}\,(\uparrow^t) \qquad \frac{\Gamma,\alpha:A^\perp\vdash_c c}{\Gamma\vdash_t \mu\alpha.c:A}\,(\mu) \qquad \frac{\Gamma\vdash_E E:A^\perp}{\Gamma\vdash_e E:A^\perp}\,(\uparrow^e)$$

$$\frac{\Gamma,x:A\vdash_c c}{\Gamma\vdash_e \tilde{\mu}x.c:A^\perp}\,(\tilde{\mu}) \qquad \frac{\Gamma,x:A,\Gamma'\vdash_F F:A^\perp \quad \Gamma\vdash_\tau \tau:\Gamma'}{\Gamma\vdash_E \tilde{\mu}[x].\langle x\|F\rangle\tau:A^\perp}\,(\tilde{\mu}^{[]})$$

$$\frac{\Gamma\vdash_t t:A \quad \Gamma\vdash_e e:A^\perp}{\Gamma\vdash_c \langle t\|e\rangle}\,(c) \qquad \frac{\Gamma,\Gamma'\vdash_c c \quad \Gamma\vdash_\tau \tau:\Gamma'}{\Gamma\vdash_l c\tau}\,(l) \qquad \frac{}{\Gamma\vdash_\tau \varepsilon:\varepsilon}\,(\varepsilon)$$

$$\frac{\Gamma\vdash_\tau \tau:\Gamma' \quad \Gamma,\Gamma'\vdash_t t:A}{\Gamma\vdash_\tau \tau[x:=t]:\Gamma',x:A}\,(\tau_t) \qquad \frac{\Gamma\vdash_\tau \tau:\Gamma' \quad \Gamma,\Gamma'\vdash_E E:A^\perp}{\Gamma\vdash_\tau \tau[\alpha:=E]:\Gamma',\alpha:A^\perp}\,(\tau_E)$$

Fig. 2. Typing rules of the $\overline{\lambda}_{[lv\tau\star]}$-calculus

2.4 A Type System for the $\overline{\lambda}_{[lv\tau\star]}$-calculus

We have nine kinds of (one-sided) sequents, one for typing each of the nine syntactic categories. We write them with an annotation on the $\vdash$ sign, using one of the letters v, V, t, F, E, e, l, c, τ. Sequents typing values and terms are asserting a type, with the type written on the right; sequents typing contexts are expecting a type A with the type written $A^\perp$; sequents typing commands and closures are black boxes neither asserting nor expecting a type; sequents typing substitutions are instantiating a typing context. In other words, we have the following nine kinds of sequents:

$$\begin{array}{lll} \Gamma\vdash_l l & \Gamma\vdash_t t:A & \Gamma\vdash_e e:A^\perp \\ \Gamma\vdash_c c & \Gamma\vdash_V V:A & \Gamma\vdash_E E:A^\perp \\ \Gamma\vdash_\tau \tau:\Gamma' & \Gamma\vdash_v v:A & \Gamma\vdash_F F:A^\perp \end{array}$$

where types and typing contexts are defined by:

$$A,B ::= X \mid A\to B \qquad\qquad \Gamma ::= \varepsilon \mid \Gamma,x:A \mid \Gamma,\alpha:A^\perp$$

The typing rules are given on Fig. 2 where we assume that a variable x (resp. co-variable α) only occurs once in a context Γ (we implicitly assume the possibility of renaming variables by α-conversion). We also adopt the convention that constants $\mathbf{k}$ and co-constants $\boldsymbol{\kappa}$ come with a signature $\mathcal{S}$ which assigns them a type. This type system enjoys the property of subject reduction.

Theorem 1 (Subject reduction). *If $\Gamma\vdash_l c\tau$ and $c\tau\to c'\tau'$ then $\Gamma\vdash_l c'\tau'$.*

Proof. By induction on typing derivations. □

3 Normalization of the $\overline{\lambda}_{[lv\tau\star]}$-calculus

3.1 Normalization by Realizability

The proof of normalization for the $\overline{\lambda}_{[lv\tau\star]}$-calculus that we present in this section is inspired from techniques of Krivine's classical realizability [19], whose notations we borrow. Actually, it is also very close to a proof by reducibility[5]. In a nutshell, to each type A is associated a set $|A|_t$ of terms whose execution is guided by the structure of A. These terms are the ones usually called *realizers* in Krivine's classical realizability. Their definition is in fact indirect, and is done by orthogonality to a set of "correct" computations, called a *pole*. The choice of this set is central when studying models induced by classical realizability for second-order-logic, but in the present case we only pay attention to the particular pole of terminating computations. This is where lies one of the difference with usual proofs by reducibility, where everything is done with respect to SN, while our definition are parametric in the pole (which is chosen to be SN in the end). The adequacy lemma, which is the central piece, consists in proving that typed terms belong to the corresponding sets of realizers, and are thus normalizing.

More in details, our proof can be sketched as follows. First, we generalize the usual notion of closed term to the notion of closed *term-in-store*. Intuitively, this is due to the fact that we are no longer interested in closed terms and substitutions to close opened terms, but rather in terms that are closed when considered in the current store. This is based on the simple observation that a store is nothing more than a shared substitution whose content might evolve along the execution. Second, we define the notion of *pole* $\perp\!\!\!\perp$, which are sets of closures closed by anti-evaluation and store extension. In particular, the set of normalizing closures is a valid pole. This allows to relate terms and contexts thanks to a notion of orthogonality with respect to the pole. We then define for each formula A and typing level o (of e, t, E, V, F, v) a set $|A|_o$ (resp. $\|A\|_o$) of terms (resp. contexts) in the corresponding syntactic category. These sets correspond to reducibility candidates, or to what is usually called truth values and falsity values in Krivine realizability. Finally, the core of the proof consists in the adequacy lemma, which shows that any closed term of type A at level o is in the corresponding set $|A|_o$. This guarantees that any typed closure is in any pole, and in particular in the pole of normalizing closures. Technically, the proof of adequacy evaluates in each case a state of an abstract machine (in our case a closure), so that the proof also proceeds by evaluation. A more detailed explanation of this observation as well as a more introductory presentation of normalization proofs by classical realizability are given in an article by Dagand and Scherer [7].

3.2 Realizability Interpretation for the $\overline{\lambda}_{[lv\tau\star]}$-calculus

We begin by defining some key notions for stores that we shall need further in the proof.

[5] See for instance the proof of normalization for system D presented in [17, Sect. 3.2].

Definition 2 (Closed store). *We extend the notion of free variable to stores:*

$$\begin{array}{rcl} FV(\varepsilon) & \triangleq & \emptyset \\ FV(\tau[x := t]) & \triangleq & FV(\tau) \cup \{y \in FV(t) : y \notin \mathit{dom}(\tau)\} \\ FV(\tau[\alpha := E]) & \triangleq & FV(\tau) \cup \{\beta \in FV(E) : \beta \notin \mathit{dom}(\tau)\} \end{array}$$

so that we can define a closed store *to be a store τ such that $FV(\tau) = \emptyset$.*

Definition 3 (Compatible stores). *We say that two stores τ and τ' are* independent *and write $\tau \# \tau'$ when $\mathit{dom}(\tau) \cap \mathit{dom}(\tau') = \emptyset$. We say that they are* compatible *and write $\tau \diamond \tau'$ whenever for all variables x (resp. co-variables α) present in both stores: $x \in \mathit{dom}(\tau) \cap \mathit{dom}(\tau')$; the corresponding terms (resp. contexts) in τ and τ' coincide. Finally, we say that τ' is an* extension *of τ and write $\tau \lhd \tau'$ whenever $\mathit{dom}(\tau) \subseteq \mathit{dom}(\tau')$ and $\tau \diamond \tau'$.*

We denote by $\overline{\tau\tau'}$ the compatible union $\mathtt{join}(\tau\tau')$ of closed stores τ and τ', defined by:

$$\begin{array}{rcll} \mathtt{join}(\tau_0[x := t]\tau_1, \tau_0'[x := t]\tau_1') & \triangleq & \tau_0\tau_0'[x := t]\mathtt{join}(\tau_1, \tau_1') & (\text{if } \tau_0 \# \tau_0') \\ \mathtt{join}(\tau, \tau') & \triangleq & \tau\tau' & (\text{if } \tau \# \tau') \\ \mathtt{join}(\varepsilon, \tau) & \triangleq & \tau & \\ \mathtt{join}(\tau, \varepsilon) & \triangleq & \tau & \end{array}$$

The following lemma (which follows easily from the previous definition) states the main property we will use about union of compatible stores.

Lemma 4. *If τ and τ' are two compatible stores, then $\tau \lhd \overline{\tau\tau'}$ and $\tau' \lhd \overline{\tau\tau'}$. Besides, if τ is of the form $\tau_0[x := t]\tau_1$, then $\overline{\tau\tau'}$ is of the form $\tau_2[x := t]\tau_3$ with $\tau_0 \lhd \tau_2$ and $\tau_1 \lhd \tau_3$.*

Proof. This follows easily from the previous definition. □

As we explained in the introduction of this section, we will not consider closed terms in the usual sense. Indeed, while it is frequent in the proofs of normalization (*e.g.* by realizability or reducibility) of a calculus to consider only closed terms and to perform substitutions to maintain the closure of terms, this only makes sense if it corresponds to the computational behavior of the calculus. For instance, to prove the normalization of $\lambda x.t$ in typed call-by-name $\lambda\mu\tilde{\mu}$-calculus, one would consider a substitution ρ that is suitable for with respect to the typing context Γ, then a context $u \cdot e$ of type $A \to B$, and evaluates:

$$\langle \lambda x.t_\rho \| u \cdot e \rangle \quad \to \quad \langle t_\rho[u/x] \| e \rangle$$

Then we would observe that $t_\rho[u/x] = t_{\rho[x:=u]}$ and deduce that $\rho[x := u]$ is suitable for $\Gamma, x : A$, which would allow us to conclude by induction.

However, in the $\overline{\lambda}_{[lv\tau\star]}$-calculus we do not perform global substitution when reducing a command, but rather add a new binding $[x := u]$ in the store:

$$\langle \lambda x.t \| u \cdot E \rangle\tau \quad \to \quad \langle t \| E \rangle\tau[x := u]$$

Therefore, the natural notion of closed term invokes the closure under a store, which might evolve during the rest of the execution (this is to contrast with a substitution).

Definition 5 (Term-in-store). *We call* closed term-in-store *(resp.* closed context-in-store, closed closures*) the combination of a term t (resp. context e, command c) with a closed store τ such that $FV(t) \subseteq \mathtt{dom}(\tau)$. We use the notation $(t|\tau)$ (resp. $(e|\tau), (c|\tau)$) to denote such a pair.*

We should note that in particular, if t is a closed term, then $(t|\tau)$ is a term-in-store for any closed store τ. The notion of closed term-in-store is thus a generalization of the notion of closed terms, and we will (ab)use of this terminology in the sequel. We denote the sets of closed closures by $\mathcal{C}_0$, and will identify $(c|\tau)$ and the closure $c\tau$ when c is closed in τ. Observe that if $c\tau$ is a closure in $\mathcal{C}_0$ and τ' is a store extending τ, then $c\tau'$ is also in $\mathcal{C}_0$. We are now equipped to define the notion of pole, and verify that the set of normalizing closures is indeed a valid pole.

Definition 6 (Pole). *A subset $\perp\!\!\!\perp \subseteq \mathcal{C}_0$ is said to be* saturated *or* closed by anti-reduction *whenever for all $(c|\tau), (c'|\tau') \in \mathcal{C}_0$, if $c'\tau' \in \perp\!\!\!\perp$ and $c\tau \to c'\tau'$ then $c\tau \in \perp\!\!\!\perp$. It is said to be* closed by store extension *if whenever $c\tau \in \perp\!\!\!\perp$, for any store τ' extending τ: $\tau \lhd \tau'$, $c\tau' \in \perp\!\!\!\perp$. A* pole *is defined as any subset of $\mathcal{C}_0$ that is closed by anti-reduction and store extension.*

The following proposition is the one supporting the claim that our realizability proof is almost a reducibility proof whose definitions have been generalized with respect to a pole instead of the fixed set SN.

Proposition 7. *The set $\perp\!\!\!\perp_{\Downarrow} = \{c\tau \in \mathcal{C}_0 : \ c\tau \text{ normalizes} \}$ is a pole.*

Proof. As we only considered closures in $\mathcal{C}_0$, both conditions (closure by anti-reduction and store extension) are clearly satisfied:

- if $c\tau \to c'\tau'$ and $c'\tau'$ normalizes, then $c\tau$ normalizes too;
- if c is closed in τ and $c\tau$ normalizes, if $\tau \lhd \tau'$ then $c\tau'$ will reduce as $c\tau$ does (since c is closed under τ, it can only use terms in τ' that already were in τ) and thus will normalize. □

Definition 8 (Orthogonality). *Given a pole $\perp\!\!\!\perp$, we say that a term-in-store $(t|\tau)$ is* orthogonal *to a context-in-store $(e|\tau')$ and write $(t|\tau)\perp\!\!\!\perp(e|\tau')$ if τ and τ' are compatible and $\langle t\|e\rangle\overline{\tau\tau'} \in \perp\!\!\!\perp$.*

Remark 9. The reader familiar with Krivine's forcing machine [20] might recognize his definition of orthogonality between terms of the shape (t,p) and stacks of the shape (π, q), where p and q are forcing conditions[6]:

$$(t,p)\perp\!\!\!\perp(\pi,q) \Leftrightarrow (t \star \pi, p \land q) \in \perp\!\!\!\perp$$

[6] The meet of forcing conditions is indeed a refinement containing somewhat the "union" of information contained in each, just like the union of two compatible stores.

We can now relate closed terms and contexts by orthogonality with respect to a given pole. This allows us to define for any formula A the sets $|A|_v, |A|_V, |A|_t$ (resp. $\|A\|_F$,$\|A\|_E$, $\|A\|_e$) of realizers (or reducibility candidates) at level v, V, t (resp. F, E, e) for the formula A. It is to be observed that realizers are here closed terms-in-store.

Definition 10 (Realizers). *Given a fixed pole* $\perp\!\!\!\perp$, *we set:*

$$\begin{array}{rl}
|X|_v & = \{(\mathbf{k}|\tau) : \ \vdash \mathbf{k} : X\} \\
|A \to B|_v & = \{(\lambda x.t|\tau) : \forall u\tau', \tau \diamond \tau' \wedge (u|\tau') \in |A|_t \Rightarrow (t|\overline{\tau\tau'}[x := u]) \in |B|_t\} \\
\|A\|_F & = \{(F|\tau) : \forall v\tau', \tau \diamond \tau' \wedge (v|\tau') \in |A|_v \Rightarrow (v|\tau') \perp\!\!\!\perp (F|\tau)\} \\
|A|_V & = \{(V|\tau) : \forall F\tau', \tau \diamond \tau' \wedge (F|\tau') \in \|A\|_F \Rightarrow (V|\tau) \perp\!\!\!\perp (F|\tau')\} \\
\|A\|_E & = \{(E|\tau) : \forall V\tau', \tau \diamond \tau' \wedge (V|\tau') \in |A|_V \Rightarrow (V|\tau') \perp\!\!\!\perp (E|\tau)\} \\
|A|_t & = \{(t|\tau) : \forall E\tau', \tau \diamond \tau' \wedge (E|\tau') \in \|A\|_E \Rightarrow (t|\tau) \perp\!\!\!\perp (E|\tau')\} \\
\|A\|_e & = \{(e|\tau) : \forall t\tau', \tau \diamond \tau' \wedge (t|\tau') \in |A|_t \Rightarrow (t|\tau') \perp\!\!\!\perp (e|\tau)\}
\end{array}$$

Remark 11. We draw the reader attention to the fact that we should actually write $|A|_v^{\perp\!\!\!\perp}$, $\|A\|_F^{\perp\!\!\!\perp}$, etc. and $\tau \Vdash_{\perp\!\!\!\perp} \Gamma$, because the corresponding definitions are parameterized by a pole $\perp\!\!\!\perp$. As it is common in Krivine's classical realizability, we ease the notations by removing the annotation $\perp\!\!\!\perp$ whenever there is no ambiguity on the pole. Besides, it is worth noting that if co-constants do not occur directly in the definitions, they may still appear in the realizers by mean of the pole.

If the definition of the different sets might seem complex at first sight, we claim that they are quite natural in regards of the methodology of Danvy's semantics artifacts presented in [2]. Indeed, having an abstract machine in context-free form (the last step in this methodology before deriving the CPS) allows us to have both the term and the context (in a command) that behave independently of each other. Intuitively, a realizer at a given level is precisely a term which is going to behave well (be in the pole) in front of any opponent chosen in the previous level (in the hierarchy v, F, V, etc.). For instance, in a call-by-value setting, there are only three levels of definition (values, contexts and terms) in the interpretation, because the abstract machine in context-free form also has three. Here the ground level corresponds to strong values, and the other levels are somewhat defined as terms (or context) which are well-behaved in front of any opponent in the previous one. The definition of the different sets $|A|_v$, $\|A\|_F$, $|A|_V$, etc. directly stems from this intuition.

In comparison with the usual definition of Krivine's classical realizability, we only considered orthogonal sets restricted to some syntactical subcategories. However, the definition still satisfies the usual monotonicity properties of bi-orthogonal sets:

Proposition 12. *For any type A and any given pole $\perp\!\!\!\perp$, we have:*

1. $|A|_v \subseteq |A|_V \subseteq |A|_t$; *2.* $\|A\|_F \subseteq \|A\|_E \subseteq \|A\|_e$.

Proof. All the inclusions are proved in a similar way. We only give the proof for $|A|_v \subseteq |A|_V$. Let $\perp\!\!\!\perp$ be a pole and $(v|\tau)$ be in $|A|_v$. We want to show that $(v|\tau)$

is in $|A|_V$, that is to say that v is in the syntactic category V (which is true), and that for any $(F|\tau') \in \|A\|_F$ such that $\tau \diamond \tau'$, $(v|\tau) \perp\!\!\!\perp (F|\tau')$. The latter holds by definition of $(F|\tau') \in \|A\|_F$, since $(v|\tau) \in |A|_v$. □

We now extend the notion of realizers to stores, by stating that a store τ realizes a context Γ if it binds all the variables x and α in Γ to a realizer of the corresponding formula.

Definition 13. *Given a closed store τ and a fixed pole $\perp\!\!\!\perp$, we say that τ* realizes *Γ, which we write*[7] $\tau \Vdash \Gamma$, *if:*

1. *for any $(x : A) \in \Gamma$, $\tau \equiv \tau_0[x := t]\tau_1$ and $(t|\tau_0) \in |A|_t$*
2. *for any $(\alpha : A^{\perp}) \in \Gamma$, $\tau \equiv \tau_0[\alpha := E]\tau_1$ and $(E|\tau_0) \in \|A\|_E$*

In the same way than weakening rules (for the typing context) are admissible for each level of the typing system:

$$\frac{\Gamma \vdash_t t : A \quad \Gamma \subseteq \Gamma'}{\Gamma' \vdash_t t : A} \qquad \frac{\Gamma \vdash_e e : A^{\perp} \quad \Gamma \subseteq \Gamma'}{\Gamma' \vdash_e e : A^{\perp}} \quad \cdots \quad \frac{\Gamma \vdash_\tau \tau : \Gamma'' \quad \Gamma \subseteq \Gamma'}{\Gamma' \vdash_\tau \tau : \Gamma''}$$

the definition of realizers is compatible with a weakening of the store.

Lemma 14 (Store weakening). *Let τ and τ' be two stores such that $\tau \triangleleft \tau'$, let Γ be a typing context and let $\perp\!\!\!\perp$ be a pole. The following statements hold:*

1. $\overline{\tau\tau'} = \tau'$
2. *If $(t|\tau) \in |A|_t$ for some closed term $(t|\tau)$ and type A, then $(t|\tau') \in |A|_t$. The same holds for each level e, E, V, F, v of the typing rules.*
3. *If $\tau \Vdash \Gamma$ then $\tau' \Vdash \Gamma$.*

Proof. 1. Straightforward from the definition of $\overline{\tau\tau'}$.
2. This essentially amounts to the following observations. First, one remarks that if $(t|\tau)$ is a closed term, so then so is $(t|\overline{\tau\tau'})$ for any closed store τ' compatible with τ. Second, we observe that if we consider for instance a closed context $(E|\tau'') \in \|A\|_E$, then $\overline{\tau\tau'} \diamond \tau''$ implies $\tau \diamond \tau''$, thus $(t|\tau) \perp\!\!\!\perp (E|\tau'')$ and finally $(t|\overline{\tau\tau'}) \perp\!\!\!\perp (E|\tau'')$ by closure of the pole under store extension. We conclude that $(t|\tau') \perp\!\!\!\perp (E|\tau'')$ using the first statement.
3. By definition, for all $(x : A) \in \Gamma$, τ is of the form $\tau_0[x := t]\tau_1$ such that $(t|\tau_0) \in |A|_t$. As τ and τ' are compatible, we know by Lemma 4 that $\overline{\tau\tau'}$ is of the form $\tau_0'[x := t]\tau_1'$ with τ_0' an extension of τ_0, and using the first point we get that $(t|\tau_0') \in |A|_t$. □

Definition 15 (Adequacy). *Given a fixed pole $\perp\!\!\!\perp$, we say that:*

- *A typing judgment $\Gamma \vdash_t t : A$ is* adequate *(w.r.t. the pole $\perp\!\!\!\perp$) if for all stores $\tau \Vdash \Gamma$, we have $(t|\tau) \in |A|_t$.*

[7] Once again, we should formally write $\tau \Vdash_{\perp\!\!\!\perp} \Gamma$ but we will omit the annotation by $\perp\!\!\!\perp$ as often as possible.

– *More generally, we say that an inference rule*

$$\frac{J_1 \quad \cdots \quad J_n}{J_0}$$

is adequate (w.r.t. the pole $⫫$) if the adequacy of all typing judgments $J_1, \ldots, J_n$ implies the adequacy of the typing judgment J_0.

Remark 16. From the latter definition, it is clear that a typing judgment that is derivable from a set of adequate inference rules is adequate too.

We will now show the main result of this section, namely that the typing rules of Fig. 2 for the $\overline{\lambda}_{[lv\tau\star]}$-calculus without co-constants are adequate with any pole. Observe that this result requires to consider the $\overline{\lambda}_{[lv\tau\star]}$-calculus without co-constants. Indeed, we consider co-constants as coming with their typing rules, potentially giving them any type (whereas constants can only be given an atomic type). Thus, there is *a priori* no reason[8] why their types should be adequate with any pole.

However, as observed in the previous remark, given a fixed pole it suffices to check whether the typing rules for a given co-constant are adequate with this pole. If they are, any judgment that is derivable using these rules will be adequate.

Theorem 17 (Adequacy). *If Γ is a typing context, $⫫$ is a pole and τ is a store such that $\tau \Vdash \Gamma$, then the following holds in the $\overline{\lambda}_{[lv\tau\star]}$-calculus without co-constants:*

1. *If v is a strong value such that $\Gamma \vdash_v v : A$, then $(v|\tau) \in |A|_v$.*
2. *If F is a forcing context such that $\Gamma \vdash_F F : A^{\perp}$, then $(F|\tau) \in \|A\|_F$.*
3. *If V is a weak value such that $\Gamma \vdash_V V : A$, then $(V|\tau) \in |A|_V$.*
4. *If E is a catchable context such that $\Gamma \vdash_E E : A^{\perp}$, then $(E|\tau) \in \|A\|_F$.*
5. *If t is a term such that $\Gamma \vdash_t t : A$, then $(t|\tau) \in |A|_t$.*
6. *If e is a context such that $\Gamma \vdash_e e : A^{\perp}$, then $(e|\tau) \in \|A\|_e$.*
7. *If c is a command such that $\Gamma \vdash_c c$, then $c\tau \in ⫫$.*
8. *If τ' is a store such that $\Gamma \vdash_\tau \tau' : \Gamma'$, then $\tau\tau' \Vdash \Gamma, \Gamma'$.*

Proof. The different statements are proved by mutual induction over typing derivations. We only give the most important cases here.

Rule $(\rightarrow_l)$. Assume that

$$\frac{\Gamma \vdash_t u : A \quad \Gamma \vdash_E E : B^{\perp}}{\Gamma \vdash_F u \cdot E : (A \rightarrow B)^{\perp}} \ (\rightarrow_l)$$

and let $⫫$ be a pole and τ a store such that $\tau \Vdash \Gamma$. Let $(\lambda x.t|\tau')$ be a closed term in the set $|A \rightarrow B|_v$ such that $\tau \diamond \tau'$, then we have:

$$\langle \lambda x.t \| u \cdot E \rangle \overline{\tau\tau'} \quad \rightarrow \quad \langle u \| \tilde{\mu} x.\langle t \| E \rangle \rangle \overline{\tau\tau'} \quad \rightarrow \quad \langle t \| E \rangle \overline{\tau\tau'}[x := u]$$

[8] Think for instance of a co-constant of type $(A \rightarrow B)^{\perp}$, there is no reason why it should be orthogonal to any function in $|A \rightarrow B|_v$.

By definition of $|A \to B|_v$, this closure is in the pole, and we can conclude by anti-reduction.

Rule (x). Assume that

$$\frac{(x : A) \in \Gamma}{\Gamma \vdash_V x : A}\;(x)$$

and let $\perp\!\!\!\perp$ be a pole and τ a store such that $\tau \Vdash \Gamma$. As $(x : A) \in \Gamma$, we know that τ is of the form $\tau_0[x := t]\tau_1$ with $(t|\tau_0) \in |A|_t$. Let $(F|\tau')$ be in $\|A\|_F$, with $\tau \diamond \tau'$. By Lemma 4, we know that $\overline{\tau\tau'}$ is of the form $\overline{\tau_0}[x := t]\overline{\tau_1}$. Hence we have:

$$\langle x\|F\rangle\overline{\tau_0}[x := t]\overline{\tau_1} \quad\to\quad \langle t\|\tilde{\mu}[x].\langle x\|F\rangle\overline{\tau_1}\rangle\overline{\tau_0}$$

and it suffices by anti-reduction to show that the last closure is in the pole $\perp\!\!\!\perp$. By induction hypothesis, we know that $(t|\tau_0) \in |A|_t$ thus we only need to show that it is in front of a catchable context in $\|A\|_E$. This corresponds exactly to the next case that we shall prove now.

Rule $(\tilde{\mu}^{[]})$. Assume that

$$\frac{\Gamma, x : A, \Gamma' \vdash_F F : A \quad \Gamma, x : A \vdash \tau' : \Gamma'}{\Gamma \vdash_E \tilde{\mu}[x].\langle x\|F\rangle\tau' : A}\;(\tilde{\mu}^{[]})$$

and let $\perp\!\!\!\perp$ be a pole and τ a store such that $\tau \Vdash \Gamma$. Let $(V|\tau_0)$ be a closed term in $|A|_V$ such that $\tau_0 \diamond \tau$. We have that:

$$\langle V\|\tilde{\mu}[x].\langle x\|F\rangle\overline{\tau'}\rangle\overline{\tau_0\tau} \quad\to\quad \langle V\|F\rangle\overline{\tau_0\tau}[x := V]\tau'$$

By induction hypothesis, we obtain $\tau[x := V]\tau' \Vdash \Gamma, x : A, \Gamma'$. Up to α-conversion in F and τ', so that the variables in τ' are disjoint from those in τ_0, we have that $\overline{\tau_0\tau} \Vdash \Gamma$ (by Lemma 14) and then $\tau'' \triangleq \overline{\tau_0\tau}[x := V]\tau' \Vdash \Gamma, x : A, \Gamma'$. By induction hypothesis again, we obtain that $(F|\tau'') \in \|A\|_F$ (this was an assumption in the previous case) and as $(V|\tau_0) \in |A|_V$, we finally get that $(V|\tau_0)\perp\!\!\!\perp(F|\tau'')$ and conclude again by anti-reduction. □

Corollary 18. *If $c\tau$ is a closure such that $\vdash_l c\tau$ is derivable, then for any pole $\perp\!\!\!\perp$ such that the typing rules for co-constants used in the derivation are adequate with $\perp\!\!\!\perp$, $c\tau \in \perp\!\!\!\perp$.*

We can now put our focus back on the normalization of typed closures. As we already saw in Proposition 7, the set $\perp\!\!\!\perp_{\Downarrow}$ of normalizing closure is a valid pole, so that it only remains to prove that any typing rule for co-constants is adequate with $\perp\!\!\!\perp_{\Downarrow}$.

Lemma 19. *Any typing rule for co-constants is adequate with the pole $\perp\!\!\!\perp_{\Downarrow}$,* i.e. *if Γ is a typing context, and τ is a store such that $\tau \Vdash \Gamma$, if $\boldsymbol{\kappa}$ is a co-constant such that $\Gamma \vdash_F \boldsymbol{\kappa} : A^{\perp}$, then $(\boldsymbol{\kappa}|\tau) \in \|A\|_F$.*

Proof. This lemma directly stems from the observation that for any store τ and any closed strong value $(v|\tau') \in |A|_v$, $\langle v \| \kappa \rangle \overline{\tau\tau'}$ does not reduce and thus belongs to the pole $\perp\!\!\!\perp_{\Downarrow}$.

As a consequence, we obtain the normalization of typed closures of the full calculus.

Theorem 20. *If $c\tau$ is a closure of the $\overline{\lambda}_{[lv\tau\star]}$-calculus such that $\vdash_l c\tau$ is derivable, then $c\tau$ normalizes.*

This is to be contrasted with Okasaki, Lee and Tarditi's semantics for the call-by-need λ-calculus, which is not normalizing in the simply-typed case, as shown in Ariola *et al.* [2].

3.3 Extension to 2nd-Order Type Systems

We focused in this article on simply-typed versions of the $\overline{\lambda}_{lv}$ and $\overline{\lambda}_{[lv\tau\star]}$ calculi. But as it is common in Krivine classical realizability, first and second-order quantifications (in Curry style) come for free through the interpretation. This means that we can for instance extend the language of types to first and second-order predicate logic:

$$\begin{aligned} e_1, e_2 &::= x \mid f(e_1, \ldots, e_k) \\ A, B &::= X(e_1, \ldots, e_k) \mid A \to B \mid \forall x.A \mid \forall X.A \end{aligned}$$

We can then define the following introduction rules for universal quantifications:

$$\frac{\Gamma \vdash_v v : A \quad x \notin FV(\Gamma)}{\Gamma \vdash_v v : \forall x.A}\ (\forall_r^1) \qquad\qquad \frac{\Gamma \vdash_v v : A \quad X \notin FV(\Gamma)}{\Gamma \vdash_v v : \forall X.A}\ (\forall_r^2)$$

Observe that these rules need to be restricted at the level of strong values, just as they are restricted to values in the case of call-by-value[9]. As for the left rules, they can be defined at any levels, let say the more general e:

$$\frac{\Gamma \vdash_e e : (A[n/x])^{\perp}}{\Gamma \vdash_e e : (\forall x.A)^{\perp}}\ (\forall_l^1) \qquad\qquad \frac{\Gamma \vdash_e e : (A[B/X])^{\perp}}{\Gamma \vdash_e e : (\forall X.A)^{\perp}}\ (\forall_l^2)$$

where n is any natural number and B any formula. The usual (call-by-value) interpretation of the quantification is defined as an intersection over all the possible instantiations of the variables within the model. We do not wish to enter into too many details[10] on this topic here, but first-order variable are to be instantiated by integers, while second order are to be instantiated by subset of terms at the lower level, *i.e.* closed strong-values in store (which we write $\mathcal{V}_0$):

$$|\forall x.A|_v = \bigcap_{n \in \mathbb{N}} |A[n/x]|_v \qquad\qquad |\forall X.A|_v = \bigcap_{S \in \mathbb{N}^k \to \mathcal{P}(\mathcal{V}_0)} |A[S/X]|_v$$

[9] For further explanation on the need for a value restriction in Krivine realizability, we refer the reader to [29] or [25].

[10] Once again, we advise the interested reader to refer to [29] or [25] for further details.

where the variable X is of arity k. It is then routine to check that the typing rules are adequate with the realizability interpretation.

4 Conclusion and Further Work

In this paper, we presented a system of simple types for a call-by-need calculus with control, which we proved to be safe in that it satisfies subject reduction (Theorem 1) and that typed terms are normalizing (Theorem 20). We proved the normalization by means of realizability-inspired interpretation of the $\overline{\lambda}_{[lv\tau\star]}$-calculus. Incidentally, this opens the doors to the computational analysis (in the spirit of Krivine realizability) of classical proofs using control, laziness and shared memory.

In further work, we intend to present two extensions of the present paper. First, following the definition of the realizability interpretation, we managed to type the continuation-and-store passing style translation for the $\overline{\lambda}_{[lv\tau\star]}$-calculus (see [2]). Interestingly, typing the translation emphasizes its computational content, and in particular, the store-passing part is reflected in a Kripke forcing-like manner of typing the extensibility of the store [28, Chap. 6].

Second, on a different aspect, the realizability interpretation we introduced could be a first step towards new ways of realizing axioms. In particular, the first author used in his Ph.D. thesis [28, Chap. 8] the techniques presented in this paper to give a normalization proof for dPA^{ω}, a proof system developed by the second author [15]. Indeed, this proof system allows to define a proof for the axiom of dependent choice thanks to the use of streams that are lazily evaluated, and was lacking a proper normalization proof.

Finally, to determine the range of our technique, it would be natural to investigate the relation between our framework and the many different presentations of call-by-need calculi (with or without control). Amongst other calculi, we could cite Chang-Felleisen presentation of call-by-need [4], Garcia *et al.* lazy calculus with delimited control [10] or Kesner's recent paper on normalizing by-need terms characterized by an intersection type system [16]. To this end, we might rely on Pédrot and Saurin's classical by-need [33]. They indeed relate (classical) call-by-need with linear head-reduction from a computational point of view, and draw the connections with the presentations of Ariola *et al.* [2] and Chang-Felleisen [4]. Ariola *et al.* $\overline{\lambda}_{lv}$-calculus being close to the $\overline{\lambda}_{[lv\tau\star]}$-calculus (see [2] for further details), our technique is likely to be adaptable to their framework, and thus to Pédrot and Saurin's system.

References

1. Ariola, Z., Felleisen, M.: The call-by-need lambda calculus. J. Funct. Program. **7**(3), 265–301 (1993)
2. Ariola, Z.M., Downen, P., Herbelin, H., Nakata, K., Saurin, A.: Classical call-by-need sequent calculi: the unity of semantic artifacts. In: Schrijvers, T., Thiemann, P. (eds.) FLOPS 2012. LNCS, vol. 7294, pp. 32–46. Springer, Heidelberg (2012). https://doi.org/10.1007/978-3-642-29822-6_6

3. Barbanera, F., Berardi, S.: A symmetric λ-calculus for classical program extraction. Inf. Comput. **125**(2), 103–117 (1996)
4. Chang, S., Felleisen, M.: The call-by-need lambda calculus, revisited. In: Seidl, H. (ed.) ESOP 2012. LNCS, vol. 7211, pp. 128–147. Springer, Heidelberg (2012). https://doi.org/10.1007/978-3-642-28869-2_7
5. Crolard, T.: A confluent lambda-calculus with a catch/throw mechanism. J. Funct. Program. **9**(6), 625–647 (1999)
6. Curien, P.-L., Herbelin, H.: The duality of computation. In: Proceedings of ICFP 2000, SIGPLAN Notices, vol. 35, no. 9, pp. 233–243. ACM (2000)
7. Dagand, P.-É., Scherer, G.: Normalization by realizability also evaluates. In: Baelde, D., Alglave, J. (eds.) Proceedings of JFLA 2015, Le Val d'Ajol, France, January 2015
8. Felleisen, M., Friedman, D.P., Kohlbecker, E.E., Duba, B.F.: Reasoning with continuations. In: Proceedings of LICS 1986, Cambridge, Massachusetts, USA, 16–18 June 1986, pp. 131–141. IEEE Computer Society (1986)
9. Gallier, J.: On girard's "candidats de reductibilité". In: Odifreddi, P. (ed.) Logic and Computer Science, pp. 123–203. Academic Press (1900)
10. Garcia, R., Lumsdaine, A., Sabry, A.: Lazy evaluation and delimited control. Log. Methods Comput. Sci. **6**(3) (2010)
11. Girard, J.-Y.: Une extension de L'interpretation de gödel a L'analyse, et son application a L'elimination des coupures dans L'analyse et la theorie des types. In: Fenstad, J.E., (ed.) Proceedings of the Second Scandinavian Logic Symposium. Studies in Logic and the Foundations of Mathematics, vol. 63, pp. 63–92. Elsevier (1971)
12. Guillermo, M., Miquel, A.: Specifying peirce's law in classical realizability. Math. Struct. Comput. Sci. **26**(7), 1269–1303 (2016)
13. Guillermo, M., Miquey, É.: Classical realizability and arithmetical formulæ. Math. Struct. Comput. Sci. 1–40 (2016)
14. Herbelin, H.: C'est maintenant qu'on calcule: au cœur de la dualité. Habilitation thesis, University Paris 11, December 2005
15. Herbelin, H.: A constructive proof of dependent choice, compatible with classical logic. In: Proceedings of the 27th Annual IEEE Symposium on Logic in Computer Science, LICS 2012, Dubrovnik, Croatia, 25–28 June 2012, pp. 365–374. IEEE Computer Society (2012)
16. Kesner, D.: Reasoning about call-by-need by means of types. In: Jacobs, B., Löding, C. (eds.) FoSSaCS 2016. LNCS, vol. 9634, pp. 424–441. Springer, Heidelberg (2016). https://doi.org/10.1007/978-3-662-49630-5_25
17. Krivine, J.-L.: Lambda-calculus, Types and Models. Ellis Horwood series in computers and their applications. Ellis Horwood, Masson (1993)
18. Krivine, J.-L.: Dependent choice, 'quote' and the clock. Theor. Comp. Sc. **308**, 259–276 (2003)
19. Krivine, J.-L.: Realizability in classical logic. Panoramas et synthèses **27**, 197–229 (2009). Interactive models of computation and program behaviour
20. Krivine, J.-L.: Realizability algebras: a program to well order r. Log. Methods Comput. Sci. **7**(3) (2011)
21. Krivine, J.-L.: Realizability algebras II: new models of ZF + DC. Log. Methods Comput. Sci. **8**(1:10), 1–28 (2012)
22. Krivine, J.-L.: On the structure of classical realizability models of ZF (2014)
23. Lafont, Y., Reus, B., Streicher, T.: Continuations semantics or expressing implication by negation. Technical report 9321, Ludwig-Maximilians-Universität, München (1993)

24. Lang, F.: Explaining the lazy Krivine machine using explicit substitution and addresses. High.-Order Symbolic Comput. **20**(3), 257–270 (2007)
25. Lepigre, R.: A classical realizability model for a semantical value restriction. In: Thiemann, P. (ed.) ESOP 2016. LNCS, vol. 9632, pp. 476–502. Springer, Heidelberg (2016). https://doi.org/10.1007/978-3-662-49498-1_19
26. Maraist, J., Odersky, M., Wadler, P.: The call-by-need lambda calculus. J. Funct. Program. **8**(3), 275–317 (1998)
27. Miquel, A.: Existential witness extraction in classical realizability and via a negative translation. Log. Methods Comput. Sci. **7**(2), 188–202 (2011)
28. Miquey, É.: Classical realizability and side-effects. Ph.D. thesis, Université Paris-Diderot, Universidad de la República (Uruguay) (2017)
29. Munch-Maccagnoni, G.: Focalisation and classical realisability. In: Grädel, E., Kahle, R. (eds.) CSL 2009. LNCS, vol. 5771, pp. 409–423. Springer, Heidelberg (2009). https://doi.org/10.1007/978-3-642-04027-6_30
30. Okasaki, C., Lee, P., Tarditi, D.: Call-by-need and continuation-passing style. Lisp Symbolic Comput. **7**(1), 57–82 (1994)
31. Parigot, M.: Free deduction: an analysis of "computations" in classical logic. In: Voronkov, A. (ed.) RCLP -1990. LNCS, vol. 592, pp. 361–380. Springer, Heidelberg (1992). https://doi.org/10.1007/3-540-55460-2_27
32. Parigot, M.: Strong normalization of second order symmetric λ-calculus. In: Kapoor, S., Prasad, S. (eds.) FSTTCS 2000. LNCS, vol. 1974, pp. 442–453. Springer, Heidelberg (2000). https://doi.org/10.1007/3-540-44450-5_36
33. Pédrot, P.-M., Saurin, A.: Classical by-need. In: Thiemann, P. (ed.) ESOP 2016. LNCS, vol. 9632, pp. 616–643. Springer, Heidelberg (2016). https://doi.org/10.1007/978-3-662-49498-1_24
34. Plotkin, G.D.: Call-by-name, call-by-value and the lambda-calculus. Theor. Comput. Sci. **1**(2), 125–159 (1975)
35. Polonovski, E.: Strong normalization of $\overline{\lambda}\mu\widetilde{\mu}$-calculus with explicit substitutions. In: Walukiewicz, I. (ed.) FoSSaCS 2004. LNCS, vol. 2987, pp. 423–437. Springer, Heidelberg (2004). https://doi.org/10.1007/978-3-540-24727-2_30
36. Tait, W.W.: Intensional interpretations of functionals of finite type I. J. Symbolic Log. **32**(2), 198–212 (1967)

7

A Hierarchy of Scheduler Classes for Stochastic Automata

Pedro R. D'Argenio[1,2,3], Marcus Gerhold[4], Arnd Hartmanns[4(✉)] and Sean Sedwards[5]

[1] Universidad Nacional de Córdoba, Córdoba, Argentina
dargenio@famaf.unc.edu.ar
[2] CONICET, Córdoba, Argentina
[3] Saarland University, Saarbrücken, Germany
[4] University of Twente, Enschede, The Netherlands
{m.gerhold,a.hartmanns}@utwente.nl
[5] University of Waterloo, Waterloo, Canada
sean.sedwards@uwaterloo.ca

Abstract. Stochastic automata are a formal compositional model for concurrent stochastic timed systems, with general distributions and nondeterministic choices. Measures of interest are defined over *schedulers* that resolve the nondeterminism. In this paper we investigate the power of various theoretically and practically motivated classes of schedulers, considering the classic complete-information view and a restriction to non-prophetic schedulers. We prove a hierarchy of scheduler classes w.r.t. unbounded probabilistic reachability. We find that, unlike Markovian formalisms, stochastic automata distinguish most classes even in this basic setting. Verification and strategy synthesis methods thus face a tradeoff between powerful and efficient classes. Using lightweight scheduler sampling, we explore this tradeoff and demonstrate the concept of a useful approximative verification technique for stochastic automata.

1 Introduction

The need to analyse continuous-time stochastic models arises in many practical contexts, including critical infrastructures [4], railway engineering [36], space mission planning [7], and security [28]. This has led to a number of discrete event simulation tools, such as those for networking [34,35,42], whose probabilistic semantics is founded on generalised semi-Markov processes (GSMP [21,33]). Nondeterminism arises through inherent concurrency of independent processes [11], but may also be deliberate underspecification. Modelling such uncertainty with probability is convenient for simulation, but not always adequate [3,29]. Various models and formalisms have thus been proposed to extend continuous-time stochastic processes with nondeterminism [8,10,19,23,27,38]. It is then possible to *verify* such systems by considering the extremal probabilities of a property. These are the supremum and infimum of the probabilities of the property in the purely stochastic systems induced by classes of *schedulers* (also called *strategies*, *policies* or *adversaries*) that resolve all nondeterminism. If the nondeterminism is considered controllable, one may alternatively be interested in the *planning* problem of synthesising a scheduler that satisfies certain probability bounds.

We consider closed systems of stochastic automata (SA [16]), which extend GSMP and feature both generally distributed stochastic delays as well as discrete nondeterministic choices. The latter may arise from non-continuous distributions (e.g. deterministic delays), urgent edges, and edges waiting on multiple clocks. Numerical verification algorithms exist for very limited subclasses of SA only: Buchholz et al. [13] restrict to phase-type or matrix-exponential distributions, such that nondeterminism cannot arise (as each edge is guarded by a single clock). Bryans et al. [12] propose two algorithms that require an a priori fixed scheduler, continuous bounded distributions, and that all active clocks be reset when a location is entered. The latter forces regeneration on every edge, making it impossible to use clocks as memory between locations. Regeneration is central to the work of Ballarini et al. [6], however they again exclude nondeterminism. The only approach that handles nondeterminism is the region-based approximation scheme of Kwiatkowska et al. [30] for a model closely related to SA, but restricted to bounded continuous distributions. Without that restriction [22], error bounds and convergence guarantees are lost.

Evidently, the combination of nondeterminism and continuous probability distributions is a particularly challenging one. With this paper, we take on the underlying problem from a fundamental perspective: we investigate the power of, and relationships between, different classes of schedulers for SA. Our motivation is, on the one hand, that a clear understanding of scheduler classes is crucial to design verification algorithms. For example, Markov decision process (MDP) model checking works well because memoryless schedulers suffice for reachability, and the efficient time-bounded analysis of continuous-time MDP (CTMDP) exploits a relationship between two scheduler classes that are sufficiently simple, but on their own do not realise the desired extremal probabilities [14]. When it comes to planning problems, on the other hand, practitioners desire *simple* solutions, i.e. schedulers that need little information and limited memory, so as to be explainable and suitable for implementation on e.g. resource-constrained embedded systems. Understanding the capabilities of scheduler classes helps decide on the tradeoff between simplicity and the ability to attain optimal results.

We use two perspectives on schedulers from the literature: the classic complete-information *residual lifetimes* semantics [9], where optimality is defined via history-dependent schedulers that see the entire current state, and *non-prophetic* schedulers [25] that cannot observe the timing of *future* events. Within each perspective, we define classes of schedulers whose views of the state and history are variously restricted (Sect. 3). We prove their relative ordering w.r.t. achieving optimal reachability probabilities (Sect. 4). We find that SA distinguish most classes. In particular, memoryless schedulers suffice in the complete-information setting (as is implicit in the method of Kwiatkowska et al. [30]), but turn out to be suboptimal in the more realistic non-prophetic case. Considering only the relative order of clock expiration times, as suggested by the first algorithm of Bryans et al. [12], surprisingly leads to partly suboptimal, partly incomparable classes. Our distinguishing SA are small and employ a common nondeterministic gadget. They precisely pinpoint the crucial differences and how schedulers interact with the various features of SA, providing deep insights into the formalism itself.

Our study furthermore forms the basis for the application of *lightweight scheduler sampling* (LSS) to SA. LSS is a technique to use Monte Carlo simulation/statistical model checking with nondeterministic models. On every LSS simulation step, a pseudo-random number generator (PRNG) is re-seeded with a hash of the identifier of the current scheduler and the (restricted) information about the current state (and previous states, for history-dependent schedulers) that the scheduler's class may observe. The PRNG's first iterate then determines the scheduler's action deterministically. LSS has been successfully applied to MDP [18,31,32] and probabilistic timed automata [15,26]. Using only constant memory, LSS samples schedulers uniformly from a selected scheduler class to find "near-optimal" schedulers that conservatively approximate the true extremal probabilities. Its principal advantage is that it is largely indifferent to the size of the state space and of the scheduler space; in general, sampling efficiency depends only on the likelihood of selecting near-optimal schedulers. However, the mass of *near*-optimal schedulers in a scheduler class that also includes the optimal scheduler may be *less* than the mass in a class that does *not* include it. Given that the mass of optimal schedulers may be vanishingly small, it may be advantageous to sample from a class of less powerful schedulers. We explore these tradeoffs and demonstrate the concept of LSS for SA in Sect. 5.

Other Related Work. Alur et al. first mention nondeterministic stochastic systems similar to SA in [2]. Markov automata (MA [19]), interactive Markov chains (IMC [27]) and CTMDP are special cases of SA restricted to exponential distributions. Song et al. [37] look into partial information distributed schedulers for MA, combining earlier works of de Alfaro [1] and Giro and D'Argenio [20] for MDP. Their focus is on information flow and hiding in parallel specifications. Wolf et al. [39] investigate the power of classic (time-abstract, deterministic and memoryless) scheduler classes for IMC. They establish (non-strict) subset relationships for almost all classes w.r.t. trace distribution equivalence, a very strong measure. Wolovick and Johr [41] show that the class of measurable schedulers for CTMDP is complete and sufficient for reachability problems.

2 Preliminaries

For a given set S, its power set is $\mathcal{P}(S)$. We denote by $\mathbb{R}$, $\mathbb{R}^+$, and $\mathbb{R}_0^+$ the sets of real numbers, positive real numbers and non-negative real numbers, respectively. A (discrete) *probability distribution* over a set Ω is a function $\mu\colon \Omega \to [0,1]$, such that $\mathrm{support}(\mu) \stackrel{\text{def}}{=} \{\, \omega \in \Omega \mid \mu(\omega) > 0 \,\}$ is countable and $\sum_{\omega \in \mathrm{support}(\mu)} \mu(\omega) = 1$. $\mathrm{Dist}(\Omega)$ is the set of probability distributions over Ω. We write $\mathcal{D}(\omega)$ for the *Dirac* distribution for ω, defined by $\mathcal{D}(\omega)(\omega) = 1$. Ω is *measurable* if it is endowed with a σ-algebra $\sigma(\Omega)$: a collection of *measurable* subsets of Ω. A (continuous) *probability measure* over Ω is a function $\mu\colon \sigma(\Omega) \to [0,1]$, such that $\mu(\Omega) = 1$ and $\mu(\cup_{i\in I} B_i) = \sum_{i\in I} \mu(B_i)$ for any countable index set I and pairwise disjoint measurable sets $B_i \subseteq \Omega$. $\text{Prob}(\Omega)$ is the set of probability measures over Ω. Each $\mu \in \text{Dist}(\Omega)$ induces a probability measure. Given probability measures μ_1 and μ_2, we denote by $\mu_1 \otimes \mu_2$ the *product measure*: the unique probability measure such that $(\mu_1 \otimes \mu_2)(B_1 \times B_2) = \mu_1(B_1) \cdot \mu_2(B_2)$, for all measurable B_1 and B_2. For a collection of measures $(\mu_i)_{i\in I}$, we analogously denote the product measure by $\bigotimes_{i\in I} \mu_i$. Let $Val \stackrel{\text{def}}{=} V \to \mathbb{R}_0^+$ be the set of valuations for an (implicit) set V of (non-negative real-valued) variables. $\mathbf{0} \in Val$ assigns value zero to all variables. Given $X \subseteq V$ and $v \in Val$, we write $v[X]$ for the valuation defined by $v[X](x) = 0$ if $x \in X$ and $v[X](y) = v(y)$ otherwise. For $t \in \mathbb{R}_0^+$, $v + t$ is the valuation defined by $(v+t)(x) = v(x) + t$ for all $x \in V$.

Stochastic Automata [16] extend labelled transition systems with stochastic *clocks*: real-valued variables that increase synchronously with rate 1 over time and expire some random amount of time after having been *restarted*. Formally:

Definition 1. *A* stochastic automaton *(SA) is a tuple* $\langle Loc, \mathcal{C}, A, E, F, \ell_{init}\rangle$, *where Loc is a countable set of* locations, $\mathcal{C}$ *is a finite set of* clocks, A *is the finite* action alphabet, *and* $E\colon Loc \to \mathcal{P}(\mathcal{P}(\mathcal{C}) \times A \times \mathcal{P}(\mathcal{C}) \times \text{Dist}(Loc))$ *is the* edge function, *which maps each location to a finite set of edges that in turn consist of a* guard set *of clocks, a label, a* restart set *of clocks and a distribution over target locations.* $F\colon \mathcal{C} \to \text{Prob}(\mathbb{R}_0^+)$ *is the* delay measure function *that maps each clock to a probability measure, and* $\ell_{init} \in Loc$ *is the* initial location.

We also write $\ell \xrightarrow{G,a,R}_E \mu$ for $\langle G, a, R, \mu\rangle \in E(\ell)$. W.l.o.g. we restrict to SA where edges are fully characterised by source state and action label, i.e. whenever $\ell \xrightarrow{G_1,a,R_1}_E \mu_1$ and $\ell \xrightarrow{G_2,a,R_2}_E \mu_2$, then $G_1 = G_2$, $R_1 = R_2$ and $\mu_1 = \mu_2$.

Intuitively, an SA starts in ℓ_{init} with all clocks expired. An edge $\ell \xrightarrow{G,a,R}_E \mu$ may be taken only if all clocks in G are expired. If any edge is enabled, some edge must be taken (i.e. all actions are *urgent* and thus the SA is *closed*). When an edge is taken, its action is a, all clocks in R are restarted, other expired clocks remain expired, and we move to successor location ℓ' with probability $\mu(\ell')$. There, another edge may be taken immediately or we may need to wait until some further clocks expire, and so on. When a clock c is restarted, the time until it expires is chosen randomly according to the probability measure $F(c)$.

Example 1. We show an example SA, M_0, in Fig. 1. Its initial location is ℓ_0. It has two clocks, x and y, with $F(x)$ and $F(y)$ both being the continuous uniform distribution over the interval $[0,1]$. No time can pass in locations ℓ_0 and ℓ_1, since they have outgoing edges with empty guard sets. We omit action labels and assume every edge to have a unique label. On entering ℓ_1, both clocks are restarted. The choice of going to either ℓ_2 or ℓ_3 from ℓ_1 is nondeterministic, since

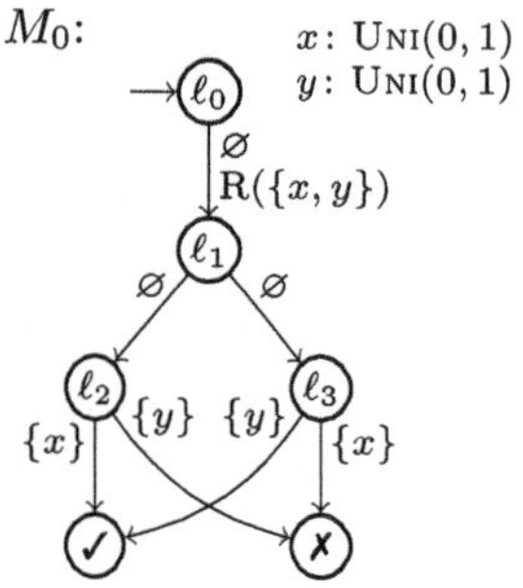

Fig. 1. Example SA M_0

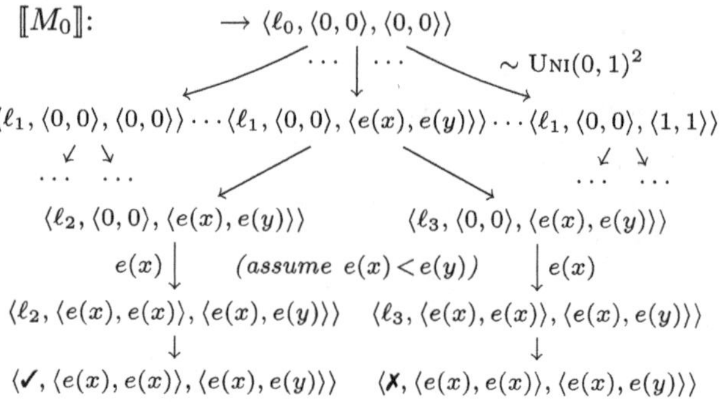

Fig. 2. Excerpt of the TPTS semantics of M_0

the two edges are always enabled at the same time. In ℓ_2, we have to wait until the first of the two clocks expires. If that is x, we have to move to location ✓; if it is y, we have to move to ✗. The probability that both expire at the same time is zero. Location ℓ_3 behaves analogously, but with the target states interchanged.

Timed Probabilistic Transition Systems form the semantics of SA. They are finitely-nondeterministic uncountable-state transition systems:

Definition 2. *A (finitely nondeterministic)* timed probabilistic transition system *(TPTS) is a tuple $\langle S, A', T, s_{init} \rangle$. S is a measurable set of states. $A' = \mathbb{R}^+ \uplus A$ is the* alphabet, *partitioned into* delays *in $\mathbb{R}^+$ and* jumps *in A. $T \colon S \to \mathcal{P}(A' \times \text{Prob}(S))$ is the* transition function, *which maps each state to a finite set of transitions, each consisting of a label in A' and a measure over target states. The initial state is $s_{init} \in S$. For all $s \in S$, we require $|T(s)| = 1$ if $\exists \langle t, \mu \rangle \in T(s) \colon t \in \mathbb{R}^+$, i.e. states admitting delays are deterministic.*

We also write $s \xrightarrow{a}_T \mu$ for $\langle a, \mu \rangle \in T(s)$. A *run* is an infinite alternating sequence $s_0 a_0 s_1 a_1 \ldots \in (S \times A')^\omega$, with $s_0 = s_{init}$. A *history* is a finite prefix of a run ending in a state, i.e. an element of $(S \times A')^* \times S$. Runs resolve all nondeterministic and probabilistic choices. A *scheduler* resolves only the nondeterminism:

Definition 3. *A measurable function $\mathfrak{s} \colon (S \times A')^* \times S \to \text{Dist}(A' \times \text{Prob}(S))$ is a* scheduler *if, for all histories $h \in (S \times A')^* \times S$, $\langle a, \mu \rangle \in \text{support}(\mathfrak{s}(h))$ implies $lst_h \xrightarrow{a}_T \mu$, where lst_h is the last state of h.*

Once a scheduler has chosen $s_i \xrightarrow{a}_T \mu$, the successor state s_{i+1} is picked randomly according to μ. Every scheduler $\mathfrak{s}$ defines a probability measure $\mathbb{P}_\mathfrak{s}$ on the space of all runs. For a formal definition, see [40]. As is usual, we restrict to *non-Zeno* schedulers that make time diverge with probability one: we require $\mathbb{P}_\mathfrak{s}(\Pi_\infty) = 1$, where Π_∞ is the set of runs where the sum of delays is ∞. In the remainder of this paper we consider extremal probabilities of reaching a set of goal locations G:

Definition 4. *For $G \subseteq Loc$, let $J_G \stackrel{\text{def}}{=} \{ \langle \ell, v, e \rangle \in S \mid \ell \in G \}$. Let $\mathfrak{S}$ be a class of schedulers. Then $\mathrm{P}^{\mathfrak{S}}_{\min}(G)$ and $\mathrm{P}^{\mathfrak{S}}_{\max}(G)$ are the minimum and maximum* reachability probabilities *for G under $\mathfrak{S}$, defined as $\mathrm{P}^{\mathfrak{S}}_{\min}(G) = \inf_{\mathfrak{s} \in \mathfrak{S}} \mathbb{P}_\mathfrak{s}(\Pi_{J_G})$ and $\mathrm{P}^{\mathfrak{S}}_{\max}(G) = \sup_{\mathfrak{s} \in \mathfrak{S}} \mathbb{P}_\mathfrak{s}(\Pi_{J_G})$, respectively.*

Semantics of Stochastic Automata. We present here the residual lifetimes semantics of [9], simplified for closed SA: any delay step must be of the minimum delay that makes some edge become enabled.

Definition 5. *The semantics of an SA* $M = \langle Loc, \mathcal{C}, A, E, F, \ell_{init} \rangle$ *is the TPTS*

$$[\![M]\!] = \langle Loc \times Val \times Val, A \uplus \mathbb{R}^+, T_M, \langle \ell_{init}, \mathbf{0}, \mathbf{0} \rangle \rangle$$

where the states are triples $\langle \ell, v, e \rangle$ *of the current location* ℓ*, a valuation* v *assigning to each clock its current value, and a valuation* e *keeping track of all clocks' expiration times.* T_M *is the smallest transition function satisfying inference rules*

$$\frac{\ell \xrightarrow{G,a,R}_E \mu \quad \mathrm{En}(G, v, e)}{\langle \ell, v, e \rangle \xrightarrow{a}_{T_M} \mu \otimes \mathcal{D}(v[R]) \otimes \mathrm{Sample}_e^R}$$

$$\frac{t \in \mathbb{R}^+ \quad \exists \ell \xrightarrow{G,a,R}_E \mu \colon \mathrm{En}(G, v + t, e) \quad \forall t' \in [0, t), \ell \xrightarrow{G,a,R}_E \mu \colon \neg\, \mathrm{En}(G, v + t', e)}{\langle \ell, v, e \rangle \xrightarrow{t}_{T_M} \mathcal{D}(\langle \ell, v + t, e \rangle)}$$

with $\mathrm{En}(G, v, e) \stackrel{\text{def}}{=} \forall x \in G \colon v(x) \geq e(x)$ *characterising the enabled edges and*

$$\mathrm{Sample}_e^R \stackrel{\text{def}}{=} \bigotimes_{c \in \mathcal{C}} \begin{cases} F(c) & \text{if } c \in R \\ \mathcal{D}(e(c)) & \text{if } c \notin R. \end{cases}$$

The second rule creates *delay* steps of t time units if no edge is enabled from now until just before t time units have elapsed (third premise) but then, after exactly t time units, some edge becomes enabled (second premise). The first rule applies if an edge $\ell \xrightarrow{G,a,R}_E \mu$ is enabled: a transition is taken with the edge's label, the successor state's location is chosen by μ, v is updated by resetting the clocks in R to zero, and the expiration times for the restarted clocks are resampled. All other expiration times remain unchanged. Notice that $[\![M]\!]$ is also a nondeterministic labelled Markov process [40] (a proof can be found in [17]).

Example 2. Figure 2 outlines the semantics of M_0. The first step from ℓ_0 to all the states in ℓ_1 is a single transition. Its probability measure is the product of $F(x)$ and $F(y)$, sampling the expiration times of the two clocks. We exemplify the behaviour of all of these states by showing it for the case of expiration times $e(x)$ and $e(y)$, with $e(x) < e(y)$. In this case, to maximise the probability of reaching ✓, we should take the transition to the state in ℓ_2. If a scheduler $\mathfrak{s}$ can see the expiration times, noting that only their order matters here, it can always make the optimal choice and achieve $\mathrm{P}_{\max}^{\{\mathfrak{s}\}}(\{✓\}) = 1$.

3 Classes of Schedulers

We now define classes of schedulers for SA with restricted information, hiding in various combinations the history and parts of states such as clock values and expiration times. All definitions consider TPTS as in Definition 5 with states $\langle \ell, v, e \rangle$ and we require for all $\mathfrak{s}$ that $\langle a, \mu \rangle \in \mathrm{support}(\mathfrak{s}(h)) \Rightarrow lst_h \xrightarrow{a}_T \mu$, as in Definition 3.

3.1 Classic Schedulers

We first consider the "classic" complete-information setting where schedulers can in particular see expiration times. We start with restricted classes of history-dependent schedulers. Our first restriction hides the values of all clocks, only revealing the total time since the start of the history. This is inspired by the step-counting or time-tracking schedulers needed to obtain optimal step-bounded or time-bounded reachability probabilities on MDP or Markov automata:

Definition 6. *A classic history-dependent* global-time *scheduler is a measurable function* $\mathfrak{s}\colon (S|_{\ell,t,e} \times A')^* \times S|_{\ell,t,e} \to \mathrm{Dist}(A' \times \mathrm{Prob}(S))$, *where* $S|_{\ell,t,e} \stackrel{\text{def}}{=} Loc \times \mathbb{R}_0^+ \times Val$ *with the second component being the total time t elapsed since the start of the history. We write* $\mathfrak{S}^{hist}_{\ell,t,e}$ *for the set of all such schedulers.*

We next hide the values of all clocks, revealing only their expiration times:

Definition 7. *A classic history-dependent* location-based *scheduler is a measurable function* $\mathfrak{s}\colon (S|_{\ell,e} \times A')^* \times S|_{\ell,e} \to \mathrm{Dist}(A' \times \mathrm{Prob}(S))$, *where* $S|_{\ell,e} \stackrel{\text{def}}{=} Loc \times Val$, *with the second component being the clock expiration times e. We write* $\mathfrak{S}^{hist}_{\ell,e}$ *for the set of all such schedulers.*

Having defined three classes of classic history-dependent schedulers, $\mathfrak{S}^{hist}_{\ell,v,e}$, $\mathfrak{S}^{hist}_{\ell,t,e}$ and $\mathfrak{S}^{hist}_{\ell,e}$, noting that $\mathfrak{S}^{hist}_{\ell,v,e}$ denotes all schedulers of Definition 3, we also consider them with the restriction that they only see the relative order of clock expiration, instead of the exact expiration times: for each pair of clocks c_1, c_2, these schedulers see the relation $\sim\, \in \{<, =, >\}$ in $e(c_1) - v(c_1) \sim e(c_2) - v(c_2)$. E.g. in ℓ_1 of Example 2, the scheduler would not see $e(x)$ and $e(y)$, but only whether $e(x) < e(y)$ or vice-versa (since $v(x) = v(y) = 0$, and equality has probability 0 here). We consider this case because the expiration order is sufficient for the first algorithm of Bryans et al. [12], and would allow optimal decisions in M_0 of Fig. 1. We denote the relative order information by o, and the corresponding scheduler classes by $\mathfrak{S}^{hist}_{\ell,v,o}$, $\mathfrak{S}^{hist}_{\ell,t,o}$ and $\mathfrak{S}^{hist}_{\ell,o}$. We now define memoryless schedulers, which only see the current state and are at the core of e.g. MDP model checking. On most formalisms, they suffice to obtain optimal reachability probabilities.

Definition 8. *A classic* memoryless *scheduler is a measurable function* $\mathfrak{s}\colon S \to \mathrm{Dist}(A' \times \mathrm{Prob}(S))$. *We write* $\mathfrak{S}^{ml}_{\ell,v,e}$ *for the set of all such schedulers.*

We apply the same restrictions as for history-dependent schedulers:

Definition 9. *A classic memoryless global-time scheduler is a measurable function* $\mathfrak{s}\colon S|_{\ell,t,e} \to \mathrm{Dist}(A' \times \mathrm{Prob}(S))$, *with* $S|_{\ell,t,e}$ *as in Definition 6. We write* $\mathfrak{S}^{ml}_{\ell,t,e}$ *for the set of all such schedulers.*

Definition 10. *A classic memoryless location-based scheduler is a measurable function* $\mathfrak{s}\colon S|_{\ell,e} \to \mathrm{Dist}(A' \times \mathrm{Prob}(S))$, *with* $S|_{\ell,e}$ *as in Definition 7. We write* $\mathfrak{S}^{ml}_{\ell,e}$ *for the set of all such schedulers.*

Again, we also consider memoryless schedulers that only see the expiration order, so we have memoryless scheduler classes $\mathfrak{S}^{ml}_{\ell,v,e}$, $\mathfrak{S}^{ml}_{\ell,t,e}$, $\mathfrak{S}^{ml}_{\ell,e}$, $\mathfrak{S}^{ml}_{\ell,v,o}$, $\mathfrak{S}^{ml}_{\ell,t,o}$ and $\mathfrak{S}^{ml}_{\ell,o}$. Class $\mathfrak{S}^{ml}_{\ell,o}$ is particularly attractive because it has a compact finite domain.

3.2 Non-prophetic Schedulers

Consider the SA M_0 in Fig. 1. No matter which of the previously defined scheduler classes we choose, we always find a scheduler that achieves probability 1 to reach ✓, and a scheduler that achieves probability 0. This is because they can all see the expiration times or expiration order of x and y when in ℓ_1. When in ℓ_1, x and y have not yet expired—this will only happen later, in ℓ_2 or ℓ_3—yet the schedulers already know which clock will "win". The classic schedulers can thus be seen to make decisions based on the timing of *future* events. This *prophetic* scheduling has already been observed in [9], where a "fix" in the form of the *spent lifetimes* semantics was proposed. Hartmanns et al. [25] have shown that this not only still permits prophetic scheduling, but even admits *divine* scheduling, where a scheduler can *change* the future. The authors propose a complex *non-prophetic* semantics that provably removes all prophetic and divine behaviour.

Much of the complication of the non-prophetic semantics of [25] is due to it being specified for open SA that include delayable actions. For the closed SA setting of this paper, prophetic scheduling can be more easily excluded by hiding from the schedulers all information about what will happen in the future of the system's evolution. This information is only contained in the expiration times e or the expiration order o. We can thus keep the semantics of Sect. 2 and modify the definition of schedulers to exclude prophetic behaviour by construction.

In what follows, we thus also consider all scheduler classes of Sect. 3.1 with the added constraint that the expiration times, resp. the expiration order, are not visible, resulting in the *non-prophetic* classes $\mathfrak{S}^{hist}_{\ell,v}$, $\mathfrak{S}^{hist}_{\ell,t}$, $\mathfrak{S}^{hist}_{\ell}$, $\mathfrak{S}^{ml}_{\ell,v}$, $\mathfrak{S}^{ml}_{\ell,t}$ and $\mathfrak{S}^{ml}_{\ell}$. Any non-prophetic scheduler can only reach ✓ of M_0 with probability $\frac{1}{2}$.

4 The Power of Schedulers

Now that we have defined a number of classes of schedulers, we need to determine what the effect of the restrictions is on our ability to optimally control an SA. We thus evaluate the power of scheduler classes w.r.t. unbounded reachability probabilities (Definition 4) on the semantics of SA. We will see that this simple setting already suffices to reveal interesting differences between scheduler classes.

For two scheduler classes $\mathfrak{S}_1$ and $\mathfrak{S}_2$, we write $\mathfrak{S}_1 \succcurlyeq \mathfrak{S}_2$ if, for all SA and all sets of goal locations G, $\mathrm{P}^{\mathfrak{S}_1}_{\min}(G) \leq \mathrm{P}^{\mathfrak{S}_2}_{\min}(G)$ and $\mathrm{P}^{\mathfrak{S}_1}_{\max}(G) \geq \mathrm{P}^{\mathfrak{S}_2}_{\max}(G)$. We write $\mathfrak{S}_1 \succ \mathfrak{S}_2$ if additionally there exists at least one SA and set G' where $\mathrm{P}^{\mathfrak{S}_1}_{\min}(G') < \mathrm{P}^{\mathfrak{S}_2}_{\min}(G')$ or $\mathrm{P}^{\mathfrak{S}_1}_{\max}(G') > \mathrm{P}^{\mathfrak{S}_2}_{\max}(G')$. Finally, we write $\mathfrak{S}_1 \approx \mathfrak{S}_2$ for $\mathfrak{S}_1 \succcurlyeq \mathfrak{S}_2 \wedge \mathfrak{S}_2 \succcurlyeq \mathfrak{S}_1$, and $\mathfrak{S}_1 \not\approx \mathfrak{S}_2$, i.e. the classes are incomparable, for $\mathfrak{S}_1 \not\succcurlyeq \mathfrak{S}_2 \wedge \mathfrak{S}_2 \not\succcurlyeq \mathfrak{S}_1$. Unless noted otherwise, we omit proofs for $\mathfrak{S}_1 \succcurlyeq \mathfrak{S}_2$ when it is obvious that the information available to $\mathfrak{S}_1$ includes the information available to $\mathfrak{S}_2$. All our distinguishing examples are based on the resolution of a single nondeterministic choice between two actions to eventually reach one of two locations. We therefore prove only w.r.t. the maximum probability, $p_{\max}$, for these examples since the minimum probability is given by $1 - p_{\max}$ and an analogous proof for $p_{\min}$ can be made by relabelling locations. We may write $\mathrm{P}_{\max}(\mathfrak{S}^y_x)$ for $\mathrm{P}^{\mathfrak{S}^y_x}_{\max}(\{✓\})$ to improve readability.

$$
\begin{array}{ccccccc}
\mathfrak{S}^{ml}_{\ell,o} & \prec & \mathfrak{S}^{ml}_{\ell,t,o} & \prec & \mathfrak{S}^{ml}_{\ell,v,o} & \prec & \mathfrak{S}^{hist}_{\ell,o} \\
\not\curlywedge & & \not\curlywedge & & \curlywedge & & \wr \\
\mathfrak{S}^{ml}_{\ell,e} & \prec & \mathfrak{S}^{ml}_{\ell,t,e} & \prec & \mathfrak{S}^{ml}_{\ell,v,e} & \succ & \mathfrak{S}^{hist}_{\ell,t,o} \\
\curlywedge & & \curlywedge & & \wr & & \wr \\
\mathfrak{S}^{hist}_{\ell,e} & \approx & \mathfrak{S}^{hist}_{\ell,t,e} & \approx & \mathfrak{S}^{hist}_{\ell,v,e} & \succ & \mathfrak{S}^{hist}_{\ell,v,o}
\end{array}
$$

Fig. 3. Hierarchy of classic scheduler classes

$$
\begin{array}{ccccc}
\mathfrak{S}^{ml}_{\ell} & \prec & \mathfrak{S}^{ml}_{\ell,t} & \prec & \mathfrak{S}^{ml}_{\ell,v} \\
\curlywedge & & \curlywedge & & \curlywedge \\
\mathfrak{S}^{hist}_{\ell} & \approx & \mathfrak{S}^{hist}_{\ell,t} & \approx & \mathfrak{S}^{hist}_{\ell,v}
\end{array}
$$

Fig. 4. Non-prophetic classes

4.1 The Classic Hierarchy

We first establish that all classic history-dependent scheduler classes are equivalent:

Proposition 1. $\mathfrak{S}^{hist}_{\ell,v,e} \approx \mathfrak{S}^{hist}_{\ell,t,e} \approx \mathfrak{S}^{hist}_{\ell,e}$.

Proof. From the transition labels in $A' = A \uplus \mathbb{R}^+$ in the history $(S' \times A')^*$, with $S' \in \{ S, S|_{\ell,t,e}, S|_{\ell,e} \}$ depending on the scheduler class, we can reconstruct the total elapsed time as well as the values of all clocks: to obtain the total elapsed time, sum the labels in $\mathbb{R}^+$ up to each state; to obtain the values of all clocks, do the same per clock and perform the resets of the edges identified by the actions.

The same argument applies among the expiration-order history-dependent classes:

Proposition 2. $\mathfrak{S}^{hist}_{\ell,v,o} \approx \mathfrak{S}^{hist}_{\ell,t,o} \approx \mathfrak{S}^{hist}_{\ell,o}$.

However, the expiration-order history-dependent schedulers are strictly less powerful than the classic history-dependent ones:

Proposition 3. $\mathfrak{S}^{hist}_{\ell,v,e} \succ \mathfrak{S}^{hist}_{\ell,v,o}$.

Proof. Consider the SA M_1 in Fig. 5. Note that the history does not provide any information for making the choice in ℓ_1: we always arrive after having spent zero time in ℓ_0 and then having taken the single edge to ℓ_1. We can analytically determine that $\mathrm{P}_{\max}(\mathfrak{S}^{hist}_{\ell,v,e}) = \frac{3}{4}$ by going from ℓ_1 to ℓ_2 if $e(x) \leq \frac{1}{2}$ and to ℓ_3 otherwise. We would obtain a probability equal to $\frac{1}{2}$ by always going to either ℓ_2 or ℓ_3 or by picking either edge with equal probability. This is the best we can do if e is not visible, and thus $\mathrm{P}_{\max}(\mathfrak{S}^{hist}_{\ell,v,o}) = \frac{1}{2}$: in ℓ_1, $v(x) = v(y) = 0$ and the expiration order is always "y before x" because y has not yet been started.

Just like for MDP and unbounded reachability probabilities, the classic history-dependent and memoryless schedulers with complete information are equivalent:

Proposition 4. $\mathfrak{S}^{hist}_{\ell,v,e} \approx \mathfrak{S}^{ml}_{\ell,v,e}$.

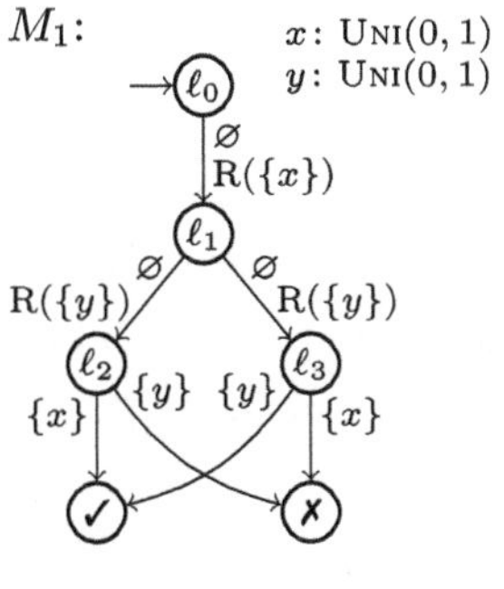

Fig. 5. SA M_1

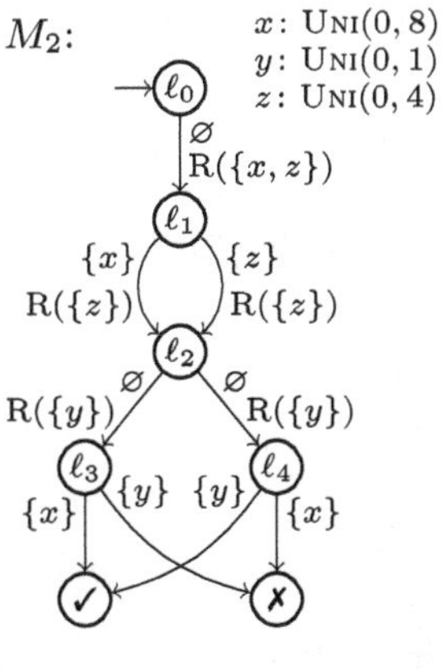

Fig. 6. SA M_2

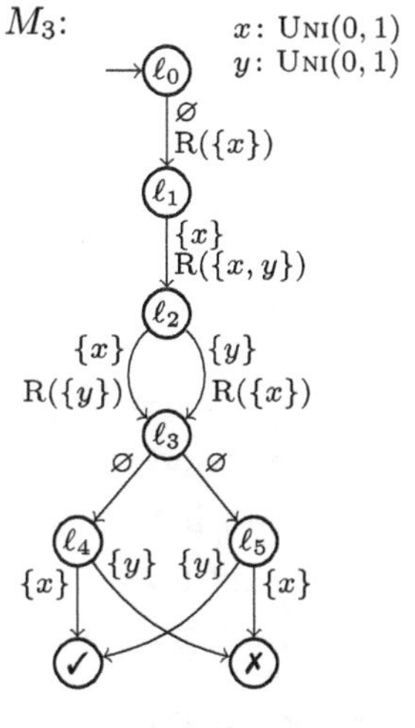

Fig. 7. SA M_3

Proof sketch. Our definition of TPTS only allows finite nondeterministic choices, i.e. we have a very restricted form of continuous-space MDP. We can thus adapt the argument of the corresponding proof for MDP [5, Lemma 10.102]: For each state (of possibly countably many), we construct a notional optimal memoryless (and deterministic) scheduler in the same way, replacing the summation by an integration for the continuous measures in the transition function. It remains to show that this scheduler is indeed measurable. For TPTS that are the semantics of SA, this follows from the way clock values are used in the guard sets so that optimal decisions are constant over intervals of clock values and expiration times (see e.g. the arguments in [12] or [30]).

On the other hand, when restricting schedulers to see the expiration order only, history-dependent and memoryless schedulers are no longer equivalent:

Proposition 5. $\mathfrak{S}^{hist}_{\ell,v,o} \succ \mathfrak{S}^{ml}_{\ell,v,o}$.

Proof. Consider the SA M_2 in Fig. 6. Let $\mathfrak{s}^{opt}_{ml(l,v,o)}$ be the (unknown) optimal scheduler in $\mathfrak{S}^{ml}_{\ell,v,o}$ w.r.t. the max. probability of reaching ✓. Define $\mathfrak{s}^{better}_{hist(l,v,o)} \in \mathfrak{S}^{hist}_{\ell,v,o}$ as: when in ℓ_2 and the last edge in the history is the left one (i.e. x is expired), go to ℓ_3; otherwise, behave like $\mathfrak{s}^{opt}_{ml(l,v,o)}$. This scheduler distinguishes $\mathfrak{S}^{hist}_{\ell,v,o}$ and $\mathfrak{S}^{ml}_{\ell,v,o}$ (by achieving a strictly higher max. probability than $\mathfrak{s}^{opt}_{ml(l,v,o)}$) if and only if there are some combinations of clock values (aspect v) and expiration orders (aspect o) in ℓ_2 that can be reached with positive probability via the left edge into ℓ_2, for which $\mathfrak{s}^{opt}_{ml(l,v,o)}$ must nevertheless decide to go to ℓ_4.

All possible clock valuations in ℓ_2 can be achieved via either the left or the right edge, but taking the left edge implies that x expires before z in ℓ_2. It is thus sufficient to show that $\mathfrak{s}^{opt}_{ml(l,v,o)}$ must go to ℓ_4 in *some* cases where x

expires before z. The general form of schedulers in $\mathfrak{S}^{ml}_{\ell,v,o}$ in ℓ_2 is "go to ℓ_3 iff (a) x expires before z and $v(x) \in S_1$ or (b) z expires before x and $v(x) \in S_2$" where the S_i are measurable subsets of $[0, 8]$. S_2 is in fact *irrelevant*: whatever $\mathfrak{s}^{opt}_{ml(l,v,o)}$ does when (b) is satisfied will be mimicked by $\mathfrak{s}^{better}_{hist(l,v,o)}$ because z can only expire before x when coming via the right edge into ℓ_2. Conditions (a) and (b) are independent.

With $S_1 = [0, 8]$, the max. probability is $\frac{77}{96} = 0.80208\bar{3}$. Since this is the only scheduler in $\mathfrak{S}^{ml}_{\ell,v,o}$ that is *relevant* for our proof and never goes to l_4 when x expires before z, it remains to show that the max. probability under $\mathfrak{s}^{opt}_{ml(l,v,o)}$ is $> \frac{77}{96}$. With $S_1 = [0, \frac{35}{12})$, we have a max. probability of $\frac{7561}{9216} \approx 0.820421$. Thus $\mathfrak{s}^{opt}_{ml(l,v,o)}$ must sometimes go to l_4 even when the left edge was taken, so $\mathfrak{s}^{better}_{hist(l,v,o)}$ achieves a higher probability and thus distinguishes the classes.

Knowing only the global elapsed time is less powerful than knowing the full history or the values of all clocks:

Proposition 6. *$\mathfrak{S}^{hist}_{\ell,t,e} \succ \mathfrak{S}^{ml}_{\ell,t,e}$ and $\mathfrak{S}^{ml}_{\ell,v,e} \succ \mathfrak{S}^{ml}_{\ell,t,e}$.*

Proof sketch. Consider the SA M_3 in Fig. 7. We have $\mathrm{P}_{\max}(\mathfrak{S}^{hist}_{\ell,t,e}) = 1$: when in ℓ_3, the scheduler sees from the history which of the two incoming edges was used, and thus knows whether x or y is already expired. It can then make the optimal choice: go to ℓ_4 if x is already expired, or to ℓ_5 otherwise. We also have $\mathrm{P}_{\max}(\mathfrak{S}^{ml}_{\ell,v,e}) = 1$: the scheduler sees that either $v(x) = 0$ or $v(y) = 0$, which implies that the other clock is already expired, and the argument above applies. However, $\mathrm{P}_{\max}(\mathfrak{S}^{ml}_{\ell,t,e}) < 1$: the distribution of elapsed time t on entering ℓ_3 is itself independent of which edge is taken. With probability $\frac{1}{4}$, exactly one of $e(x)$ and $e(y)$ is below t in ℓ_3, which implies that that clock has just expired and thus the scheduler can decide optimally. Yet with probability $\frac{3}{4}$, the expiration times are not useful: they are both positive and drawn from the same distribution, but one unknown clock is expired. The wait for x in ℓ_1 ensures that comparing t with the expiration times in e does not reveal further information in this case.

In the case of MDP, knowing the total elapsed time (i.e. steps) does not make a difference for unbounded reachability. Only for step-bounded properties is that extra knowledge necessary to achieve optimal probabilities. With SA, however, it makes a difference even in the unbounded case:

Proposition 7. *$\mathfrak{S}^{ml}_{\ell,t,e} \succ \mathfrak{S}^{ml}_{\ell,e}$.*

Proof. Consider SA M_4 in Fig. 8. We have $\mathrm{P}_{\max}(\mathfrak{S}^{ml}_{\ell,t,e}) = 1$: in ℓ_2, the remaining time until y expires is $e(y)$ and the remaining time until x expires is $e(x) - t$ for the global time value t as ℓ_2 is entered. The scheduler can observe all of these quantities and thus optimally go to ℓ_3 if x will expire first, or to ℓ_4 otherwise. However, $\mathrm{P}_{\max}(\mathfrak{S}^{ml}_{\ell,e}) < 1$: $e(x)$ only contains the absolute expiration time of x, but without knowing t or the expiration time of z in ℓ_1, and thus the current value $v(x)$, this scheduler cannot know with certainty which of the clocks will expire first and is therefore unable to make an optimal choice in ℓ_2.

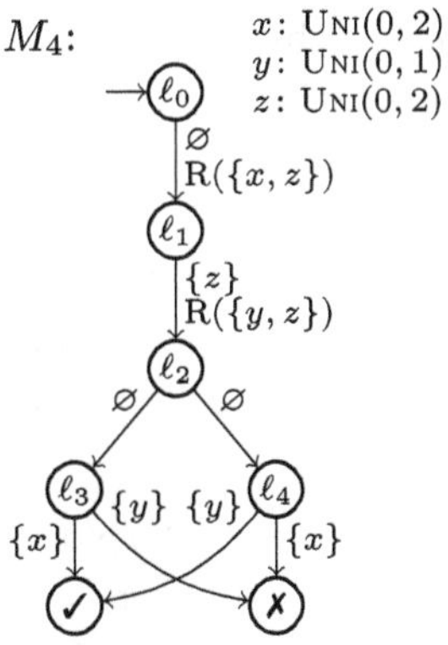

Fig. 8. SA M_4

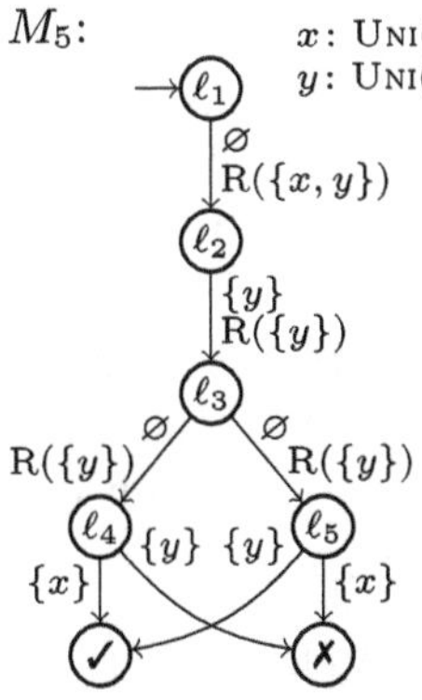

Fig. 9. SA M_5

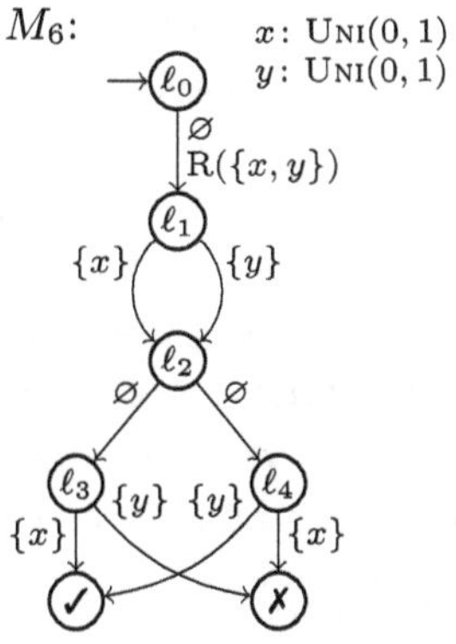

Fig. 10. SA M_6

Finally, we need to compare the memoryless schedulers that see the clock expiration times with memoryless schedulers that see the expiration order. As noted in Sect. 3.1, these two views of the current state are incomparable unless we also see the clock values:

Proposition 8. $\mathfrak{S}^{ml}_{\ell,v,e} \succ \mathfrak{S}^{ml}_{\ell,v,o}$.

Proof. $\mathfrak{S}^{ml}_{\ell,v,e} \not\preccurlyeq \mathfrak{S}^{ml}_{\ell,v,o}$ follows from the same argument as in the proof of Proposition 3. $\mathfrak{S}^{ml}_{\ell,v,e} \succcurlyeq \mathfrak{S}^{ml}_{\ell,v,o}$ is because knowing the current clock values v and the expiration times e is equivalent to knowing the expiration order, since that is precisely the order of the differences $e(c) - v(c)$ for all clocks c.

Proposition 9. $\mathfrak{S}^{ml}_{\ell,t,e} \not\approx \mathfrak{S}^{ml}_{\ell,t,o}$.

Proof. $\mathfrak{S}^{ml}_{\ell,t,e} \not\preccurlyeq \mathfrak{S}^{ml}_{\ell,t,o}$ follows from the same argument as in the proof of Proposition 3. For $\mathfrak{S}^{ml}_{\ell,t,e} \not\succcurlyeq \mathfrak{S}^{ml}_{\ell,t,o}$, consider the SA M_3 of Fig. 7. We know from the proof of Proposition 6 that $\mathrm{P}_{\max}(\mathfrak{S}^{ml}_{\ell,t,e}) < 1$. However, if the scheduler knows the order in which the clocks will expire, it knows which one has already expired (the first one in the order), and can thus make the optimal choice in ℓ_3 to achieve $\mathrm{P}_{\max}(\mathfrak{S}^{ml}_{\ell,t,o}) = 1$.

Proposition 10. $\mathfrak{S}^{ml}_{\ell,e} \not\approx \mathfrak{S}^{ml}_{\ell,o}$.

Proof. The argument of Proposition 9 applies by observing that, in M_3 of Fig. 7, we also have $\mathrm{P}_{\max}(\mathfrak{S}^{ml}_{\ell,e}) < 1$ via the same argument as for $\mathfrak{S}^{ml}_{\ell,t,e}$ in the proof of Proposition 6.

Among the expiration-order schedulers, the hierarchy is as expected:

Proposition 11. $\mathfrak{S}^{ml}_{\ell,v,o} \succ \mathfrak{S}^{ml}_{\ell,t,o} \succ \mathfrak{S}^{ml}_{\ell,o}$.

Proof sketch. Consider M_5 of Fig. 9. To maximise the probability, in ℓ_3 we should go to ℓ_4 whenever x is already expired or close to expiring, for which the amount of time spent in ℓ_2 is an indicator. $\mathfrak{S}^{ml}_{\ell,o}$ only knows that x may have expired when the expiration order is "x before y", but definitely has not expired when it is "y before x". Schedulers in $\mathfrak{S}^{ml}_{\ell,t,o}$ can do better: They also see the amount of time spent in ℓ_2. Thus $\mathfrak{S}^{ml}_{\ell,t,o} \succ \mathfrak{S}^{ml}_{\ell,o}$. If we modify M_5 by adding an initial delay on x from a new ℓ_0 to ℓ_1 as in M_3, then the same argument can be used to prove $\mathfrak{S}^{ml}_{\ell,v,o} \succ \mathfrak{S}^{ml}_{\ell,t,o}$: the extra delay makes knowing the elapsed time t useless with positive probability, but the exact time spent in l_2 is visible to $\mathfrak{S}^{ml}_{\ell,v,o}$ as $v(x)$.

We have thus established the hierarchy of classic schedulers shown in Fig. 3, noting that some of the relationships follow from the propositions by transitivity.

4.2 The Non-prophetic Hierarchy

Each non-prophetic scheduler class is clearly dominated by the classic and expiration-order scheduler classes that otherwise have the same information, for example $\mathfrak{S}^{hist}_{\ell,v,e} \succ \mathfrak{S}^{hist}_{\ell,v}$ (with very simple distinguishing SA). We show that the non-prophetic hierarchy follows the shape of the classic case, including the difference between global-time and pure memoryless schedulers, with the notable exception of memoryless schedulers being weaker than history-dependent ones.

Proposition 12. $\mathfrak{S}^{hist}_{\ell,v} \approx \mathfrak{S}^{hist}_{\ell,t} \approx \mathfrak{S}^{hist}_{\ell}$.

Proof. This follows from the argument of Proposition 1.

Proposition 13. $\mathfrak{S}^{hist}_{\ell,v} \succ \mathfrak{S}^{ml}_{\ell,v}$.

Proof. Consider the SA M_6 in Fig. 10. It is similar to M_4 of Fig. 8, and our arguments are thus similar to the proof of Proposition 7. On M_6, we have $\mathrm{P}_{\max}(\mathfrak{S}^{hist}_{\ell,v}) = 1$: in ℓ_2, the history reveals which of the two incoming edges was used, i.e. which clock is already expired, thus the scheduler can make the optimal choice. However, if neither the history nor e is available, we get $\mathrm{P}_{\max}(\mathfrak{S}^{ml}_{\ell,v}) = \frac{1}{2}$: the only information that can be used in ℓ_2 are the values of the clocks, but $v(x) = v(y)$, so there is no basis for an informed choice.

Proposition 14. $\mathfrak{S}^{hist}_{\ell,t} \succ \mathfrak{S}^{ml}_{\ell,t}$ *and* $\mathfrak{S}^{ml}_{\ell,v} \succ \mathfrak{S}^{ml}_{\ell,t}$.

Proof. Consider the SA M_3 in Fig. 7. We have $\mathrm{P}_{\max}(\mathfrak{S}^{hist}_{\ell,t}) = \mathrm{P}_{\max}(\mathfrak{S}^{ml}_{\ell,v}) = 1$, but $\mathrm{P}_{\max}(\mathfrak{S}^{ml}_{\ell,t}) = \frac{1}{2}$ by the same arguments as in the proof of Proposition 6.

Proposition 15. $\mathfrak{S}^{ml}_{\ell,t} \succ \mathfrak{S}^{ml}_{\ell}$.

Proof. Consider the SA M_4 in Fig. 8. The schedulers in $\mathfrak{S}^{ml}_{\ell}$ have no information but the current location, so they cannot make an informed choice in ℓ_2. This and the simple loop-free structure of M_4 make it possible to analytically calculate the resulting probability: $\mathrm{P}_{\max}(\mathfrak{S}^{ml}_{\ell}) = \frac{17}{24} = 0.708\overline{3}$. If information about the global elapsed time t in ℓ_2 is available, however, the value of x is revealed. This allows making a better choice, e.g. going to ℓ_3 when $t \leq \frac{1}{2}$ and to ℓ_4 otherwise, resulting in $\mathrm{P}_{\max}(\mathfrak{S}^{ml}_{\ell,t}) \approx 0.771$ (statistically estimated with high confidence).

We have thus established the hierarchy of non-prophetic schedulers shown in Fig. 4, where some relationships follow from the propositions by transitivity.

5 Experiments

We have built a prototype implementation of lightweight scheduler sampling for SA by extending the MODEST TOOLSET's [24] MODES simulator, which already supports deterministic stochastic timed automata (STA [8]). With some care, SA can be encoded into STA. Using the original algorithm for MDP of [18], our prototype works by providing to the schedulers a discretised view of the continuous components of the SA's semantics, which, we recall, is a continuous-space MDP. The currently implemented discretisation is simple: for each real-valued quantity (the value $v(c)$ of clock c, its expiration time $e(c)$, and the global elapsed time t), it identifies all values that lie within the same interval $[\frac{i}{n}, \frac{i+1}{n})$, for integers i, n. We note that better static discretisations are almost certainly possible, e.g. a region construction for the clock values as in [30].

We have modelled M_1 through M_6 as STA in MODEST. For each scheduler class and model in the proof of a proposition, and discretisation factors $n \in \{1, 2, 4\}$, we sampled 10 000 schedulers and performed statistical model checking for each of them in the lightweight manner. In Fig. 11 we report the min. and max. estimates, $(\hat{p}_{\min}, \hat{p}_{\max})_{\ldots}$, over all sampled schedulers. Where different discretisations lead to different estimates, we report the most extremal values. The subscript denotes the discretisation factors that achieved the reported estimates. The analysis for each sampled scheduler was performed with a number of simulation runs sufficient for the overall max./min. estimates to be within $\pm\,0.01$ of the true maxima/minima of the *sampled* set of schedulers with probability $\geq$0.95 [18]. Note that $\hat{p}_{\min}$ is an upper bound on the true minimum probability and $\hat{p}_{\max}$ is a lower bound on the true maximum probability.

Increasing the discretisation factor or increasing the scheduler power generally increases the number of decisions the schedulers *can* make. This may also increase the number of *critical* decisions a scheduler *must* make to achieve the extremal probability. Hence, the sets of discretisation factors associated to specific experiments may be informally interpreted in the following way:

- $\{1, 2, 4\}$: Fine discretisation is not important for optimality and optimal schedulers are not rare.
- $\{1, 2\}$: Fine discretisation is not important for optimality, but increases rarity of optimal schedulers.
- $\{2, 4\}$: Fine discretisation is important for optimality, optimal schedulers are not rare.
- $\{1\}$: Optimal schedulers are very rare.
- $\{2\}$: Fine discretisation is important for optimality, but increases rarity of schedulers.
- $\{4\}$: Fine discretisation is important for optimality and optimal schedulers are not rare.

M_1:

Proposition 3:
$\mathfrak{S}^{hist}_{\ell,v,e}$: $(0.24, 0.76)_{2,4}$
$\mathfrak{S}^{hist}_{\ell,v,o}$: $(0.49, 0.51)_{1,2,4}$

Proposition 8:
$\mathfrak{S}^{ml}_{\ell,v,e}$: $(0.24, 0.76)_{2,4}$
$\mathfrak{S}^{ml}_{\ell,v,o}$: $(0.49, 0.51)_{1,2,4}$

Proposition 9:
$\mathfrak{S}^{ml}_{\ell,t,e}$: $(0.24, 0.76)_{2,4}$
$\mathfrak{S}^{ml}_{\ell,t,o}$: $(0.49, 0.51)_{1,2,4}$

Proposition 10:
$\mathfrak{S}^{ml}_{\ell,e}$: $(0.24, 0.76)_{2,4}$
$\mathfrak{S}^{ml}_{\ell,o}$: $(0.49, 0.51)_{1,2,4}$

M_3:

Proposition 6:
$\mathfrak{S}^{hist}_{\ell,t,e}$: $(0.00, 1.00)_{1}$
$\mathfrak{S}^{ml}_{\ell,v,e}$: $(0.12, 0.86)_{4}$
$\mathfrak{S}^{ml}_{\ell,t,e}$: $(0.37, 0.65)_{2}$

Proposition 9:
$\mathfrak{S}^{ml}_{\ell,t,e}$: $(0.37, 0.65)_{2}$
$\mathfrak{S}^{ml}_{\ell,t,o}$: $(0.00, 1.00)_{1,2}$

Proposition 10:
$\mathfrak{S}^{ml}_{\ell,e}$: $(0.34, 0.67)_{4}$
$\mathfrak{S}^{ml}_{\ell,o}$: $(0.00, 1.00)_{1,2,4}$

Proposition 14:
$\mathfrak{S}^{hist}_{\ell,t}$: $(0.00, 1.00)_{1,2}$
$\mathfrak{S}^{ml}_{\ell,v}$: $(0.21, 0.78)_{4}$
$\mathfrak{S}^{ml}_{\ell,t}$: $(0.49, 0.51)_{1,2,4}$

M_2:

Proposition 5:
$\mathfrak{S}^{hist}_{\ell,o}$: $(0.06, 0.94)_{1,2,4}$
$\mathfrak{S}^{ml}_{\ell,v,o}$: $(0.18, 0.83)_{1}$

M_4:

Proposition 7:
$\mathfrak{S}^{ml}_{\ell,t,e}$: $(0.25, 0.79)_{1}$
$\mathfrak{S}^{ml}_{\ell,e}$: $(0.29, 0.71)_{1}$

Proposition 15:
$\mathfrak{S}^{ml}_{\ell,t}$: $(0.22, 0.78)_{2,4}$
$\mathfrak{S}^{ml}_{\ell}$: $(0.28, 0.72)_{1,2,4}$

M_5:

Proposition 11:
$\mathfrak{S}^{ml}_{\ell,t,o}$: $(0.15, 0.86)_{4}$
$\mathfrak{S}^{ml}_{\ell,o}$: $(0.16, 0.84)_{1,2,4}$

M_6:

Proposition 13:
$\mathfrak{S}^{hist}_{\ell,v}$: $(0.00, 1.00)_{1,2}$
$\mathfrak{S}^{ml}_{\ell,v}$: $(0.49, 0.51)_{1,2,4}$

Fig. 11. Results from the prototype of lightweight scheduler sampling for SA

The results in Fig. 11 respect and differentiate our hierarchy. In most cases, we found schedulers whose estimates were within the statistical error of calculated optima or of high confidence estimates achieved by alternative statistical techniques. The exceptions involve M_3 and M_4. We note that M_4 makes use of an additional clock, increasing the dimensionality of the problem and potentially making near-optimal schedulers rarer. The best result for M_3 and class $\mathfrak{S}^{ml}_{l,t,e}$ was obtained using discretisation factor $n = 2$: a compromise between nearness to optimality and rarity. A greater compromise was necessary for M_4 and classes $\mathfrak{S}^{ml}_{l,t,e}$, $\mathfrak{S}^{ml}_{l,e}$, where we found near-optimal schedulers to be very rare and achieved best results using discretisation factor $n = 1$.

The experiments demonstrate that lightweight scheduler sampling can produce useful and informative results with SA. The present theoretical results will allow us to develop better abstractions for SA and thus to construct a refinement algorithm for efficient lightweight verification of SA that will be applicable to realistically sized case studies. As is, they already demonstrate the importance of selecting a proper scheduler class for efficient verification, and that restricted classes are useful in planning scenarios.

6 Conclusion

We have shown that the various notions of information available to a scheduler class, such as history, clock order, expiration times or overall elapsed time, almost all make distinct contributions to the power of the class in SA. Our choice of notions was based on classic scheduler classes relevant for other stochastic models, previous literature on the character of nondeterminism in and verification of SA, and the need to synthesise simple schedulers in planning. Our distinguishing examples clearly expose how to exploit each notion to improve the probability of reaching a goal. For verification of SA, we have demonstrated the feasibility of lightweight scheduler sampling, where the different notions may be used to finely control the power of the lightweight schedulers. To solve stochastic timed planning problems defined via SA, our analysis helps in the case-by-case selection of an appropriate scheduler class that achieves the desired tradeoff between optimal probabilities and ease of implementation of the resulting plan.

We expect the arguments of this paper to extend to steady-state/frequency measures (by adding loops back from absorbing to initial states in our examples), and that our results for classic schedulers transfer to SA with delayable actions. We propose to use the results to develop better abstractions for SA, the next goal being a refinement algorithm for efficient lightweight verification of SA.

References

1. de Alfaro, L.: The verification of probabilistic systems under memoryless partial-information policies is hard. Technical report, DTIC Document (1999)
2. Alur, R., Courcoubetis, C., Dill, D.: Model-checking for probabilistic real-time systems. In: Albert, J.L., Monien, B., Artalejo, M.R. (eds.) ICALP 1991. LNCS, vol. 510, pp. 115–126. Springer, Heidelberg (1991). https://doi.org/10.1007/3-540-54233-7_128
3. Andel, T.R., Yasinsac, A.: On the credibility of MANET simulations. IEEE Comput. **39**(7), 48–54 (2006)
4. Avritzer, A., Carnevali, L., Ghasemieh, H., Happe, L., Haverkort, B.R., Koziolek, A., Menasché, D.S., Remke, A., Sarvestani, S.S., Vicario, E.: Survivability evaluation of gas, water and electricity infrastructures. Electr. Notes Theor. Comput. Sci. **310**, 5–25 (2015)
5. Baier, C., Katoen, J.P.: Principles of Model Checking. MIT Press, Cambridge (2008)
6. Ballarini, P., Bertrand, N., Horváth, A., Paolieri, M., Vicario, E.: Transient analysis of networks of stochastic timed automata using stochastic state classes. In: Joshi, K., Siegle, M., Stoelinga, M., D'Argenio, P.R. (eds.) QEST 2013. LNCS, vol. 8054, pp. 355–371. Springer, Heidelberg (2013). https://doi.org/10.1007/978-3-642-40196-1_30
7. Bisgaard, M., Gerhardt, D., Hermanns, H., Krčál, J., Nies, G., Stenger, M.: Battery-aware scheduling in low orbit: the GomX–3 case. In: Fitzgerald, J., Heitmeyer, C., Gnesi, S., Philippou, A. (eds.) FM 2016. LNCS, vol. 9995, pp. 559–576. Springer, Cham (2016). https://doi.org/10.1007/978-3-319-48989-6_34
8. Bohnenkamp, H.C., D'Argenio, P.R., Hermanns, H., Katoen, J.P.: MoDeST: a compositional modeling formalism for hard and softly timed systems. IEEE Trans. Softw. Eng. **32**(10), 812–830 (2006)
9. Bravetti, M., D'Argenio, P.R.: Tutte le algebre insieme: concepts, discussions and relations of stochastic process algebras with general distributions. In: Baier, C., Haverkort, B.R., Hermanns, H., Katoen, J.-P., Siegle, M. (eds.) Validation of Stochastic Systems. LNCS, vol. 2925, pp. 44–88. Springer, Heidelberg (2004). https://doi.org/10.1007/978-3-540-24611-4_2
10. Bravetti, M., Gorrieri, R.: The theory of interactive generalized semi-Markov processes. Theor. Comput. Sci. **282**(1), 5–32 (2002)

11. Brázdil, T., Krčál, J., Křetínský, J., Řehák, V.: Fixed-delay events in generalized semi-Markov processes revisited. In: Katoen, J.-P., König, B. (eds.) CONCUR 2011. LNCS, vol. 6901, pp. 140–155. Springer, Heidelberg (2011). https://doi.org/10.1007/978-3-642-23217-6_10
12. Bryans, J., Bowman, H., Derrick, J.: Model checking stochastic automata. ACM Trans. Comput. Log. **4**(4), 452–492 (2003)
13. Buchholz, P., Kriege, J., Scheftelowitsch, D.: Model checking stochastic automata for dependability and performance measures. In: DSN, pp. 503–514. IEEE Computer Society (2014)
14. Butkova, Y., Hatefi, H., Hermanns, H., Krčál, J.: Optimal continuous time Markov decisions. In: Finkbeiner, B., Pu, G., Zhang, L. (eds.) ATVA 2015. LNCS, vol. 9364, pp. 166–182. Springer, Cham (2015). https://doi.org/10.1007/978-3-319-24953-7_12
15. D'Argenio, P.R., Hartmanns, A., Legay, A., Sedwards, S.: Statistical approximation of optimal schedulers for probabilistic timed automata. In: Ábrahám, E., Huisman, M. (eds.) IFM 2016. LNCS, vol. 9681, pp. 99–114. Springer, Cham (2016). https://doi.org/10.1007/978-3-319-33693-0_7
16. D'Argenio, P.R., Katoen, J.P.: A theory of stochastic systems part I: stochastic automata. Inf. Comput. **203**(1), 1–38 (2005)
17. D'Argenio, P.R., Lee, M.D., Monti, R.E.: Input/output stochastic automata. In: Fränzle, M., Markey, N. (eds.) FORMATS 2016. LNCS, vol. 9884, pp. 53–68. Springer, Cham (2016). https://doi.org/10.1007/978-3-319-44878-7_4
18. D'Argenio, P.R., Legay, A., Sedwards, S., Traonouez, L.M.: Smart sampling for lightweight verification of Markov decision processes. STTT **17**(4), 469–484 (2015)
19. Eisentraut, C., Hermanns, H., Zhang, L.: On probabilistic automata in continuous time. In: LICS, pp. 342–351. IEEE Computer Society (2010)
20. Giro, S., D'Argenio, P.R.: Quantitative model checking revisited: neither decidable nor approximable. In: Raskin, J.-F., Thiagarajan, P.S. (eds.) FORMATS 2007. LNCS, vol. 4763, pp. 179–194. Springer, Heidelberg (2007). https://doi.org/10.1007/978-3-540-75454-1_14
21. Haas, P.J., Shedler, G.S.: Regenerative generalized semi-Markov processes. commun. stat. Stochast. Models **3**(3), 409–438 (1987)
22. Hahn, E.M., Hartmanns, A., Hermanns, H.: Reachability and reward checking for stochastic timed automata. In: Electronic Communications of the EASST, AVoCS 2014, vol. 70 (2014)
23. Harrison, P.G., Strulo, B.: SPADES - a process algebra for discrete event simulation. J. Log. Comput. **10**(1), 3–42 (2000)
24. Hartmanns, A., Hermanns, H.: The Modest Toolset: an integrated environment for quantitative modelling and verification. In: Ábrahám, E., Havelund, K. (eds.) TACAS 2014. LNCS, vol. 8413, pp. 593–598. Springer, Heidelberg (2014). https://doi.org/10.1007/978-3-642-54862-8_51
25. Hartmanns, A., Hermanns, H., Krčál, J.: Schedulers are no Prophets. In: Probst, C.W., Hankin, C., Hansen, R.R. (eds.) Semantics, Logics, and Calculi. LNCS, vol. 9560, pp. 214–235. Springer, Cham (2016). https://doi.org/10.1007/978-3-319-27810-0_11
26. Hartmanns, A., Sedwards, S., D'Argenio, P.: Efficient simulation-based verification of probabilistic timed automata. In: WSC. IEEE (2017). https://doi.org/10.1109/WSC.2017.8247885
27. Hermanns, H.: Interactive Markov Chains: The Quest for Quantified Quality. LNCS, vol. 2428. Springer, Heidelberg (2002). https://doi.org/10.1007/3-540-45804-2

28. Hermanns, H., Krämer, J., Krčál, J., Stoelinga, M.: The value of attack-defence diagrams. In: Piessens, F., Viganò, L. (eds.) POST 2016. LNCS, vol. 9635, pp. 163–185. Springer, Heidelberg (2016). https://doi.org/10.1007/978-3-662-49635-0_9
29. Kurkowski, S., Camp, T., Colagrosso, M.: MANET simulation studies: the incredibles. Mob. Comput. Commun. Rev. **9**(4), 50–61 (2005)
30. Kwiatkowska, M., Norman, G., Segala, R., Sproston, J.: Verifying quantitative properties of continuous probabilistic timed automata. In: Palamidessi, C. (ed.) CONCUR 2000. LNCS, vol. 1877, pp. 123–137. Springer, Heidelberg (2000). https://doi.org/10.1007/3-540-44618-4_11
31. Legay, A., Sedwards, S., Traonouez, L.M.: Estimating rewards & rare events in nondeterministic systems. In: Electronic Communications of the EASST, AVoCS 2015, vol. 72 (2015)
32. Legay, A., Sedwards, S., Traonouez, L.-M.: Scalable verification of Markov decision processes. In: Canal, C., Idani, A. (eds.) SEFM 2014. LNCS, vol. 8938, pp. 350–362. Springer, Cham (2015). https://doi.org/10.1007/978-3-319-15201-1_23
33. Matthes, K.: Zur Theorie der Bedienungsprozesse. In: 3rd Prague Conference on Information Theory, Stat. Dec. Fns. and Random Processes, pp. 513–528 (1962)
34. NS-3 Consortium: ns-3: A Discrete-event Network Simulator for Internet Systems. https://www.nsnam.org/
35. Pongor, G.: OMNeT: objective modular network testbed. In: MASCOTS, pp. 323–326. The Society for Computer Simulation (1993)
36. Ruijters, E., Stoelinga, M.: Better railway engineering through statistical model checking. In: Margaria, T., Steffen, B. (eds.) ISoLA 2016. LNCS, vol. 9952, pp. 151–165. Springer, Cham (2016). https://doi.org/10.1007/978-3-319-47166-2_10
37. Song, L., Zhang, L., Godskesen, J.C.: Late weak bisimulation for Markov automata. CoRR abs/1202.4116 (2012)
38. Strulo, B.: Process algebra for discrete event simulation. Ph.D. thesis, Imperial College of Science, Technology and Medicine. University of London, October 1993
39. Wolf, V., Baier, C., Majster-Cederbaum, M.E.: Trace semantics for stochastic systems with nondeterminism. Electr. Notes Theor. Comput. Sci. **164**(3), 187–204 (2006)
40. Wolovick, N.: Continuous probability and nondeterminism in labeled transition systems. Ph.D. thesis, Universidad Nacional de Córdoba, Córdoba, Argentina (2012)
41. Wolovick, N., Johr, S.: A characterization of meaningful schedulers for continuous-time Markov decision processes. In: Asarin, E., Bouyer, P. (eds.) FORMATS 2006. LNCS, vol. 4202, pp. 352–367. Springer, Heidelberg (2006). https://doi.org/10.1007/11867340_25
42. Zeng, X., Bagrodia, R.L., Gerla, M.: Glomosim: a library for parallel simulation of large-scale wireless networks. In: PADS, pp. 154–161. IEEE Computer Society (1998)

8

Differential Calculus with Imprecise Input and Its Logical Framework

Abbas Edalat[1] and Mehrdad Maleki[2(✉)]

[1] Department of Computing, Imperial College London, London SW7 2RH, UK
a.edalat@imperial.ac.uk
[2] Institute for Research in Fundamental Sciences (IPM), Niavaran, Tehran, Iran
m.maleki@ipm.ir

Abstract. We develop a domain-theoretic Differential Calculus for locally Lipschitz functions on finite dimensional real spaces with imprecise input/output. The inputs to these functions are hyper-rectangles and the outputs are compact real intervals. This extends the domain of application of Interval Analysis and exact arithmetic to the derivative. A new notion of a tie for these functions is introduced, which in one dimension represents a modification of the notion previously used in the one-dimensional framework. A Scott continuous sub-differential for these functions is then constructed, which satisfies a weaker form of calculus compared to that of the Clarke sub-gradient. We then adopt a Program Logic viewpoint using the equivalence of the category of stably locally compact spaces with that of semi-strong proximity lattices. We show that given a localic approximable mapping representing a locally Lipschitz map with imprecise input/output, a localic approximable mapping for its sub-differential can be constructed, which provides a logical formulation of the sub-differential operator.

Keywords: Imprecise input/output · Interval analysis
Exact computation · Lipschitz maps · Clarke gradient
Domain theory · Stone duality

1 Introduction

A well-known hurdle in numerical computation is caused by accumulation of round-off errors in floating point arithmetic, which can create havoc and lead to catastrophic errors in compound calculations. In safety and critical systems, where reliability of numerical computation is of utmost importance, one way to avoid the pitfalls of floating point arithmetic is to use interval analysis or exact arithmetic. In both interval analysis and exact arithmetic as well as in computable analysis, a real number is represented by a nested shrinking sequence of compact intervals whose intersections is the real number. Similarly, a real n-vector can be represented by a nested sequence of hyper-rectangles in $\mathbb{R}^n$. This leads to a framework in numerical computation and a framework for computational geometry where the inputs of algorithms or programmes are imprecise real numbers or real n-vectors; see for example [3,5,6,9,10,14,15,17,21–23,27].

All frameworks for interval analysis and exact real computation are based on functions whose input and output are real intervals. When we compose two such functions, the output of the first function serves as the input to the second function. An implementation of these frameworks in a functional programming language follows this same pattern; see for example the lazy Haskell implementation of IC-Reals for Exact Real Computation [1], which uses linear fractional transformations as developed in [14,22].

An important feature of working with a calculus consisting of functions with interval or imprecise input/output is that even when we deal with elementary functions such as polynomials we cannot restrict ourselves to their canonical (maximal) extensions to intervals [21]. These canonical extensions take a compact interval to its forward image under the function. In fact, these extensions are not closed under, for example, multiplication. Thus, the real-valued map of a real variable $x \mapsto x^2$ when implemented with interval input by $x \mapsto x \times x$, using multiplication of two copies of the input interval, is not the canonical extension of the quadratic map of real numbers: it evaluates for example $[-1,1]^2$ to $[-1,1]$ rather than $[0,1]$, which is what the canonical extension of the quadratic map evaluates to. In general, we need to work with any Scott continuous map of type $\mathbf{I}\mathbb{R} \to \mathbf{I}\mathbb{R}$ or, in higher dimension, of type $\mathbf{I}\mathbb{R}^n \to \mathbf{I}\mathbb{R}$, where $\mathbf{I}\mathbb{R}^n$ denotes the domain of hyper-rectangles of $\mathbb{R}^n$.

In the past 60 years, interval analysis has grown as a distinct interdisciplinary subject to impact on nearly all areas of mathematical and numerical analysis including computer arithmetic, linear algebra, integration, solution of initial value problems and partial differential equations to correct solutions in mathematical optimisation and robotics; see [20]. It is natural to ask if the domain of application of interval analysis and exact computation can be extended to the derivative of functions, i.e., whether one can take a kind of derivative of a map which takes a compact interval or a compact hyper-rectangle as input.

In [11], the notion of a domain-theoretic sub-differentiation of maps which have non-empty and compact intervals as inputs and outputs was introduced. The restriction of these maps to real numbers turns out to be locally Lipschitz maps of type $\mathbb{R} \to \mathbb{R}$ and the sub-differential restricted to real numbers has been shown to be the same as the Clarke sub-gradient [8]. A major problem, however, is that the framework in [11], which only deals with one-dimensional maps of type $\mathbf{I}\mathbb{R} \to \mathbf{I}\mathbb{R}$ is not accompanied with a Stone duality framework and thus, even in dimension one, cannot be used in order to handle program logic and predicate transformers.

In [7], a typed lambda calculus in the framework of an extension of Real PCF [6,17,22] was introduced in which in particular continuously differentiable and more generally Lipschitz functions can be defined. Given an expression representing a real-valued function of a real variable in this language, one is able to evaluate the expression on an argument, representing an interval, but also evaluate the generalised derivative, i.e., the L-derivative, equivalently the Clarke gradient, of the expression on an interval. The operational semantics of the language, which is equipped with min and a weighed average, enjoys adequacy and a definability result proving that any computable Lipschitz map is definable in it. The denotational semantics is based on domain theory which in principle allows a program logic formulation of the computation, although this challenge has not been taken up yet.

In [13], a point free framework for sub-differentiation of real-valued locally Lipschitz functions on finite dimensional Euclidean spaces has been developed which provides a Stone duality for the Clarke gradient and thus enables a program logic view of differentiation. However, the induced logical framework cannot be employed for the class of functions with imprecise input/output used in exact computation since, as already pointed out, this class necessarily contains general extensions of real-valued locally Lipschitz maps of finite dimensional Euclidean spaces.

In this paper, we formulate a new notion of a tie of functions with imprecise input/output, which, in one dimension, represents a modification of the corresponding notion in [12]. This allows us to develop a Scott continuous sub-differential for functions with hyper-rectangles in $\mathbb{R}^n$ as inputs and compact intervals in $\mathbb{R}$ as output, which are used in exact computation. We show that a weaker calculus compared to that for the Clarke sub-gradient is satisfied in this interval framework. In addition we construct a logical framework for sub-differentiation of locally Lipschitz maps of type $\mathbf{I}\mathbb{R}^n \to \mathbf{I}\mathbb{R}$. The basic Stone duality results developed in [13] are then extended to sub-differentiation of such interval maps.

1.1 Background

We assume the reader is familiar with basic elements of topology and domain theory. Following the definition in [18], by a domain we mean a continuous dcpo (directed complete partial order). All the domains we use in this paper are bounded complete as well. By $\mathbf{C}(\mathbb{R}^n)$, we denote the domain of non-empty convex and compact subsets of $\mathbb{R}^n$ ordered with reverse inclusion and augmented with $\bot = \mathbb{R}^n$ as the bottom element. If $C_1, C_2 \in \mathbf{C}(\mathbb{R}^n)$ then the way-below relation is given by $C_1 \ll C_2$ iff $C_1^\circ \supset C_2$, where S° is the interior of the set S. By $\mathbf{I}\mathbb{R}^n$, we denote the sub-domain of non-empty compact hyper-rectangles with faces parallel to coordinate hyper-planes of $\mathbb{R}^n$. The Euclidean norm of $x \in \mathbb{R}^n$ is denoted by $\|x\|$.

The lattice of open subsets of a topological space X is denoted by $\Omega(X)$. The Scott topology of a domain D is, however, written as σ_D. The closure of $S \subset X$ is denoted by $\overline{S}$. The upper topology, equivalently the Scott-topology, of $\mathbf{C}(\mathbb{R}^n)$ has a basis of the form

$$\Box O = \{C \in \mathbf{C}(\mathbb{R}^n) : C \subset O\},$$

where O belongs to a basis of open and convex subsets of $\mathbb{R}^n$.

Given an open set $a \subset X$ of a topological space and an element $b \in D$ of a domain D, the single-step function $b\chi_a : X \to D$ is defined by $b\chi_a(x) = b$ if $x \in a$ and $\bot$ otherwise. A non-empty compact real interval x is written as $x = [x^-, x^+]$. For a map $f : X \to Y$ of topological spaces, $f[S]$ denotes the image of the set $S \subset X$.

The three operations of addition of two vectors, scalar multiplication of a vector and a real number, and the inner product of two vectors can be extended to $\mathbf{C}(\mathbb{R}^n)$ to obtain the following three Scott continuous maps:

(i) $- + - : \mathbf{C}(\mathbb{R}^n) \times \mathbf{C}(\mathbb{R}^n) \to \mathbf{C}(\mathbb{R}^n)$ with $A + B = \{a + b : a \in A, b \in B\}$,
(ii) $- \times - : \mathbb{R} \times \mathbf{C}(\mathbb{R}^n) \to \mathbf{C}(\mathbb{R}^n)$ with $rA = \{rx : x \in A\}$, and,
(iii) $- \cdot - : \mathbf{C}(\mathbb{R}^n) \times \mathbf{C}(\mathbb{R}^n) \to \mathbf{I}\mathbb{R}$ with $A \cdot B = \{a \cdot b : a \in A, b \in B\}$.

These three operations have well-defined restrictions to $\mathbf{I}\mathbb{R}^n$. In addition, in this paper, we will consider their higher order extension to sets of sets. For example, if $a_1, a_2 \in \Omega(\mathbb{R})$ are open subsets, then $\Box a_1, \Box a_2 \in \sigma_{\mathbf{C}(\mathbb{R}^n)}$ and we have:

$$(\Box a_1) \cdot (\Box a_2) := \{x_1 \cdot x_2 : x_1 \in \Box a_1, x_2 \in \Box a_2\}$$

Moreover:

Proposition 1. *(i) The modal operator $\Box : \Omega(\mathbb{R}^n) \to \sigma_{\mathbf{C}(\mathbb{R}^n)}$ preserves meets, i.e., $\Box O_1 \wedge \Box O_2 = \Box(O_1 \wedge O_2)$ for all $O_1, O_2 \in \Omega(\mathbb{R}^n)$.*
(ii) The way-below relation satisfies $O_1 \ll O_2$ if and only if $\Box O_1 \ll \Box O_2$ for all $O_1, O_2 \in \Omega(\mathbb{R}^n)$.
(iii) If $O_1, O_2 \subset \mathbb{R}^n$ are open hyper-rectangles, then $\Box(O_1 + O_2) = \Box O_1 + \Box O_2$.
(iv) If $O \subset \mathbb{R}^n$ is a convex open set and $a \subset \mathbb{R}^n$ is a hyper-rectangle, then $\Box(O \cdot a) = (\Box O) \cdot (\Box a)$.

Next, we present the notion of Clarke's sub-gradient [4]. Recall that a map $f : U \subset \mathbb{R}^n \to \mathbb{R}$, where U is an open set, is locally Lipschitz if all points in U have an open neighbourhood $O \subset U$ with a constant $k \geq 0$ such that $|f(x) - f(y)| \leq k\|x - y\|$ for all $x, y \in O$. The generalized directional derivative of a locally Lipschitz f at x in the direction of v is defined as follow:

$$f^\circ(x; v) = \limsup_{y \to x \; t \to 0^+} \frac{f(y + tv) - f(y)}{t}$$

The Clarke subgradient of f at x, denoted by $\partial f(x)$ is a convex and compact subset of $\mathbb{R}^n$ and is defined by:

$$\partial f(x) = \{w \in \mathbb{R}^n : f^\circ(x; v) \geq w \cdot v \text{ for all } v \in \mathbb{R}^n\} \quad (1)$$

The sub-gradient function $\partial f : U \subset \mathbb{R}^n \to \mathbf{C}(\mathbb{R}^n)$ is upper continuous, equivalently Scott continuous. Moreover, the Clarke sub-gradient satisfies a weak calculus. For locally Lipschitz maps $f, g : U \subseteq \mathbb{R}^n \to \mathbb{R}$,

(i) Sum: $\partial f(x) + \partial g(x) \supseteq \partial(f + g)(x)$.
(ii) Product: $(\partial f(x))g(x) + f(x)(\partial g(x)) \supseteq \partial(f \cdot g)(x)$

(iii) Chain rule: For $f, g : \mathbb{R} \to \mathbb{R}, \partial f(g(x)) \cdot \partial g(x) \supseteq \partial(f \circ g)(x)$.

The notion of the L-derivative, equivalent to the Clarke sub-gradient, for real-valued functions on finite dimensional Euclidean spaces has the following ingredients [8]. A function $f : U \subset \mathbb{R}^n \to \mathbb{R}$ has a non-empty generalized Lipschitz constant $b \in \mathbf{C}(\mathbb{R}^n)$ in a non-empty convex open set $a \subset \mathbb{R}^n$ if for all $x, y \in a$ we have $f(x) - f(y) \in b \cdot (x - y)$. The collection of all functions that have generalized Lipschitz constant b in a is denoted by $\delta(a, b)$, called the tie of a with b. The collection of all single-step functions $b\chi_a$ with $a \subset U$ and $f \in \delta(a, b)$ is bounded in $(U \to \mathbf{C}(\mathbb{R}^n))$ and thus the L-derivative of f defined as

$$\mathcal{L}f = \sup\{b\chi_a : f \in \delta(a, b)\}$$

is Scott-continuous function. Moreover, we have $\mathcal{L}f = \partial f$.

1.2 Stably Locally Compact Space and Semi-strong Proximity Lattice

We recall that in geometric logic one uses the open sets of a topological space as propositions or semi-decidable properties [25, 26]. If X is a topological space and $\Omega(X)$ its lattice of open sets, a propositional geometric theory is constructed as follows: For every open set $a \in \Omega(X)$, define a proposition P_a, i.e., every open set of X provides a property or predicate. For open sets a and b with $a \subseteq b$ stipulate: (i) $P_a \vdash P_b$. For a family of open sets S, stipulate: (ii) $P_{\cup S} \vdash \bigvee_{a \in S} P_a$. For a finite family of open sets S, stipulate: (iii) $\bigwedge_{a \in S} P_a \vdash P_{\cap S}$. The converses of (ii) and (iii) follow from (i). The nullary disjunction in (ii) is interpreted as **false** and the nullary conjunction in the converse of (iii) is interpreted as **truth**, i.e., $P_\emptyset \vdash$ **false** and $P_X \vdash$ **truth**.

We regard $x \in X$ as a model of the theory in which P_a is interpreted as **true** iff $x \in a$, i.e., $x \models a$ iff $x \in a$, or, a point is a model of a proposition if it is in the open set representing the proposition. It is possible that different points give rise to the same model, i.e., satisfy the same open sets, and it is also possible that a model does not arise by points in X in this way. For so-called sober spaces, as we will define below, we do have a one-to-one correspondence between points and models.

A topological space X is called *stably locally compact* [2, 18] if it is sober, locally compact and if the intersection of two compact saturated sets is compact. Recall that X is sober if its points are in bijection with the completely prime filters of its lattice of open sets. (A set is saturated if it is the intersection of its open neighbourhoods.) Equivalently, X is stably locally compact if and only if its lattice of open sets is a distributive continuous lattice which is also arithmetic, i.e., its way-below relation satisfies:

$$O \ll O_1, O_2 \Rightarrow O \ll O_1 \wedge O_2$$

The spaces $\mathbb{R}^n$, $\mathbf{I}\mathbb{R}^n$ and $\mathbf{C}(\mathbb{R}^n)$ are all stably locally compact spaces. The way-below relation for $\Omega(\mathbb{R}^n)$ is given by $O_1 \ll O_2$ iff $\overline{O_1}$ is compact and $\overline{O_1} \subset O_2$, whereas the way-below relation in $\mathbf{C}(\mathbb{R}^n)$, and thus $\mathbf{I}\mathbb{R}^n$, is given by Proposition 1. We can obtain a finitary representation of these spaces by a sub-lattice of open sets as we will now describe.

A *semi-strong proximity lattice* [13] consists of a tuple $(B; \vee, \wedge, 0, 1; \prec)$ in which $(B; \vee, \wedge, 0, 1)$ is a distributive lattice such that $\prec$ is a binary relation on B with $\prec = \prec \circ \prec$ satisfying:

1. $\forall a \in B\ M \subset_f B.\, M \prec a \Leftrightarrow \bigvee M \prec a.$
2. $\forall a \in B.\, a \neq 1 \Rightarrow a \prec 1.$
3. $\forall a, a_1, a_2 \in B.\, a \prec a_1, a_2 \Leftrightarrow a \prec a_1 \wedge a_2.$
4. $\forall a, x, y \in B.\, a \prec x \vee y \Rightarrow$
   $\exists x', y' \in B.\, x' \prec x \,\&\, y' \prec y \,\&\, a \prec x' \vee y'.$

Here, $M \subset_f B$ means that M is a finite (possibly empty) subset of B, and $M \prec a$ means that $\forall m \in M.\, m \prec a$.

The relation $R \subseteq B_1 \times B_2$, between two semi-strong proximity lattice, is a *localic approximable mapping* if it satisfies:

1. $R \circ \prec_2 = R$
2. $\prec_1 \circ R = R.$
3. $\forall M \subset_f B_1 \forall b \in B_2.\, M\, R\, b \iff \bigvee M\, R\, b.$
4. $\forall a \in B_1.\, a \neq 1 \Rightarrow a\, R\, 1.$
5. $\forall a \in B_1 \forall a_1, a_2 \in B_2.\, a\, R\, a_1 \,\&\, a\, R\, a_2 \Leftrightarrow a\, R\, a_1 \wedge a_2.$
6. $\forall a \in B_1 \forall M \subset_f B_2.\, a\, R \bigvee M \Rightarrow$
   $\exists N \subset_f B_1.\, a \prec_1 \bigvee N \,\&\, \forall n \in N \exists m \in M.\, n\, R\, m.$

The identity approximable mapping on B is $\prec_B$ and composition of approximable mappings is the usual composition of the relations in the same order as for functions.

Let **SL-Compact** denote the category of all stably locally compact spaces and continuous functions and let **Semi-Strong PL** denote the category of semi-strong proximity lattice and approximable mappings. The following functors between these categories establish an equivalence between them [13,19].

$$A : \textbf{SL-Compact} \to \textbf{Semi-Strong PL}$$
$$G : \textbf{Semi-Strong PL} \to \textbf{SL-Compact}$$

Given a stably locally compact space X, fix a basis B of its topology which is closed under finite intersections and let $A(X)$ be the semi-strong proximity lattice based on B. Given a continuous function $f : X_1 \to X_2$ between two stably locally compact spaces, we have a localic approximable mapping $A_f : A(X_1) \to A(X_2)$ given by $a\, A_f\, b$ iff $a \ll f^{-1}(b)$.

Given a semi-strong proximity lattice B, the spectrum $\mathsf{spec(B)}$ of B is the set of all prime filters of B. For $x \in B$ let $\mathcal{O}_x = \{F \in \mathsf{spec(B)} : x \in F\}$. The collection of $\mathcal{O}_x$'s, $x \in B$, is a base of a topology over $\mathsf{spec(B)}$. Put,

$$G(B) = spec(B)$$

Given a localic approximable mapping $R : B_1 \to B_2$ define,

$$G_R : \mathsf{spec}(\mathsf{B}_1) \to \mathsf{spec}(\mathsf{B}_2)$$

by $G_R(F) = \{b_2 \in B_2 : \exists b_1 \in F.b_1 \, R \, b_2\}$. We have, $A_{G_R} = R$ and $G_{A_f} = f$. Thus, the category of semi-strong proximity lattice with approximable mappings is equivalent to the category of stably locally compact spaces and continuous functions [13].

We now construct some canonical bases of $\mathbf{C}(\mathbb{R}^n)$ and $\mathbf{I}\mathbb{R}^n$, which provide us with the semi-strong proximity lattices these spaces can be represented by. Let $B^0_{\mathbb{R}^n}$, respectively B^0_U, for $U \subset \mathbb{R}^n$, be any basis of $\mathbb{R}^n$, respectively U, that consists of bounded convex open sets and is closed under finite intersections. We let $B_{\mathbb{R}^n}$, respectively B_U, denote the semi-strong proximity lattice generated by $B^0_{\mathbb{R}}$, respectively B^0_U. This means that every element of $B_{\mathbb{R}}$, respectively B_U, is a finite join of elements of $B^0_{\mathbb{R}^n}$, respectively B^0_U [13].

It now follows, by Proposition 1, that $B^0_{\mathbf{C}(\mathbb{R}^n)} = \{\Box a : a \in B^0_{\mathbb{R}^n}\}$ is a basis of the Scott topology $\sigma_{\mathbf{C}(\mathbb{R}^n)}$, which is closed under finite intersections. Let $B_{\mathbf{C}(\mathbb{R}^n)}$ be the semi-strong proximity lattice generated by $B^0_{\mathbf{C}(\mathbb{R}^n)}$. Thus, each element of the semi-strong proximity lattice $B_{\mathbf{C}(\mathbb{R}^n)}$ is the finite join of elements of $B^0_{\mathbf{C}(\mathbb{R}^n)}$.

Finally, let $\mathcal{T}(U)$ be a basis of $U \subset \mathbb{R}^n$ consisting of open hyper-rectangles in U with faces parallel to the coordinate planes and let $\mathcal{T} := \mathcal{T}(\mathbb{R}^n)$. Then $B^0_{\mathbf{I}\mathbb{R}^n} = \{\Box a : a \in \mathcal{T}\}$ is a basis for $\sigma_{\mathbf{I}\mathbb{R}^n}$. By using $\mathcal{T}(U)$, we similarly obtain a basis $B^0_{\mathbf{I}U}$ for $\mathbf{I}U \subset \mathbf{I}\mathbb{R}^n$. Again by Proposition 1(i) these bases are closed under finite intersections. We let $B_{\mathbf{I}\mathbb{R}^n}$, respectively, $B_{\mathbf{I}U}$ be the semi-strong proximity lattices generated by $B^0_{\mathbf{I}\mathbb{R}^n}$, respectively, $B^0_{\mathbf{I}U}$. Thus, each element of $B_{\mathbf{I}\mathbb{R}^n}$, respectively, $B_{\mathbf{I}U}$, is the finite join of elements of $B^0_{\mathbf{I}\mathbb{R}^n}$, respectively, $B^0_{\mathbf{I}U}$.

The functors A and G thus provide a bijection between the two hom-sets:

$$(\mathbf{I}U \to \mathbf{I}\mathbb{R}) \underset{\mathrm{A}}{\overset{\mathrm{G}}{\leftrightarrows}} (B_{\mathbf{I}U} \to B_{\mathbf{I}\mathbb{R}})$$

and between the two hom-sets:

$$(\mathbf{I}U \to \mathbf{C}(\mathbb{R}^n)) \underset{\mathrm{A}}{\overset{\mathrm{G}}{\leftrightarrows}} (B_{\mathbf{I}U} \to B_{\mathbf{C}(\mathbb{R}^n)})$$

These bijections are used later to deduce our Stone duality results.

1.3 Related Work

Differentiation in logical form for functions of type $U \subseteq \mathbb{R}^n \to \mathbb{R}$ was introduced in [13]. These maps were represented by localic approximable mappings of type $B_U \to B_{\mathbb{R}}$, and the localic approximable mapping of the L-derivative of these functions have the type $B_U \to B_{\mathbf{C}(\mathbb{R}^n)}$. The strong tie of a with b, denoted by $\delta_s(a, b)$, was defined as the collection of all functions $f : a \subseteq U \to \mathbb{R}$ such that there exists $a' \in B^0_{\mathbb{R}}$ and $b' \in \mathbf{C}(\mathbb{R}^n)$ with $a \ll a'$, $b \ll b'$ and $f \in \delta(a', b')$.

The approximable mappings $R : B_U \to B_{\mathbb{R}}$ has Lipschitz constant $O \in B_{\mathbf{C}(\mathbb{R}^n)}$ in $a \in B_U$, denoted by $R \in \Delta(a, O)$, if we have:

$$\forall a_1, a_2 \prec a, (a_1, a_2) \in \mathsf{Sep}, \exists a_1', a_2' \in B_{\mathbb{R}}.$$
$$a_1 \, R \, a_1', a_2 \, R \, a_2', a_1' - a_2' \prec O \cdot (a_1 - a_2)$$

where the separation predicate $\mathsf{Sep} \subset B_U \times B_U$ means $(a_1, a_2) \in \mathsf{Sep}$ if there exists a_1', a_2' such that $a_1 \prec a_1', a_2 \prec a_2'$ and $a_1' \wedge a_2' = 0$. The strong knot $\Delta_s(a, O)$ is defined as the set of approximable mappings $R : B_U \to B_{\mathbb{R}}$ such that there exists $a' \in B_U$, $O' \in B_{\mathbf{C}(\mathbb{R}^n)}$ with $a \prec a'$, $O' \prec O$ and $R \in \Delta(a', O')$.

The strong ties and strong knots are dual to each others, i.e., $R \in \Delta_s(a, O)$ iff $G_R \in \delta_s(a, \overline{O})$. The Lipschitzian derivative of $R : B_U \to B_{\mathbb{R}}$ is defined as the approximable mapping

$$\mathsf{L}(R) = \sup\{A_{\overline{O}\chi_a} : R \in \Delta_s(a, O)\}$$

It turns out that $\mathsf{L}(R) = A_{\mathcal{L}G_R}$ and we have a weak calculus which matches that for the Clarke sub-gradient stated after Eq. (1), i.e., $\mathsf{L}(R_1) + \mathsf{L}(R_2) \subseteq \mathsf{L}(R_1 + R_2)$ and $R_1 \cdot \mathsf{L}(R_2) + R_2 \cdot \mathsf{L}(R_1) \subseteq \mathsf{L}(R_1 \cdot R_2)$, and if at least one of R_1 and R_2 is a continuously differentiable approximable mapping then equality holds. A weak form of the chain rule also holds for composition of approximable mappings corresponding to that for the Clarke sub-gradient.

2 L-derivative with Imprecise Inputs

We start by defining a notion of tie for Scott continuous map of type $f : \mathbf{I}U \to \mathbf{I}\mathbb{R}$, for an open convex subset $U \subset \mathbb{R}^n$. From now on, in the rest of the paper, we assume $f : \mathbf{I}U \to \mathbf{I}\mathbb{R}$ is Scott-continuous.

Definition 1. *Let $f : \mathbf{I}U \subseteq \mathbf{I}\mathbb{R}^n \to \mathbf{I}\mathbb{R}$ where $U \subset \mathbb{R}^n$ is an open set, be Scott continuous and $a \in \mathcal{T}(U)$, an open hyper-rectangle in U, and $b \in \mathbf{C}(\mathbb{R}^n)$. We say f has a* generalized Lipschitz constant *b in $\Box a$ and write $\delta(\Box a, b)$ if we have:*

$$\forall x, y \in \Box a, x \cap y = \emptyset. \, f(x) - f(y) \subseteq b \cdot (x - y)$$

In the one dimensional case, this new notion is a modification of that in [12] as we in Definition 1, require the hyper-rectangles x and y to be disjoint, i.e., inconsistent in $\mathbf{I}U$. Thus, the condition for membership of a tie is weaker. We will need this weaker condition in order to develop the Stone duality result later in the paper.

We show that despite this weaker notion, if $f \in \delta(\Box a, b)$ with $b \neq \bot$, then f preserves maximal elements and its restriction to maximal elements gives a Lipschitz map. In other words f is the extension of a classical Lipschitz function in $\mathbf{I}a$.

Proposition 2. *Let $f \in \delta(\Box a, b)$, where $a \subset \mathbb{R}^n$ is a open hyper-rectangle and $b \in \mathbf{C}(\mathbb{R}^n) \setminus \{\bot\}$, then for each $x \in a$, $f(\{x\}) \in \mathbf{I}\mathbb{R}$ is maximal and the induced function $\hat{f} : a \subset \mathbb{R}^n \to \mathbb{R}$ is Lipschitz and satisfies:*

$$\forall x_1, x_2 \in a. (b \cdot (x_1 - x_2))^- \leq \hat{f}(x_1) - \hat{f}(x_2) \leq (b \cdot (x_1 - x_2))^+ \tag{2}$$

$$\forall x_1, x_2 \in a. |\hat{f}(x_1) - \hat{f}(x_2)| \leq \|b\| \|x_1 - x_2\|, \tag{3}$$

where $\|b\| = \max\{\|L\| | L \in b\}$.

Corollary 1. *If $f \in \delta(\Box a, b)$ then $\hat{f} \in \delta(a, b)$.*

Definition 2. *We say a Scott continuous function of type $\mathbf{I}U \subset \mathbf{I}\mathbb{R}^n \to \mathbf{I}\mathbb{R}$ is* locally Lipschitz *in $\Box a$, for $a \in \mathcal{T}(U)$, if it belongs to a tie $\delta(\Box a, b)$ with $b \neq \bot$.*

Given a continuous function $f : U \subseteq \mathbb{R}^n \to \mathbb{R}$, its maximal extension to a Scott continuous function $\mathbf{I}U \subseteq \mathbf{I}\mathbb{R}^n \to \mathbf{I}\mathbb{R}$ is denoted by $\mathbf{I}f$ with $\mathbf{I}f(x) = f[x]$ for $x \in \mathbf{I}U$ when $x \neq \bot$ and $\mathbf{I}f(\bot) = \bot$.

Corollary 2. *$f \in \delta(a, b)$ iff $\mathbf{I}f \in \delta(\Box a, b)$.*

If $(A, \sqsubseteq)$ is a dcpo then the consistency predicate $\mathsf{Con}_{(A,\sqsubseteq)}$ and $\mathsf{Con}_{(A,\ll)}$ for a finite subset $\{a_i : i \in I\}$ with respect to $\sqsubseteq$ and $\ll$ are defined as follow:

$$\mathsf{Con}_{(A,\sqsubseteq)}\{a_i : i \in I\} \iff \exists a \in A, \forall i \in I. a_i \sqsubseteq a$$

and

$$\mathsf{Con}_{(A,\ll)}\{a_i : i \in I\} \iff \exists a \in A, \forall i \in I. a_i \ll a$$

For the collection $(b_i \chi_{a_i})_{i \in I}$ or $(b_i \chi_{\Box a_i})_{i \in I}$ for finite indexing set I where $a_i \in \Omega(\mathbb{R}^n)$ are open hyper-rectangles and $b_i \in (D, \sqsubseteq)$, the function space consistency predicate $\mathsf{Con}_{\mathbb{R}^n \to D}$ or $\mathsf{Con}_{\mathbf{I}\mathbb{R}^n \to D}$ is defined as follows:

$$\mathsf{Con}_{\mathbb{R}^n \to D}(b_i \chi_{a_i})_{i \in I} \iff \forall J \subseteq I. [\mathsf{Con}_{(\Omega(\mathbb{R}^n),\gg)}\{a_i : i \in J\} \Rightarrow \mathsf{Con}_{(D,\sqsubseteq)}\{b_i : i \in J\}]$$

$$\mathsf{Con}_{\mathbf{I}\mathbb{R}^n \to D}(b_i \chi_{\Box a_i})_{i \in I} \iff \forall J \subseteq I. [\mathsf{Con}_{(\Omega(\mathbf{I}\mathbb{R}^n),\gg)}\{\Box a_i : i \in J\} \Rightarrow \mathsf{Con}_{(D,\sqsubseteq)}\{b_i : i \in J\}].$$

It follows that the supremum $\sup_{i \in I} b_i \chi_{a_i}$ exists iff $\mathsf{Con}_{\mathbb{R}^n \to D}(b_i \chi_{a_i})_{i \in I}$ and $\sup_{i \in I} b_i \chi_{\Box a_i}$ exists iff $\mathsf{Con}_{\mathbf{I}\mathbb{R}^n \to D}(b_i \chi_{\Box a_i})_{i \in I}$.

Proposition 3. *For any indexing set J the family of step functions $(b_j \chi_{\Box a_j})_{j \in J}$ is consistent if $\bigcap_{j \in J} \delta(\Box a_j, b_j) \neq \emptyset$.*

Proof. Suppose $f \in \bigcap_{j \in J} \delta(\Box a_j, b_j)$ then $\hat{f} \in \bigcap_{j \in J} \delta(a_j, b_j)$, and hence $(b_j \chi_{a_j})_{j \in J}$ is consistent, which implies $(b_j \chi_{\Box a_j})_{j \in J}$ is consistent. ■

Recall that a crescent in $\mathbb{R}^n$ is the intersection of a closed and an open set. Given two points $p, q \in \mathbb{R}^n$, we denote the closed, respectively open, line segment between them by $[p, q] = \{\lambda p + (1 - \lambda)q : 0 \leq \lambda \leq 1\}$, respectively $(p, q) = \{\lambda p + (1 - \lambda)q : 0 < \lambda < 1\}$.

Proposition 4. *We have* $\delta(\Box a, b) \supseteq \bigcap_{j\in J} \delta(\Box a_j, b_j)$ *if* $b\chi_{\Box a} \sqsubseteq \sup_{j\in J} b_j\chi_{\Box a_j}$.

Proof. Let $g := \sup_{j\in J} b_j\chi_{\Box a_j}$. Suppose $b\chi_{\Box a} \sqsubseteq \sup_{j\in J} b_j\chi_{\Box a_j}$, then $\Box a \subset \bigcup_{j\in J} \Box a_j$ and thus $a \subset \bigcup_{j\in J} a_j$. In addition, by considering the restriction of g to the maximal elements of $\mathbf{I}\mathbb{R}^n$, we find that a is partitioned by the open sets a_j, $j \in J$, into a finite number of disjoint crescents c_i, $i \in I$, with

$$g(\{r\}) = \sup_{c_i \subset a_j} b_j \sqsupseteq b$$

for $r \in c_i$. Let $f \in \bigcap_{j\in J} \delta(\Box a_j, b_j)$. We show that $f \in \delta(\Box a, b)$. Suppose we have two hyper-rectangles $x, y \in \Box a$ with $x \cap y = \emptyset$. Let the points $p \in x$ and $q \in y$ be such that $\|p - q\|$ is the minimum distance between x and y. Then $[p, q]$ is partitioned by the crescents c_i, $i \in I$, into a finite number of one-dimensional intervals such that the one-dimensional interior of each is contained in c_i for some $i \in I$. Let $r_0, r_1, \ldots, r_k \in \mathbb{R}^n$ be the boundary points of these intervals ordered from p to q. Then, using the continuity of $\hat{f}$, we have:

$$f(\{r_t\}) - f(\{r_{t+1}\}) \subseteq \sup_{(r_t, r_{t+1}) \subseteq c_j} b_j \cdot (\{r_t\} - \{r_{t+1}\}) \subseteq b \cdot (\{r_t\} - \{r_{t+1}\})$$

for $0 \leq t \leq n - 1$. Since $x \in \Box a$, there exists $j \in J$ with $x \in \Box a_j$. Moreover, $x \subseteq a_j$ iff $r_0 \in \overline{a_j}$. Similarly, $y \subseteq a_j$ iff $r_k \in \overline{a_j}$. From these relations, we obtain:

$$f(x) - f(\{r_0\}) \subseteq \sup_{x \subset a_j} b_j \cdot (x - \{r_0\}), \quad f(\{r_k\}) - f(y) \subseteq \sup_{y \subset a_j} b_j \cdot (\{r_k\} - y)$$

Thus,

$$\begin{aligned} f(x) - f(y) &= f(x) - f(\{r_0\}) + f(\{r_0\}) - \cdots - f(\{r_k\}) + f(\{r_k\}) - f(y) \\ &\subseteq b \cdot \left(x - \left(\sum_{t=0}^{k-1} f(\{r_t\}) - f(\{r_t\})\right) - y\right) = b \cdot (x - y) \; \blacksquare \end{aligned}$$

Definition 3. *The derivative of a Scott continuous map* $f : \mathbf{I}U \subset \mathbf{I}\mathbb{R}^n \to \mathbf{I}\mathbb{R}$ *is the map:*

$$\mathcal{L}f = \sup_{f \in \delta(\Box a, b)} b\chi_{\Box a} : \mathbf{I}U \to \mathbf{C}(\mathbb{R}^n)$$

where U *is a convex open subset of* $\mathbb{R}^n$.

Theorem 1. *(i)* $\mathcal{L}f$ *is well-defined and Scott continuous.*
(ii) $f \in \delta(\Box a, b)$ *iff* $b\chi_{\Box a} \sqsubseteq \mathcal{L}f$.

Proof. (i) Let the indexing set J be defined by $j \in J \iff f \in \delta(\Box a_j, b_j)$, then $f \in \bigcap_{j\in J} \delta(\Box a_j, b_j)$. Thus, by Proposition 3 $(b_j\chi_{\Box a_j})_{j\in J}$ is consistent therefore, $\mathcal{L}f = \sup_{f\in\delta(\Box a, b)} b\chi_{\Box a}$ exists and is Scott continuous.

(ii) If $f \in \delta(\Box a, b)$ then clearly $b\chi_{\Box a} \sqsubseteq \mathcal{L}f$. Now take $a' \ll a$ and $b' \ll b$. Then $b'\chi_{\Box a'} \ll b\chi_{\Box a} \sqsubseteq \mathcal{L}f$ and there exists a finite indexing set J such that $b'\chi_{\Box a'} \sqsubseteq \sup_{j\in J} b_j\chi_{\Box a_j}$ and $f \in \delta(\Box a_j, b_j)$ for $j \in J$. Now by Proposition 4, we have $\bigcap_{j\in J} \delta(\Box a_j, b_j) \subseteq \delta(\Box a', b')$, and thus, $f \in \delta(\Box a', b')$. From this, it follows that $f \in \delta(\Box a, b)$. ■

If $f : U \subseteq \mathbb{R}^n \to \mathbb{R}$ is a locally Lipschitz map, then the Clarke sub-gradient $\mathcal{L}f : U \to \mathbf{C}(\mathbb{R}^n)$ extends, by Scott's extension theory for densely injective spaces [24], to a Scott continuous map $\mathbf{I}(\mathcal{L}f) : \mathbf{I}U \to \mathbf{C}(\mathbb{R}^n)$. We then have:

Proposition 5.

$$\mathcal{L}(\mathbf{I}f) = \mathbf{I}(\mathcal{L}f)$$

Proof. This follows from the relation:

$$f \in \delta(a, b) \iff \mathbf{I}f \in \delta(\Box a, b),$$

for all $a \in \Omega(U)$ and $b \in \mathbf{C}(\mathbb{R}^n)$. ∎

The following example shows that in the context of the L-derivative of interval functions, Clarke's weak calculus no longer holds for Sum.

Example 1. Let $f, g : \mathbf{I}\mathbb{R} \to \mathbf{I}\mathbb{R}$ defined by $f(x) = x$ and $g(x) = -x$, then $\mathcal{L}f(x) = \{1\}$ and $\mathcal{L}g(x) = \{-1\}$ and thus $\mathcal{L}f(x) + \mathcal{L}g(x) = \{0\}$. On the other hand, $(f + g)(x) = f(x) + g(x) = x - x$ and it follows that $f + g \notin \delta(\Box a, \{0\})$, for any open set $a \subset \mathbb{R}$, and consequently $\mathcal{L}(f + g) \neq \{0\}$. Hence, $\mathcal{L}(f + g)(x) \nsubseteq \mathcal{L}f(x) + \mathcal{L}g(x)$.

We say an interval $[r^-, r^+]$ is *positive* , respectively *negative*, if $r^- > 0$, respectively $r^+ < 0$. The above counter-example is the consequence of the fact that in interval arithmetic, while the relation $(u + v)w \subseteq uw + vw$ always holds for $u, v, w \in \mathbf{I}\mathbb{R}$, the converse relation $(u + v)w \supseteq uw + vw$ may fail. However, if u and v are both positive or both negative then the converse also holds [21, p. 13].

We can obtain a weak calculus for sum and product of two functions f and g if we first use an operation that is routinely performed in interval analysis, namely to approximate the values $\mathcal{L}f(x)$ and $\mathcal{L}g(x)$ with the smallest axes aligned hyper-rectangle containing it, and then assume that the two induced hyper-rectangles have the same sign in each of their components. We now formalise this procedure.

Let $H : \mathbf{C}(\mathbb{R}^n) \to \mathbf{I}\mathbb{R}^n$ be the map that takes every convex compact set to the smallest axes aligned hyper-rectangle containing it. Then, it is easy to check that H is Scott continuous. Let $\pi_i : \mathbb{R}^n \to \mathbb{R}$ be the projection of the ith coordinate and extend it pointwise to its maximal extension $\mathbf{I}\pi_i : \mathbf{I}\mathbb{R}^n \to \mathbf{I}\mathbb{R}$. Define the predicate $\mathsf{Sgn} \subset (\mathbf{I}\mathbb{R}^n)^2$ by $(x, y) \in \mathsf{Sgn}$ if for each $i = 1, \ldots, n$ the two intervals $\mathbf{I}\pi_i(x)$ and $\mathbf{I}\pi_i(y)$ are either both positive or both negative.

Suppose $x, y, z \in \mathbf{I}\mathbb{R}^n$ and $(y, z) \in \mathsf{Sgn}$, then the interval $\mathbf{I}\pi_i(y)\mathbf{I}\pi_i(z)$ is positive for each $i = 1 \ldots, n$ and we have $x(y + z) = xy + xz$. In fact,

$$\mathbf{I}\pi_i(x)(\mathbf{I}\pi_i(y) + \mathbf{I}\pi_i(z)) = \mathbf{I}\pi_i(x)\mathbf{I}\pi_i(y) + \mathbf{I}\pi_i(x)\mathbf{I}\pi_i(z),$$

and hence:

$$\begin{aligned} x(y + z) &= \sum_{i=1}^{n} \mathbf{I}\pi_i(x)(\mathbf{I}\pi_i(y) + \mathbf{I}\pi_i(z)) = \sum_{i=1}^{n} \mathbf{I}\pi_i(x)\mathbf{I}\pi_i(y) + \mathbf{I}\pi_i(x)\mathbf{I}\pi_i(z) \\ &= \sum_{i=1}^{n} \mathbf{I}\pi_i(x)\mathbf{I}\pi_i(y) + \sum_{i=1}^{n} \mathbf{I}\pi_i(x)\mathbf{I}\pi_i(z) = xy + xz \end{aligned}$$

Proposition 6. *Suppose $f, g : \mathbf{I}U \subseteq \mathbf{I}\mathbb{R}^n \to \mathbf{I}\mathbb{R}$ are locally Lipschitz functions and $x \in \mathbf{I}U$ is such that $(H(\mathcal{L}f(x)), H(\mathcal{L}g(x))) \in \mathsf{Sgn}$. Then:*

1.
$$H(\mathcal{L}f(x)) + H(\mathcal{L}g(x)) \supseteq H(\mathcal{L}(f+g)(x))$$

2. *If, in addition, $(f(x), g(x)) \in \mathsf{Sgn}$, then we also have:*
$$f(x)H(\mathcal{L}g(x)) + g(x)H(\mathcal{L}f(x)) \supseteq H(\mathcal{L}(fg)(x))$$

We will provide the proof for a weak form of the chain rule, which is more involved compared to sum and product. First consider the extended scalar multiplication $M : \mathbf{C}(\mathbb{R}^n) \times \mathbf{I}\mathbb{R}^+ \to \mathbf{C}(\mathbb{R}^n)$, where $\mathbb{R}^+$ is the set of non-negative reals, with $M(b, x) = \{ur : u \in b, r \in x\}$. Then, M is well-defined and Scott continuous. For ease of presentation, we write $M(b, x) = bx$.

Proposition 7. *If $g : \mathbf{I}U_1 \subseteq \mathbf{I}\mathbb{R}^n \to \mathbf{I}\mathbb{R}$ and $f : \mathbf{I}U_2 \subseteq \mathbf{I}\mathbb{R} \to \mathbf{I}\mathbb{R}$ and $\mathsf{Im}(g) \subset \mathbf{I}U_2$ with $(\mathcal{L}f)(g(x)) \in \mathbf{I}\mathbb{R}^+$, are Scott-continuous, then:*

$$((\mathcal{L}f) \circ g)(x)\mathcal{L}g(x) \supseteq \mathcal{L}(f \circ g)(x)$$

3 Lipschitzian Approximable Mapping

Recall that, since $\mathbf{I}\mathbb{R}^n$, $\mathbf{C}(\mathbb{R}^n)$ and $\mathbb{R}^n$ are stably locally compact space and the category of stably locally compact spaces with continuous functions and the category of semi-strong proximity lattice with approximable mappings are equivalent, any continuous function $f : \mathbf{I}U \subset \mathbf{I}\mathbb{R}^n \to \mathbf{I}\mathbb{R}$ defines an approximable mapping $A_f : B_{\mathbf{I}U} \to B_{\mathbf{I}\mathbb{R}}$ by $\Box a A_f \Box a' \iff \Box a \ll f^{-1}(\Box a')$. On the other hand any approximable mapping with type $R : B_{\mathbf{I}\mathbb{R}^n} \to B_D$, where D is either $\mathbf{I}\mathbb{R}$ or $\mathbf{I}\mathbb{R}^n$ or $\mathbf{C}(\mathbb{R}^n)$, gives us a continuous function $G_R : \mathbf{I}\mathbb{R}^n \to D$.

Lemma 1. *Let $f : \mathbf{I}U \subset \mathbf{I}\mathbb{R}^n \to \mathbf{I}\mathbb{R}$ be a Scott continuous function such that $f(\{x\})$ is singleton for all $x \in U$. Suppose a_1 is an open hyper-rectangle in U and a_2 is an open interval. If $\hat{f} : U \subset \mathbb{R}^n \to \mathbb{R}$ is the induced function with $f(\{x\}) = \{\hat{f}(x)\}$ then:*

$$\Box a_1 \ll f^{-1}(\Box a_2) \Rightarrow a_1 \ll \hat{f}^{-1}(a_2) \qquad \Box a_1\ A_f\ \Box a_2 \Rightarrow a_1\ A_{\hat{f}}\ a_2$$

Recall the definition of the predicate $\mathsf{Sep} \subset B_{\mathbb{R}} \times B_{\mathbb{R}}$ from Subsect. 1.3.

Definition 4. *We say an approximable mapping $R : B_{\mathbf{I}U} \to B_{\mathbf{I}\mathbb{R}}$, where $U \subset \mathbb{R}^n$ is a convex open set, has Lipschitzian constant O in $\Box a$, with $O \in B^0_{\mathbb{R}^n}$ and $a \in \mathcal{T}(U)$, if:*

$$\forall a_1, a_2 \in \mathcal{T}(U).\, a_1, a_2 \prec a \,\&\, (a_1, a_2) \in \mathsf{Sep}\ \exists a_1', a_2' \in B_{\mathbb{R}}.$$
$$\Box a_1\, R\, \Box a_1', \Box a_2\, R\, \Box a_2' \ \&\ a_1' - a_2' \prec O \cdot (a_1 - a_2),$$

and we say R is Lipschitzian *in $\Box a$. The set of all approximable mappings with the above property is denoted by $\Delta(\Box a, O)$, called the* knot *of $\Box a$ and O.*

Note that, by Proposition 1, the last formula in Definition 4 is equivalent to $\Box a_1' - \Box a_2' \prec \Box O \cdot (\Box a_1 - \Box a_2)$. Given this equivalence, it is simpler to use the formula without the modal operator $\Box$ as we have done in this definition. By Proposition 1 and Stone duality, we have:

Proposition 8. *Suppose $f : \mathbf{I}U \to \mathbf{I}\mathbb{R}$ is a Scott continuous function such that $f(\{x\})$ is singleton for every $x \in U$. Then we have: $A_{\hat{f}} \in \Delta(a, O)$ if $A_f \in \Delta(\Box a, O)$.*

From $\Delta(\Box a, O)$, a Lipschitz property of G_R can be deduced as follows.

Proposition 9. *If $R : B_{\mathbf{I}U} \to B_{\mathbf{I}\mathbb{R}}$ is an approximable mapping such that $R \in \Delta(\Box a, O)$ then:*

$$\forall x, y \in \Box a.\, x \cap y = \emptyset \Rightarrow G_R(x) - G_R(y) \subseteq \overline{O} \cdot (x - y)$$

Proof. Let $x, y \in \Box a$ and $x \cap y = \emptyset$, then consider $a_1, a_2 \in \mathcal{T}(U)$ such that $(a_1, a_2) \in \mathsf{Sep}$ and $x \in \Box a_1, y \in \Box a_2$. Hence, there exist $a_1', a_2' \in B_{\mathbb{R}}$ such that $\Box a_i \, R \, \Box a_i', i = 1, 2$ and:

$$a_1' - a_2' \prec O \cdot (a_1 - a_2)$$

By Stone duality we have $R = R_{G_R}$. Hence $\Box a_i \prec G_R^{-1}(\Box a_i'), i = 1, 2$, and thus:,

$$G_R(x) - G_R(y) \subseteq O \cdot (a_1 - a_2).$$

Since this holds for all sufficiently small a_1 and a_2 that contain x and y respectively, we obtain: $G_R(x) - G_R(y) \subseteq \overline{O} \cdot (x - y)$. ■

Corollary 3. *If $R \in \Delta(\Box a, O)$ then $G_R \in \delta(\Box a, \overline{O})$.*

Thus, if A_f is a Lipschitzian approximable mapping of type $B_{\mathbf{I}U} \to B_{\mathbf{I}\mathbb{R}}$ then f is a Lipschitz function of type $\mathbf{I}U \to \mathbf{I}\mathbb{R}$ and hence $f(\{x\})$ is a singleton for every $x \in U$ and the induced function $\hat{f} : U \to \mathbb{R}$ is also Lipschitz.

Now we are in a position to obtain duality results similar to those in [13] for functions of type $\mathbf{I}U \subseteq \mathbf{I}\mathbb{R}^n \to \mathbf{I}\mathbb{R}$.

Proposition 10. *Let $f \in \delta(\Box a, b)$ then for every $a_0 \in \mathcal{T}$ such that $a_0 \prec a$ and every $O \in B^0_{\mathbb{R}^n}$ such that $b \subset O$ we have $A_f \in \Delta(\Box a_0, O)$.*

Proof. Suppose $a_0 \prec a$. Let $a_1, a_2 \in \mathcal{T}(U)$ with $(a_1, a_2) \in \mathsf{Sep}$ and $a_1, a_2 \prec a_0$. Then, since $\overline{a_1}, \overline{a_2} \in \mathbf{I}U$, from definition of the tie $\delta(\Box a, b)$, we have,

$$\begin{aligned} f(\overline{a_1}) - f(\overline{a_2}) &\subseteq b \cdot (\overline{a_1} - \overline{a_2}) \\ &\subseteq O \cdot (a_1 - a_2). \end{aligned}$$

Since $f(\overline{a_1}), f(\overline{a_2}) \in \mathbf{I}\mathbb{R}$ are compact, there exist open hyper-rectangles $a_1', a_2' \in B_{\mathbb{R}}$ such that $f(\overline{a_i}) \subseteq a_i', i = 1, 2$, and $a_1' - a_2' \prec O \cdot (a_1 - a_2)$. This implies $A_f \in \Delta(\Box a_0, O)$. ■

Example 2. Let $f : \mathbf{I}\mathbb{R} \to \mathbf{I}\mathbb{R}$ be given by:

$$f([x_1, x_2]) = [x_1 - \delta(x_2 - x_1), x_2 + \delta(x_2 - x_1)]$$

for $\delta > 0$. The restriction $\hat{f}$ of f to the maximal elements of $\mathbf{I}\mathbb{R}$ is the identity function of type $\hat{f} = \mathrm{Id} : \mathbb{R} \to \mathbb{R}$. Since $\mathbf{I}\mathrm{Id} \neq f$, the map f is not the maximal extension of the identity map Id. On the other hand, $A_f : B_{\mathbf{I}\mathbb{R}} \to B_{\mathbf{I}\mathbb{R}}$ satisfies $A_f \in \Delta(\Box\mathbb{R}, O)$ iff $(1-\delta, 1+\delta) \subseteq O$. However, $A_{\hat{f}} \in \Delta(\mathbb{R}, O)$ iff $1 \in O$.

The following two propositions represent a domain isomorphism between the function space $(\mathbf{I}U \to \mathbf{C}(\mathbb{R}^n))$ and the domain of approximable mappings $(B_{\mathbf{I}U} \to B_{\mathbf{C}(\mathbb{R}^n)})$ ordered by inclusion.

Proposition 11. *1. For $f_1, f_2 : \mathbf{I}U \to \mathbf{C}(\mathbb{R}^n)$ we have:*

$$f_1 \sqsubseteq f_2 \iff A_{f_1} \subseteq A_{f_2}$$

2. For $R_1, R_2 : B_{\mathbf{I}U} \to B_{\mathbf{C}(\mathbb{R}^n)}$ we have:

$$R_1 \subseteq R_2 \iff G_{R_1} \sqsubseteq G_{R_2}$$

Proposition 12. *1. If $(f_i)_{i\in I}$ is a directed set in $\mathbf{I}U \to \mathbf{C}(\mathbb{R}^n)$, with supremum $f = \sup_{i\in I} f_i$, then $\bigcup_{i\in I} A_{f_i} = A_f$ in $\mathsf{App}(B_{\mathbf{I}U}, B_{\mathbf{C}(\mathbb{R}^n)})$.*
2. If $(R_i)_{i\in I}$ is a directed set in $\mathsf{App}(B_{\mathbf{I}U}, B_{\mathbf{C}(\mathbb{R}^n)})$ then $\sup_{i\in I} G_{R_i} = G_R$ in $(\mathbf{I}U \to \mathbf{C}(\mathbb{R}^n))$ where $R = \sup_{i\in I} R_i$.

Definition 5. *If a is an open hyper-rectangle and O is a basic convex open set then the single-step approximable mapping $\eta_{(\Box a, O)}$ is defined as $\eta_{(\Box a, O)} = A_{\overline{O}\chi_{\Box a}} : B_{\mathbf{I}U} \to B_{\mathbf{C}(\mathbb{R}^n)}$.*

For defining the Lipschitzian derivative of an approximable mapping we first need to define the notions of a strong tie and a strong knot.

Definition 6. *We say $f : \mathbf{I}U \to \mathbf{I}\mathbb{R}$ has a* strong set-valued Lipschitz constant *$b \in \mathbf{C}(\mathbb{R}^n)$ in $\Box a$, for $a \in \mathcal{T}(U)$, denoted by $f \in \delta_s(\Box a, b)$, if there exist $a' \prec a$ and $b' \in \mathbf{C}(\mathbb{R}^n)$ with $b \ll_{\mathbf{C}(\mathbb{R}^n)} b'$ such that $f \in \delta(\Box a', b')$. We call $\delta_s(\Box a, b)$ the strong single-tie of $\Box a$ with b.*

From general results about single-step functions, [16] we know that if $b\chi_{\Box a} \ll \mathcal{L}f$, then for every $x \in \Box a$ we have $b \ll \mathcal{L}f(x)$, and hence, $\mathcal{L}f(x) \in \Uparrow b$. This means $\mathcal{L}f(\Box a) \subseteq \Uparrow b$. Moreover $\Box a \ll (\mathcal{L}f)^{-1}(\Uparrow b)$.

Similar to Proposition VII.3 in [13] and its corollary, we have:

Proposition 13. *If $f : \mathbf{I}U \to \mathbf{I}\mathbb{R}$ is locally Lipschitz, then:*

$$f \in \delta_s(\Box a, b) \iff b\chi_{\Box a} \ll \mathcal{L}f$$

$$\mathcal{L}f = \sup\{b\chi_{\Box a} : b\chi_{\Box a} \ll \mathcal{L}f\} = \sup\{b\chi_{\Box a} : f \in \delta_s(\Box a, b)\}$$

Definition 7. *We say an approximable mapping $R : B_{\mathbf{I}U} \to B_{\mathbf{I}\mathbb{R}}$ has* strong Lipschitz constant *O in $\square a$, for $O \in B^0_{\mathbb{R}^n}$ and $a \in \mathcal{T}(U)$, denoted by $R \in \Delta_s(\square a, O)$, if there exist $a' \in \mathcal{T}(U)$ with $a \prec a'$ and $O' \in B^0_{\mathbb{R}^n}$ with $O' \prec O$ such that $R \in \Delta(\square a', O')$.*

Proposition 14. *1. If $f \in \delta_s(\square a, b)$ then for all $O \in B^0_{\mathbb{R}^n}$ with $b \subset O$ we have $A_f \in \Delta_s(\square a, O)$.*
2. If $A_f \in \Delta_s(\square a, O)$ then there exists $b \subset O$ such that $f \in \delta_s(\square a, b)$.

Proof. 1. Let $f \in \delta_s(\square a, b)$ and $b \subset O$, then there exists $a' \in \mathcal{T}(U)$ with $a \prec a'$ and b' with $b \ll b'$ such that $f \in \delta(\square a', b')$. By the interpolation property of $\prec$ there exists a_0 with $a \prec a_0 \prec a'$ and O_0 with $b \subset O_0 \prec O$. By Proposition 10 we have $A_f \in \Delta(\square a_0, O_0)$ and thus $A_f \in \Delta_s(\square a, O)$.
2. Let $A_f \in \Delta_s(\square a, O)$ then by the definition of strong knot there exists a' with $a \prec a'$ and O' with $O' \prec O$ such that $A_f \in \Delta(\square a', O')$. By Corollary 3, $f \in \delta(\square a', \overline{O'})$. By the interpolation property, there exists O'' with, $O' \prec O'' \prec O$. Let $b' = \overline{O'}$ and $b = \overline{O''}$ then $b \prec b'$ and $f \in \delta(\square a', b')$. Hence, $f \in \delta_s(\square a, b)$. ■

Finally, we obtain the duality between strong ties and strong knots extending the main result in [13] to functions with interval input and output.

Corollary 4. *We have $R \in \Delta_s(\square a, O)$ iff $G_R \in \delta_s(\square a, \overline{O})$. Dually, we have $f \in \delta_s(\square a, b)$ iff $A_f \in \Delta_s(\square a, b^\circ)$.*

Definition 8. *Let $R : B_{\mathbf{I}U} \to B_{\mathbf{I}\mathbb{R}}$ be a Lipschitzian approximable mapping. The Lipschitzian derivative of R is defied as:*

$$L(R) = \sup\{\eta_{(\square a, O)} : R \in \Delta_s(\square a, O)\}$$

which is of type $B_{\mathbf{I}U} \to B_{\mathbf{C}(\mathbb{R}^n)}$.

The following theorem extends Theorem VII.12 in [13] to functions with interval input and output.

Theorem 2. *The Lipschitzian derivative of a Lipschitzian approximable mapping $R : B_{\mathbf{I}U} \to B_{\mathbf{I}\mathbb{R}}$ is an approximable mapping and we have: $L(R) = A_{\mathcal{L}G_R}$.*

4 Conclusion

We have developed a notion of sub-differentiation for Scott continuous maps which take hyper-rectangles in a finite dimensional Euclidean spaces to compact real intervals and is itself a Scott continuous map. This extends the domain of application of Interval Analysis to the classical derivative. It also extends Clarke's theory and that of the L-derivative to functions with imprecise input/output as one encounters in interval analysis and exact real number computation. The classical Clarke operator commutes with the extension operator that extends a non-empty convex and compact valued map of a finite dimensional Euclidean spaces to the space of the hyper-rectangles of the Euclidean space. We have derived a calculus for sub-differentiation of interval maps which is weaker than the corresponding Clarkes calculus for point maps. A Stone duality framework for sub-differentiation of interval maps is also constructed which allows for a program logic view of sub-differentiation. We envisage several areas for immediate further work, namely an implementation of this work in Haskell, an implementation in a theorem prover such as Coq and a derivation of a weak calculus for constructors of approximable mappings which would match the calculus for the interval functions.

References

1. Haskell Implementation of IC-Reals for Exact Real Computation. Imperial College London. http://www.doc.ic.ac.uk/exact-computation/Haskell
2. Abramsky, S., Jung, A.: Domain theory. In: Abramsky, S., Gabbay, D.M., Maibaum, T.S.E. (eds.) Handbook of Logic in Computer Science, vol. 3. Clarendon, Oxford (1994)
3. Bauer, A., Escardó, M.H., Simpson, A.: Comparing functional paradigms for exact real-number computation. In: Widmayer, P., Eidenbenz, S., Triguero, F., Morales, R., Conejo, R., Hennessy, M. (eds.) ICALP 2002. LNCS, vol. 2380, pp. 488–500. Springer, Heidelberg (2002). https://doi.org/10.1007/3-540-45465-9_42
4. Clarke, F.H.: Optimization and Nonsmooth Analysis. Wiley, New York (1983)
5. Di Gianantonio, P.: A functional approach to real number computation. Ph.D. thesis, University of Pisa (1993)
6. Di Gianantonio, P.: Real number computability and domain theory. Inf. Comput. **127**(1), 11–25 (1996)
7. Di Gianantonio, P., Edalat, A.: A language for differentiable functions. In: Proceedings of the 16th International Conference on Foundations of Software Science and Computation Structures (FoSSaCS) (2013)
8. Edalat, A.: A continuous derivative for real-valued functions. In: Cooper, S.B., Löwe, B., Sorbi, A. (eds.) CiE 2007. LNCS, vol. 4497, pp. 248–257. Springer, Heidelberg (2007). https://doi.org/10.1007/978-3-540-73001-9_26
9. Edalat, A., Escardó, M.: Integration in real PCF. In: Eleventh Annual IEEE Symposium on Logic in Computer Science (LICS). IEEE (1996)
10. Edalat, A., Heckmann, R.: Computing with real numbers. In: Barthe, G., Dybjer, P., Pinto, L., Saraiva, J. (eds.) APPSEM 2000. LNCS, vol. 2395, pp. 193–267. Springer, Heidelberg (2002). https://doi.org/10.1007/3-540-45699-6_5
11. Edalat, A., Lieutier, A.: Domain theory and differential calculus (functions of one variable). In: LICS. IEEE (2002). www.doc.ic.ac.uk/~ae/papers/diffcal.ps. Full paper to appear in MSCS
12. Edalat, A., Lieutier, A.: Foundation of a computable solid modelling. Theoret. Comput. Sci. **284**(2), 319–345 (2002)
13. Edalat, A., Maleki, M.: Differentiation in logical form. In: Proceedings of 32th ACM/IEEE Symposium on Logic in Computer Science (LICS 2017). ACM/IEEE (2017)
14. Edalat, A., Potts, P.J.: A new representation for exact real numbers. In: Proceedings of Mathematical Foundations of Programming Semantics 13, Electronic Notes in Theoretical Computer Science, vol. 6. Elsevier Science B.V. (1997). www.elsevier.nl/locate/entcs/volume6.html

15. Edalat, A., Potts, P.J., Sünderhauf, P.: Lazy computation with exact real numbers. In: Proceedings of the Third ACM SIGPLAN International Conference on Functional Programming, pp. 185–194. ACM (1998)
16. Erker, T., Escardó, M., Keimel, K.: The way-below relation of function spaces over semantic domains. Topol. Appl. **89**(1–2), 61–74 (1998)
17. Escardó, M.H.: PCF extended with real numbers. Theor. Comput. Sci. **162**(1), 79–115 (1996)
18. Gierz, G., Hofmann, K.H., Keimel, K., Lawson, J.D., Mislove, M., Scott, D.S.: Continuous Lattices and Domains. Cambridge University Press, Cambridge (2003)
19. Jung, A., Sünderhauf, P.: On the duality of compact vs. open. Ann. New York Acad. Sci. **806**(1), 214–230 (1996)
20. Moore, R., Kearfott, R., Cloud, M.: Introduction to Interval Analysis. Society for Industrial and Applied Mathematics, Philadelphia (2009)
21. Moore, R.E.: Interval Analysis. Prentice-Hall, Englewood Cliffs (1966)
22. Potts, P.J., Edalat, A., Escardó, M.: Semantics of exact real arithmetic. In: Twelfth Annual IEEE Symposium on Logic in Computer Science. IEEE (1997)
23. Pour-El, M.B., Richards, J.I.: Computability in Analysis and Physics. Springer, New York (1988)
24. Scott, D.S.: Continuous lattices. In: Lawvere, F.W. (ed.) Toposes, Algebraic Geometry and Logic. LNM, vol. 274, pp. 97–136. Springer, Heidelberg (1972). https://doi.org/10.1007/BFb0073967
25. Smyth, M.B.: Effectively given domains. Theor. Comput. Sci. **5**, 257–274 (1977)
26. Vickers, S.J.: Geometric logic in computer science. In: Burn, G.L., Gay, S.J., Ryan, M.D. (eds.) Theory and Formal Methods, pp. 37–54. Springer, Heidelberg (1993). https://doi.org/10.1007/978-1-4471-3503-6_4
27. Weihrauch, K.: Computable Analysis (An Introduction). Springer, Heidelberg (2000). https://doi.org/10.1007/978-3-642-56999-9

9

Categorical Combinatorics for Non-Deterministic Strategies on Simple Games

Clément Jacq(✉) and Paul-André Melliès

Institut de Recherche en Informatique Fondamentale,
Université Paris Diderot, Paris, France
Clement.Jacq@irif.fr

Abstract. The purpose of this paper is to define in a clean and conceptual way a non-deterministic and sheaf-theoretic variant of the category of simple games and deterministic strategies. One thus starts by associating to every simple game a presheaf category of non-deterministic strategies. The bicategory of simple games and non-deterministic strategies is then obtained by a construction inspired by the recent work by Melliès and Zeilberger on type refinement systems. We show that the resulting bicategory is symmetric monoidal closed and cartesian. We also define a 2-comonad which adapts the Curien-Lamarche exponential modality of linear logic to the 2-dimensional and non deterministic framework. We conclude by discussing in what sense the bicategory of simple games defines a model of non deterministic intuitionistic linear logic.

1 Introduction

A new generation of 2-categorical and sheaf-theoretic game semantics is currently emerging in the field of programming language semantics. The games and strategies which determine them are more sophisticated mathematically, and also more difficult to define rigorously, than they were in the deterministic case. For that reason, it is timely to examine more closely the 2-categorical and sheaf-theoretic frameworks available to us in order to formulate these games and strategies in a suitably clean and conceptual way. In this investigation, one benefits from the efforts made in the past twenty-five years to give a clearer mathematical status to the previous generation of game semantics, which was (to a large extent) based on the notion of arena game. We recognize three main lines of work here:

1. the logical approach advocated by Girard, and formulated in ludics [3], polarized linear logic [7] or tensorial logic [12] with its connection to continuations and string diagrams,
2. the combinatorial approach advocated by Hyland, inspired by algebraic topology, and based on the combinatorial description of the structure of pointers in arena games [4],

3. the concurrent and asynchronous approach advocated by Melliès, based on the description of arena games as asynchronous games, and of strategies as causal concurrent structures playing on them, either in an alternated [9–11] or in a non-alternated way [18].

Interestingly, all the sheaf-theoretic frameworks designed for game semantics today are offsprings of the third approach based on asynchronous games: on the one hand, the notion of concurrent strategy in [19] is a sheaf-theoretic transcription of the notion of receptive ingenuous strategy formulated in [18]; on the other hand, the sheaf-theoretic notion of non-deterministic innocent strategy in [13, 17] relies on the diagrammatic and local definition of innocence in alternated asynchronous games [11]. For that reason, our purpose in this paper is to investigate the connection with the second approach, different in spirit and design, and to define a bicategory of simple games and non-deterministic strategies in the sheaf-theoretic style of Harmer et al. [4]. As we will see, our work also integrates a number of elements coming from the first approach, and more specifically, the discovery by Melliès that strategies are presented by generators and relations, and for that reason, are prone to factorisation theorems [14, 15]. Since we are interested in sheaf-theoretic models of computations, we should not forget to mention the pioneering work by Hirschowitz and Pous on models of process calculi [5], and its recent connection to game semantics [2].

In the present paper, we start from the category $\mathcal{G}$ of simple games and deterministic strategies between them, and we explain how to turn $\mathcal{G}$ into a bicategory $\mathcal{S}$ of simple games and *non-deterministic* strategies. As we will see, the construction of $\mathcal{S}$ relies on the discovery of a number of elementary but fundamental fibrational properties of the original category $\mathcal{G}$. Since our work is built on [4], let us recall that a simple game A is defined there as a contravariant presheaf $A : \omega^{op} \to \mathbf{Set}$ over the order category $\omega = 0 \to 1 \to 2 \to \cdots$ associated to the infinite countable ordinal ω. A simple game A is thus a family of sets A_n together with a function $\pi_n : A_{n+1} \to A_n$ for all $n \in \mathbb{N}$, depicted as:

$$A_0 \xleftarrow{\pi_0} A_1 \xleftarrow{\pi_1} A_2 \longleftarrow \quad \cdots \quad \longleftarrow A_n \xleftarrow{\pi_n} A_{n+1} \longleftarrow \cdots$$

One requires moreover that A_0 is the singleton set. The intuition is that A is a rooted tree; that A_n contains its plays (or branches) of length n; and that π_n is the prefix function which transports every play of length $n+1$ to its prefix of length n. In particular, every simple game A contains only one play of length 0, which should be thought as the empty play. Every simple game A should be moreover understood as alternating: here, the intuition is that every play of odd length $2n+1$ ends with an Opponent move, and that every play of even length $2n$ ends with a Player move if $n > 0$.

Terminology: An element $a \in A_n$ is called a position of degree n in the game A. The position $a \in A_n$ is called a P-position when its degree n is even, and a O-position when its degree n is odd. Given a position $a \in A_{n+1}$, we write $\pi(a)$ for the position $\pi_n(a)$; similarly, given a position $a \in A_{n+2}$, we write $\pi^2(a)$ for the position $\pi_n \circ \pi_{n+1}(a)$. A simple game A is called O-branching when the function $\pi : A_{2n+2} \to A_{2n+1}$ is injective, for all $n \in \mathbb{N}$. This means that every Opponent position $a \in A_{2n+1}$ can be extended in at most one way into a Player position $b \in A_{2n+2}$, for all $n \in \mathbb{N}$.

We start the paper by formulating a sheaf-theoretic notion of non-deterministic P-strategy on a simple game A. Recall that a deterministic P-strategy σ of a simple game A is defined in [4] as a family of subsets $\sigma_{2n} \subseteq A_{2n}$ of P-positions, satisfying the following properties, for all $n \in \mathbb{N}$:

(i) Unique empty play — σ_0 is equal to the singleton set A_0,
(ii) Closure under even prefixes — if $a \in \sigma_{2n+2}$ then $\pi^2(a) \in \sigma_{2n}$,
(iii) Determinacy — if $a, b \in \sigma_{2n}$ with $\pi(a) = \pi(b)$, then $a = b$.

In order to generalize this definition to non-deterministic P-strategies, we find convenient to consider the full subcategory ω_P of ω consisting of the strictly positive even numbers, of the form $2n$ for $n > 0$; and the inclusion functor $\iota_P : \omega_P \to \omega$. Define the presheaf $A_P = A \circ \iota_P$ as the simple game A obtained as the restriction of the presheaf $A : \omega^{op} \to \mathbf{Set}$ to the subcategory ω_P:

$$A_P \quad = \quad \omega_P^{op} \xrightarrow{\ \iota_P\ } \omega^{op} \xrightarrow{\ A\ } \mathbf{Set}$$

The collection A_P thus consists of all the Player positions in A, except for the initial one $* \in A(0)$. This leads us to the following definition of (non-deterministic) P-strategy on a simple game A:

Definition 1. *A P-strategy σ on a simple game A is a presheaf $S : \omega_P^{\mathrm{op}} \to \mathbf{Set}$ over the category ω_P together with a morphism of presheaves $\sigma : S \to A_P$. We write $\sigma : A$ in that case. The presheaf S is called the* support *of the strategy σ and the elements of S_{2n} are called the runs of degree $2n$ of the strategy, for $n \geq 0$.*

In other words, a P-strategy σ on A is a family of sets S_{2n} indexed by strictly positive numbers $n > 0$, related between them by functions $(\pi_P)_{2n} : S_{2n+2} \to S_n$ pictured as:

$$S_2 \xleftarrow{\ \pi_P\ } S_4 \longleftarrow \quad \cdots \quad \longleftarrow S_{2n} \xleftarrow{\ \pi_P\ } S_{2n+2} \longleftarrow \cdots$$

together with a family of functions $\sigma_{2n} : S_{2n} \to A_{2n}$ making the diagram below commute, for all $n > 0$:

$$\begin{array}{ccccc} S_{2n} & & \xleftarrow{\qquad \pi_P \qquad} & & S_{2n+2} \\ \downarrow{\scriptstyle \sigma_{2n}} & & & & \downarrow{\scriptstyle \sigma_{2n+2}} \\ A_{2n} & \xleftarrow{\ \pi\ } & A_{2n+1} & \xleftarrow{\ \pi\ } & A_{2n+2} \end{array}$$

To every simple game A, we associate the category $\mathcal{P}(A)$ of P-strategies over A, defined as the slice category

$$\mathcal{P}(A) = [\omega_P^{op}, \mathbf{Set}] / A_P \tag{1}$$

whose objects are thus the strategies over A, and whose morphisms $\theta : \sigma \to \tau$ between two strategies $\sigma : S \to A$ and $\tau : T \to A$ are the morphisms $\theta : S \to T$ of presheaves satisfying the expected equation: $\sigma = \tau \circ \theta$. We will call those simulations. One main contribution of the paper is the observation that the family of categories $\mathcal{P}(A)$ can be organised into a pseudofunctor

$$\mathcal{P} : \mathcal{G} \longrightarrow \mathbf{Cat}$$

from the category $\mathcal{G}$ of simple games and deterministic strategies. The pseudofunctor $\mathcal{P}$ is moreover monoidal, in the sense that there exists a family of functors

$$m_{A,B} : \mathcal{P}(A) \times \mathcal{P}(B) \longrightarrow \mathcal{P}(A \otimes B)$$

indexed by simple games A, B. As a symmetric monoidal closed category, the category $\mathcal{G}$ is enriched over itself, with the simple game $\mathcal{G}(A, B) = A \multimap B$ constructed from the simple games A and B. Here comes the nice point of the construction: the bicategory $\mathcal{S}$ is simply defined as the bicategory with simple games A, B as objects, and with

$$\mathcal{S}(A, B) = \mathcal{P}(A \multimap B)$$

as category of morphisms between two simple games A and B. In other words, a morphism $\sigma : A \to B$ in $\mathcal{S}$ is a P-strategy $\sigma : A \multimap B$, and a 2-cell $\theta : \sigma \Rightarrow \tau : A \to B$ is a morphism $\theta : \sigma \to \tau$ in the category $\mathcal{P}(A \multimap B)$. At this point, the fact that $\mathcal{S}$ defines a bicategory is easily derived from the lax monoidal structure of the pseudofunctor $\mathcal{P}$. Recall that, as a symmetric monoidal closed category, the category $\mathcal{G}$ is enriched over itself. From a conceptual point of view, the construction of the bicategory $\mathcal{S}$ thus amounts to a change of enrichment category along the lax monoidal pseudofunctor $\mathcal{P} : \mathcal{G} \to \mathbf{Cat}$, transforming the $\mathcal{G}$-enriched category $\mathcal{G}$ into the (weak) $\mathbf{Cat}$-enriched category $\mathcal{S}$.

Besides the construction of $\mathcal{S}$, a great care will be devoted to the analysis of the Curien-Lamarche exponential comonad ! on the category $\mathcal{G}$ and to the recipe to turn it into an exponential 2-comonad on the bicategory $\mathcal{S}$. The construction relies on the existence of a family of functors

$$p_A \quad : \quad \mathcal{P}(A) \longrightarrow \mathcal{P}(!A)$$

called "promotion" functors, and natural in the simple game A in the category $\mathcal{G}$. In particular, the functorial part of the exponential 2-comonad $! : \mathcal{S} \to \mathcal{S}$ is defined as the composite:

$$\mathcal{P}(A \multimap B) \xrightarrow{p_{A \multimap B}} \mathcal{P}(!(A \multimap B)) \xrightarrow{\mathcal{P}(n_{A,B})} \mathcal{P}(!A \multimap !B)$$

where $n_{A,B} : !(A \multimap B) \to !A \multimap !B$ is the canonical morphism in $\mathcal{G}$ which provides the structure of a lax monoidal functor to the original comonad $! : \mathcal{G} \to \mathcal{G}$.

2 Non-deterministic P-strategies as P-cartesian Transductions

As explained in the introduction, a P-strategy $\sigma \in \mathcal{P}(A)$ over a simple game A is defined as an object of the slice category (1) in the category $[\omega_P^{op}, \mathbf{Set}]$ of contravariant presheaves over ω_P. We will use the fact that the slice category is equivalent to the category of contravariant presheaves

$$\mathcal{P}(A) \quad = \quad [\omega_P^{op}\,,\,\mathbf{Set}]\,/\,A_P \;\; \cong \;\; [\,\mathbf{tree}(A_P)^{op}, \mathbf{Set}]$$

over the Grothendieck category $\mathbf{tree}(A_P)$ generated by the presheaf $A_P \in [\omega_P^{op}, \mathbf{Set}]$. The category $\mathbf{tree}(A_P)$ has the P-positions of the simple game A as objects, and a morphism $a \to a'$ between $a \in A_{2p}$ and $a' \in A_{2q}$ precisely when $p \leq q$ and $\pi^{2q-2p}(a') = a$. In other words, it is the order category associated to the tree of P-positions of the simple game A.

We find convenient for later purposes to reformulate non-deterministic P-strategies in the following way. This paves the way to a comprehension theorem for the pseudofunctor $\mathcal{P}$, which will be established in the next section. A transduction $\theta : A \to B$ between two simple games $A, B : \omega^{op} \to \mathbf{Set}$ is defined as a natural transformation between the presheaves A and B, given by a family of functions $\theta_n : A_n \to B_n$ making the square $\square_n$ diagram below commute, for all $n \in \mathbb{N}$:

$$\begin{array}{ccc} A_n & \xleftarrow{\quad \pi_n \quad} & A_{n+1} \\ {\scriptstyle \theta_n}\big\downarrow & \square_n & \big\downarrow{\scriptstyle \theta_{n+1}} \\ B_n & \xleftarrow[\quad \pi_n \quad]{} & B_{n+1} \end{array}$$

A transduction $\theta : A \to B$ is called P-cartesian when $\square_{2n}$ is a pullback square for all $n \in \mathbb{N}$; and O-cartesian when $\square_{2n+1}$ is a pullback square for all $n \in \mathbb{N}$. We write $\mathcal{T}$ for the category of simple games and transductions between them, and $\mathcal{T}_P$ (resp. $\mathcal{T}_O$) for the subcategory of P-cartesian (resp. O-cartesian) transductions. Note that the restriction functor

$$(-)_P \quad : \quad [\omega^{op}, \mathbf{Set}] \quad \longrightarrow \quad [\omega_P^{op}, \mathbf{Set}]$$

is a fibration, and that a transduction $\theta : A \to B$ between simple games is P-cartesian precisely when it defines a cartesian morphism with respect to the fibration $(-)_P$. For that reason, a P-cartesian transduction $\theta : A \to B$ is entirely characterized by the family of functions $\theta_{2n} : A_{2n} \longrightarrow B_{2n}$ on the P-positions of the simple games A and B, for $n \in \mathbb{N}$. From this follows easily that

Proposition 1. *A P-strategy σ on a simple game A is the same thing as a simple game S together with a P-cartesian transduction $S \to A$. The simple game S is uniquely determined by σ up to isomorphism. It is called the support (or run-tree) of σ, and noted $\{A \,|\, \sigma\}$, while the P-cartesian transduction is noted* $\mathsf{supp}_\sigma : \{A \,|\, \sigma\} \longrightarrow A$.

Note that the definition applies the general principle formulated in [18] that a strategy σ of a game A is a specific kind of map (here a P-cartesian transduction) $S \to A$ from a given game $S = \{A \,|\, \sigma\}$ to the game A of interest. One benefit of this principle is that it unifies the two concepts of game and of strategy, by regarding a strategy σ of a game A as a game S "embedded" in an appropriate way by $S \to A$ inside the simple game A. This insight coming from [18] underlies for instance the construction in [19] of a category of non-deterministic strategies between asynchronous games.

Typically, consider the simple game $A = \mathbb{B}_1 \multimap \mathbb{B}_2$ where $\mathbb{B}$ is the simple boolean game with a unique initial Opponent move q and two Player moves tt for true and ff for false; and where the indices 1, 2 are here to indicate the component of the boolean game $\mathbb{B}$. The simple game A may be represented as the decision tree below:

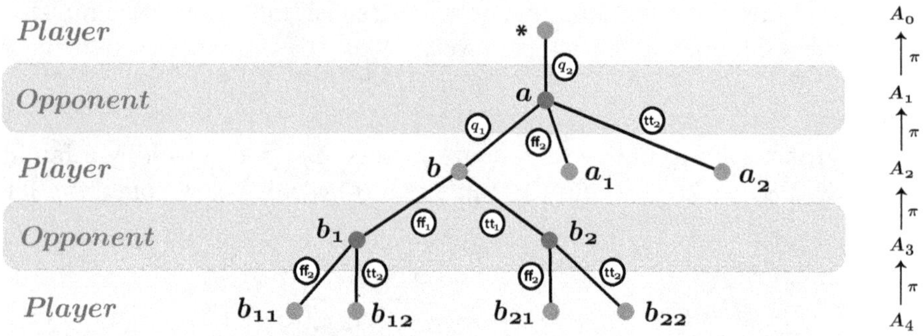

where the sets of positions are defined as:

$$A_1 = \{a\} \qquad A_2 = \{b, a_1, a_2\} \qquad A_3 = \{b_1, b_2\} \qquad A_4 = \{b_{11}, b_{12}, b_{21}, b_{22}\}$$

and where the branches are induced by the prefix functions $\pi_n : A_{n+1} \to A_n$ depicted on the picture above. For the reader's convenience, we label every edge of A by the name of the move which would be used in the more familiar definition of simple games, where plays are defined as sequences of moves [1,6]. Note that every position $a \in A_n$ of degree n is determined by its occurrence, defined as the sequence of n moves from the root $*$ to the position a in the tree A. Typically, the P-position $b \in A_2$ has occurrence $q_2 \cdot q_1$ and the P-position $b_{21} \in A_4$ has occurrence $q_2 \cdot q_1 \cdot \mathtt{tt}_1 \cdot \mathsf{ff}_2$.

By way of illustration, we define the P-strategy $\sigma \in \mathcal{P}(A)$ as the presheaf below

$$\begin{array}{c} * \mapsto \{*\} \quad a_1 \mapsto \emptyset \quad a_2 \mapsto \{x''\} \\ b \mapsto \{x'\} \quad b_{11} \mapsto \emptyset \quad b_{12} \mapsto \emptyset \quad b_{21} \mapsto \{z'\} \quad b_{22} \mapsto \{z'', z'''\} \end{array}$$

on the Grothendieck category $\mathbf{tree}(A_P)$ associated to the presheaf A_P of P-positions in A. As explained in Proposition 1, the P-strategy σ may be equivalently defined as the simple game $S = \{A \,|\, \sigma\}$ below

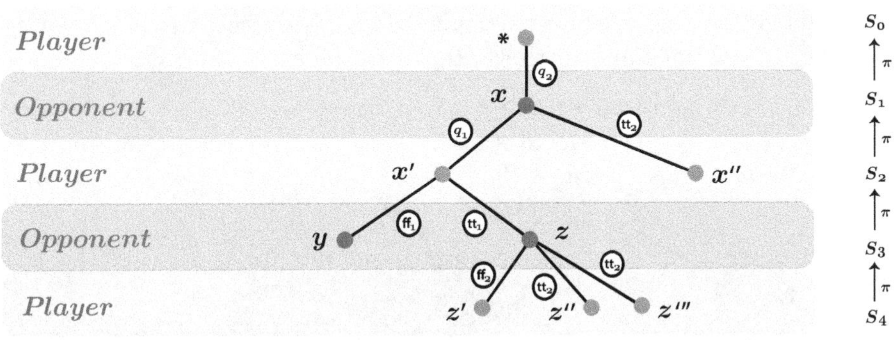

together with the P-cartesian transduction $\mathsf{supp}_\sigma : \{A \,|\, \sigma\} \to A$ described as:

$$x \mapsto a \qquad x' \mapsto b \qquad x'' \mapsto a_2 \qquad y \mapsto b_1 \qquad z' \mapsto b_{21} \qquad z'' \mapsto b_{22} \qquad z''' \mapsto b_{22}$$

It is worth mentioning that the transduction supp_σ may be recovered from the moves labelled on the run-tree $S = \{A \,|\, \sigma\}$. This pictorial description provides a convenient way to describe how the non-deterministic P-strategy σ plays on A. Typically, when questioned by the initial move q_2 of the game, the non-deterministic P-strategy σ answers tt_2 with the run $x'' \in S_2$ or asks the value of the input boolean by playing the move q_1; when the Opponent answers with the move tt_1, the P-strategy reacts by playing the value ff_2 with the run $z' \in S_4$ or by playing the value ff_2 with the runs $z'', z''' \in S_4$. Note in particular that the P-strategy σ is allowed to play two different runs $z'', z''' \in S_4$ of the same play $b_{22} \in A_4$.

3 P-cartesian Transductions as Deterministic Strategies

In the previous section, we have seen how to regard every non-deterministic P-strategy $\sigma \in \mathcal{P}(B)$ as a P-cartesian transduction $\mathsf{supp}_\sigma : \{B \,|\, \sigma\} \to B$ into the simple game B. Our purpose here is to show that every P-cartesian transduction $\theta : A \to B$ can be seen as a particular kind of deterministic strategy of the simple game $A \multimap B$.

Definition 2 (Total strategies). *A deterministic strategy σ of a simple game A is total when for every O-position s such that the P-position $\pi(s)$ is an element of σ, there exists a P-position t in the strategy σ such that $\pi(t) = s$.*

Definition 3 (Back-and-forth strategies). *Given two simple games A and B, a back-and-forth strategy f of the simple game $A \multimap B$ is a deterministic and total strategy whose positions are all of the form (c, a, b) where $c : n \to n$ is a copycat schedule.*

Back-and-forth strategies compose, and thus define a subcategory of $\mathcal{G}$:

Definition 4 (The category $\mathcal{BF}$). *The category $\mathcal{BF}$ of back-and-forth strategies is the subcategory of $\mathcal{G}$ whose objects are the simple games and whose morphisms $f : A \to B$ are the back-and-forth strategies of $A \multimap B$.*

As a matter of fact, we will be particularly interested here in the subcategory $\mathcal{BF}^+$ of *functional* back-and-forth strategies in the category $\mathcal{BF}$.

Definition 5 (Functional strategies). *A functional strategy f of the simple game $A \multimap B$ is a back-and-forth strategy such that for every position $a \in A_n$ of degree n in the simple game A, there exists a unique position $b \in B_n$ of same degree in B such that $(c, a, b) \in f$, where $c : n \to n$ is the copycat schedule.*

The following basic observation justifies our interest in the notion of functional strategy:

Proposition 2. *For all simple games A, B, there is a one-to-one correspondence between the P-cartesian transductions $A \to B$ and the functional strategies in $A \multimap B$.*

Proof. See Appendix E.

For that reason, we will identify P-cartesian transductions and functional strategies from now on. Put together with Proposition 1, this leads us to the following correspondence, which holds for every simple game A:

Proposition 3. *The category $\mathcal{P}(A)$ is equivalent to the slice category $\mathcal{BF}^+/A$.*

The result may be understood as a preliminary form of comprehension: it states that every non-deterministic P-strategy $\sigma \in \mathcal{P}(A)$ may be equivalently seen as a functional P-strategy

$$\mathsf{supp}_\sigma \quad : \quad \{A \,|\, \sigma\} \quad \longrightarrow \quad A \tag{2}$$

in the category $\mathcal{G}$ of simple games and deterministic strategies, obtained by composing the equivalences stated in Propositions 1 and 3. Note that the simple game $\{A \,|\, \sigma\}$ coincides with the run-tree S of the non-deterministic strategy σ formulated in Proposition 1 and that the functional strategy supp_σ coincides with the P-cartesian transduction which "projects" the support S on the simple game A. The property (Proposition 3) is important from a methodological point of view, because it enables us to use the rich toolbox developed for simple games and deterministic strategies, in order to handle non-deterministic strategies *inside* the category $\mathcal{G}$.

4 The Pseudofunctor $\mathcal{P}$

Suppose given a P-strategy $\sigma \in \mathcal{P}(A)$ over the simple game A and a morphism $f : A \to B$ in the category $\mathcal{G}$.

Definition 6. *The P-strategy $\mathcal{P}(f)(\sigma) \in \mathcal{P}(B)$ over the simple game B is defined as the contravariant presheaf over $\mathbf{tree}(B_P)$ which transports every P-position b of the simple game B to the disjoint union defined below:*

$$\mathcal{P}(f)(\sigma) \quad : \quad b \quad \mapsto \quad \coprod_{(e,a,b) \in f} \quad \sigma(a). \tag{3}$$

The fact that (3) defines a presheaf over $\mathcal{P}(B)$ and that $\mathcal{P}$ is a pseudofunctor (see Definition 24) is established in the Appendix F.

This construction equips the family of presheaf categories $\mathcal{P}(A)$ with the structure of a pseudofunctor $\mathcal{P} : \mathcal{G} \longrightarrow \mathbf{Cat}$. Moreover, the pseudo-functor $\mathcal{P}$ has comprehension in the sense of Lawvere [8]. For every simple game B, the *comprehension functor* is defined as the composite

$$\{B\,|\,-\} \quad : \quad \mathcal{P}(B) \quad \longrightarrow \quad \mathcal{BF}^{+}/B \quad \longrightarrow \quad \mathcal{G}/B$$

which transports every non-deterministic P-strategy to the morphism (2) seen as an object of $\mathcal{G}/B$. One establishes that

Theorem 1 (Comprehension). *For every simple game B, the comprehension functor*

$$\{B\,|\,-\} \quad : \quad \mathcal{P}(B) \quad \longrightarrow \quad \mathcal{G}/B$$

has a left adjoint functor

$$\mathsf{image} \quad : \quad \mathcal{G}/B \quad \longrightarrow \quad \mathcal{P}(B).$$

Given a deterministic strategy $f : A \to B$, the contravariant presheaf $\mathsf{image}(f)$ over the category $\mathbf{tree}(B_P)$ transports every P-position b of the game B to the set below:

$$\mathsf{image}(f) \quad : \quad b \quad \mapsto \quad \left\{ \quad (e,a,b) \quad \middle| \quad (e,a,b) \in f \quad \right\}$$

Note that the presheaf $\mathsf{image}(f)$ may be also described by the formula

$$\mathsf{image}(f) \quad = \quad \mathcal{P}(f)(*_A) \quad \in \quad \mathcal{P}(B)$$

where $*_A$ is the terminal object in the category $\mathcal{P}(A)$ of P-strategies over A. Note that the run-tree $\{A\,|\,*_A\}$ of the P-strategy $*_A \in \mathcal{P}(A)$ is the simple game A itself, with supp_{*_A} the identity $i_A : A \to A$. In other words, the P-strategy $*_A$ has exactly one run over each position of the simple game A.

Also note that we will occasionally note positions of $\mathsf{image}(f)$ $b_{(e,a)}$ when there is need to emphasize the fact that $\mathsf{image}(f)$ is a contravariant presheaf over $\mathbf{tree}(B_P)$.

5 The Slender-Functional Factorisation Theorem

In order to establish the comprehension theorem, we prove a factorization theorem in the original category $\mathcal{G}$, which involves slender and functional strategies.

Definition 7. *A deterministic strategy f in a simple game $A \multimap B$ is slender when for every P-position b in the simple game B, there exists exactly one P-position a of the simple game A and exactly one schedule e such that $(e,a,b) \in f$.*

By extension, we say that a morphism $f : A \to B$ in the category $\mathcal{G}$ is slender when the deterministic strategy f is slender in $A \multimap B$. Note that every isomorphism $f : A \to B$ in the category $\mathcal{G}$ is both slender and functional.

Proposition 4. *Suppose that A and B are two simple games and that f is a deterministic strategy of $A \multimap B$. Then, there exists a slender strategy $g : A \to C$ and a functional strategy $h : C \to B$ such that $f = h \circ g$.*

The simple game C is defined as $\{B \,|\, \mathsf{image}(f)\}$ while the slender strategy $g : A \to C$ is defined as

$$g \quad = \quad \left\{ \quad (e, a, (e, a, b)) \quad \middle| \quad (e, a, b) \in f \quad \right\}$$

and $h : C \to B$ is the functional strategy $\mathsf{supp}_{\mathsf{image}(f)}$ associated in Proposition 3 to the P-strategy $\mathsf{image}(f) \in \mathcal{P}(B)$.

Proposition 5. *Suppose that $s : U \to V$ and $f : A \to B$ are two morphisms of the category $\mathcal{G}$. Suppose moreover that s is slender and that f is functional. Then, $s : X \to Y$ is orthogonal to $f : A \to B$ in the sense that for all morphisms $u : X \to A$ and $v : Y \to B$ making the diagram (a) commute, there exists a unique morphism $h : Y \to B$ making the diagram (b) commute in the category $\mathcal{G}$:*

$$(a) \quad \begin{array}{ccc} X & \xrightarrow{u} & A \\ {\scriptstyle s}\downarrow & & \downarrow{\scriptstyle f} \\ Y & \xrightarrow{v} & B \end{array} \qquad\qquad (b) \quad \begin{array}{ccc} X & \xrightarrow{u} & A \\ {\scriptstyle s}\downarrow & \nearrow^{h} & \downarrow{\scriptstyle f} \\ Y & \xrightarrow{v} & B \end{array}$$

The deterministic strategy $h : Y \to A$ is defined as

$$\begin{aligned} h = & \left\{ (e, y, a) \;\middle|\; \begin{array}{l} \exists x \in X, b \in B, e', e'' \in \Upsilon, \\ (e, y, b) \in v \ \wedge (c, a, b) \in f \ \wedge (e', x, y) \in s \ \wedge (e'', x, a) \in u \end{array} \right\} \\ \uplus & \left\{ (e, y, a) \;\middle|\; \begin{array}{l} \exists x \in X, b \in B, e', e'' \in \Upsilon, \\ (e, y, b) \in v \ \wedge (c, a, b) \in f \ \wedge (e', x, \pi y) \in s \ \wedge (e'', x, \pi a) \in u \end{array} \right\} \end{aligned}$$

Note that the position b is uniquely determined by the position a because f is functional, and that the pair (e', x) is uniquely determined by the position y because s is slender. Moreover, by determinism of $u = h \circ s$, the schedule e'' is entirely determined by the schedules e and e'.

Theorem 2 (Factorization theorem). *The classes $\mathcal{S}$ of slender morphisms and $\mathcal{F}$ of functional morphisms define a factorization system $(\mathcal{S}, \mathcal{F})$ in the category $\mathcal{G}$.*

It is a folklore result that, in that situation, the comprehension theorem (Theorem 1) follows from the factorization theorem. The reason is that the category $\mathcal{P}(B)$ is equivalent (by Proposition 3) to the full subcategory $\mathcal{BF}^+/B$ of functional strategies in the slice category $\mathcal{G}/B$. Seen from that point of view, the comprehension functor $\{B\,|\,-\}$ coincides with the embedding of $\mathcal{BF}^+/B$ into $\mathcal{G}/B$. It is worth noting that for every P-strategy $\sigma \in \mathcal{P}(A)$, one has an isomorphism

$$\sigma \quad \cong \quad \mathsf{image}(\mathsf{supp}_{\sigma})$$

in the category $\mathcal{P}(A)$, and that one has an isomorphism

$$\mathcal{P}(f)(\sigma) \quad \cong \quad \mathsf{image}(f \circ \mathsf{supp}_{\sigma}) \tag{4}$$

in the category $\mathcal{P}(B)$, for every morphism $f : A \to B$ in the category $\mathcal{G}$. This provides an alternative way to define the pseudofunctor $\mathcal{P}$.

6 The Bicategory $\mathcal{S}$ of Simple Games and Non-deterministic Strategies

In this section, we explain how to construct a bicategory $\mathcal{S}$ of simple games and non-deterministic strategies, starting from the category $\mathcal{G}$. The first step is to equip the pseudofunctor $\mathcal{P}$ with a lax monoidal structure (See Definition 25), based on the definition of tensor product in the category $\mathcal{G}$ formulated in [4], see Appendix B for details. We start by observing that

Proposition 6. *Suppose given two morphisms $f : A \to B$ and $g : C \to D$ in the category $\mathcal{G}$ of simple games and deterministic strategies. The morphism*

$$f \otimes g : A \otimes C \longrightarrow B \otimes D$$

is slender when f and g are slender, and functional when f and g are functional.

Proof. See Appendix G.

Note that the isomorphism $\mathsf{image}(f \otimes g) \cong \mathsf{image}(f) \otimes \mathsf{image}(g)$ follows immediately from this statement and from the factorization theorem (Theorem 2), for every pair of morphisms $f : A \to B$ and $g : C \to D$ in the category $\mathcal{G}$. The tensor product $\sigma \otimes \tau$ of two P-strategies σ and τ is defined in the same spirit, using comprehension:

Definition 8. *Suppose that $\sigma \in \mathcal{P}(A)$ is a P-strategy of a simple game A and that $\tau \in \mathcal{P}(B)$ is a P-strategy of a simple game B. The tensor product $\sigma \otimes \tau$ is the P-strategy of the simple game $A \otimes B$ defined as*

$$\sigma \otimes \tau \quad = \quad \mathsf{image}(\,\mathsf{supp}_{\sigma} \otimes \mathsf{supp}_{\tau}\,).$$

Here, the morphism $\mathsf{supp}_\sigma \otimes \mathsf{supp}_\tau : \{A \,|\, \sigma\} \otimes \{B \,|\, \tau\} \to A \otimes B$ denotes the tensor product (computed in the original category $\mathcal{G}$) of the morphisms supp_σ and supp_τ. A direct description of $\sigma \otimes \tau \in \mathcal{P}(A \otimes B)$ is also possible, as the presheaf which transports every position (e, a, b) of the simple game $A \otimes B$ to the set-theoretic product below:

$$\sigma \otimes \tau \quad : \quad (e, a, b) \quad \mapsto \quad \sigma(a) \times \tau(b).$$

As indicated in the introduction, the tensor product of P-strategies defines a family of functors $m_{A,B} : \mathcal{P}(A) \times \mathcal{P}(B) \to \mathcal{P}(A \otimes B)$ which, together with the isomorphism of categories $m_1 : 1 \to \mathcal{P}(1)$, equips the pseudofunctor $\mathcal{P}$ with a lax monoidal structure:

Theorem 3. *The pseudofunctor $\mathcal{P}$ equipped with the family of functors $m_{A,B}$ and m_1 defines a lax monoidal pseudofunctor from $(\mathcal{G}, \otimes, 1)$ to $(\mathbf{Cat}, \times, 1)$.*

Proof. See Appendix H.

The bicategory $\mathcal{S}$ of simple games and non-deterministic strategies is deduced from the lax monoidal pseudofunctor $\mathcal{P}$ in the following generic way, inspired by the idea of monoidal refinement system [16].

Definition 9. *The bicategory $\mathcal{S}$ has simple games A, B, C as objects, with the hom-category $\mathcal{S}(A, B)$ defined as*

$$\mathcal{S}(A, B) \quad = \quad \mathcal{P}(A \multimap B)$$

the composition functor

$$\circ_{A,B,C} : \mathcal{P}(B \multimap C) \times \mathcal{P}(A \multimap B) \longrightarrow \mathcal{P}(A \multimap C)$$

defined as the composite

$$\mathcal{P}(B \multimap C) \times \mathcal{P}(A \multimap B) \xrightarrow{m_{B \multimap C, A \multimap B}} \mathcal{P}((B \multimap C) \otimes (A \multimap B)) \xrightarrow{\mathcal{P}(comp_{A,B,C})} \mathcal{P}(A \multimap C)$$

where $comp_{A,B,C} : (B \multimap C) \otimes (A \multimap B) \longrightarrow (A \multimap C)$ is the morphism which internalizes composition in the symmetric monoidal closed category $\mathcal{G}$. In the same way, the identity in $\mathcal{P}(A \multimap A)$ is defined as the composite

$$1 \xrightarrow{\ m_1\ } \mathcal{P}(1) \xrightarrow{\mathcal{P}(id_A)} \mathcal{P}(A \multimap A)$$

where the morphism $id_A : 1 \to (A \multimap A)$ internalizes the identity morphism in $\mathcal{G}$.

Proposition 7. *The bicategory $\mathcal{S}$ is symmetric monoidal closed in the sense that there exists a family of isomorphisms*

$$\Phi_{A,B,C} \quad : \quad \mathcal{S}(A \otimes B, C) \quad \cong \quad \mathcal{S}(B, A \multimap C).$$

The isomorphism $\Phi_{A,B,C}$ is defined as the image by the pseudofunctor $\mathcal{P}$ of the isomorphism

$$\varphi_{A,B,C} \quad : \quad (A \otimes B) \multimap C \quad \cong \quad B \multimap (A \multimap C)$$

in the category $\mathcal{G}$ between the underlying simple games. One benefit of our conceptual approach is that the monoidal closed structure of $\mathcal{S}$ is neatly deduced from the monoidal closed structure of the original category $\mathcal{G}$.

7 The Exponentional Modality on the Category $\mathcal{G}$

Now that the monoidal bicategory $\mathcal{S}$ has been defined, we analyze how the exponential modality defined in [4] adapts to our sheaf-theoretic framework.

Definition 10. *Let A be a simple game. $!A$ is the simple game whose set $(!A)_n$ of positions of degree n consists of the pairs $(\phi, \overline{a})$ such that:*

- *ϕ is a O-heap over n and $\overline{a} = (a_1, \ldots, a_n)$ is a sequence of positions of A,*
- *for each $k \in \{1, \ldots, n\}$, the sequence of positions in $\overline{a} = (a_1, \ldots, a_n)$ corresponding to the branch of k in ϕ defines a play*

$$\{a_k, a_{\phi(k)}, a_{\phi^2(k)}, \ldots\}$$

of the simple game A.

The predecessor function $\pi_n : (!A)_{n+1} \to (!A)_n$ is defined as $\pi(\phi, \overline{a}) = (\phi \restriction (n), \overline{a} \restriction (n))$.

Definition 11. *Let f be a deterministic strategy of $A \multimap B$. The deterministic strategy $!f$ of $!A \multimap !B$ consists of the positions $(e, (\phi, \overline{a}), (\psi, \overline{b}))$ such that $\phi = e^*\psi$ and, for each branch of (ϕ, e, π), the positions associated to that branch are played by f.*

It is worth observing that the construction of $!f : !A \to !B$ can be decomposed in the following way. Consider the morphism

$$n_{A,B} \quad : \quad !(A \multimap B) \quad \longrightarrow \quad !A \multimap !B$$

obtained by currying the composite morphism

$$!(A \multimap B) \otimes !A \xrightarrow{\ lax\ monoidal\ } !((A \multimap B) \otimes A) \xrightarrow{\ !evaluation\ } !B$$

in the symmetric monoidal closed category $\mathcal{G}$, where we use the coercion morphism which provides the exponential modality $! : \mathcal{G} \to \mathcal{G}$ with the structure of a lax monoidal functor.

Definition 12 **($\#f$).** *Given a deterministic strategy f of a simple game A, the deterministic strategy $\#f$ of the simple game $!A$ has positions the pairs $(\phi, \overline{a})$ such that for each branch of $(\phi, \overline{a})$, the positions associated to that branch are played by the deterministic strategy f.*

Proposition 8. *Given a morphism $f : A \to B$ of the category $\mathcal{G}$ and its curried form $\lambda a.f : 1 \to A \multimap B$, the composite morphism*

$$1 \xrightarrow{\#\lambda a:A.f} !\,(A \multimap B) \xrightarrow{n_{A,B}} !\,A \multimap !\,B$$

is the curried form $\lambda x : !A.\ !f$ in the category $\mathcal{G}$ of the morphism $!f : !A \longrightarrow !B$.

More details about the original exponential modality in $\mathcal{G}$ will be found in Appendix C. By analogy with Proposition 6, we establish that

Proposition 9. *Suppose that $f : A \to B$ is a morphism in the category $\mathcal{G}$. Then, the morphism*

$$!f \quad : \quad !A \quad \longrightarrow \quad !B$$

is slender when f is slender, and functional when f is functional.

Proof. See Appendix I.

8 The Exponential Modality on the Bicategory $\mathcal{S}$

In this section, we define the linear exponential modality $! : \mathcal{S} \to \mathcal{S}$ on the symmetric monoidal closed bicategory $\mathcal{S}$, in order to define a bicategorical model of intuitionistic linear logic. The construction is inspired by the observation made in the previous section (Proposition 8).

Definition 13. *Given a P-strategy $\sigma \in \mathcal{P}(A)$ of a simple game A, the P-strategy $\#\sigma$ of the simple game $!A$ is defined as the image in $\mathcal{P}(!A)$ of the morphism*

$$!\,\mathsf{supp}_{\sigma} \quad : \quad !\,\{A \,|\, \sigma\} \quad \longrightarrow \quad !A.$$

Note that the definition of $\#\sigma$ induces a commutative diagram in the category $\mathcal{G}$

$$\begin{array}{ccc} !\,\{A \,|\, \sigma\} & \xrightarrow{\ isomorphism\ } & \{!A \,|\, \#\sigma\} \\ & {\scriptstyle !\mathsf{supp}_{\sigma}} \searrow \quad \swarrow {\scriptstyle \mathsf{supp}_{\#\sigma}} & \\ & !A & \end{array}$$

where the top arrow is an isomorphism. Moreover, the definition of $\#\sigma$ coincides with the previous definition (Definition 12) when the P-strategy $\sigma = f$ happens to be deterministic.Consequently, for two games A, B and a deterministic strategy $f : A \multimap B$, we have $\mathsf{image}(!f) \cong \#^{\mathcal{S}}\mathsf{image}(f)$ and $\#^{\mathcal{S}} f = \#f$.

As mentioned in the introduction, this construction $\sigma \mapsto \#\sigma$ defines a functor

$$p_A \quad : \quad \mathcal{P}(A) \quad \longrightarrow \quad \mathcal{P}(!A).$$

Now, remember that a morphism $\sigma : A \to B$ of the bicategory $\mathcal{S}$ is defined as a P-strategy

$$\sigma \in \mathcal{P}(A \multimap B).$$

For that reason, every such morphism $\sigma : A \to B$ induces a P-strategy

$$\#\sigma \in \mathcal{P}(!(A \multimap B)).$$

In order to turn the P-strategy $\#\sigma$ into a P-strategy

$$!\sigma \in \mathcal{P}(\,!A \multimap !B\,)$$

we apply the functor

$$\mathcal{P}(n_{A,B}) \quad : \quad \mathcal{P}(\,!(A \multimap B)\,) \quad \longrightarrow \quad \mathcal{P}(\,!A \multimap !B\,)$$

to the P-strategy $\#\sigma$, where

$$n_{A,B} \quad : \quad !\,(A \multimap B) \quad \longrightarrow \quad !A \multimap !B$$

denotes the structural morphism of $\mathcal{G}$ defined in the previous section. The construction may be summarized as follows:

Definition 14. *The morphism $!\sigma : !A \to !B$ of the bicategory $\mathcal{S}$ associated to the morphism $\sigma : A \to B$ is defined as the P-strategy*

$$\mathcal{P}(n_{A,B})(\#\sigma) \quad \in \quad \mathcal{P}(!A \multimap !B).$$

Theorem 4. *With this definition, $! : \mathcal{S} \to \mathcal{S}$ defines a pseudofunctor from the bicategory $\mathcal{S}$ to itself.*

Proof. See Appendix J.

The family of morphisms

$$\delta_A : !A \to !!\,A \qquad\qquad \varepsilon_A : !A \to A$$

are defined with the same deterministic strategies in $\mathcal{P}(!A \multimap !!\,A)$ and $\mathcal{P}(!A \multimap A)$ as in the original category $\mathcal{G}$. One checks that the families δ and ε define natural transformations between pseudonatural functors on $\mathcal{S}$ (as defined in Definition 26), and that the 2-functor $! : \mathcal{S} \to \mathcal{S}$ defines a 2-comonad in the appropriate bicategorical sense (see Definition 27). The family of morphisms

$$d_A : !A \to !A \otimes !A \qquad\qquad e_A : !A \to 1$$

are defined with the same deterministic strategies in $\mathcal{P}(!A \multimap !A \otimes !A)$ and $\mathcal{P}(!A \multimap 1)$ as in the original category $\mathcal{G}$, and one checks that they define natural transformations between pseudonatural functors on $\mathcal{S}$. One obtains in this way that

Theorem 5. *The bicategory p equipped with the exponential modality* $! : \mathcal{S} \to \mathcal{S}$ *defines a bicategorical model of multiplicative intuitionistic linear logic.*

The formal and rigorous verification of these facts would be extremely tedious if done directly on the bicategory $\mathcal{S}$ of nondeterministic strategies. Our proof relies on the fact that the constructions of the model (Definitions 9, 14) are performed by "push" functors $\mathcal{P}(f)$ above a structural morphism f living in the original category $\mathcal{G}$. The interested reader will find part of the detailed proof in Appendix K.

9 Conclusion

We construct a bicategory $\mathcal{S}$ of simple games and non-deterministic strategies, which is symmetric monoidal closed in the extended 2-dimensional sense. We then equip the bicategory $\mathcal{S}$ with a linear exponential modality $! : \mathcal{S} \to \mathcal{S}$ which defines a bicategorical model of intuitionistic linear logic. This provides, as far as we know, the first sheaf-theoretic and non-deterministic game semantics of intuitionistic linear logic — including, in particular, a detailed description of the exponential modality.

A The Category $\mathcal{G}$ of Simple Games and Deterministic Strategies

We recall the construction of the category Υ of schedules performed in [4] and how we deduce from it the category $\mathcal{G}$ of simple games and deterministic strategies.

Definition 15 (Schedule). *A schedule is defined as a function* $e : \{1, \ldots, n\} \to \{0, 1\}$ *verifying* $e(1) = 1$ *and* $e(2k+1) = e(2k)$ *whenever* $1 \leq 2k \leq n-1$. *The number of* 0*'s and* 1*'s in* e *are noted* $|e|_0$ *and* $|e|_1$ *respectively. A schedule* e *is noted* $e : |e|_0 \to |e|_1$.

A schedule $e : p \to q$ may be equivalently seen as a couple $l : (p) \to (p+q)$ and $r : (q) \to (p+q)$ of order-preserving and globally surjective functions, such that $r(1) = 1$ and

$$l(i)\,\text{odd} \Rightarrow l(i+1) = l(i)+1 \qquad\qquad r(j)\,\text{even} \Rightarrow r(j+1) = r(j)+1$$

for all $1 \leq i \leq p-1$ and $1 \leq j \leq q-1$, where (n) stands for the finite ordinal $(n) = \{1, \ldots, n\}$.

Definition 16. *The category of schedules Υ has the natural numbers as objects, the schedules $e : p \to q$ as morphisms from p to q.*

The identity morphism $c : p \to p$ is the copycat schedule c characterized by the fact that $c(2k+1) \neq c(2k+2)$ for all $1 \leq 2k \leq 2p$. Details on the composition of two schedules $e : p \to r$ and $e' : r \to q$ as a schedule $e \centerdot e' : p \to q$ can be found in [4]. Now, we explain how we derive the category $\mathcal{G}$ from the category Υ. We start by defining the simple game $A \multimap B$ of linear maps from A to B:

Definition 17. *The simple game $A \multimap B$ is defined as the set $(A \multimap B)_n$ of all the triples (e, a, b) consisting of a schedule $e : p \to q$ with $p + q = n$, a position $a \in A_p$ and $b \in B_q$. The predecessor function π is defined as*

$$\pi(e, a, b) = \begin{cases} (\, e \restriction (n-1)\, ,\, \pi(a)\, ,\, b\,) & if\ \ e(n) = 0 \\ (\, e \restriction (n-1)\, ,\, a\, ,\, \pi(b)\,) & if\ \ e(n) = 1 \end{cases}$$

Definition 18. *The category $\mathcal{G}$ has simple games A, B as objects, and deterministic P-strategies f, g of $A \multimap B$ as morphisms from A to B. Note that we use latin letters instead of greek letters for deterministic strategies. The identity morphism $i_A : A \to A$ is defined as the P-strategy of $A \multimap A$ whose positions of degree $2n$ are the triples (c, a, a) where $c : n \to n$ is the copycat schedule, and $a \in A_n$. The composite $g \circ f : A \to C$ of two deterministic P-strategies $f : A \to B$ and $g : B \to C$ is the deterministic P-strategy whose set of positions of degree $2n$ is defined as*

$$(g \circ f)_{2n} = \coprod_{\substack{e : p \to r,\, e' : r \to q \\ p+q=2n}} \left\{ (e \centerdot e', a, c) \;\middle|\; \exists b \in B_r\, ,\, (e, a, b) \in \sigma_{p+r}\, ,\, (e', b, c) \in \tau_{r+q} \right\}$$

B The Tensor Product in the Category $\mathcal{G}$

Definition 19 (Tensorial schedule). *A $\otimes$-schedule is a function e : $\{1, \ldots, n\} \to \{0, 1\}$ verifying $e(2k+1) = e(2k+2)$ whenever $0 \leq 2k \leq n-2$.*

Definition 20 ($A \otimes B$). *The positions of the simple game $A \otimes B$ of degree n are the triples (e, a, b) where $e : p \otimes q$ is a $\otimes$-schedule with $p + q = n$, $a \in A_p$ and $b \in B_q$. The predecessor function π is defined as*

$$\pi(e, a, b) = \begin{cases} (e \restriction (n-1), \pi(a), b)\ if\ e(n) = 0 \\ (e \restriction (n-1), a, \pi(b)\,)\ if\ e(n) = 1 \end{cases}$$

The simple game 1 is the simple game with a unique position $*$, of degree 0.

We can also define $\otimes$ on strategies. Intuitively, for $f : A \to B$ and $g : C \to D$ two morphisms of the category $\mathcal{G}$, the plays of the strategy $f \otimes g$ of the simple game $(A \otimes C) \multimap (B \otimes D)$ are obtained by combining through a tensorial schedule plays of f and g.

The intuition is that, once we know the structure of f and g, the structure of plays of $f \otimes g$ is entirely directed by what happens in $B \otimes D$. The only agency that Opponent really has is to decide at some points whether to play on B or D, the rest being handled by the plays of f, g and the structure of $(A \otimes C) \multimap (B \otimes D)$. Formally, this gives the proposition:

Proposition 10. *Let $f : A \multimap B, g : C \multimap D$ be two deterministic strategies. Assuming a valid play of $f \otimes g : A \otimes C \multimap B \otimes D$ and the associated schedules $e : A \otimes C \to B \otimes D, t_1 : A \times C, t_2 : B \times D, e_1 : A \to B, e_2 : C \to D$, the knowledge of t_2, e_1, e_2 is enough to reconstruct e and t_1.*

Proof. The first O move of such a play is in $B \otimes D$ to follow the structure of $A \otimes C \multimap B \otimes D$. This is given to us by t_2. Let us assume it is a move in D (The other case is handled similarly).

The P move after that will necessarily be a move in C or D, as playing a move in A, B would break the structure of $A \multimap B, B \otimes D$ respectively. e_2 gives us the information.

- If it is a move in D, We go back to a situation equivalent to the initial one. We have also started to reconstruct e, which starts by 11.
- If it is a move in C, we start to reconstruct both e which starts by 10 and t_1 which starts by 1.

In this last case, the following O move will be a move in C as a move in A, B, D would break the structure of $A \multimap B, B \otimes D, C \multimap D$ respectively. e is then at 100 and t_1 at 11.

Finally, the following P move will be a move in either C or D as a move in A, B would break the structure of $A \multimap B, B \otimes D$ respectively. e_2 gives us this information.

- If it is a move in D, We go back to a situation equivalent to the initial one. We have also started to reconstruct e, which starts by 1001 and t_1 which starts by 11. We've also played the first two moves of t_2 which is at 11.
- If it is a move in C, we go back to the precedent situation (the one with a fixed O move in C) with e at 1000 and t_1 at 111.

To sum up the described construction, once an opponent move in B or D is played, the play is stuck playing in either $A \multimap B$ or $C \multimap D$ until a player move is played in B, D respectively. t_2 decides whether to play the opponent move in B or D and e_1 guides the play in $A \multimap B$ in the first case, e_2 guides it in $C \multimap D$ in the second. This guides us through the whole play and allows us to reconstruct both e and t_1.

In particular, any compatible plays of $f, g, B \otimes D$ induce a play of $f \otimes g$.

This proposition and its proof are key in several proofs we will make in the rest of the paper.

Proposition 11. *The category $(\mathcal{G}, \otimes, 1, \multimap)$ is symmetric monoidal closed.*

C The Exponential Modality on the Category $\mathcal{G}$

In this section, we recall the combinatorial structures introduced in [4] to construct the linear exponential comonad $! : \mathcal{G} \to \mathcal{G}$ on the symmetric monoidal closed category $\mathcal{G}$.

Definition 21 (Pointer function). *A pointer function on n is a parity-reversing function*

$$\phi \quad : \quad \{1, \ldots, n\} \quad \longrightarrow \quad \{0, \ldots, n-1\}$$

such that $\phi(i) < i$ for all i. A pointer function ϕ is called an O-heap if $\phi(2k) = 2k - 1$ for all k, and a P-heap if $\phi(2k+1) = 2k$ for all k. The set $\{k, \phi(k), \phi^2(k), ...\}$ will be called the branch of ϕ associated to the integer k. Note that the predecessor function π defined as $\pi(i) = i - 1$ for all i is both an O-heap and a P-heap.

Definition 22. *Suppose that $e : p \to q$ is a schedule, that ϕ is a O-heap over q and that ψ is a P-heap over p. The O-heap (ϕ, e, ψ) on $p + q$ is defined as follows:*

$$(\phi, e, \psi)(k) \quad = \quad \begin{cases} r(\phi(j)) & \text{if } k = r(j) \text{ is odd} \\ l(\psi(i)) & \text{if } k = l(i) \text{ is odd} \\ k - 1 & \text{otherwise} \end{cases}$$

where the schedule e is represented as a pair (l, r) as explained in Appendix A. Intuitively, the O-heap (ϕ, e, ψ) points alongside ϕ when the schedule e is at 1 and alongside ψ otherwise. The fact that (ϕ, e, ψ) defines an O-heap is ensured by the even case.

We recall the partial order over the set of pointer functions introduced in [4].

Definition 23 (Generalization). *Given two pointer functions ϕ, ψ, we say that ϕ is a generalization of ψ, and note $\phi \succeq \psi$, if the branch of ϕ associated to $k \in \{1, .., n\}$ can be injected in the branch of ψ associated to k, or, in other words, if for all k, there exists j such that $\phi(k) = \psi^j(k)$.*

Further in the paper, and in certain proofs, we will also need to look into the structure of $!!A$. Intuitively, positions of $!!A$ are pairs $(\phi, \overline{u})$ where $\overline{u}$ is a sequence of positions of $!A$ and ϕ an O-heap. It is equivalent to another representation using only a sequence of positions of A:

Proposition 12. *A position $(\phi, \overline{u})$ of $!!A$ is equivalent to $(\phi, \psi, \overline{a})$ with $\phi \succeq \psi$, ψ an O-heap, $\overline{a}$ a sequence of positions of A, verifying*

$$\forall i, j \in \{1, \ldots, n\}, (i \neq j) \Rightarrow \exists k, a_{\phi^k(i)} \neq a_{\phi^k(j)}$$

The moves alongside the branches of ψ are then plays of the simple game A.

From this follows a description of the strategy

$$!!f \quad : \quad !!A \quad \longrightarrow \quad !!B$$

for a deterministic strategy $f : A \multimap B$. The positions of $!!f$ are of the form

$$(e, (\phi, \psi, \overline{a}), (\phi', \psi', \overline{b}))$$

where $e^*\phi' = \phi, e^*\psi' = \psi$ and each thread of (ψ, e, π) is a play of the strategy f.

D Some Bicategorical Definitions

In this section, we recall a few definitions required by our bicategorical setting.

Definition 24. *A pseudofunctor is a mapping between bicategories $\mathcal{C}$ and $\mathcal{D}$ where the usual functorial equations $F(f \circ g) = F(f) \circ F(g)$ and $F(Id_A) = Id_{F(A)}$ are only valid up to natural bijectve 2-morphisms in $\mathcal{D}$.*

Definition 25. *Let $(\mathcal{C}, \otimes_\mathcal{C}, 1_\mathcal{C})$ and $(\mathcal{D}, \otimes_\mathcal{D}, 1_\mathcal{D})$ be two monoidal bicategories. A lax monoidal pseudofunctor between them is given by:*

- *a pseudofunctor $F : \mathcal{C} \to \mathcal{D}$*
- *a morphism $\epsilon : 1_\mathcal{D} \to F(1_{\mathcal{C})}$*
- *for every pair of objects $A, B \in \mathcal{C}$, a natural transformation $\mu_{A,B} : F(A) \otimes_\mathcal{D} F(B) \to F(A \otimes_\mathcal{C} B)$*

satisfying the following conditions:

- *associativity: For every triple of objects $A, B, C \in \mathcal{C}$, the following diagram commutes:*

$$\begin{array}{ccc}
(F(A) \otimes_\mathcal{D} F(B)) \otimes_\mathcal{D} F(C) & \xrightarrow{a^\mathcal{D}_{F(A),F(B),F(C)}} & F(A) \otimes_\mathcal{D} (F(B) \otimes_\mathcal{D} F(C)) \\
\downarrow{\scriptstyle \mu_{A,B} \otimes id} & & \downarrow{\scriptstyle id \otimes \mu_{B,C}} \\
F(A \otimes_\mathcal{C} B) \otimes_\mathcal{D} F(C) & & F(A) \otimes_\mathcal{D} F(B \otimes_\mathcal{C} C) \\
\downarrow{\scriptstyle \mu_{A \otimes B, C}} & & \downarrow{\scriptstyle \mu_{A, B \otimes C}} \\
F((A \otimes_\mathcal{C} B) \otimes_\mathcal{C} C) & \xrightarrow{F(a^\mathcal{C}_{A,B,C})} & F(A \otimes_\mathcal{C} (B \otimes_\mathcal{C} C))
\end{array}$$

  where the two morphisms $a^\mathcal{C}, a^\mathcal{D}$ denote the associators of the two tensor products.
- *unality: For every object $A \in \mathcal{C}$, the following diagram and its right symmetry both commute:*

$$\begin{array}{ccc}
1_\mathcal{D} \otimes_\mathcal{D} F(A) & \xrightarrow{\epsilon \otimes id} & F(1_\mathcal{C}) \otimes_\mathcal{D} F(A) \\
\downarrow{\scriptstyle l^\mathcal{D}_{F(A)}} & & \downarrow{\scriptstyle \mu_{1_\mathcal{C}, A}} \\
F(A) & \xleftarrow{F(l^\mathcal{C}{}_A)} & F(1_\mathcal{C} \otimes_\mathcal{C} A)
\end{array}$$

  where $l^\mathcal{C}, l^\mathcal{D}$ denote the left unitors of the two tensor products.

Definition 26. *Let F, G be two pseudofunctors between two bicategories $\mathcal{C}$ and $\mathcal{D}$. A pseudonatural transformation $\phi : F \to G$ is given by:*

- *for every object A of $\mathcal{C}$, a morphism $\phi(A) : F(A) \to G(A)$ of $\mathcal{D}$.*
- *for every morphism $f : A \to B$ of $\mathcal{C}$, a bijective 2−morphism $\phi(f) : \phi(B) \circ F(f) \Rightarrow G(f) \circ \phi(A)$*

such that

- *ϕ respects composition of morphisms, meaning that we have an equivalence between*

$$(\phi(A) \triangleleft G(f, g)) \cdot (\phi(f) \triangleright G(g)) \cdot (F(f) \triangleleft \phi(g))$$

and

$$\phi(g \circ f) \cdot (F(f, g) \triangleright \phi(C)),$$

both being 2-morphisms from

$$\phi(C) \circ F(g) \circ F(f) \Rightarrow G(g \circ f) \circ \phi(A),$$

where $\cdot$ is the vertical composition between 2-morphisms, $\triangleleft, \triangleright$ the two versions of the horizontal composition between a morphism and a 2-morphism, (also called whiskering), anf $F(f, g) : F(g) \circ F(f) \Rightarrow F(g \circ f)$ is the bijective 2-morphism coming from the pseudofunctor F.
- *ϕ respects the identity morphisms, meaning we have an equivalence between*

$$L^{\mathcal{D}}_{\phi(A)} \cdot \epsilon^{F}_{id_A} \triangleright \phi(A)$$

and

$$R^{\mathcal{D}}_{\phi(A)} \cdot \phi(A) \triangleleft \epsilon^{G}_{id_A} \cdot \phi(id_A)$$

both being 2-morphisms from

$$\phi(A) \circ F(id_A) \Rightarrow \phi(A)$$

where $L^{\mathcal{D}}_{\phi(A)} : \phi(A) \circ id_{F(A)} \Rightarrow \phi(A)$ is the left unitor coming from the bicategory $\mathcal{D}$ and $\epsilon^{F}_{id_A} : F(id_A) \Rightarrow id_{F(A)}$ is the bijective 2-morphism coming from the pseudofunctor F.
- *ϕ is natural in the following sense: for every 2-morphism $\psi : f \Rightarrow g$ with $f, g : A \to B$, we have an equivalence between*

$$\phi(g) \cdot F(\psi) \triangleright \phi(B)$$

and

$$\phi(A) \triangleleft G(\psi) \cdot \phi(f).$$

Definition 27. *A fully weak comonad G on a bicategory $\mathcal{C}$ is a pseudofunctor, along with pseudonatural transformations δ and ϵ that satisfy the usual laws of a comonad up to natural bijectiive 2-morphisms in $\mathcal{C}$.*

E Proof of Proposition 2

Proof. Let A, B be two games.

Let σ be a P-cartesian transduction between A and B. The associated deterministic strategy f_σ is simply given by:

$$f_\sigma(2n) = \{(c, a, \sigma(a)) | a \in A(n)\}$$

This definition clearly gives a functional strategy, the determinism being given by the fact that σ is P-cartesian.

Conversely, let f be a functional strategy of $A \multimap B$. The associated P-cartesian transduction σ_f is given by:

$$\sigma_f(2n)(a) = b \text{ s.t. } (c, a, b) \in f(4n)$$

Such a b is unique by functionality of f.

F Proof that $\mathcal{P}$ is a pseudofunctor

Proof. First we need to complete the definition of $\mathcal{P}$ by detailling why, for f a deterministic strategy of $A \to B$ and σ a P-strategy over A, $\mathcal{P}(f)(\sigma)$ is indeed a P-strategy over B, and thus a presheaf over $\mathbf{tree}(B_P)$. For this, we need to define the collection of projector functions $\pi_{2n} : \mathcal{P}(f)(\sigma)(2n) \to \mathcal{P}(f)(\sigma)(2n-2)$ as follows:

For $x \in \mathcal{P}(f)(\sigma)(2n)$ over b (meaning $x \in \mathcal{P}(f)(\sigma)(b)$ and $b \in B_{2n}$), there exists by definition a unique e, a such that $(e, a, b) \in f$ and $x \in \sigma(a)$. From this, we define:

$$\pi_{2n}(x) = \pi_\sigma^k(x), (\pi^{2k+2}(e), \pi_A^{2k}(a), \pi_B^2(b)) \in f.$$

By determinism of f, there is only one such k. Moreover, we also have $\pi_\sigma^k(x) \in \sigma(\pi_A^{2k}(a))$. Consequently, by definition of $\mathcal{P}(f)(\sigma)$, we have $\pi_\sigma^k(x) \in \mathcal{P}(f)(\sigma)(\pi_B^2(b))$ as expected.

Next step is to show that, for a strategy $f : A \to B$, $\mathcal{P}(f)$ is a functor from $\mathcal{P}(A)$ to $\mathcal{P}(B)$. For that, we need to define its effects on simulations. For $\alpha : \sigma \to \tau$, $\mathcal{P}(f)(\alpha) : \mathcal{P}(f)(\sigma) \to \mathcal{P}(f)(\tau)$ is simply defined by applying α to all positions of $\mathcal{P}(f)(\sigma)$, as all those are induced from positions of σ by definition. With this, it is easy to verify that $\mathcal{P}(f)$ preserves identities and composition of simulations.

Finally, let us show that $\mathcal{P}$ is a pseudofunctor.

First, $\mathcal{P}(Id_A)\sigma$ associates to a position a of A the set:

$$\mathcal{P}(Id_A)(\sigma) \quad : \quad a \quad \mapsto \quad \coprod_{(c,a,a) \in Id_A} \sigma(a).$$

which is instantly isomorphic to $\sigma(a)$. Factoring the effect on simulations, it is easy to build a bijective natural natural transformation between $\mathcal{P}(Id_A) \cong Id_{\mathcal{P}(A)}$. Thus $\mathcal{P}(Id_A) \cong Id_{\mathcal{P}(A)}$.

Next, let $f : A \to B$ and $g : B \to C$ two deterministic strategies and σ a P-strategy of A. We have:

$$\mathcal{P}(g)(\mathcal{P}(f)(\sigma) \quad : \quad c \quad \mapsto \quad \coprod_{(e_2, b, c) \in g} \; \coprod_{(e_1, a, b) \in f} \sigma(a).$$

This is easily isomorphic to $\mathcal{P}(g \circ f)\sigma$ which is given by:

$$\mathcal{P}(g \circ f)(\sigma) \quad : \quad c \quad \mapsto \quad \coprod_{(e, a, c) \in g \circ f} \sigma(a).$$

This isomorphism is a consequence of the definition of composition for deterministic strategies, as there is only one triple e_1, e_2, b such that $(e_1, a, b) \in f$, $(e_2, b, c) \in g$ and $e = e_1 \cdot e_2$ for a position $(e, a, c) \in g \circ f$.

This extends into a natural isomorphism between the functors $\mathcal{P}(g \circ f)$ and $\mathcal{P}(g)(\mathcal{P}(f)$, giving us the fact that $\mathcal{P}$ is indeed a pseudofunctor.

G Proof of Proposition 6

Proof. – Let $f : A \multimap B, g : C \multimap D$ be two slender strategies. Let (t_2, b, d)be a player position of $B \otimes D$. Since f and g are slender, there exist unique e_f, a, e_g, c such that $(e_f, a, b) \in f, (e_g, c, d) \in g$. Using t_2, e_f, e_g and Proposition 10, we reconstruct e, t_1 such that $(e, (t_1, a, c), (t_2, b, d))$ is a position of $f \otimes g$. This position is unique as the reconstruction of Proposition 10 is unique, and thus $f \otimes g$ is a slender strategy.

– Let $f : A \multimap B, g : C \multimap D$ be two functional strategies. Let (t_1, a, c) be an opponent position of $A \otimes C$. Since f and g are functional strategies, there exist unique b, d such that $(cp_f, a, b) \in f, (cp_g, c, d) \in g$. The study of $f \otimes g$ done in the proof of Proposition 10 gives us that any valid position of $f \otimes g$ would have a copycat schedule (as the schedule is built from sequences $1.0^k.1$ of cp_f and cp_g. This implies immediately that the only possible position is $cp, (t_1, a, c), (t_1, b, d)$ as no other play would verify the needed structures, and thus $f \otimes g$ is a functional strategy.

H Proof of Theorem 3

Proof. First, we can note that the unit 1 of $\mathcal{G}$ has a unique P-strategy, the empty strategy. Consequently, $\mathcal{P}(1)$ is the singleton category, which is the unit of the cartesian product in **Cat**.

Moreover, to extend $\mathcal{P}$ as a lax monoidal pseudofunctor, we need a transformation $\mu_{A,B} : \mathcal{P}(A) \times \mathcal{P}(B) \to \mathcal{P}(A \otimes B)$ natural in A and B.

Since the morphisms of that transformation live in **Cat**, they are functors. We thus define:

for σ an object of $\mathcal{P}(A)$ and τ an object of $\mathcal{P}(B)$,

$$\mu_{A,B}(\sigma, \tau) = \sigma \otimes \tau$$

for $\alpha : \sigma \to \sigma'$ a morphism of $\mathcal{P}(A)$ and $\beta : \tau \to \tau'$ a morphism of $\mathcal{P}(B)$, $\mu_{A,B}(\alpha, \beta) : \sigma \otimes \tau \to \sigma' \otimes \tau'$ is defined by:

$$\mu_{A,B}(\alpha, \beta)(t, x, y) = (t, \alpha(x), \beta(y))$$

We now need to prove that this transformation is natural in A and B, and that it verifies the two commutative diagrams of a lax monoidal functor (associativity and unitality), up to bijective simulations. Those last two are easy to verify and use similar arguments, so we will focus on the naturality.

We need our transformation to verify the following commutative diagram for A, B, A', B' four games and $f : A \multimap A', g : B \multimap B'$ two deterministic strategies:

$$\begin{array}{ccc} \mathcal{P}(A) \times \mathcal{P}(B) & \xrightarrow{\mu_{A,B}} & \mathcal{P}(A \otimes B) \\ \downarrow {\scriptstyle \mathcal{P}(f) \times \mathcal{P}(g)} & & \downarrow {\scriptstyle \mathcal{P}(f \otimes g)} \\ \mathcal{P}(A') \times \mathcal{P}(B') & \xrightarrow{\mu_{A',B'}} & \mathcal{P}(A' \otimes B') \end{array}$$

Let σ be a P-strategy of A and τ a P-strategy of B. Verifying the commutative diagram amounts to finding two reciprocal morphisms between: $\mathcal{P}(f)(\sigma) \otimes \mathcal{P}(g)(\tau)$ and $\mathcal{P}(f \otimes g)(\sigma \otimes \tau)$.

$$\mathcal{P}(f)(\sigma) \otimes \mathcal{P}(g)(\tau) \cong \mathsf{image}(f \circ \mathsf{supp}_{\sigma}) \otimes \mathsf{image}(g \circ \mathsf{supp}_{\tau})$$
$$\mathcal{P}(f)(\sigma) \otimes \mathcal{P}(g)(\tau) \cong \mathsf{image}(f \circ \mathsf{supp}_{\sigma} \otimes g \circ \mathsf{supp}_{\tau}) \text{ by consequences of prop 6}$$

$$\mathcal{P}(f \otimes g)(\sigma \otimes \tau) \cong \mathsf{image}((f \otimes g) \circ \mathsf{supp}_{\sigma \otimes \tau})$$
$$\mathcal{P}(f \otimes g)(\sigma \otimes \tau) \cong \mathsf{image}((f \otimes g) \circ \mathsf{supp}_{\sigma} \otimes \mathsf{supp}_{\tau}) \text{ by consequences of prop 6}$$

By bifunctoriality of $\otimes$, we have $f \circ \mathsf{supp}_{\sigma} \otimes g \circ \mathsf{supp}_{\tau} \cong (f \otimes g) \circ \mathsf{supp}_{\sigma} \otimes \mathsf{supp}_{\tau}$, giving us the equality of the images we need, up to bijective simulations.

I Proof of Proposition 9

Proof. – Let $(\psi, \bar{b} = b_1, ...b_n)$ a P position of $!B$. Since f is slender, for all b_i player positions of $\bar{b}$, there exists a unique pair (e_i, a_i) such that $(e_i, a_i, b_i) \in f$.

We use a method similar to the one used in the proof of Proposition 10. Instead of using the tensorial schedule to guide us in reconstructing the play of $!A \multimap !B$, we use ψ, which indicates us what is the next player move b_i to get to (starting from b_{i-2}, and assuming we have reconstructed e and ϕ so far), and then use the play (e_i, a_i, b_i) to construct the play.

The sequence of moves we add is the suffix of the play (e_i, a_i, b_i) looking like $b_{i-1}a_i^1....a_i^k b_i$ (with $a_i^k = a_i$) as any other move in the play (e_i, a_i, b_i) has already been played (since in particular any b move prior to b_{i-1} has been played.

Player cannot backtrack in the middle of the sequence $b_{i-1}a_i^1....a_i^k b_i$ without breaking the fact that the full play is associated to a O-heap in $!(A \multimap B)$.

This allows us to extend e into $e.1.0^k.1$ and ϕ by linking a_i^1 to its predecessor in A of the play (e_i, a_i, b_i).

This method constructs a valid position of $!f$ as all branches are played following f and ϕ is a O-Heap. It is the only possible position including $\psi, \overline{b}$ as everything we have done was determined by ψ, f and $\overline{b}$. Thus $!f$ is a slender strategy.

- Let $(\phi, \overline{a} = a_1, ...a_n)$ an O position of $!A$. Since f is a functional strategy, for all a_i opponent positions of $\overline{a}$, there exists a unique b_i such that $(c, a_i, b_i) \in f$. By determinism of f, it is also true for all player positions of $\overline{a}$. By using ϕ as a guide, this easily allows us to construct the position of $!f$: $(c, (\phi, \overline{a}), (\phi, \overline{b} = b_1, ...b_n))$.

  It is the unique such position for $(\phi, \overline{a})$ for reasons similar to the ones evoked in the proof for slender strategies. Thus $!f$ is a functional strategy.

J Proof of Theorem 4

Proof. – For a game A, we have by construction:

$$(!_{\mathcal{P}})_{A,B}(Id_A) = \mathcal{P}(n_{A,B}) \circ \#^{\mathcal{S}}(Id_A)$$

$$(!_{\mathcal{P}})_{A,B}(Id_A) = \mathcal{P}(n_{A,B})(\# Id_A) = Id_{!A}$$

- Let A, B, C be three games and σ a P-strategy of $A \multimap B$, τ a P-strategy of $B \multimap C$. We need to prove that there is a natural isomorphic simulation between $!_{\mathcal{P}}(\tau \circ \sigma)$ and $!_{\mathcal{P}}(\tau) \circ\ !_{\mathcal{P}}(\sigma)$.

  First we will simplify those two strategies through the various properties we have seen so far:

  First $!_{\mathcal{P}}(\tau \circ \sigma)$:

$$!_{\mathcal{P}}(\tau \circ \sigma) = \mathcal{P}(n_{A,C})(\#^{\mathcal{S}}(\tau \circ \sigma))$$
$$!_{\mathcal{P}}(\tau \circ \sigma) \cong \mathsf{image}(n_{A,C} \circ \mathsf{supp}_{\#^{\mathcal{S}}(\tau\circ\sigma)}) \text{ by equation 4}$$
$$!_{\mathcal{P}}(\tau \circ \sigma) \cong \mathsf{image}(n_{A,C} \circ\ !\mathsf{supp}_{\tau\circ\sigma}) \text{ by consequence of def 13}$$
$$!_{\mathcal{P}}(\tau \circ \sigma) \cong \mathsf{image}(n_{A,C} \circ\ !\mathsf{supp}_{\mathcal{P}(comp_{A,B,C})(\sigma\otimes\tau)}) \text{ by definition 9}$$
$$!_{\mathcal{P}}(\tau \circ \sigma) \cong \mathsf{image}(n_{A,C} \circ\ !\mathsf{supp}_{\mathsf{image}(comp_{A,B,C} \circ \mathsf{supp}_{\sigma\otimes\tau})}) \text{ by equation 4}$$
$$!_{\mathcal{P}}(\tau \circ \sigma) \cong \mathsf{image}(n_{A,C} \circ \mathsf{supp}_{\mathsf{image}(!(comp_{A,B,C} \circ \mathsf{supp}_{\sigma\otimes\tau}))}) \text{ by consequence of def 13}$$
$$!_{\mathcal{P}}(\tau \circ \sigma) \cong \mathsf{image}(n_{A,C} \circ\ !(comp_{A,B,C} \circ \mathsf{supp}_{\sigma\otimes\tau})) \text{ by theorem 1}$$
$$!_{\mathcal{P}}(\tau \circ \sigma) \cong \mathsf{image}(n_{A,C} \circ\ !comp_{A,B,C} \circ \mathsf{supp}_{\#^{\mathcal{S}}(\sigma\otimes\tau)}) \text{ by functoriality of ! and consequence of def 13}$$

Then, $!_{\mathcal{P}}(\tau) \circ\ !_{\mathcal{P}}(\sigma)$:

$$!_{\mathcal{P}}(\tau) \circ\ !_{\mathcal{P}}(\sigma) = \mathcal{P}(n_{B,C})(\#^{s}\tau) \circ \mathcal{P}(n_{A,B})(\#^{s}\sigma)$$

$$!_{\mathcal{P}}(\tau) \circ !_{\mathcal{P}}(\sigma) \cong \mathsf{image}(n_{B,C} \circ \mathsf{supp}_{\#^{s}(\tau)}) \circ \mathsf{image}(n_{A,B} \circ \mathsf{supp}_{\#^{s}(\sigma)}) \text{ by equation 4}$$

$$!_{\mathcal{P}}(\tau) \circ !_{\mathcal{P}}(\sigma) \cong \mathcal{P}(comp_{!A,!B,!C})(\mathsf{image}(n_{A,B} \circ \mathsf{supp}_{\#^{s}(\sigma)}) \otimes \mathsf{image}(n_{B,C} \circ \mathsf{supp}_{\#^{s}(\tau)})) \text{ by definition 9}$$

$$!_{\mathcal{P}}(\tau) \circ !_{\mathcal{P}}(\sigma) \cong \mathcal{P}(comp_{!A,!B,!C})(\mathsf{image}(n_{A,B} \circ \mathsf{supp}_{\#^{s}(\sigma)} \otimes n_{B,C} \circ \mathsf{supp}_{\#^{s}(\tau)})) \text{ by consequence of prop 6}$$

$$!_{\mathcal{P}}(\tau) \circ !_{\mathcal{P}}(\sigma) \cong \mathsf{image}(comp_{!A,!B,!C} \circ (\mathsf{supp}_{\mathsf{image}(n_{A,B} \circ \mathsf{supp}_{\#^{s}(\sigma)} \otimes n_{B,C} \circ \mathsf{supp}_{\#^{s}(\tau)})})) \text{ by equation 4}$$

$$!_{\mathcal{P}}(\tau) \circ !_{\mathcal{P}}(\sigma) \cong \mathsf{image}(comp_{!A,!B,!C} \circ (n_{A,B} \circ \mathsf{supp}_{\#^{s}(\sigma)} \otimes n_{B,C} \circ \mathsf{supp}_{\#^{s}(\tau)})) \text{ by theorem 1}$$

$$!_{\mathcal{P}}(\tau) \circ !_{\mathcal{P}}(\sigma) \cong \mathsf{image}(comp_{!A,!B,!C} \circ n_{A,B} \otimes n_{B,C} \circ \mathsf{supp}_{\#^{s}(\sigma)} \otimes \mathsf{supp}_{\#^{s}(\tau)}) \text{ by bifunctoriality of } \otimes$$

$$!_{\mathcal{P}}(\tau) \circ !_{\mathcal{P}}(\sigma) \cong \mathsf{image}(comp_{!A,!B,!C} \circ n_{A,B} \otimes n_{B,C} \circ !\mathsf{supp}_{(\sigma)} \otimes !\mathsf{supp}_{(\tau)}) \text{ by consequence of def 13}$$

We intend to prove that those two images are isomorphic. For that, we will make the following remark:
! is lax monoidal in $\mathcal{G}$, meaning that there exists a transformation $\mu_{A,B} : !A \otimes !B \to !(A \otimes B)$ natural in A and B. Thus we have the following diagram with the top square commuting by naturality of μ:

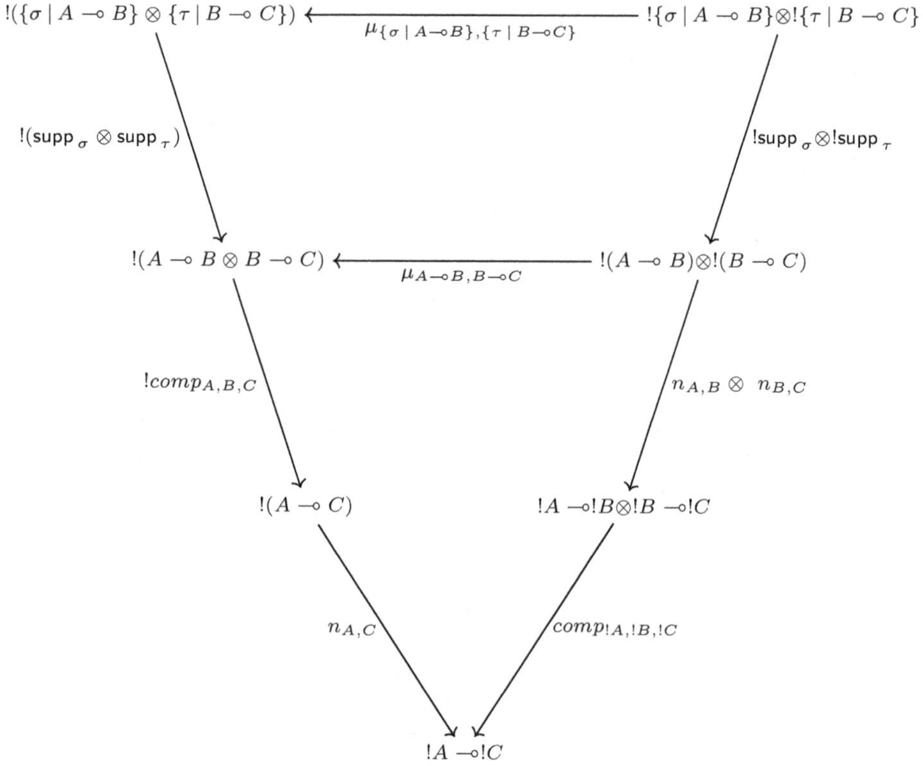

In more details, positions of $\mu_{A,B}$ are of the form: $(e, (t, \phi, \overline{a}, \psi, \overline{b}), (\Phi, \overline{t', a, b}))$, where, for a position $(\Phi, \overline{t', a, b})$ of $!(A \otimes B)$, one can rebuild the unique associated position by playing the moves in order and building the tensorial schedule and the O-heaps incrementally, the general structure ensuring that we do get them in the end. Consequently $\mu_{A,B}$ is slender and induces a transduction from B to A.

Note that it is not bijective as the play of $!(A \otimes B)$ where we play in B, then backtrack to play in A would produce the same play in $!A\otimes!B$ than playing in B then in A without backtracking.
Thus, we have, since $\mu_{\{\sigma \mid A\multimap B\},\{\tau \mid B\multimap C\}}$ is slender:

$$\mathsf{image}(n_{A,C} \circ\ !comp_{A,B,C} \circ\ \mathsf{supp}_{\#^{\mathrm{s}}(\sigma\otimes\tau)}) \cong \mathsf{image}(n_{A,C} \circ\ !comp_{A,B,C} \circ \mathsf{supp}_{\#^{\mathrm{s}}(\sigma\otimes\tau)} \circ\ \mu_{\{\sigma \mid A\multimap B\},\{\tau \mid B\multimap C\}})$$

Then, by naturality,

$$\mathsf{image}(n_{A,C} \circ\ !comp_{A,B,C} \circ\ \mathsf{supp}_{\#^{\mathrm{s}}(\sigma\otimes\tau)}) \cong \mathsf{image}(n_{A,C} \circ\ !comp_{A,B,C} \circ \mu_{A\multimap B,B\multimap C} \circ\ \mathsf{supp}_{\#^{\mathrm{s}}\sigma\otimes\#^{\mathrm{s}}\tau})$$

Consequently,

$$\mathsf{image}(n_{A,C} \circ\ !comp_{A,B,C} \circ\ \mathsf{supp}_{!(\sigma\otimes\tau)}) \cong \mathsf{image}(comp_{!A,!B,!C} \circ n_{A,B} \otimes\ n_{B,C} \circ !\mathsf{supp}_{(\sigma)} \otimes !\mathsf{supp}_{(\tau)})$$

if and only if

$$\mathsf{image}(n_{A,C} \circ\ !comp_{A,B,C} \circ\ \mu_{A\multimap B,B\multimap C} \circ\ \mathsf{supp}_{!\sigma\otimes!\tau}) \cong \mathsf{image}(comp_{!A,!B,!C} \circ n_{A,B} \otimes\ n_{B,C} \circ !\mathsf{supp}_{(\sigma)} \otimes !\mathsf{supp}_{(\tau)})$$

meaning if and only if

$$\mathsf{image}(n_{A,C} \circ\ !comp_{A,B,C} \circ\ \mu_{A\multimap B,B\multimap C}) \cong \mathsf{image}(comp_{!A,!B,!C} \circ n_{A,B} \otimes\ n_{B,C})$$

An important remark is that $\mu_{A\multimap B,B\multimap C}$ transfers plays p of $(!(A \multimap B)\otimes!(B \multimap C))$ such that there exists $(e, (\phi, \overline{a}), (\psi, \overline{c}))_p \in \mathsf{image}(comp_{!A,!B,!C} \circ n_{A,B} \otimes\ n_{B,C})$ to plays p' of $!(A \multimap B \otimes B \multimap C)$ such that there exists $(e, (\phi, \overline{a}), (\psi, \overline{c}))'_p \in \mathsf{image}(n_{A,C} \circ\ !comp_{A,B,C})$.

In other words μ, when restricted to plays that play a role in the images we outlined, acts as a function from the set of plays of $(!(A \multimap B)\otimes!(B \multimap C))$ to the set of plays of $!(A \multimap B \otimes B \multimap C)$. This can be proved by looking at the respective structures of the plays and induces one half of the isomorphism we need.

We do a similar study by introducing a P-strategy of $!(A \multimap B \otimes B \multimap C) \multimap (!(A \multimap B)\otimes!(B \multimap C))$ that acts as a converse of $\mu_{A\multimap B,B\multimap C}$ for such plays and thus get a converse to our morphism, which will give us the second half of the isomorphism we need. Here is how we proceed:
Let $(t, (\phi, \overline{e, a, b}), (\psi, \overline{f, b, c}))$ be a play of $(!(A \multimap B)\otimes!(B \multimap C))$ such that there exists

$$(e_{!A\multimap!C}, (\phi_{!A}, \overline{a}), (\phi_{!C}, \overline{c}))_{e,(t,\phi,\overline{e,a,b},\psi,\overline{f,b,c})} \in \mathsf{image}(comp_{!A,!B,!C} \circ n_{A,B} \otimes n_{B,C}).$$

In particular, that implies that, since $n_{A,B} \otimes \overline{n_{B,C}}$ doesn't change the order of moves, the sequence of moves of $(t, \overline{(\phi, e, a, b)}, \overline{(\psi, f, b, c)})$ must be able to be the left projection of $comp_{!A,!B,!C}$. This restricts the way the moves can be played.

In particular, B moves from the two components must must answer each other right away, giving sequences without backtrack of the form $c(b_r.b_l.b_l.b_r) * c$, with similar structures for sequences starting and/or finishing with a A move. In addition, there cannot be any backtrack in A or any of the two B component that would not be initiated by a backtrack in a C component.

The idea is that a backtrack in C induces a backtrack in B which is mirrored on the left component and induces a backtrack in A. Those backtracks give us a heap structure and the moves inside a sequence follow a proper tensor schedule, so it can be seen as a play of $!(A \multimap B \otimes B \multimap C)$ and it is easy to verify that this play would produce an element of $\mathsf{image}(n_{A,C} \circ\ !comp_{A,B,C} \circ \mu_{A \multimap B, B \multimap C})$ and that the P-strategy of $!(A \multimap B \otimes B \multimap C) \multimap (!(A \multimap B) \otimes !(B \multimap C))$ built by reorganizing structure without changing order of moves is a converse to $\mu_{A \multimap B, B \multimap C}$.

Consequently, we have the bijection of images we needed and thus an isomorphic simulation between $!_{\mathcal{P}}(\tau \circ \sigma)$ and $!_{\mathcal{P}}(\tau) \circ\ !_{\mathcal{P}}(\sigma)$. It is natural since μ and the isomorphisms involved in the manipulation of images are natural.
The few additional diagrams that must be checked are easy to verify with similar methods, and thus we have that $!_{\mathcal{P}}$ is a pseudofunctor.

K Proof that ! Is a Pseudocomonad

In the following section, we'll detail the construction of the pseudonatural transformations δ and ϵ and prove their naturality. From those definitions, verifying that ! is a pseudocomonad is easy as the morphism part of the two natural transformations coincides with their definition in the deterministic case, making the diagrams commute instantly. After that, we may do a similar study on d, e to give ! the necessary structure to be a linear exponential modality.

We will handle here the case of δ_σ for a P-strategy $\sigma : A \to B$. This is, by Definiton 26, a bijective 2-morphism between $!_{\mathcal{P}}!_{\mathcal{P}}\sigma \circ \delta_A$ and $\delta_B \circ\ !_{\mathcal{P}}\sigma$, both being P-strategies of $!A \multimap !!B$.

First note that

$$!_{\mathcal{P}}!_{\mathcal{P}}\sigma \circ \delta_A = \mathsf{image}(comp_{!A,!!A,!!B} \circ \ \mathsf{supp}_{!_{\mathcal{P}}!_{\mathcal{P}}\sigma} \otimes \mathsf{supp}_{\delta_A})$$

and that

$$\delta_B \circ\ !_{\mathcal{P}}\sigma = \mathsf{image}(comp_{!A,!B,!!B} \circ \ \mathsf{supp}_{\delta_B} \otimes \mathsf{supp}_{!_{\mathcal{P}}\sigma}).$$

We want to study the structure of both images to find an isomorphic simulation between them.

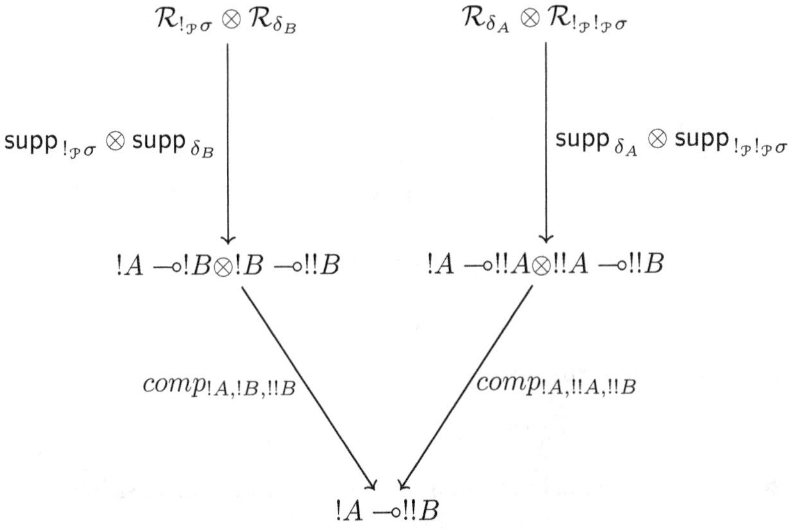

What we will do is start from a position

$$e, (\phi_A, \overline{a}), (\psi_B, \phi_B, \overline{b})$$

of $!A \multimap !!B$ and go back along the arrows to see what structure the positions that produce this position must have.

First, on the left branch, the presence of $comp_{!A,!B,!!B}$ indicates that the position in $!A \multimap !B \otimes !B \multimap !!B$ must be of the form

$$t, (e_1, (\phi_A, \overline{a}), (\Phi_B, \overline{b'}), (e_2, (\Phi_B, \overline{b'}), (\psi_B, \phi_B, \overline{b})))$$

for some $t, e_1, e_2, \Phi_B, \overline{b'}$ such that $e_1 \cdot e_2 = e$.

Since the right component of this position comes from δ_B, we actually have $\overline{b'} = \overline{b}$, $\Phi_B = \phi_B$, $e_2 = c$ and thus $e_1 = e$ and we actually have the position

$$t, (e, (\phi_A, \overline{a}), (\phi_B, \overline{b}), (c, (\phi_B, \overline{b}), (\psi_B, \phi_B, \overline{b})))$$

for some t which is fixed by the two components for the composition to work.

And thus, this gives us the following position of $\mathcal{R}_{!_{\mathcal{P}}\sigma} \otimes \mathcal{R}_{\delta_B}$:

$$(t, ((\phi_A, e, \pi), \overline{x}), (c, (\phi_B, \overline{b}), (\psi_B, \phi_B, \overline{b})))$$

where $\overline{x}$ is a sequence of moves that gets projected to the sequence of moves of $(e, (\phi_A, \overline{a}), (\phi_B, \overline{b}))$. There is no modification of the order the moves are played in this step, just a reorganization of the structure.

Thus a position of $\mathcal{R}_{\delta_B \circ\, !_{\mathcal{P}}\sigma}$ is of the form

$$(e, (\phi_A, \overline{a}), (\psi_B, \phi_B, \overline{b}))_{(t,((\phi_A,e,\pi),\overline{x}),(c,(\phi_B,\overline{b}),(\psi_B,\phi_B,\overline{b})))}.$$

We apply a similar reasoning to the right branch to obtain the form of a position of $\mathcal{R}_{!_{\mathcal{P}}!_{\mathcal{P}}\sigma \circ \delta_A}$:

$$(e, (\phi_A, \overline{a}), (\psi_B, \phi_B, \overline{b}))_{(t',(c,(\phi_A,\overline{a}),(e*\psi_B,\phi_A,\overline{a})),((e*\psi_B,e,\pi),(\phi_A,e,\pi),\overline{x'}))}$$

where t' is fixed by the composition and the sequence of moves $\overline{x'}$ gets projected to the same sequence of moves than $\overline{x}$ in the left branch. In particular, both sequences have the same length.

Since everything is fixed from the initial position $(e, (\phi_A, \overline{a}), (\psi_B, \phi_B, \overline{b}))$ but the two sequences $\overline{x}$ and $\overline{x'}$, we can then build δ_σ as the simulation sending one position to the other one sharing that same initial structure and the same sequence $\overline{x}$.

With a simlar study, we build ϵ_σ as the simulation that sends positions of the form

$$(e, (\pi, \overline{a}), b)_{t,(c,(\pi,\overline{a}),a),x)}$$

to positions of the form

$$(e, (\pi, \overline{a}), b)_{t',(\pi,\overline{x}),(c,(\pi,\overline{b}),b)}).$$

where t, t' are fixed by construction and $\overline{x}$ is the branch of positions finishing in x in $\mathcal{R}_\sigma$.

Proof. We will now prove the pseudonaturality of ϵ, δ is handled in a similar way. Let us look at the naturality first. Let A, B be two games, σ, τ two P-strategies of $A \multimap B$ and $\alpha : \sigma \to \tau$ a simulation We require that the two following pasting diagrams are equivalent:

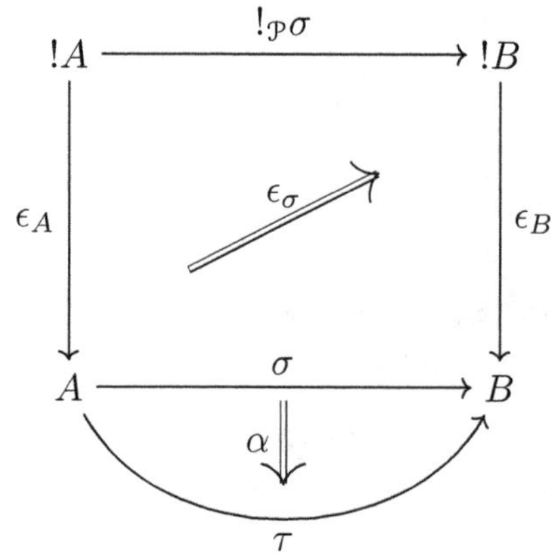

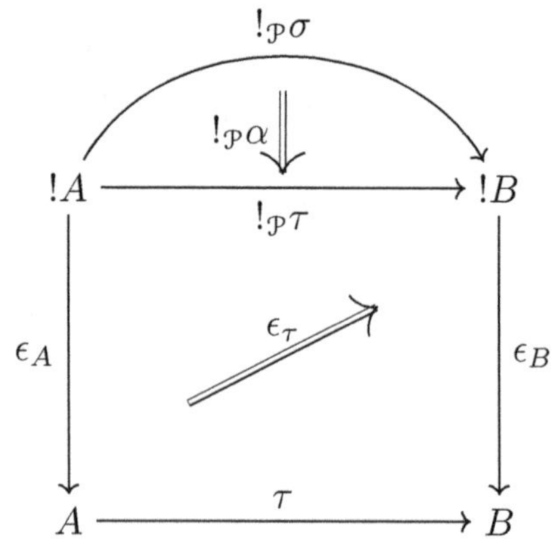

This amounts to the following equality of simulations:

$$(\epsilon_A \lhd \alpha) \cdot \epsilon_\sigma^{-1} = \epsilon_\tau^{-1} \cdot (!_{\mathcal{P}}\alpha \rhd \epsilon_B)$$

where $\lhd, \rhd$ indicate the whiskering that results from the composition of P-strategies and $\cdot$ indicates the vertical composition which is simply the composition of functions. Thus, for a position

$$(e, (\pi, \overline{a}), b)_{t', (\pi, \overline{x}), (c, (\pi, \overline{b}), b)}$$

of $\epsilon_B \circ\ !_{\mathcal{P}}\sigma$, we have:

$$(\epsilon_A \lhd \alpha) \cdot \epsilon_\sigma^{-1}\ ((e, (\pi, \overline{a}), b)_{t', (\pi, \overline{x}), (c, (\pi, \overline{b}), b)}) = (\epsilon_A \lhd \alpha)\ ((e, (\pi, \overline{a}), b)_{t, (c, (\pi, \overline{a}), a), x}) \text{ by def of } \epsilon_\sigma$$

$$(\epsilon_A \lhd \alpha) \cdot \epsilon_\sigma^{-1}\ ((e, (\pi, \overline{a}), b)_{t', (\pi, \overline{x}), (c, (\pi, \overline{b}), b)}) = (e, (\pi, \overline{a}), b)_{t, (c, (\pi, \overline{a}), a), \alpha(x)} \text{ by def of } \mathcal{P}, \epsilon_A$$

On the other hand,

$$\begin{aligned} &\epsilon_\tau^{-1} \cdot (!_{\mathcal{P}}\alpha \rhd \epsilon_B)\ ((e, (\pi, \overline{a}), b)_{t', (\pi, \overline{x}), (c, (\pi, \overline{b}), b)}) \\ &\quad = \epsilon_\tau^{-1}\ ((e, (\pi, \overline{a}), b)_{t', (\pi, \overline{\alpha(x)}), (c, (\pi, \overline{b}), b)}) \text{ by def of } \mathcal{P}, \epsilon_B, !_{\mathcal{P}} \end{aligned}$$

$$\begin{aligned} &\epsilon_\tau^{-1} \cdot (!_{\mathcal{P}}\alpha \rhd \epsilon_B)\ ((e, (\pi, \overline{a}), b)_{t', (\pi, \overline{x}), (c, (\pi, \overline{b}), b)}) \\ &\quad = (e, (\pi, \overline{a}), b)_{t, (c, (\pi, \overline{a}), a), \alpha(x)}) \text{ by def of } \epsilon_\tau \end{aligned}$$

And thus, we have the equivalence we require. The other diagram equalitiies we need to verify are done in a similar way.

The key point to remember from this proof and the similar ones that need to be done, is that, while the form of the positions is a bit heavy, the structures that underly them do most of the work for us, making most of the needed verifications very easy, once the positions have been properly described.

We apply those methods to verify that ! is indeed a pseudocomonad, to define and verify that d_A, e_A are proper pseudonatural transformations and to check that !, along with those transformations, does have the structure of a linear exponential modality.

References

1. Curien, P.-L.: On the symmetry of sequentiality. In: Brookes, S., Main, M., Melton, A., Mislove, M., Schmidt, D. (eds.) MFPS 1993. LNCS, vol. 802, pp. 29–71. Springer, Heidelberg (1994). https://doi.org/10.1007/3-540-58027-1_2
2. Eberhart, C., Hirschowitz, T.: Justified sequences in string diagrams: a comparison between two approached to concurrent game semantics (2016)
3. Girard, J.Y.: Locus Solum: from the rules of logic to the logic of rules. Math. Struct. Comput. Sci. **11**(03), 301–506 (2001)
4. Harmer, R., Hyland, J.M.E., Melliès, P.-A.: Categorical combinatorics for innocent strategies. In: LICS, pp. 379–388 (2007)

5. Hirschowitz, T., Pous, D.: Innocent strategies as presheaves and interactive equivalences for CCS. Sci. Ann. Comput. Sci. (2012)
6. Hyland, M.: Game semantics. In: Semantics of Logics and Computation, Publications of the Newton Institute, pp. 131–184. Cambridge University Press (1997)
7. Laurent, O.: Polarized games. Ann. Pure Appl. Logic **130**(1–3), 79–123 (2004)
8. Lawvere, F.W.: Equality in hyperdoctrines and comprehension schema as an adjoint functor. In: Proceedings of the New York Symposium on Applications of Categorical Algebra, pp. 1–14 (1970)
9. Melliès, P.-A.: Asynchronous games 3: an innocent model of linear logic. In: Category Theory and Computer Science, pp. 171–192 (2004)
10. Melliès, P.-A.: Asynchronous games 4: a fully complete model of propositional linear logic. In: LICS 2005 (2005)
11. Melliès, P.-A.: Asynchronous games 2: the true concurrency of innocence. Theor. Comput. Sci. **358**, 200–228 (2006)
12. Melliès, P.-A.: Game semantics in string diagrams. In: LICS 2012 (2012)
13. Melliès, P.-A.: Tensorial logic with algebraic effects. Talk at the Institut Henri Poincaré, June 2014
14. Melliès, P.-A.: Dialogue categories and chiralities. In: Publications of the Research Institute in Mathematical Sciences (2015)
15. Melliès, P.-A.: Une étude micrologique de la négation. Habilitation thesis (2017)
16. Mellies, P.-A., Zeilberger, N.: Functors are type refinement systems (2015)
17. Ong, C.H.L., Tsukada, T.: Nondeterminism in game semantics via sheaves. In: LICS 2016 (2016)
18. Melliès, P.-A., Mimram, S.: Asynchronous games: innocence without alternation. In: Caires, L., Vasconcelos, V.T. (eds.) CONCUR 2007. LNCS, vol. 4703, pp. 395–411. Springer, Heidelberg (2007). https://doi.org/10.1007/978-3-540-74407-8_27
19. Rideau, S., Winskel, G.: Concurrent strategies. In: LICS 2011 (2011)

10

The Equational Theory of the Natural Join and Inner Union is Decidable

Luigi Santocanale(✉)

LIS, CNRS UMR 7020, Aix-Marseille Université, Marseille, France
luigi.santocanale@lis-lab.fr

Abstract. The natural join and the inner union operations combine relations of a database. Tropashko and Spight [25] realized that these two operations are the meet and join operations in a class of lattices, known by now as the relational lattices. They proposed then lattice theory as an algebraic approach to the theory of databases, alternative to the relational algebra.

Previous works [17,23] proved that the quasiequational theory of these lattices—that is, the set of definite Horn sentences valid in all the relational lattices—is undecidable, even when the signature is restricted to the pure lattice signature.

We prove here that the equational theory of relational lattices is decidable. That, is we provide an algorithm to decide if two lattice theoretic terms t, s are made equal under all interpretations in some relational lattice. We achieve this goal by showing that if an inclusion $t \leq s$ fails in any of these lattices, then it fails in a relational lattice whose size is bound by a triple exponential function of the sizes of t and s.

1 Introduction

The natural join and the inner union operations combine relations (i.e. tables) of a database. SQL-like languages construct queries by making repeated use of the natural join and of the union. The inner union is a mathematically well behaved variant of the union—for example, it does not introduce empty cells. Tropashko and Spight realized [25,26] that these two operations are the meet and join operations in a class of lattices, known by now as the class of relational lattices. They proposed then lattice theory as an algebraic approach, alternative to Codd's relational algebra [4], to the theory of databases.

Roughly speaking, elements of the relational lattice $\mathsf{R}(D, A)$ are tables of a database, where A is a set of columns' names and D is the set of possible cells' values. Let us illustrate the two operations with examples. The natural join takes two tables and constructs a new one whose columns are indexed by the union of the headers, and whose rows are glueings of the rows along identical values in common columns:

Author	Area
Santocanale	Logic
Santocanale	CS

$\bowtie$

Area	Reviewer
CS	Turing
Logic	Gödel

$=$

Author	Area	Reviewer
Santocanale	Logic	Gödel
Santocanale	CS	Turing

The inner union restricts two tables to the common columns and lists all the rows of the two tables. The following example suggests how to construct, using this operation, a table of users given two (or more) tables of people having different roles.

Author		
Name	Surname	Conf
Luigi	Santocanale	FOSSACS

$\cup$

Reviewer		
Name	Surname	Area
Alan	Turing	CS
Kurt	Gödel	Logic

$=$

User	
Name	Surname
Luigi	Santocanale
Alan	Turing
Kurt	Gödel

Since we shall focus on lattice-theoretic considerations, we shall use the symbols $\wedge$ and $\vee$, in place of the symbols $\bowtie$ for $\cup$ used by database theorists.

A first important attempt to axiomatize these lattices was done by Litak et al. [17]. They proposed an axiomatization, comprising equations and quasiequations, in a signature that extends the pure lattice signature with a constant, the header constant. A main result of that paper is that the quasiequational theory of relational lattices is undecidable in this extended signature. Their proof mimics Maddux's proof that the equational theory of cylindric algebras of dimension $n \geq 3$ is undecidable [18].

Their result was further refined by us in [23]: the quasiequational theory of relational lattices is undecidable even when the signature considered is the least one, comprising only the meet (natural join) and the join operations (inner union). Our proof relied on a deeper algebraic insight: we proved that it is undecidable whether a finite subdirectly irreducible lattice can be embedded into a relational lattice—from this kind of result, undecidability of the quasiequational theory immediately follows. We proved the above statement by reducing to it an undecidable problem in modal logic, the coverability problem of a frame by a universal $\mathbf{S5}^3$-product frame [12]. In turn, this problem was shown to be undecidable by reducing it to the representability problem of finite simple relation algebras [11].

We prove here that the equational theory of relational lattices is decidable. That is, we prove that it is decidable whether two lattice terms t and s are such that $[\![t]\!]_v = [\![s]\!]_v$, for any valuation $v : \mathbb{X} \longrightarrow \mathsf{R}(D, A)$ of variables in a relational lattice $\mathsf{R}(D, A)$. We achieve this goal by showing that this theory has a kind of finite model property of bounded size. Out main result, Theorem 25, sounds as follows: *if an inclusion $t \leq s$ fails in a relational lattice $\mathsf{R}(D, A)$, then such inclusion fails in a finite lattice $\mathsf{R}(E, B)$, such that B is bound by an exponential function in the size of t and s, and E is linear in the size of t.* It follows that the size of $\mathsf{R}(E, B)$ can be bound by a triple exponential function in the size of t and s. In algebraic terms, our finite model theorem can be stated by saying that the variety generated by the relational lattices is actually generated by its finite generators, the relational lattices that are finite.

In our opinion, our results are significant in two respects. Firstly, the algebra of the natural join and of the inner union has a direct connection to the widespread SQL-like languages, see e.g. [17]. We dare to say that most of programmers that use a database—more or less explicitly, for example within server-side web programs—are using these operations. In view of the widespread use of these languages, the decidability status of this algebraic system deserved being settled. Moreover, we believe that the mathematical insights contained in our decidability proof shall contribute to understand further the algebraic system. For example, it is not known yet whether a complete finite axiomatic basis exists for relational lattices; finding it could eventually yield applications, e.g. on the side of automated optimization of queries.

Secondly, our work exhibits the equational theory of relational lattices as a decidable one within a long list of undecidable logical theories [11,12,17,18,23] that are used to model the constructions of relational algebra. We are exploring limits of decidability, a research direction widely explored in automata theoretic settings starting from [3]. We do this, within logic and with plenty of potential applications, coming from the undecidable side and crossing the border: after the quasiequational theory, undecidable, the next natural theory on the list, the equational theory of relational lattices, is decidable.

On the technical side, our work relies on [22] where the duality theory for finite lattices developed in [21] was used to investigate equational axiomatizations of relational lattices. A key insight from [22] is that relational lattices are, in some sense, duals of generalized ultrametric spaces over a powerset algebra. It is this perspective that made it possible to uncover the strong similarity between the lattice-theoretic methods and tools from modal logic—in particular the theory of combination of modal logics, see e.g. [15]. We exploit here this similarity to adapt filtrations techniques from modal logic [8] to lattice theory. Also, the notion of generalized ultrametric spaces over a powerset algebra and the characterization of injective objects in the category of these spaces have been fundamental tools to prove the undecidability of the quasiequational theory [23] as well as, in the present case, the decidability of the equational theory.

The paper is organised as follows. We recall in Sect. 2 some definitions and facts about lattices. The relational lattices $\mathsf{R}(D, A)$ are introduced in Sect. 3. In Sect. 4 we show how to construct a lattice $\mathsf{L}(X, \delta)$ from a generalized ultrametric space (X, δ). This construction generalizes the construction of the lattice $\mathsf{R}(D, A)$: if $X = D^A$ is the set of all functions from A to D and δ is as a sort of Hamming distance, then $\mathsf{L}(X, \delta) = \mathsf{R}(D, A)$. We use the functorial properties of L to argue that when a finite space (X, δ) has the property of being pairwise-complete, then $\mathsf{L}(X, \delta)$ belongs to the variety generated by the relational lattices. In Sect. 5 we show that if an inclusion $t \leq s$ fails in a lattice $\mathsf{R}(D, A)$, then we can construct a finite subset $T(f, t) \subseteq D^A$, a "tableau" witnessing the failure, such that if $T(f, t) \subseteq T$ and T is finite, then $t \leq s$ fails in a finite lattice of the form $\mathsf{L}(T, \delta_B)$, where the distance δ_B takes values in a finite powerset algebra $P(B)$. In Sect. 6, we show how to extend $T(f, t)$ to a finite bigger set G, so that (G, δ_B) as a space over the powerset algebra $P(B)$ is pairwise-complete. This lattice $\mathsf{L}(\mathsf{G}, \delta_B)$ fails the inclusion $t \leq s$; out of it, we build a lattice of the form $\mathsf{R}(E, B)$, which fails the same inclusion; the sizes of E and B can be bound by functions of the sizes of the terms t and s. Perspectives for future research directions appear in the last Sect. 7.

2 Elementary Notions on Orders and Lattices

We assume some basic knowledge of order and lattice theory as presented in standard monographs [5,9]. Most of the lattice theoretic tools we use originate from the monograph [7].

A *lattice* is a poset L such that every finite non-empty subset $X \subseteq L$ admits a smallest upper bound $\bigvee X$ and a greatest lower bound $\bigwedge X$. A lattice can also be understood as a structure $\mathfrak{A}$ for the functional signature $(\vee, \wedge)$, such that the interpretations of these two binary function symbols both give $\mathfrak{A}$ the structure of an idempotent commutative semigroup, the two semigroup structures being connected by the absorption laws $x \wedge (y \vee x) = x$ and $x \vee (y \wedge x) = x$. Once a lattice is presented as such structure, the order is recovered by stating that $x \leq y$ holds if and only if $x \wedge y = x$.

A lattice L is *complete* if any subset $X \subseteq L$ admits a smallest upper bound $\bigvee X$. It can be shown that this condition implies that any subset $X \subseteq L$ admits a greatest lower bound $\bigwedge X$. A lattice is *bounded* if it has a least element $\bot$ and a greatest element $\top$. A complete lattice (in particular, a finite lattice) is bounded, since $\bigvee \emptyset$ and $\bigwedge \emptyset$ are, respectively, the least and greatest elements of the lattice.

If P and Q are partially ordered sets, then a function $f : P \longrightarrow Q$ is *order-preserving* (or *monotone*) if $p \leq p'$ implies $f(p) \leq f(p')$. If L and M are lattices, then a function $f : L \longrightarrow M$ is a *lattice morphism* if it preserves the lattice operations $\vee$ and $\wedge$. A lattice morphism is always order-preserving. A lattice morphism $f : L \longrightarrow M$ between bounded lattices L and M is *bound-preserving* if $f(\bot) = \bot$ and $f(\top) = \top$. A function $f : P \longrightarrow Q$ is said to be *left adjoint* to an order-preserving $g : Q \longrightarrow P$ if $f(p) \leq q$ holds if and only if $p \leq g(q)$ holds, for every $p \in P$ and $q \in Q$; such a left adjoint, when it exists, is unique. Dually, a function $g : Q \longrightarrow P$ is said to be *right adjoint* to an order-preserving $f : P \longrightarrow Q$ if $f(p) \leq q$ holds if and only if $p \leq g(q)$ holds; clearly, f is left adjoint to g if and only if g is right adjoint to f, so we say that f and g form an adjoint pair. If P and Q are complete lattices, the property of being a left adjoint (resp., right adjoint) to some g (resp., to some f) is equivalent to preserving all (possibly infinite) joins (resp., all meets).

A *Moore family on* $P(U)$ is a collection $\mathcal{F}$ of subsets of U which is closed under arbitrary intersections. Given a Moore family $\mathcal{F}$ on $P(U)$, the correspondence sending $Z \subseteq U$ to $\overline{Z} := \bigcap\{Y \in \mathcal{F} \mid Z \subseteq Y\}$ is a *closure operator* on $P(U)$, that is, an order-preserving inflationary and idempotent endofunction of $P(U)$. The subsets in $\mathcal{F}$, called the *closed sets*, are exactly the fixpoints of this closure operator. A Moore family $\mathcal{F}$ has the structure of a complete lattice where

$$\bigwedge X := \bigcap X\,, \qquad \bigvee X := \overline{\bigcup X}\,. \tag{1}$$

The notion of Moore family can also be defined for an arbitrary complete lattice L. Moore families on L turns out to be in bijection with closure operators on L. We shall actually consider the dual notion: a *dual Moore family on a complete lattice* L is a subset $\mathcal{F} \subseteq L$ that is closed under arbitrary joins. Such an $\mathcal{F}$ determines an interior operator (an order-preserving decreasing and idempotent endofunction on L) by the formula $x^\circ = \bigvee\{ y \in \mathcal{F} \mid y \leq x \}$ and has the structure of a complete lattice, where $\bigvee_{\mathcal{F}} X := \bigvee_L X$ and $\bigwedge_{\mathcal{F}} X := (\bigwedge_L X)^\circ$. Dual Moore families on L are in bijection with interior operators on L. Finally, let us mention that closure (resp., interior) operators arise from adjoint pairs f and g (with f left adjoint to g) by the formula $\overline{x} = g(f(x))$ (resp., $x^\circ = f(g(x))$);

3 The Relational Lattices $\mathsf{R}(D, A)$

Throughout this paper we use the Y^X for the set of functions of domain Y and codomain X.

Let A be a collection of attributes (or column names) and let D be a set of cell values. A *relation* on A and D is a pair (α, T) where $\alpha \subseteq A$ and $T \subseteq D^\alpha$. Elements of the relational lattice[1] $\mathsf{R}(D, A)$ are relations on A and D. Informally, a relation (α, T) represents a table of a relational database, with α being the header, i.e. the collection of names of columns, while T is the collection of rows.

Before we define the natural join, the inner union operations, and the order on $\mathsf{R}(D, A)$, let us recall some key operations. If $\alpha \subseteq \beta \subseteq A$ and $f \in D^\beta$, then we shall use $f\restriction_\alpha \in D^\alpha$ for the restriction of f to α; if $T \subseteq D^\beta$, then $T\Vert_\alpha$ shall denote projection to α, that is, the direct image of T along restriction, $T\Vert_\alpha := \{ f\restriction_\alpha \mid f \in T \}$; if $T \subseteq D^\alpha$, then $i_\beta(T)$ shall denote cylindrification to β, that is, the inverse image of restriction, $i_\beta(T) := \{ f \in D^\beta \mid f_{\restriction\alpha} \in T \}$. Recall that i_β is right adjoint to $\Vert_\alpha$. With this in mind, the natural join and the inner union of relations are respectively described by the following formulas:

$$
\begin{aligned}
(\alpha_1, T_1) \wedge (\alpha_2, T_2) &:= (\alpha_1 \cup \alpha_2, T) \\
\text{where } T &= \{ f \mid f\restriction_{\alpha_i} \in T_i, i = 1, 2 \} \\
&= i_{\alpha_1 \cup \alpha_2}(T_1) \cap i_{\alpha_1 \cup \alpha_2}(T_2)\,, \\
(\alpha_1, T_1) \vee (\alpha_2, T_2) &:= (\alpha_1 \cap \alpha_2, T) \\
\text{where } T &= \{ f \mid \exists i \in \{ 1, 2 \}, \exists g \in T_i \text{ s.t. } g\restriction_{\alpha_1 \cap \alpha_2} = f \} \\
&= T_1\Vert_{\alpha_1 \cap \alpha_2} \cup T_2\Vert_{\alpha_1 \cap \alpha_2}\,.
\end{aligned}
$$

The order is then given by $(\alpha_1, T_1) \leq (\alpha_2, T_2)$ iff $\alpha_2 \subseteq \alpha_1$ and $T_1\Vert_{\alpha_2} \subseteq T_2$.

A convenient way of describing these lattices was introduced in [17, Lemma 2.1]. The authors showed that the relational lattices $\mathsf{R}(D, A)$ are isomorphic to the lattices of closed subsets of $A \cup D^A$, where $Z \subseteq A \cup D^A$ is said to be closed if it is a fixed-point of the closure operator $\overline{(-)}$ defined as

$$
\overline{Z} := Z \cup \{ f \in D^A \mid A \setminus Z \subseteq Eq(f, g), \text{for some } g \in Z \}\,,
$$

[1] In [17] such a lattice is called *full* relational lattice. The wording "class of relational lattices" is used there for the class of lattices that have an embedding into some lattice of the form $\mathsf{R}(D, A)$.

where in the formula above $Eq(f,g)$ is the equalizer of f and g. Letting $\delta(f,g) := \{ x \in A \mid f(x) \neq g(x) \}$, the above definition of the closure operator is obviously equivalent to the following one:

$$\overline{Z} := \alpha \cup \{ f \in D^A \mid \delta(f,g) \subseteq \alpha, \text{ for some } g \in Z \cap D^A \}, \text{ with } \alpha = Z \cap A.$$

From now on, we rely on this representation of relational lattices.

4 Lattices from Metric Spaces

Generalized ultrametric spaces over a Boolean algebra $P(A)$ turn out to be a convenient tool for studying relational lattices [17,22]. Metrics are well known tools from graph theory, see e.g. [10]. Generalized ultrametric spaces over a Boolean algebra $P(A)$ were introduced in [20] to study equivalence relations.

Definition 1. *An* ultrametric space over $P(A)$ *(briefly, a* space*) is a pair* (X, δ)*, with* $\delta : X \times X \longrightarrow P(A)$ *such that, for every* $f, g, h \in X$*,*

$$\delta(f,f) \subseteq \emptyset\,, \qquad \delta(f,g) \subseteq \delta(f,h) \cup \delta(h,g)\,, \tag{2}$$

$$\delta(f,g) = \emptyset \text{ implies } f = g\,, \qquad \delta(f,g) = \delta(g,f)\,. \tag{3}$$

That is, we have defined an ultrametric space over $P(A)$ as a category (with a small set of objects) enriched over $(P(A)^{op}, \emptyset, \cup)$ (equation (2), see [16]) which moreover is *reduced* and *symmetric* (conditions (3)) .

A *morphism* of spaces[2] $\psi : (X, \delta_X) \longrightarrow (Y, \delta_Y)$ is a function $\psi : X \longrightarrow Y$ such that $\delta_Y(\psi(f), \psi(g)) \leq \delta_X(f,g)$, for each $f, g \in X$. Obviously, spaces and their morphisms form a category. If $\delta_Y(\psi(f), \psi(g)) = \delta_X(f,g)$, for each $f, g \in X$, then ψ is said to be an *isometry.* A space (X, δ) is said to be *pairwise-complete*, see [2], or *convex*, see [19], if, for each $f, g \in X$ and $\alpha, \beta \subseteq A$,

$$\delta(f,g) \subseteq \alpha \cup \beta \text{ implies } \delta(f,h) \subseteq \alpha \text{ and } \delta(h,g) \subseteq \beta\,, \quad \text{for some } h \in X.$$

Proposition 2 (see [2,20]). *If A is finite, then a space is injective in the category of spaces if and only if it is pairwise-complete.*

If (X, δ_X) is a space and $Y \subseteq X$, then the restriction of δ_X to Y induces a space (Y, δ_X); we say then that (Y, δ_X) is a *subspace* of X. Notice that the inclusion of Y into X yields an isometry of spaces.

Our main example of space over $P(A)$ is (D^A, δ), with D^A the set of functions from A to D and the distance defined by

$$\delta(f,g) := \{ a \in A \mid f(a) \neq g(a) \}\,. \tag{4}$$

A second example is a slight generalization of the previous one. Given a surjective function $\pi : D \longrightarrow A$, let Sec_π denote the set of all the functions $f : A \longrightarrow D$ such

[2] As $P(A)$ is not totally ordered, we avoid calling a morphism "*non-expanding map*" as it is often done in the literature.

that $\pi \circ f = id_A$. Then $\mathtt{Sec}_\pi \subseteq D^A$, so $\mathtt{Sec}_\pi$ with the distance inherited from (D^A, δ) can be made into a space. Considering the first projection $\pi_1 : A \times D \longrightarrow A$, we see that (D^A, δ) is isomorphic to the space $\mathtt{Sec}_{\pi_1}$. By identifying $f \in \mathtt{Sec}_\pi$ with a vector $\langle f(a) \in \pi^{-1}(a) \mid a \in A \rangle$, we see that

$$\mathtt{Sec}_\pi = \prod_{a \in A} D_a\,, \qquad \text{where } D_a := \pi^{-1}(a). \tag{5}$$

That is, the spaces of the form $\mathtt{Sec}_\pi$ are naturally related to Hamming graphs in combinatorics [13], dependent function types in type theory [6,14], universal $\mathbf{S5}^A$-product frames in modal logic [12].

Theorem 3 (see [23]). *Spaces of the form $\mathtt{Sec}_\pi$ are, up to isomorphism, exactly the injective objects in the category of spaces.*

4.1 The Lattice of a Space

The construction of the lattice $\mathsf{R}(D, A)$ can be carried out from any space. Namely, for a space (X, δ) over $P(A)$, say that $Z \subseteq X$ is *α-closed* if $g \in Z$ and $\delta(f, g) \subseteq \alpha$ implies $f \in Z$. Clearly, α-closed subsets of X form a Moore family so, for $Z \subseteq X$, we denote by $\overline{Z}^\alpha$ the least α-closed subset of X containing Z. Observe that $f \in \overline{Z}^\alpha$ if and only if $\delta(f, g) \subseteq \alpha$ for some $g \in Z$. Next and in the rest of the paper, we shall exploit the obvious isomorphism between $P(A) \times P(X)$ and $P(A \cup X)$ (where we suppose A and X disjoint) and notationally identify a pair $(\alpha, Z) \in P(A) \times P(X)$ with its image $\alpha \cup X \in P(A \cup X)$. Let us say then that (α, Z) is closed if Z is α-closed. Closed subsets of $P(A \cup X)$ form a Moore family, whence a complete lattice where the order is subset inclusion.

Definition 4. *For a space (X, δ), the lattice $\mathsf{L}(X, \delta)$ is the lattice of closed subsets of $P(A \cup X)$.*

Clearly, for the space (D^A, δ), we have $\mathsf{L}(D^A, \delta) = \mathsf{R}(D, A)$. Let us mention that meets and joins $\mathsf{L}(X, \delta)$ are computed using the formulas in (1). In particular, for joins,

$$(\alpha, Y) \vee (\beta, Z) = (\alpha \cup \beta, \overline{Y \cup Z}^{\alpha \cup \beta}).$$

The above formula yields that, for any $f \in X$, $f \in (\alpha, Y) \vee (\beta, Z)$ if and only if $\delta(f, g) \subseteq \alpha \cup \beta$, for some $g \in Y \cup Z$.

We argue next that the above construction is functorial. Below, for a function $\psi : X \to Y$, $\psi^{-1} : P(Y) \to P(X)$ is the inverse image of ψ, defined by $\psi^{-1}(Z) := \{\, x \in X \mid \psi(x) \in Z \,\}$.

Proposition 5. *If $\psi : (X, \delta_X) \to (Y, \delta_Y)$ is a space morphism and $(\alpha, Z) \in \mathsf{L}(Y, \delta_Y)$, then $(\alpha, \psi^{-1}(Z)) \in \mathsf{L}(X, \delta_X)$. Therefore, by defining $\mathsf{L}(\psi)(\alpha, Z) := (\alpha, \psi^{-1}(Z))$, the construction L lifts to a contravariant functor from the category of spaces to the category of complete meet-semilattices.*

Proof. Let $f \in X$ be such that, for some $g \in \psi^{-1}(Z)$ (i.e. $\psi(g) \in Z$), we have $\delta_X(f,g) \subseteq \alpha$. Then $\delta_Y(\psi(f),\psi(g)) \subseteq \delta_X(f,g) \subseteq \alpha$, so $\psi(f) \in Z$, since Z is α-closed, and $f \in \psi^{-1}(Z)$. In order to see that $\mathsf{L}(\psi)$ preserves arbitrary intersections, recall that ψ^{-1} does. □

Notice that $\mathsf{L}(\psi)$ might not preserve arbitrary joins.

Proposition 6. *The lattices* $\mathsf{L}(\mathsf{Sec}_\pi)$ *generate the same lattice variety of the lattices* $\mathsf{R}(D,A)$.

That is, a lattice equation holds in all the lattices $\mathsf{L}(\mathsf{Sec}_\pi)$ if and only if it holds in all the relation lattices $\mathsf{R}(D,A)$.

Proof. Clearly, each lattice $\mathsf{R}(D,A)$ is of the form $\mathsf{L}(\mathsf{Sec}_\pi)$. Thus we only need to argue that every lattice of the form $\mathsf{L}(\mathsf{Sec}_\pi)$ belongs to the lattice variety generated by the $\mathsf{R}(D,A)$, that is, the least class of lattices containing the lattices $\mathsf{R}(D,A)$ and closed under products, sublattices, and homomorphic images. We argue as follows.

As every space Sec_π embeds into a space (D^A,δ) and a space Sec_π is injective, we have maps $\iota : \mathsf{Sec}_\pi \longrightarrow (D^A,\delta)$ and $\psi : (D^A,\delta) \longrightarrow \mathsf{Sec}_\pi$ such that $\psi \circ \iota = id_{\mathsf{Sec}_\pi}$. By functoriality, $\mathsf{L}(\iota) \circ \mathsf{L}(\psi) = id_{\mathsf{L}(\mathsf{Sec}_\pi)}$. Since $\mathsf{L}(\iota)$ preserves all meets, it has a left adjoint $\ell : \mathsf{L}(\mathsf{Sec}_\pi) \longrightarrow \mathsf{L}(D^A,\delta) = \mathsf{R}(D,A)$. It is easy to see that $(\ell, \mathsf{L}(\psi))$ is an EA-duet in the sense of [24, Definition 9.1] and therefore $\mathsf{L}(\mathsf{Sec}_\pi)$ is a homomorphic image of a sublattice of $\mathsf{R}(D,A)$, by [24, Lemma 9.7]. □

Remark 7. For the statement of [24, Lemma 9.7] to hold, additional conditions are necessary on the domain and the codomain of an EA-duet. Yet the implication that derives being a homomorphic image of a sublattice from the existence of an EA-duet is still valid under the hypothesis that the two arrows of the EA-duet preserve one all joins and, the other, all meets.

4.2 Extension from a Boolean Subalgebra

We suppose that $P(B)$ is a Boolean subalgebra of $P(A)$ via an inclusion $i : P(B) \longrightarrow P(A)$. If (X,δ_B) is a space over $P(B)$, then we can transform it into a space (X,δ_A) over $P(A)$ by setting $\delta_A(f,g) = i(\delta_B(f,g))$. We have therefore two lattices $\mathsf{L}(X,\delta_B)$ and $\mathsf{L}(X,\delta_A)$.

Proposition 8. *Let* $\beta \subseteq B$ *and* $Y \subseteq X$. *Then* Y *is* β*-closed if and only if it is* $i(\beta)$*-closed. Consequently the map* i_**, sending* $(\beta,Y) \in \mathsf{L}(X,\delta_B)$ *to* $i_*(\beta,Y) := (i(\beta),Y) \in \mathsf{L}(X,\delta_A)$*, is a lattice embedding.*

Proof. Observe that $\delta_B(f,g) \subseteq \beta$ if and only if $\delta_A(f,g) = i(\delta_B(f,g)) \subseteq i(\beta)$. This immediately implies the first statement of the Lemma, but also that, for $Y \subseteq X$, $\overline{Y}^{\beta} = \overline{Y}^{i(\beta)}$. Using the fact that meets are computed as intersections and that i preserves intersections, it is easily seen that i_* preserves meets. For joins let us compute as follows:

$$\begin{aligned} i_*(\beta_1, Y_1) \vee i_*(\beta_2, Y_2) &= (i(\beta_1) \cup i(\beta_2), \overline{Y_1 \cup Y_2}^{i(\beta_1) \cup i(\beta_2)}) \\ &= (i(\beta_1 \cup \beta_2), \overline{Y_1 \cup Y_2}^{i(\beta_1 \cup \beta_2)}) = (i(\beta_1 \cup \beta_2), \overline{Y_1 \cup Y_2}^{\beta_1 \cup \beta_2}) \\ &= i_*(\beta_1 \cup \beta_2, \overline{Y_1 \cup Y_2}^{\beta_1 \cup \beta_2}) = i_*((\beta_1, Y_1) \vee (\beta_2, Y_2)). \end{aligned}$$ □

5 Failures from Big to Small Lattices

The set of lattice terms is generated by the following grammar:

$$t := x \mid \top \mid t \wedge t \mid \bot \mid t \vee t\,,$$

where x belongs to a set of variables $\mathbb{X}$. For lattice terms $t_1, \ldots, t_n$, we use $Vars(t_1, \ldots, t_n)$ to denote the set of variables (which is finite) occurring in any of these terms. The size of a term t is the number of nodes in the representation of t as a tree. If $v : \mathbb{X} \longrightarrow L$ is a valuation of variables into a lattice L, the value of a term t w.r.t. the valuation v is defined by induction in the obvious way; here we shall use $[\![t]\!]_v$ for it.

For t, s two lattice terms, the inclusion $t \leq s$ is the equation $t \vee s = s$. Any lattice-theoretic equation is equivalent to a pair of inclusions, so the problem of deciding the equational theory of a class of lattices reduces to the problem of decing inclusions. An inclusion $t \leq s$ is valid in a class of lattices $\mathcal{K}$ if, for any valuation $v : \mathbb{X} \longrightarrow L$ with $L \in \mathcal{K}$, $[\![v]\!]_v \leq [\![s]\!]_v$; it fails in $\mathcal{K}$ if for some $L \in \mathcal{K}$ and $v : \mathbb{X} \longrightarrow L$ we have $[\![t]\!]_v \not\leq [\![s]\!]_v$.

From now on, our goal shall be proving that if an inclusion $t \leq s$ fails in a lattice $\mathsf{R}(D, A)$, then it fails in a lattice $\mathsf{L}(\mathtt{Sec}_\pi)$, where $\mathtt{Sec}_\pi$ is a finite space over some finite Boolean algebra $P(B)$. The size of B and of the space $\mathtt{Sec}_\pi$, shall be inferred from of the sizes of t and s.

From now on, we us fix terms t and s, a lattice $\mathsf{R}(D, A)$, and a valuation $v : \mathbb{X} \longrightarrow \mathsf{R}(D, A)$ such that $[\![t]\!]_v \not\subseteq [\![s]\!]_v$.

Lemma 9. *If, for some $a \in A$, $a \in [\![t]\!]_v \setminus [\![s]\!]_v$, then the inclusion $t \leq s$ fails in the lattice $\mathsf{R}(E, B)$ with $B = \emptyset$ and E a singleton.*

Proof. The map sending $(\alpha, X) \in \mathsf{R}(D, A)$ to $\alpha \in P(A)$ is lattice morphism. Therefore if $t \leq s$ fails because of $a \in A$, then it already fails in the Boolean lattice $P(A)$. Since $P(A)$ is distributive, $t \leq s$ fails in the two elements lattice. Now, when $B = \emptyset$ and E is a singleton $\mathsf{R}(E, B)$ is (isomorphic to) the 2 elements lattice, so the same equation fails in $\mathsf{R}(E, B)$. □

Because of the Lemma, we shall focus on functions $f \in D^A$ such that $f \in [\![t]\!]_v \setminus [\![s]\!]_v$. In this case we shall say that f *witnesses the failure of* $t \leq s$ (in $\mathsf{R}(D, A)$, w.r.t. the valuation v).

5.1 The Lattices $\mathsf{R}(D, A)_T$

Let T be a subset of D^A and consider the subspace (T, δ) of D^A induced by the inclusion $i_T : T \subseteq D^A$. According to Proposition 5, the inclusion i_T induces a complete meet-semilattice homomorphism $\mathsf{L}(i_T) : \mathsf{R}(D, A) = \mathsf{L}(D^A, \delta) \to \mathsf{L}(T, \delta)$. Such a map has a right adjoint $j_T : \mathsf{L}(T, \delta) \to \mathsf{L}(D^A, \delta)$, which is a complete join-semilattice homomorphism; moreover j_T is injective, since $\mathsf{L}(i_T)$ is surjective.

Proposition 10. *For a subset $T \subseteq D^A$ and $(\alpha, X) \in \mathsf{R}(D, A)$, $(\alpha, \overline{X \cap T}^{\alpha}) = j_T(\mathsf{L}(i_T(\alpha, X))$. The set of elements of the form $(\alpha, \overline{X \cap T}^{\alpha})$, for $\alpha \subseteq A$ and $X \subseteq D^A$, is a complete sub-join-semilattice of $\mathsf{R}(D, A)$.*

Proof. It is easily seen that $\mathsf{L}(i_T)(\alpha, X) = (\alpha, X \cap T)$ and that, for $(\beta, Y) \in \mathsf{L}(T, \delta)$, $(\beta, Y) \subseteq (\alpha, X \cap T)$ if and only if $(\beta, \overline{Y}^{\beta}) \subseteq (\alpha, X)$, so $j_T(\beta, Y) = (\beta, \overline{Y}^{\beta})$.

It follows that the elements of the form $(\alpha, \overline{X \cap T}^{\alpha})$, where $(\alpha, X) \in \mathsf{R}(D, A)$, form a sub-complete join-semilattice of $\mathsf{R}(D, A)$: indeed, they are the image of lattice $\mathsf{L}(T, \delta)$ under the complete join-semilattice homomorphism j_T. We argue next that, for any pair (α, X) (we do not require that X is α-closed) there is a $Z \subseteq D^A$ which is α-closed and such that $\overline{X \cap T}^{\alpha} = \overline{Z \cap T}^{\alpha}$. Indeed, the equality

$$\overline{X \cap T}^{\alpha} = \overline{\overline{X \cap T}^{\alpha} \cap T}^{\alpha}$$

is easily verified, so we can let $Z = \overline{X \cap T}^{\alpha}$. □

Therefore, the set of pairs of the form $(\alpha, \overline{X \cap T}^{\alpha})$ is a dual Moore family and a complete lattice, where joins are computed as in $\mathsf{R}(D, A)$, and where meets are computed in a way that we shall make explicit. For the moment, let us fix the notation.

Definition 11. $\mathsf{R}(D, A)_T$ *is the lattice of elements of the form* $(\alpha, \overline{X \cap T}^{\alpha})$.

By the proof of Proposition 10, the lattice $\mathsf{R}(D, A)_T$ is isomorphic to the latttice $\mathsf{L}(T, \delta)$. We shall use the symbol $\bigwedge\!\!\!\!\bigwedge$ for meets in $\mathsf{R}(D, A)_T$; these are computed by the formula

$$\bigwedge\!\!\!\!\bigwedge_{i \in I}(\alpha_i, X_i) = (\bigcap_{i \in I} \alpha_i, \bigcap_{i \in I} X_i)^{\circ},$$

where, for each $(\alpha, X) \in \mathsf{R}(D, A)$, $(\alpha, X)^{\circ}$ is the greatest pair in $\mathsf{R}(D, A)_T$ that is below (α, X). Standard theory on adjoints yields

$$(\alpha, X)^{\circ} = (j_T \circ \mathsf{L}(i_T))(\alpha, X) = (\alpha, \overline{X \cap T}^{\alpha}).$$

We obtain in this way the explicit formula for the binary meet in $\mathsf{R}(D, A)_T$:

$$(\alpha, \overline{X \cap T}^{\alpha}) \bigwedge\!\!\!\!\bigwedge (\beta, \overline{Y \cap T}^{\beta}) = (\alpha \cap \beta, \overline{\overline{X \cap T}^{\alpha} \cap \overline{Y \cap T}^{\beta} \cap T}^{\alpha \cap \beta}).$$

Remark that we have

$$(\alpha, X) \Join (\beta, Y) \subseteq (\alpha, X) \cap (\beta, Y)$$

whenever (α, X) and (β, Y) are in $\mathsf{R}(D, A)_T$.

Lemma 12. *Let $(\alpha, X), (\beta, Y) \in \mathsf{R}(D, A)_T$ and let $f \in T$. If $f \in (\alpha, X) \cap (\beta, Y)$, then $f \in (\alpha, X) \Join (\beta, Y)$.*

Proof. This is immediate from the fact that

$$\overline{X \cap T}^{\alpha} \cap \overline{Y \cap T}^{\beta} \cap T \subseteq \overline{\overline{X \cap T}^{\alpha} \cap \overline{Y \cap T}^{\beta} \cap T}^{\alpha \cap \beta}. \qquad \square$$

5.2 Preservation of the Failure in the Lattices $\mathsf{R}(D, A)_T$

Recall that $v : \mathbb{X} \longrightarrow \mathsf{R}(D, A)$ is the valuation that we have fixed.

Definition 13. *For a susbset T of D^A, the valuation $v_T : \mathbb{X} \longrightarrow \mathsf{R}(D, A)_T$ is defined by the formula $v_T(x) = v(x)^{\circ}$, for each $x \in \mathbb{X}$.*

More explicitley, we have

$$v_T(x) := (\alpha, \overline{T \cap X}^{\alpha}), \quad \text{where } (\alpha, X) = v(x).$$

The valuation v_T takes values in $\mathsf{R}(D, A)_T$, while v takes value in $\mathsf{R}(D, A)$. It is possible then to evaluate a lattice term t in $\mathsf{R}(D, A)_T$ using v_T and to evaluate it in $\mathsf{R}(D, A)$ using v. To improve readability, we shall use the notation $[\![t]\!]_T$ for the result of evaluating the term in $\mathsf{R}(D, A)_T$, and the notation $[\![t]\!]$ for the result of evaluating it in $\mathsf{R}(D, A)$. Since both $[\![t]\!]$ and $[\![t]\!]_T$ are subsets of $P(A \cup X)$, it is possible to compare them using inclusion.

Lemma 14. *The relation $[\![s]\!]_T \subseteq [\![s]\!]$ holds, for each $T \subseteq D^A$ and each lattice term s.*

Proof. The proof of the Lemma is a straightforward induction, considering that $v_T(x) \subseteq v(x)$ for all $x \in \mathbb{X}$. For example, using $[\![s_i]\!]_T \subseteq [\![s_i]\!]$, for $i = 1, 2$,

$$[\![s_1 \wedge s_2]\!]_T = [\![s_1]\!]_T \Join [\![s_2]\!]_T \subseteq [\![s_1]\!]_T \cap [\![s_2]\!]_T \subseteq [\![s_1]\!] \cap [\![s_2]\!] = [\![s_1 \wedge s_2]\!]. \qquad \square$$

A straightforward induction also yields:

Lemma 15. *Let $T \subseteq D^A$ be a finite subset, let t be a lattice term and suppose that $[\![t]\!] = (\beta, Y)$. Then $[\![t]\!]_T$ is of the form (β, Y') for some $Y' \subseteq D^A$.*

Definition 16. *Let us define, for each term t and $f \in D^A$ such that $f \in [\![t]\!]$, a finite set $T(f, t) \subseteq D^A$ as follows:*

- *If t is the variable x, then we let $T(f,t) := \{ f \}$.*
- *If $t = s_1 \wedge s_2$, then $f \in [\![s_1]\!] \cap [\![s_2]\!]$, so we define $T(f,t) := T(f,s_1) \cup T(f,s_2)$.*
- *If $t = s_1 \vee s_2$ and $[\![s_i]\!] = (\alpha_i, X_i)$ for $i = 1,2$, then $f \in [\![s_1 \vee s_2]\!]$ gives that, for some $i \in \{1,2\}$ there exists $g \in X_i$ such that $\delta(f,g) \subseteq \alpha_1 \cup \alpha_2$. We set then $T(f,t) := \{ f \} \cup T(g,s_i)$.*

Obviously, we have:

Lemma 17. *For each lattice term t and $f \in D^A$ such that $f \in [\![t]\!]$, $f \in T(f,t)$.*

Proposition 18. *For each lattice term t and $f \in D^A$ such that $f \in [\![t]\!]$, if $T(f,t) \subseteq T$, then $f \in [\![t]\!]_T$.*

Proof. We prove the statement by induction on t.

- If t is the variable x and $f \in [\![x]\!] = v(x) = (\beta, Y)$, then $f \in Y$. We have $T(f,x) = \{ f \}$. Obviously, $f \in Y \cap \{ f \} = Y \cap T(f,t) \subseteq Y \cap T$, so $f \in (\beta, \overline{Y \cap T}^{\beta}) = v_T(x) = [\![t]\!]_T$.
- Suppose $t = s_1 \wedge s_2$ so $f \in [\![s_1 \wedge s_2]\!]$ yields $f \in [\![s_1]\!]$ and $f \in [\![s_2]\!]$. We have defined $T(f,t) = T(f,s_1) \cup T(f,s_2) \subseteq T$ and so, using $T(f,s_i) \subseteq T$ and the induction hypothesis, $f \in [\![s_i]\!]_T$ for $i = 1,2$. By Lemma 17 $f \in T$, so we can use Lemma 12 asserting that

$$f \in [\![s_1]\!]_T \wedge\!\!\!\wedge [\![s_2]\!]_T = [\![s_1 \wedge s_2]\!]_T \,.$$

- Suppose $t = s_1 \vee s_2$ and $f \in [\![s_1 \vee s_2]\!]$; let also $(\beta_i, Y_i) := [\![s_i]\!]$ for $i = 1,2$. We have defined $T(f,t) := \{ f \} \cup T(g,s_i)$ for some $i \in \{1,2\}$ and for some $g \in [\![s_i]\!]$ such that $\delta(f,g) \subseteq \beta_1 \cup \beta_2$. Now $g \in T(g,s_i) \subseteq T(f,t) \subseteq T$ so, by the induction hypothesis, $g \in [\![s_i]\!]_T$. According to Lemma 15, for each $i = 1,2$ $[\![s_i]\!]_T$ is of the form (β_i, Y_i'), for some subset $Y_i' \subseteq D^A$. Therefore $\delta(f,g) \subseteq \beta_1 \cup \beta_2$ and $g \in [\![s_i]\!]_T$ implies

$$f \in [\![s_1]\!]_T \vee [\![s_2]\!]_T = [\![s_1 \vee s_2]\!]_T \,.$$

□

Proposition 19. *Suppose f witnesses the failure of the inclusion $t \leq s$ in $\mathsf{R}(D,A)$ w.r.t. the valuation v. Then, for each subset $T \subseteq D^A$ such $T(f,t) \subseteq T$, f witnesses the failure of the inclusion $t \leq s$ in the lattice $\mathsf{R}(D,A)_T$ and w.r.t. valuation v_T.*

Proof. As f witnesses $t \not\leq s$ in $\mathsf{R}(D,A)$, $f \in [\![t]\!]$ and $f \notin [\![s]\!]$. By Lemma 18 $f \in [\![t]\!]_T$. If $f \in [\![s]\!]_T$, then $[\![s]\!]_T \subseteq [\![s]\!]$ (Lemma 14) implies $f \in [\![s]\!]$, a contradicition. Therefore $f \notin [\![s]\!]_T$, so f witnesses $t \not\leq s$ in $\mathsf{R}(D,A)_T$. □

5.3 Preservation of the Failure in a Finite Lattice $\mathsf{L}(X,\delta)$

From now on, we suppose that $T \subseteq D^A$ is finite and $T(f,t) \subseteq T$ with f witnessing the failure of $t \leq s$. Consider the sub-Boolean-algebra of $P(A)$ generated by the sets

$$\{ \delta(f,g) \mid f,g \in T \} \cup \{ A \cap v(x) \mid x \in Vars(t,s) \} \,. \tag{6}$$

Let us call B this Boolean algebra (yet, notice the dependency of this definition on T, as well as on t, s and v). It is well known that a Boolean algebra generated by a finite set is finite.

Remark 20. If $n = \mathrm{card}(T)$ and $m = \mathrm{card}(Vars(t,s))$, then B can have at most $2^{\frac{n(n-1)}{2}+m}$ atoms. If we let k be the maximum of the sizes of t and s, then, for $T = T(f,t)$, both $n \leq k$ and $m \leq 2k$. We obtain in this case the over-approximation $2^{\frac{k^2+3k}{2}}$ on the number of atoms of B.

Let us also recall that B is isomorphic to the powerset $P(\mathsf{at}(\mathsf{B}))$, where $\mathsf{at}(\mathsf{B})$ is the set of atoms of B. Let $i : P(\mathsf{at}(\mathsf{B})) \longrightarrow P(A)$ be an injectve homomorphism of Boolean algebras whose image is B. Since $\delta(f,g) \in \mathsf{B}$ for every $f, g \in T$, we can transform the metric space (T, δ) induced from (D^A, δ) into a metric space $(T, \delta_{\mathsf{at}(\mathsf{B})})$ whose distance takes values in the powerset algebra $P(\mathsf{at}(\mathsf{B}))$:

$$\delta_{\mathsf{at}(\mathsf{B})}(f,g) = \beta \quad \text{if and only if} \quad \delta(f,g) = i(\beta)\,.$$

Recall from Proposition 8 that there is a lattice embedding $i_* : \mathsf{L}(T, \delta_{\mathsf{at}(\mathsf{B})}) \longrightarrow \mathsf{L}(T,\delta)$, defined in the obvious way: $i_*(\alpha, Y) = (i(\beta), Y)$.

Proposition 21. *If f witnesses the failure of the inclusion $t \leq s$ in $\mathsf{R}(D,A)$ w.r.t. the valuation v, then the same inclusion fails in all the lattices $\mathsf{L}(T, \delta_{\mathsf{at}(\mathsf{B})})$, where T is a finite set and $T(f,t) \subseteq T$.*

Proof. By Proposition 19 the inclusion $t \leq s$ fails in the lattice $\mathsf{R}(D,A)_T$. This lattice is isomorphic to the lattice $\mathsf{L}(T,\delta)$ via the map sending $(\alpha, X) \in \mathsf{R}(D,A)_T$ to $(\alpha, X \cap T)$. Up to this isomorphism, it is seen that the (restriction to the variables in t and s of) the valuation v_T takes values in the image of the lattice $\mathsf{L}(T, \delta_{\mathsf{at}(\mathsf{B})})$ via i_*, so $[\![t]\!]_T, [\![s]\!]_T$ belong to this sublattice and the inclusion fails in this lattice, and therefore also in $\mathsf{L}(T, \delta_{\mathsf{at}(\mathsf{B})})$. □

6 Preservation of the Failure in a Finite Lattice $\mathsf{L}(\mathtt{Sec}_\pi)$

We have seen up to now that if $t \leq s$ fails in $\mathsf{R}(D,A)$, then it fails in many lattices of the form $\mathsf{L}(T, \delta_{\mathsf{at}(\mathsf{B})})$. Yet it is not obvious a priori that any of these lattices belongs to the variety generated by the relational lattices. We show in this section that we can extend any T to a finite set G while keeping B fixed, so that $(\mathsf{G}, \delta_{\mathsf{at}(\mathsf{B})})$ is a pairwise-complete space over $P(\mathsf{at}(\mathsf{B}))$. Thus, the inclusion $t \leq s$ fails in the finite lattice $\mathsf{L}(\mathsf{G}, \delta_{\mathsf{at}(\mathsf{B})})$. Since $(\mathsf{G}, \delta_{\mathsf{at}(\mathsf{B})})$ is isomorphic to a space of the form $\mathtt{Sec}_\pi$ with $\pi : E \longrightarrow \mathsf{at}(\mathsf{B})$, the inclusion $t \leq s$ fails in a lattice $\mathsf{L}(\mathtt{Sec}_\pi)$ which we have seen belongs to the variety generated by the relational lattices. This also leads to construct a finite relational lattice $\mathsf{R}(\mathsf{at}(\mathsf{B}), E)$ in which the equation $t \leq s$ fails. By following the chain of constructions, the sizes of $\mathsf{at}(\mathsf{B})$ and E can also be estimated, leading to decidability of the equational theory of relational lattices.

Definition 22. *A* glue of T and B *is a function* $g \in D^A$ *such that, for all* $\alpha \in \mathsf{at}(\mathsf{B})$, *there exists* $f \in T$ *with* $f\restriction\alpha = g$. *We denote by* G *the set of all functions that are glues of* T *and* B.

Observe that $T \subseteq \mathsf{G}$ and that G is finite, with

$$\mathrm{card}(\mathsf{G}) \leq \mathrm{card}(T)^{\mathrm{card}(\mathsf{at}(\mathsf{B}))}\,. \tag{7}$$

In order to prove the following Lemma, let, for each $\alpha \in \mathsf{at}(\mathsf{B})$ and $g \in \mathsf{G}$, $f(g,\alpha) \in T$ be such that $g\restriction\alpha = f(g,\alpha)\restriction\alpha$.

Lemma 23. *If* $g_1, g_2 \in \mathsf{G}$, *then* $\delta(g_1, g_2) \in \mathsf{B}$.

Proof.

$$\delta(g_1,g_2) = \bigcup_{\alpha\in\mathsf{at}(\mathsf{B})} (\alpha \cap \delta(g_1,g_2)) = \bigcup_{\alpha\in\mathsf{at}(\mathsf{B})} (\alpha \cap \delta(f(g_1,\alpha), f(g_2,\alpha)))\,.$$

Since $\delta(f(g_1,\alpha), f(g_2,\alpha)) \in \mathsf{B}$ and α is an atom of B, each expression of the form $\alpha \cap \delta(f(g_1,\alpha), f(g_2,\alpha))$ is either $\emptyset$ or α. It follows that $\delta(g_1,g_2) \in \mathsf{B}$. □

For a Boolean subalgebra B of $P(A)$, we say that a subset T of D^A is *pairwise-complete relative to B* if, for each $f, g \in T$,

1. $\delta(f,g) \in B$,
2. $\delta(f,g) \subseteq \beta \cup \gamma$, implies $\delta(f,h) \subseteq \beta$ and $\delta(h,g) \subseteq \gamma$ for some $h \in T$, for each $\beta, \gamma \in B$.

Lemma 24. *The set* G *is pairwise-complete relative to the Boolean algebra* B.

Proof. Let $f, g \in \mathsf{G}$ be such that $\delta(f,g) \subseteq \beta \cup \gamma$. Let $h \in D^A$ be defined so that, for each $\alpha \in \mathsf{at}(\mathsf{B})$, $h\restriction\alpha = f\restriction\alpha$ if $\alpha \not\subseteq \beta$ and $h\restriction\alpha = g\restriction\alpha$, otherwise. Obviously, $h \in \mathsf{G}$.

Observe that $\alpha \not\subseteq \beta$ if and only if $\alpha \subseteq \beta^{\mathsf{c}}$, for each $\alpha \in \mathsf{at}(\mathsf{B})$, since $\beta \in \mathsf{B}$. We deduce therefore $h\restriction\alpha = f\restriction\alpha$ if $\alpha \in \mathsf{at}(\mathsf{B})$ and $\alpha \subseteq \beta^{\mathsf{c}}$, so $f(a) = h(a)$ for each $a \in \beta^{\mathsf{c}}$. Consequently $\beta^{\mathsf{c}} \subseteq Eq(f,h)$ and $\delta(f,h) \subseteq \beta$.

We also have $h\restriction\alpha = g\restriction\alpha$ if $\alpha \in \mathsf{at}(\mathsf{B})$ and $\alpha \subseteq \gamma^{\mathsf{c}}$. As before, this implies $\delta(h,g) \subseteq \gamma$. Indeed, this is the case if $\alpha \subseteq \beta$, by definition of h. Suppose now that $\alpha \not\subseteq \beta$, so $\alpha \subseteq \beta^{\mathsf{c}} \cap \gamma^{\mathsf{c}} = (\beta \cup \gamma)^{\mathsf{c}}$. Since $\delta(f,g) \subseteq \beta \cup \gamma$, then $\alpha \subseteq \delta(f,g)^{\mathsf{c}} = Eq(f,g)$, i.e. $f\restriction\alpha = g\restriction\alpha$. Together with $h\restriction\alpha = f\restriction\alpha$ (by definition of h) we obtain $h\restriction\alpha = f\restriction\alpha$. □

We can finally bring together the observations developed so far and state our main results.

Theorem 25. *If an inclusion* $t \leq s$ *fails in all the lattices* $\mathsf{R}(D,A)$, *then it fails in a finite lattice* $\mathsf{R}(E,A')$, *where* $\mathrm{card}(A') \leq 2^{p(k)}$ *with* $k = \max(size(t), size(s))$, $p(k) = \frac{2^{k^2}+3k}{2}$, *and* $\mathrm{card}(E) \leq size(t)$.

Proof. By Proposition 19 the inclusion $t \leq s$ fails in all the lattices $\mathsf{R}(D, A)_T$ where $T(f, t) \subseteq T$. Once defined B as the Boolean subalgebra of $P(A)$ generated by the sets as in the display (6) (with $T = T(f, T)$) and G as the set of glues of $T(f, t)$ and B as in Definition 22, the inclusion fails in $\mathsf{R}(D, A)_{\mathsf{G}}$, since $T(f, T) \subseteq \mathsf{G}$, and then in $\mathsf{L}(\mathsf{G}, \delta_{\mathsf{at}(\mathsf{B})})$ by Proposition 21. The condition that G is pairwise-complete relative to B is equivalent to saying that the space $(\mathsf{G}, \delta_{\mathsf{at}(\mathsf{B})})$ is pairwise-complete. This space is therefore isomorphic to a space of the form Sec_π for some surjective $\pi : F \longrightarrow \mathsf{at}(\mathsf{B})$, and $t \leq s$ fails in $\mathsf{L}(\mathsf{Sec}_\pi)$.

Equation (7) shows that, for each $\alpha \in \mathsf{at}(\mathsf{B})$, $F_\alpha = \pi^{-1}(\alpha)$ has cardinality at most $\mathrm{card}(T(f, t))$ and the size of t is an upper bound for $\mathrm{card}(T(f, t))$. We can therefore embed the space Sec_π into a space of the form $(E^{\mathsf{at}(\mathsf{B})}, \delta)$ with the size of t an upper bound for $\mathrm{card}(E)$. The proof of Proposition 6 exhibits $\mathsf{L}(\mathsf{Sec}_\pi)$ as a homomorphic image of a sublattice of $\mathsf{L}(E^{\mathsf{at}(\mathsf{B})}, \delta)$ and therefore the inclusion $t \leq s$ also fails within $\mathsf{L}(E^{\mathsf{at}(\mathsf{B})}, \delta) = \mathsf{R}(E, \mathsf{at}(\mathsf{B}))$. The upper bound on the size of $\mathsf{at}(\mathsf{B})$ has been extimated in Remark 20. □

Remark 26. In the statement of the previous Theorem, the size of the lattice $\mathsf{R}(E, A')$ can be estimated out of the sizes of E and A' considering that

$$P(E^{A'}) \subseteq \mathsf{R}(E, A') \subseteq P(A' \cup E^{A'})\,.$$

An upper bound for $\mathrm{card}(\mathsf{R}(E, A'))$ is therefore $2^{p(k)+k^{2^{p(k)}}}$ where $p(k)$ is the polynomial of degree 2 as in the statement of the Theorem and k is the maximum of $size(t), size(s)$.

A standard argument yields now:

Corollary 27. *The equational theory of the relational lattices is decidable.*

7 Conclusions

We argued that the equational theory of relational lattices is decidable. We achieved this goal by giving a finite (counter)model construction of bounded size.

Our result leaves open other questions that we might ask on relational lattices. We mentioned in the introduction the quest for a complete axiomatic base for this theory or, anyway, the need of a complete deductive system—so to develop automatic reasoning for the algebra of relational lattices. As part of future researches it is tempting to contribute achieving this goal using the mathematical insights contained in the decidability proof.

Our result also opens new research directions, in primis, the investigation of the complexity of deciding lattice-theoretic equations/inclusions on relational lattices. Of course, the obvious decision procedure arising from the finite model construction is not optimal; few algebraic considerations already suggest how the decision procedure can be improved.

Also, it would be desirable next to investigate decidability of equational theories in signatures extending of the pure lattice signature; many such extensions are proposed in [17]. It is not difficult to adapt the present decidability proof so to add to the signature the header constant.

A further interesting question is how this result translates back to the field of multidimensional modal logic [15]. We pointed out in [22] how the algebra of relational lattices can be encoded into multimodal framework; we conjecture that our decidability result yields the decidability of some positive fragments of well known undecidable logics, such as the products $\mathbf{S5}^n$ with $n \geq 3$. Moreover connections need to be established with other existing decidability results in modal logic and in database theory [1].

References

1. Abiteboul, S., Hull, R., Vianu, V.: Foundations of Databases: The Logical Level, 1st edn. Addison-Wesley Longman Publishing Co., Inc., Boston (1995)
2. Ackerman, N.: Completeness in generalized ultrametric spaces. p-Adic Numbers Ultrametric Anal. Appl. **5**(2), 89–105 (2013)
3. Caucal, D.: On infinite transition graphs having a decidable monadic theory. Theoret. Comput. Sci. **290**(1), 79–115 (2003)
4. Codd, E.F.: A relational model of data for large shared data banks. Commun. ACM **13**(6), 377–387 (1970)
5. Davey, B.A., Priestley, H.A.: Introduction to Lattices and Order. Cambridge University Press, New York (2002)
6. Dyckhoff, R., Tholen, W.: Exponentiable morphisms, partial products and pullback complements. J. Pure Appl. Algebra **49**(1–2), 103–116 (1987)
7. Freese, R., Ježek, J., Nation, J.: Free Lattices. American Mathematical Society, Providence (1995)
8. Gabbay, D.M.: Selective filtration in modal logic I. Semantic tableaux method. Theoria **36**, 323–330 (1970)
9. Grätzer, G.: General Lattice Theory. Birkhäuser Verlag, Basel (1998). New appendices by the author with B. A. Davey, R. Freese, B. Ganter, M. Greferath, P. Jipsen, H. A. Priestley, H. Rose, E. T. Schmidt, S. E. Schmidt, F. Wehrung and R. Wille
10. Hammack, R., Imrich, W., Klavzar, S.: Handbook of Product Graphs, 2nd edn. CRC Press Inc., Boca Raton (2011)
11. Hirsch, R., Hodkinson, I.: Representability is not decidable for finite relation algebras. Trans. Amer. Math. Soc. **353**, 1403–1425 (2001)
12. Hirsch, R., Hodkinson, I., Kurucz, A.: On modal logics between $\mathbf{K} \times \mathbf{K} \times \mathbf{K}$ and $\mathbf{S5} \times \mathbf{S5} \times \mathbf{S5}$. J. Symbolic Log. **67**(3), 221–234 (2002)
13. Imrich, W., Klavar, S.: Product Graphs. Wiley-Interscience Series in Discrete Mathematics and Optimization. Wiley-Interscience, New York (2000). Structure and recognition, With a foreword by Peter Winkler
14. Jacobs, B.: Categorical Logic and Type Theory. Studies in Logic and the Foundations of Mathematics, vol. 141. North-Holland Publishing Co., Amsterdam (1999)
15. Kurucz, A.: Combining modal logics. In: Patrick Blackburn, J.V.B., Wolter, F. (eds.) Handbook of Modal Logic, vol. 3 (Studies in Logic and Practical Reasoning), pp. 869–924. Elsevier (2007)

16. Lawvere, F.W.: Metric spaces, generalized logic and closed categories. Rendiconti del Seminario Matematico e Fisico di Milano XLIII, pp. 135–166 (1973)
17. Litak, T., Mikulás, S., Hidders, J.: Relational lattices: from databases to universal algebra. J. Logic. Algebraic Methods Program. **85**(4), 540–573 (2016)
18. Maddux, R.: The equational theory of CA_3 is undecidable. J. Symbolic Logic **45**(2), 311–316 (1980)
19. Pouzet, M.: Une approche métrique de la rétraction dans les ensembles ordonnés et les graphes. In: Proceedings of the Conference on Infinitistic Mathematics (Lyon, 1984), pp. 59–89. Publ. Dp. Math. Nouvelle Sér. B, 85–2, Univ. Claude-Bernard, Lyon (1985)
20. Priess-Crampe, S., Ribemboim, P.: Equivalence relations and spherically complete ultrametric spaces. C. R. Acad. Sci. Paris **320**(1), 1187–1192 (1995)
21. Santocanale, L.: A duality for finite lattices, September 2009. http://hal.archives-ouvertes.fr/hal-00432113
22. Santocanale, L.: Relational lattices via duality. In: Hasuo, I. (ed.) CMCS 2016. LNCS, vol. 9608, pp. 195–215. Springer, Cham (2016)
23. Santocanale, L.: Embeddability into relational lattices is undecidable. In: Höfner, P., Pous, D., Struth, G. (eds.) RAMICS 2017. LNCS, vol. 10226, pp. 258–273. Springer, Cham (2017). https://hal.archives-ouvertes.fr/hal-01474822
24. Santocanale, L., Wehrung, F.: The equational theory of the weak order on finite symmetric groups, P. 41, September 2014
25. Spight, M., Tropashko, V.: Relational lattice axioms (2008). http://arxiv.org/abs/0807.3795
26. Tropashko, V.: Relational algebra as non-distributive lattice (2006). http://arxiv.org/abs/cs/0501053

11

Automata for True Concurrency Properties

Paolo Baldan(✉) and Tommaso Padoan

Dipartimento di Matematica, Università di Padova, Padua, Italy
{baldan,padoan}@math.unipd.it

Abstract. We present an automata-theoretic framework for the model checking of true concurrency properties. These are specified in a fixpoint logic, corresponding to history-preserving bisimilarity, capable of describing events in computations and their dependencies. The models of the logic are event structures or any formalism which can be given a causal semantics, like Petri nets. Given a formula and an event structure satisfying suitable regularity conditions we show how to construct a parity tree automaton whose language is non-empty if and only if the event structure satisfies the formula. The automaton, due to the nature of event structure models, is usually infinite. We discuss how it can be quotiented to an equivalent finite automaton, where emptiness can be checked effectively. In order to show the applicability of the approach, we discuss how it instantiates to finite safe Petri nets. As a proof of concept we provide a model checking tool implementing the technique.

1 Introduction

Behavioural logics with the corresponding verification techniques are a cornerstone of automated verification. For concurrent and distributed systems, so called true concurrent models can be an appropriate choice, since they describe not only the possible steps in the evolution of the system but also their causal dependencies. A widely used foundational model in this class is given by Winskel's event structures [1]. They describe the behaviour of a system in terms of events in computations and two dependency relations: a partial order modelling causality and an additional relation modelling conflict. A survey on the use of such causal models can be found in [2]. Recently they have been used in the study of concurrency in weak memory models [3,4], for process mining and differencing [5], in the study of atomicity [6] and of information flow [7] properties.

Operational models can be abstracted by considering true concurrent equivalences that range from hereditary history preserving bisimilarity to the coarser pomset and step equivalences (see, e.g., [8]) and behavioural logics expressing causal properties (see, e.g., [9–14] for a necessarily partial list and [15–19] for some related verification techniques).

Event-based logics have been recently introduced [20,21], capable of uniformly characterising the equivalences in the true concurrent spectrum. Their formulae include variables which are bound to events in computations and describe their dependencies. While the relation between operational models, behavioural equivalences and event-based true concurrent logics is well understood, the corresponding model checking problem has received limited attention.

We focus on the logic referred to as $\mathcal{L}_{hp}$ in [20], corresponding to a classical equivalence in the spectrum, i.e., history preserving (hp-)bisimilarity [22–24].

Decidability of model checking is not obvious since event structure models are infinite even for finite state systems and the possibility of expressing properties that depends on the past often leads to undecidability [25]. In a recent paper [26] we proved the decidability of the problem for the alternation free fragment of the logic $\mathcal{L}_{hp}$ over a class of event structures satisfying a suitable regularity condition [27] referred to as strong regularity. The proof relies on a tableau-based model checking procedure. Despite the infiniteness of the model, a suitable stop condition can be identified, ensuring that a successful finite tableau can be generated if and only if the formula is satisfied by the model.

Besides the limitation to the alternation free fragment of $\mathcal{L}_{hp}$, a shortcoming of the approach is that a direct implementation of the procedure can be extremely inefficient. Roughly speaking, the problem is that in the search of a successful tableau, branches which are, in some sense, equivalent are explored several times.

In this paper we devise an automata-theoretic technique, in the style of [28], for model checking $\mathcal{L}_{hp}$ that works for the full logic, without constraints on the alternation depth. Besides providing an alternative approach for model-checking $\mathcal{L}_{hp}$, amenable of a more efficient implementation, this generalises the decidability result of [26] to the full logic $\mathcal{L}_{hp}$. Given a formula in $\mathcal{L}_{hp}$ and a strongly regular event structure, the procedure generates a parity tree automaton. Satisfiability is reduced to emptiness in the sense that the event structure satisfies the formula if and only if the automaton accepts a non-empty language.

The result is not directly usable for practical purposes since the automaton is infinite for any non-trivial event structure. However an equivalence on states can be defined such that the quotiented automaton accepts the same language as the original one. Whenever such equivalence is of finite index the quotiented automaton is finite, so that satisfaction of the formula can be checked effectively on the quotient. We show that for all strongly regular event structures a canonical equivalence always exists that is of finite index.

The procedure is developed abstractly on event structures. A concrete algorithm on some formalism requires the effectiveness of the chosen equivalence on states. We develop a concrete instantiation of the algorithm on finite safe Petri nets. It is implemented in a tool, wishfully called *True concurrency workbench* (TCWB), written in Haskell. Roughly, the search of an accepting run in the automaton can be seen as an optimisation of the procedure for building a successful tableau in [26] where the graph structure underlying the automaton helps in the reuse of the information discovered. Some tests reveal that the TCWB is way more efficient than the direct implementation of the tableau-based procedure (which could not manage most of the examples in the TCWB repository).

The rest of the paper is structured as follows. In Sect. 2 we review event structures, strong regularity and the logic $\mathcal{L}_{hp}$ of interest in the paper. In Sect. 3

we introduce (infinite state) parity tree automata and we show how the model checking problem for $\mathcal{L}_{hp}$ on strongly regular PES can be reduced to the non-emptiness of the language of such automata. In Sect. 4 we discuss the instantiation of the approach to Petri nets. Finally, in Sect. 5 we discuss some related work and outline directions of future research. Due to space limitations, proofs are only sketched.

2 Event Structures and True Concurrent Logic

We introduce prime event structures [1] and the subclass of strongly regular event structures on which our model checking approach will be developed. Then we present the logic for true concurrency of interest in the paper.

2.1 Prime Event Structures and Regularity

Throughout the paper $\mathbb{E}$ is a fixed countable set of events, Λ a finite set of labels ranged over by $\mathsf{a}, \mathsf{b}, \mathsf{c} \ldots$ and $\lambda : \mathbb{E} \to \Lambda$ a labelling function.

Definition 1 (prime event structure). *A (Λ-labelled)* prime event structure *(*PES*) is a tuple $\mathcal{E} = \langle E, \leq, \# \rangle$, where $E \subseteq \mathbb{E}$ is the set of* events *and $\leq$, $\#$ are binary relations on E, called* causality *and* conflict *respectively, such that: 1. $\leq$ is a partial order and $\lceil e \rceil = \{e' \in E \mid e' \leq e\}$ is finite for all $e \in E$; 2. $\#$ is irreflexive, symmetric and inherited along $\leq$, i.e., for all $e, e', e'' \in E$, if $e \# e' \leq e''$ then $e \# e''$.*

The PES *$\mathcal{E}_1 = \langle E_1, \leq_1, \#_1 \rangle$, $\mathcal{E}_2 = \langle E_2, \leq_2, \#_2 \rangle$ are* isomorphic, *written $\mathcal{E}_1 \sim \mathcal{E}_2$, when there is a bijection $\iota : E_1 \to E_2$ such that for all $e_1, e_1' \in E_1$, it holds $e_1 \leq_1 e_1'$ iff $\iota(e_1) \leq_2 \iota(e_1')$ and $e_1 \#_1 e_1'$ iff $\iota(e_1) \#_2 \iota(e_1')$ and $\lambda(e_1) = \lambda(\iota(e_1))$.*

In the following, we will assume that the components of a PES $\mathcal{E}$ are named as in the definition above, possibly with subscripts. The concept of concurrent computation for PESs is captured by the notion of configuration.

Definition 2 (configuration). *A* configuration *of a* PES *$\mathcal{E}$ is a finite set of events $C \subseteq E$* consistent *(i.e., $\neg(e \# e')$ for all $e, e' \in C$) and* causally closed *(i.e., $\lceil e \rceil \subseteq C$ for all $e \in C$). We denote by $\mathcal{C}(\mathcal{E})$ the set of configurations of $\mathcal{E}$.*

The evolution of a PES can be represented by a transition system over configurations, with the empty configuration as initial state.

Definition 3 (transition system). *Let $\mathcal{E}$ be a* PES *and let $C \in \mathcal{C}(\mathcal{E})$. Given $e \in E \setminus C$ such that $C \cup \{e\} \in \mathcal{C}(\mathcal{E})$, and $X, Y \subseteq C$ with $X \subseteq \lceil e \rceil$, $Y \cap \lceil e \rceil = \emptyset$ we write $C \xrightarrow{X, \overline{Y} < e}_{\lambda(e)} C \cup \{e\}$. The set of* enabled *events at a configuration C is defined as $en(C) = \{e \in E \mid C \xrightarrow{e} C'\}$. The* PES *is called k-*bounded *for some $k \in \mathbb{N}$ (or simply* bounded*) if $|en(C)| \leq k$ for all $C \in \mathcal{C}(\mathcal{E})$.*

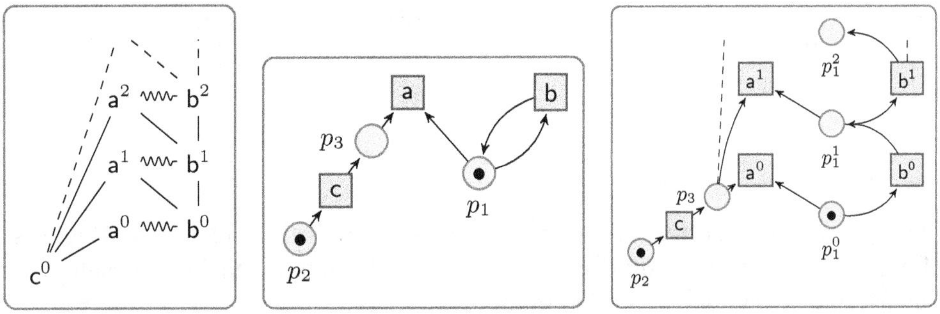

(a) $\mathcal{E}_{\mathcal{N}}$ (b) $\mathcal{N}$ (c) $\mathcal{U}(\mathcal{N})$

Fig. 1. (a) A PES $\mathcal{E}_{\mathcal{N}}$ associated with the net $\mathcal{N}$ in (b) via its unfolding (c).

Transitions are labelled by the executed event e. In addition, they report its label $\lambda(e)$, a subset of causes X and a set of events $Y \subseteq C$ concurrent with e. When X or Y are empty they are normally often, i.e., e.g., we write $C \xrightarrow{X<e}_{\lambda(e)} C'$ for $C \xrightarrow{\emptyset<e}_{\lambda(e)} C'$ and $C \xrightarrow{e}_{\lambda(e)} C'$ for $C \xrightarrow{\emptyset,\overline{\emptyset}<e}_{\lambda(e)} C'$.

The PES modelling a non-trivial system is normally infinite. We will work on a subclass identified by finitarity requirements on the possible substructures.

Definition 4 (residual). *Let $\mathcal{E}$ be a* PES. *For a configuration $C \in \mathcal{C}(\mathcal{E})$, the* residual *of $\mathcal{E}$ after C, is defined as $\mathcal{E}[C] = \{e \mid e \in E \setminus C \wedge C \cup \{e\}$ consistent$\}$.*

The residual of $\mathcal{E}$ can be seen as a PES, endowed with the restriction of causality and conflict of $\mathcal{E}$. Intuitively, it represents the PES that remains to be executed after the computation expressed by C. Given $C \in \mathcal{C}(\mathcal{E})$ and $X \subseteq C$, we denote by $\mathcal{E}[C] \cup X$ the PES obtained from $\mathcal{E}[C]$ by adding the events in X with the causal dependencies they had in the original PES $\mathcal{E}$.

Definition 5 (strong regularity). *A* PES *$\mathcal{E}$ is called* strongly regular *when it is bounded and for each $k \in \mathbb{N}$ the set $\{\mathcal{E}[C] \cup \{e_1, \ldots, e_k\} \mid C \in \mathcal{C}(\mathcal{E}) \wedge e_1, \ldots, e_k \in C\}$ is finite up to isomorphism of* PESs.

Strong regularity [26] is obtained from the notion of regularity in [27], by replacing residuals with residuals extended with a bounded number of events from the past. Intuitively, this is important since we are interested in history dependent properties. We will later show in Sect. 4 that the PESs associated with finite safe Petri nets, i.e., the regular trace PESs [27], are strongly regular.

A simple PES is depicted in Fig. 1a. Graphically, curly lines represent immediate conflicts and the causal partial order proceeds upwards along the straight lines. Events are denoted by their labels, possibly with superscripts. For instance, in $\mathcal{E}_{\mathcal{N}}$, the events a^0 and b^0, labelled by a and b, respectively, are in conflict. Event c^0 causes the events a^i and it is concurrent with b^i for all $i \in \mathbb{N}$. It is an infinite PES associated with the Petri net $\mathcal{N}$ in Fig. 1b in a way that will be discussed in Sect. 4.1, hence it is strongly regular by Corollary 1. It has five (equivalence classes of) residuals extended with an event from the past $\mathcal{E}_{\mathcal{N}}[\{\mathsf{b}^0\}] \cup \{\mathsf{b}^0\}$, $\mathcal{E}_{\mathcal{N}}[\{\mathsf{c}^0, \mathsf{b}^0\}] \cup \{\mathsf{b}^0\}$, $\mathcal{E}_{\mathcal{N}}[\{\mathsf{c}^0, \mathsf{a}^0\}] \cup \{\mathsf{c}^0\}$, $\mathcal{E}_{\mathcal{N}}[\{\mathsf{c}^0, \mathsf{a}^0\}] \cup \{\mathsf{a}^0\}$, and $\mathcal{E}_{\mathcal{N}}[\{\mathsf{c}^0, \mathsf{b}^0, \mathsf{a}^1\}] \cup \{\mathsf{b}^0\}$.

2.2 True Concurrent Logic

The logic of interest for this paper, originally defined in [20], is a Hennessy-Milner style logic that allows one to specify the dependencies (causality and concurrency) between events in computation.

Logic formulae include event variables, from a fixed denumerable set *Var*, denoted by $x, y, \ldots$. Tuples of variables like $x_1, \ldots, x_n$ will be denoted by a corresponding boldface letter $\mathbf{x}$ and, abusing the notation, tuples will be often used as sets. The logic includes diamond and box modalities. The formula $\langle\!| \mathbf{x}, \overline{\mathbf{y}} < \mathsf{a}\, z |\!\rangle\, \varphi$ holds in a configuration when an a-labelled event e is enabled which causally depends on the events bound to $\mathbf{x}$ and is concurrent with those in $\mathbf{y}$. Event e is executed and then the formula φ must hold, with e bound to variable z. Dually, $[\![\mathbf{x}, \overline{\mathbf{y}} < \mathsf{a}\, z]\!]\, \varphi$ is satisfied when all a-labelled events causally dependent on $\mathbf{x}$ and concurrent with $\mathbf{y}$ bring to a configuration where φ holds.

For dealing with fixpoint operators we fix a denumerable set $\mathcal{X}^a$ of *abstract propositions*, ranged over by $X, Y, \ldots$. Each abstract proposition X has an arity $ar(X)$ and it represents a formula with $ar(X)$ (unnamed) free event variables. Then, for $\mathbf{x}$ such that $|\mathbf{x}| = ar(X)$, we write $X(\mathbf{x})$ to indicate the abstract proposition X whose free event variables are named $\mathbf{x}$.

Definition 6 (syntax). *The syntax of $\mathcal{L}_{hp}$ over the sets of event variables Var, abstract propositions $\mathcal{X}^a$ and labels Λ is defined as follows:*

$$\begin{aligned}\varphi \; ::= \; & X(\mathbf{x}) \mid \mathsf{T} \mid \varphi \wedge \varphi \mid \langle\!| \mathbf{x}, \overline{\mathbf{y}} < \mathsf{a}\, z |\!\rangle\, \varphi \mid \nu X(\mathbf{x}).\varphi \\ & \mid \mathsf{F} \mid \varphi \vee \varphi \mid [\![\mathbf{x}, \overline{\mathbf{y}} < \mathsf{a}\, z]\!]\, \varphi \mid \mu X(\mathbf{x}).\varphi\end{aligned}$$

For a formula φ we denote by $fv(\varphi)$ its free event variables, defined in the obvious way. Just note that the modalities act as binders for the variable representing the event executed, hence $fv(\langle\!| \mathbf{x}, \overline{\mathbf{y}} < \mathsf{a}\, z |\!\rangle\, \varphi) = fv([\![\mathbf{x}, \overline{\mathbf{y}} < \mathsf{a}\, z]\!]\, \varphi) = (fv(\varphi) \setminus \{z\}) \cup \mathbf{x} \cup \mathbf{y}$. For formulae $\nu X(\mathbf{x}).\varphi$ and $\mu X(\mathbf{x}).\varphi$ we require that $fv(\varphi) = \mathbf{x}$. The free propositions in φ not bound by μ or ν, are denoted by $fp(\varphi)$. When both $fv(\varphi)$ and $fp(\varphi)$ are empty we say that φ is *closed*. When $\mathbf{x}$ or $\mathbf{y}$ are empty are omitted, e.g., we write $\langle\!| \mathsf{a}\, z |\!\rangle\, \varphi$ for $\langle\!| \emptyset, \overline{\emptyset} < \mathsf{a}\, z |\!\rangle\, \varphi$.

For example, the formula $\varphi_1 = \langle\!| \mathsf{c}\, x |\!\rangle (\langle\!| x < \mathsf{a}\, y |\!\rangle \mathsf{T} \wedge \langle\!| \overline{x} < \mathsf{b}\, z |\!\rangle \mathsf{T})$ requires that, after the execution of a c-labelled event, one can choose between a causally dependent a-labelled event and a concurrent b-labelled event. It is satisfied by $\mathcal{E}_{\mathcal{N}}$ in Fig. 1a. Instead $\varphi_2 = \langle\!| \mathsf{c}\, x |\!\rangle (\langle\!| \overline{x} < \mathsf{a}\, y |\!\rangle \mathsf{T} \wedge \langle\!| \overline{x} < \mathsf{b}\, z |\!\rangle \mathsf{T})$ requiring both events to be concurrent would be false. Moving to infinite computations, consider $\varphi_3 = [\![\mathsf{b}\, x]\!] \nu Z(x).\langle\!| \mathsf{c}\, z |\!\rangle \langle\!| \overline{z} < \mathsf{b}\, y |\!\rangle \mathsf{T} \wedge [\![x < \mathsf{b}\, y]\!] Z(y)$, expressing that all non-empty causal chains of b-labelled events reach a state where it is possible to execute two concurrent events labelled c and b, respectively. Then φ_3 holds in $\mathcal{E}_{\mathcal{N}}$. Another formula satisfied by $\mathcal{E}_{\mathcal{N}}$ is $\varphi_4 = \langle\!| \mathsf{c}\, x |\!\rangle \langle\!| \overline{x} < \mathsf{b}\, y |\!\rangle \nu X(x, y).\langle\!| y, \overline{x} < \mathsf{b}\, z |\!\rangle X(x, z)$

requiring the existence of an infinite causal chain of b-labelled events, concurrent with a c-labelled event.

The logic $\mathcal{L}_{hp}$ is interpreted over PESs. The satisfaction of a formula is defined with respect to a configuration C and a (total) function $\eta : Var \to E$, called an *environment*, that binds free variables in φ to events in C. Namely, if $Env_{\mathcal{E}}$ denotes the set of environments, the semantics of a formula will be a set of pairs in $\mathcal{C}(\mathcal{E}) \times Env_{\mathcal{E}}$. The semantics of $\mathcal{L}_{hp}$ also depends on a *proposition environment* $\pi : \mathcal{X} \to 2^{\mathcal{C}(\mathcal{E}) \times Env_{\mathcal{E}}}$ which provides an interpretation for propositions. In order to ensure that the semantics of a formula only depends on the events associated with its free variables and is independent on the naming of the variables, it is required that if $(C, \eta) \in \pi(X(\mathbf{x}))$ and $\eta'(\mathbf{y}) = \eta(\mathbf{x})$ pointwise, then $(C, \eta') \in \pi(X(\mathbf{y}))$. We denote by $PEnv_{\mathcal{E}}$ the set of proposition environments, ranged over by π.

We can now give the semantics of logic $\mathcal{L}_{hp}$. Given an event environment η and an event e we write $\eta[x \mapsto e]$ for the updated environment which maps x to e. Similarly, for a proposition environment π and $S \subseteq \mathcal{C}(\mathcal{E}) \times Env_{\mathcal{E}}$, we write $\pi[Z(\mathbf{x}) \mapsto S]$ for the corresponding update.

Definition 7 (semantics). *Let $\mathcal{E}$ be a* PES. *The denotation of a formula φ in $\mathcal{L}_{hp}$ is given by the function $\{\!|\cdot|\!\}^{\mathcal{E}} : \mathcal{L}_{hp} \to PEnv_{\mathcal{E}} \to 2^{\mathcal{C}(\mathcal{E}) \times Env_{\mathcal{E}}}$ defined inductively as follows, where we write $\{\!|\varphi|\!\}^{\mathcal{E}}_{\pi}$ instead of $\{\!|\varphi|\!\}^{\mathcal{E}}(\pi)$:*

$$\{\!|\mathsf{T}|\!\}^{\mathcal{E}}_{\pi} = \mathcal{C}(\mathcal{E}) \times Env_{\mathcal{E}} \qquad \{\!|\mathsf{F}|\!\}^{\mathcal{E}}_{\pi} = \emptyset \qquad \{\!|Z(\mathbf{y})|\!\}^{\mathcal{E}}_{\pi} = \pi(Z(\mathbf{y}))$$

$$\{\!|\varphi_1 \wedge \varphi_2|\!\}^{\mathcal{E}}_{\pi} = \{\!|\varphi_1|\!\}^{\mathcal{E}}_{\pi} \cap \{\!|\varphi_2|\!\}^{\mathcal{E}}_{\pi} \qquad \{\!|\varphi_1 \vee \varphi_2|\!\}^{\mathcal{E}}_{\pi} = \{\!|\varphi_1|\!\}^{\mathcal{E}}_{\pi} \cup \{\!|\varphi_2|\!\}^{\mathcal{E}}_{\pi}$$

$$\{\!|\langle\!|\mathbf{x}, \overline{\mathbf{y}} < \mathsf{a}\, z|\!\rangle\, \varphi|\!\}^{\mathcal{E}}_{\pi} = \{(C, \eta) \mid \exists e.\, C \xrightarrow{\eta(\mathbf{x}), \overline{\eta(\mathbf{y})} < e}_{\mathsf{a}} C' \ \wedge\ (C', \eta[z \mapsto e]) \in \{\!|\varphi|\!\}^{\mathcal{E}}_{\pi}\}$$

$$\{\!|[\![\mathbf{x}, \overline{\mathbf{y}} < \mathsf{a}\, z]\!]\, \varphi|\!\}^{\mathcal{E}}_{\pi} = \{(C, \eta) \mid \forall e.\, C \xrightarrow{\eta(\mathbf{x}), \overline{\eta(\mathbf{y})} < e}_{\mathsf{a}} C' \ \Rightarrow\ (C', \eta[z \mapsto e]) \in \{\!|\varphi|\!\}^{\mathcal{E}}_{\pi}\}$$

$$\{\!|\nu Z(\mathbf{x}).\varphi|\!\}^{\mathcal{E}}_{\pi} = gfp(f_{\varphi, Z(\mathbf{x}), \pi}) \qquad \{\!|\mu Z(\mathbf{x}).\varphi|\!\}^{\mathcal{E}}_{\pi} = lfp(f_{\varphi, Z(\mathbf{x}), \pi})$$

where $f_{\varphi, Z(\mathbf{x}), \pi} : 2^{\mathcal{C}(\mathcal{E}) \times Env_{\mathcal{E}}} \to 2^{\mathcal{C}(\mathcal{E}) \times Env_{\mathcal{E}}}$ is defined by $f_{\varphi, Z(\mathbf{x}), \pi}(S) = \{\!|\varphi|\!\}^{\mathcal{E}}_{\pi[Z(\mathbf{x}) \mapsto S]}$ and $gfp(f_{\varphi, Z(\mathbf{x}), \pi})$ (resp. $lfp(f_{\varphi, Z(\mathbf{x}), \pi})$) denotes the corresponding greatest (resp. least) fixpoint. We say that a PES *$\mathcal{E}$ satisfies a formula φ and write $\mathcal{E} \models \varphi$ if $(\emptyset, \eta) \in \{\!|\varphi|\!\}^{\mathcal{E}}_{\pi}$ for all environments η and π.*

The semantics of boolean operators is standard. The formula $\langle\!|\mathbf{x}, \overline{\mathbf{y}} < \mathsf{a}\, z|\!\rangle\, \varphi$ holds in (C, η) when configuration C enables an a-labelled event e that causally depends on (at least) the events bound to the variables in $\mathbf{x}$ and concurrent with (at least) those bound to the variables in $\mathbf{y}$ and, once executed, it produces a new configuration $C' = C \cup \{e\}$ which, paired with the environment $\eta' = \eta[z \mapsto e]$, satisfies the formula φ. Dually, $[\![\mathbf{x}, \overline{\mathbf{y}} < \mathsf{a}\, z]\!]\, \varphi$ holds when all a-labelled events executable from C, caused by $\mathbf{x}$ and concurrent with $\mathbf{y}$ bring to a configuration where φ is satisfied.

The fixpoints corresponding to the formulae $\nu Z(\mathbf{x}).\varphi$ and $\mu Z(\mathbf{x}).\varphi$ are guaranteed to exist by Knaster-Tarski theorem, since the set $2^{\mathcal{C}(\mathcal{E}) \times Env_{\mathcal{E}}}$ ordered by subset inclusion is a complete lattice and the functions $f_{\varphi, Z(\mathbf{x}), \pi}$ are monotonic.

3 Automata-Based Model Checker

We introduce nondeterministic parity tree automata and we show how the model checking problem for $\mathcal{L}_{hp}$ on strongly regular PESs can be reduced to the non-emptiness of the language of such automata. The automaton naturally generated from a PES and a formula has an infinite number of states. We discuss how the automaton can be quotiented to a finite one accepting the same language and thus potentially useful for model checking purposes.

3.1 Infinite Parity Tree Automata

Automata on infinite trees revealed to be a powerful tool to various problems in the setting of branching temporal logics. Here we focus on nondeterministic parity tree automata [29], with some (slightly) non-standard features. We work on k-trees (rather than on binary trees), a choice that will simplify the presentation, and we allow for possibly infinite state automata.

When automata are used for model checking purposes it is standard to restrict to unlabelled trees. A *k-bounded branching tree* or *k-tree*, for short, is a subset $\mathcal{T} \subseteq [1,k]^\star$, such that

1. $\mathcal{T}$ is prefix closed, i.e., if $wv \in \mathcal{T}$ then $w \in \mathcal{T}$
2. $w1 \in \mathcal{T}$ for all $w \in \mathcal{T}$
3. for all $i \in [2,k]$ if $wi \in \mathcal{T}$ then $w(i-1) \in \mathcal{T}$.

Elements of $\mathcal{T}$ are the nodes of the tree. The empty string ϵ corresponds to the root. A string of the form wi corresponds to the i-th child of w. Hence by (2) each branch is infinite and by (3) the presence of the i-th child implies the presence of the j-th children for $j \leq i$.

Definition 8 (nondeterministic parity automaton). *A k*-bounded nondeterministic parity tree automaton *(NPA) is a tuple $\mathcal{A} = \langle Q, \rightarrow, q_0, \mathcal{F}\rangle$ where Q is a set of states, $\rightarrow \subseteq Q \times \bigcup_{i=1}^{k} Q^k$ is the* transition relation, *$q_0 \in Q$ is the* initial state, *and $\mathcal{F} = (F_0, \ldots, F_h)$ is the* acceptance condition, *where $F_0, \ldots, F_h \subseteq Q$ are mutually disjoint subsets of states.*

Transitions are written as $q \rightarrow (q_1, \ldots, q_m)$ instead of $(q, (q_1, \ldots, q_m)) \in \rightarrow$.

Given a k-tree $\mathcal{T}$, a *run* of $\mathcal{A}$ on $\mathcal{T}$ is a labelling of $\mathcal{T}$ over the states $r : \mathcal{T} \rightarrow Q$ consistent with the transition relation, i.e., such that $r(\epsilon) = q_0$ and for all $u \in \mathcal{T}$, with m children, there is a transition $r(u) \rightarrow (r(u1), \ldots, r(um))$ in $\mathcal{A}$. A *path* in the run r is an infinite sequence of states $p = (q_0, q_1, \ldots)$ labelling a complete path from the root in the tree. It is called *accepting* if there exists an even number $l \in [0,h]$ such that the set $\{j \mid q_j \in F_l\}$ is infinite and the set $\{j \mid q_j \in \bigcup_{l<i\leq h} F_i\}$ is finite. The run r is *accepting* if all paths are accepting.

Definition 9 (language of an NPA). *Let $\mathcal{A}$ be an NPA. The language of $\mathcal{A}$, denoted by $L(\mathcal{A})$, consists of the trees $\mathcal{T}$ which admit an accepting run.*

Observe that for a k-bounded NPA, the language $L(\mathcal{A})$ is a set of k-trees.

The possibility of having an infinite number of states and the associated acceptance condition are somehow non-standard. However, it is easy to see that whenever an NPA is finite, the acceptance condition coincides with the standard one requiring a single state with maximal even priority to occur infinitely often.

Since NPAs are nondeterministic, different runs (possibly infinitely many) can exist for the same input tree. Still, the non-emptiness problem, also for our k-ary variant, is decidable when the number of states is finite (and solvable by a corresponding parity game [30]).

3.2 Infinite NPAs for Model Checking

We show how, given a PES and a closed formula in $\mathcal{L}_{hp}$, we can build an NPA in a way that, for strongly regular PESs, the satisfaction of φ in $\mathcal{E}$ reduces to the non-emptiness of the automaton language. The construction is inspired by that in [28] for the mu-calculus.

The acceptance condition for the automaton will refer to the fixpoint alternation in the formulae of $\mathcal{L}_{hp}$. We adapt a definition from [28]. A fixpoint formula $\alpha X(\mathbf{y}).\varphi'$, for $\alpha \in \{\nu, \mu\}$, is called an α-formula. Hereafter α ranges over $\{\nu, \mu\}$. Given an α-formula $\varphi = \alpha X(\mathbf{y}).\varphi'$, we say that a subformula ψ of φ is a *direct active subformula*, written $\psi \sqsubseteq_d \varphi$, if the abstract proposition X appears free in ψ. The transitive closure of $\sqsubseteq_d$ is a partial order and when $\psi \sqsubseteq_d^* \varphi$ we say that ψ is an *active subformula* of φ. We denote by $\mathsf{sf}(\varphi)$ the set of subformulae of a formula φ and by $\mathsf{sf}_\alpha(\varphi)$ the set of active α-subformulae.

The *alternation depth* of a formula φ in $\mathcal{L}_{hp}$, written $\mathsf{ad}(\varphi)$, is defined, for a ν-formula φ, as $\mathsf{ad}(\varphi) = \max\{1 + \mathsf{ad}(\psi) \mid \psi \in \mathsf{sf}_\mu(\varphi)\}$ and dually, for a μ-formula φ, as $\mathsf{ad}(\varphi) = \max\{1 + \mathsf{ad}(\psi) \mid \psi \in \mathsf{sf}_\nu(\varphi)\}$. For any other formula φ, $\mathsf{ad}(\varphi) = max\{\mathsf{ad}(\psi) \mid \psi \in \mathsf{sf}(\varphi) \setminus \{\varphi\}\}$. It is intended that $\max \emptyset = 0$. E.g., by the first clause above, the alternation depth of $\nu X(\mathbf{x}).\,\varphi$ is 0 in absence of active μ-subformulae.

Hereafter we assume that in every formula different bound propositions have different names, so that we can refer to the fixpoint subformula quantifying an abstract proposition. This requirement can always be fulfilled by alpha-renaming.

Hereafter, if X and X' are abstract propositions quantified in α-subformulae $\alpha X(\mathbf{x}).\,\varphi$ and $\alpha' X'(\mathbf{x}').\,\varphi'$, we will write $\mathsf{ad}(X)$ for $\mathsf{ad}(\alpha X(\mathbf{x}).\,\varphi)$ and $X \sqsubseteq_d X'$ for $\alpha X(\mathbf{x}).\,\varphi \sqsubseteq_d \alpha' X'(\mathbf{x}').\,\varphi'$. Moreover, given a PES $\mathcal{E}$, for a pair $(C, \eta) \in \mathcal{C}(\mathcal{E}) \times Env_{\mathcal{E}}$ and variables $\mathbf{x}$, $\mathbf{y}$, z, we define $(\mathbf{x}, \overline{\mathbf{y}} < \mathsf{a}z)$-successors of (C, η), as

$$\mathsf{Succ}^{\mathbf{x},\overline{\mathbf{y}}<\mathsf{a}z}(C, \eta) = \{(C', \eta[z \mapsto e]) \mid C \xrightarrow{\eta(\mathbf{x}),\overline{\eta(\mathbf{y})}<e}_{\mathsf{a}} C'\}.$$

We can now illustrate the construction of the NPA for a formula and a PES.

Definition 10 (NPA for a formula). *Let $\mathcal{E}$ be a bounded* PES *and let $\varphi \in \mathcal{L}_{hp}$ be a closed formula. The NPA for $\mathcal{E}$ and φ is $\mathcal{A}_{\mathcal{E},\varphi} = \langle Q, \rightarrow, q_0, \mathcal{F}\rangle$ defined* *as follows. The set of states* $Q \subseteq \mathcal{C}(\mathcal{E}) \times Env_{\mathcal{E}} \times \mathsf{sf}(\varphi)$ *is* $Q = \{(C, \eta, \psi) \mid \eta(fv(\psi)) \subseteq C\}$. *The initial state* $q_0 = (\emptyset, \eta, \varphi)$, *for some chosen* $\eta \in Env_{\mathcal{E}}$. *The transition relation is defined, for any state* $q = (C, \eta, \psi) \in Q$, *by:*

- *if* $\psi = \mathsf{T}$ *or* $\psi = \mathsf{F}$, *then* $q \to (q)$;
- *if* $\psi = \psi_1 \wedge \psi_2$, *then* $q \to (q_1, q_2)$ *where* $q_i = (C, \eta, \psi_i)$, $i \in \{1, 2\}$;
- *if* $\psi = \psi_1 \vee \psi_2$, *then* $q \to (q_1)$ *and* $q \to (q_2)$ *where* $q_i = (C, \eta, \psi_i)$, $i \in \{1, 2\}$;
- *if* $\psi = [\![\mathbf{x}, \overline{\mathbf{y}} < \mathsf{a}\, z]\!]\psi'$ *and* $\mathsf{Succ}^{\mathbf{x}, \overline{\mathbf{y}} < \mathsf{a} z}(C, \eta) = \{(C_1, \eta_1), \ldots, (C_n, \eta_n)\} \neq \emptyset$ *then* $q \to (q_1, \ldots, q_n)$ *where* $q_i = (C_i, \eta_i, \psi')$ *for* $i \in [1, n]$, *otherwise* $q \to (q)$;
- *if* $\psi = \langle\!| \mathbf{x}, \overline{\mathbf{y}} < \mathsf{a}\, z |\!\rangle\psi'$ *and* $\mathsf{Succ}^{\mathbf{x}, \overline{\mathbf{y}} < \mathsf{a} z}(C, \eta) = \{(C_1, \eta_1), \ldots, (C_n, \eta_n)\} \neq \emptyset$ *then* $q \to (q_i)$ *where* $q_i = (C_i, \eta_i, \psi')$ *for* $i \in [1, n]$, *otherwise* $q \to (q)$;
- *if* $\psi = \alpha X(\mathbf{x}).\psi'$ *then* $q \to (q')$ *where* $q' = (C, \eta, X(\mathbf{x}))$;
- *if* $\psi = X(\mathbf{y})$ *and* $\psi' \in \mathsf{sf}(\varphi)$ *is the unique subformula such that* $\psi' = \alpha X(\mathbf{x}).\psi''$ *then* $q \to (q')$ *where* $q' = (C, \eta[\mathbf{x} \mapsto \eta(\mathbf{y})], \psi'')$.

The acceptance condition is $\mathcal{F} = (F_0, \ldots, F_h)$ *where* $h = \mathsf{ad}(\varphi) + 1$ *and the* F_i *are as follows. Consider* $A_0, \ldots, A_h \subseteq \mathsf{sf}(\varphi)$ *such that for* $i \in [0, h]$, *if* i *is even (odd) then* A_i *contains exactly all propositions quantified in* ν*-subformulae (*μ*-subformulae) with alternation depth* i *or* $i - 1$. *Then* $F_0 = (\mathcal{C}(\mathcal{E}) \times Env_{\mathcal{E}} \times (A_0 \cup \{\mathsf{T}\})) \cup B$ *where* $B = \{(C, \eta, [\![\mathbf{x}, \overline{\mathbf{y}} < \mathsf{a}\, z]\!]\psi) \mid \mathsf{Succ}^{\mathbf{x}, \overline{\mathbf{y}} < \mathsf{a} z}(C, \eta) = \emptyset\}$ *is the set of all subformulae of* φ *in a context where they are trivially true, and* $F_i = \mathcal{C}(\mathcal{E}) \times Env_{\mathcal{E}} \times A_i$, *for* $i \in [1, h]$.

States of $\mathcal{A}_{\mathcal{E},\varphi}$ are triples (C, η, φ) consisting of a configuration C, an environment η and a subformula ψ of the original formula φ. The intuition is that a transition reduces the satisfaction of a formula in a state to that of subformulae in possibly updated states. It can just decompose the formula, as it happens for $\wedge$ or $\vee$, check the satisfaction of a modal operator, thus changing the state consequently, or unfold a fixpoint.

The automaton $\mathcal{A}_{\mathcal{E},\varphi}$ is bounded but normally infinite (whenever the PES $\mathcal{E}$ is infinite and the formula φ includes some non-trivial fixpoint).

We next show that for a strongly regular PES the satisfaction of the formula φ on the PES $\mathcal{E}$ reduces to the non-emptiness of the language of $\mathcal{A}_{\mathcal{E},\varphi}$.

Theorem 1 (model checking via non-emptiness). *Let* $\mathcal{E}$ *be a strongly regular* PES *and let* $\check{\varphi}$ *be a closed formula in* $\mathcal{L}_{hp}$. *Then* $L(\mathcal{A}_{\mathcal{E},\check{\varphi}}) \neq \emptyset$ *iff* $\mathcal{E} \models \check{\varphi}$.

We next provide an outline of the proof. A basic ingredient is an equivalence that can be defined on the NPA. As a first step we introduce a generalised notion of residual in which the relation with some selected events in the past is kept.

Definition 11 (pointed residual). *Given a* PES $\mathcal{E}$ *and a set* X, *a* X-pointed configuration *is a pair* $\langle C, \zeta \rangle$ *where* $C \in \mathcal{C}(\mathcal{E})$ *and* $\zeta : X \to C$ *is a function. We say that the* X*-pointed configurations* $\langle C, \zeta \rangle$, $\langle C', \zeta' \rangle$ *have isomorphic pointed residuals, written* $\mathcal{E}[\langle C, \zeta \rangle] \approx \mathcal{E}[\langle C', \zeta' \rangle]$ *if there is an isomorphism of* PESs $\iota : \mathcal{E}[C] \to \mathcal{E}[C']$ *such that for all* $x \in X$, $e \in \mathcal{E}[C]$ *we have* $\zeta(x) \leq e$ *iff* $\zeta'(x) \leq \iota(e)$.

Then two states are deemed equivalent if they involve the same subformula (up to renaming of the event variables) and the configurations, pointed by the free variables in the formulae, have isomorphic residuals. This resembles the notion of contextualised equivalence used on tableau judgments in [26].

Definition 12 (future equivalence). *Let $\mathcal{E}$ be a* PES*, φ be a formula and let $q_i = (C_i, \eta_i, \psi_i)$, $i \in \{1, 2\}$ be two states of the NPA $\mathcal{A}_{\mathcal{E},\varphi}$. We say that q_1 and q_2 are* future equivalent*, written $q_1 \approx_f q_2$, if there exists a formula ψ and substitutions $\sigma_i : fv(\psi) \to fv(\psi_i)$ such that $\psi\sigma_i = \psi_i$, for $i \in \{1, 2\}$, and the $fv(\psi)$-pointed configurations $\langle C_i, \eta_i \circ \sigma_i \rangle$ have isomorphic pointed residuals.*

It can be shown that, given $q_i = (C_i, \eta_i, \psi_i)$, $i \in \{1, 2\}$ as above, for all proposition environments π (satisfying a technical property of saturation) we have that $(C_1, \eta_1) \in \{\!|\psi_1|\!\}^{\mathcal{E}}_{\pi}$ if and only if $(C_2, \eta_2) \in \{\!|\psi_2|\!\}^{\mathcal{E}}_{\pi}$. Additionally, using strong regularity, one can prove that the semantics of fixpoint formulae is properly captured by finite approximants and that equivalence $\approx_f$ is of finite index. These are fundamental building bricks in the proof of Theorem 1 which, roughly, proceeds as follows.

Assume that the language $L(\mathcal{A}_{\mathcal{E},\varphi}) \neq \emptyset$. Then there is an accepting run r over some k-tree $\mathcal{T}$. Since φ is finite, in each infinite path there are infinitely many states $q_{i_h} = (C_{i_h}, \eta_{i_h}, \psi_{i_h})$ where ψ_{i_h} is the same subformula, up to renaming. Since $\approx_f$ is of finite index, infinitely many such states are equivalent. Then one deduces that, for some h, the subformula ψ_{i_h} is satisfied in (C_{i_h}, η_{i_h}). For fixpoint subformulae, this requires to show that, since the run is accepting, the subformula of maximal alternation depth that repeats infinitely often is a ν-formula and use the fact that, as mentioned before, its semantics can be finitely approximated. Then, by a form of backward soundness of the transitions, we get that all the nodes, including the root, contain formulae which are satisfied.

For the converse implication, assume that $\mathcal{E} \models \varphi$. Starting from the initial state $q_0 = (\emptyset, \eta, \varphi)$ where the formula is satisfied, and using the automaton transitions, we can build a k-tree $\mathcal{T}$ and a run where for each state (C', η', ψ) the subformula ψ is satisfied in (C', η') and such run can be proved to be accepting.

3.3 Quotienting the Automaton

In order to have an effective procedure for checking the satisfaction of a formula we need to build a suitable quotient of the NPA, with respect to an equivalence which preserves emptiness. A simple but important observation is that it is sufficient to require that the equivalence is a bisimulation in the following sense. An analogous notion is studied in [31] in the setting of nondeterministic tree automata over finite trees.

Definition 13 (bisimulation). *Given an NPA $\mathcal{A}$, a symmetric relation $R \subseteq Q \times Q$ over the set of states is a bisimulation if for all $(q, q') \in R$*

1. *for all $i \in [0, h]$, $q \in F_i \iff q' \in F_i$;*
2. *if $q \to (q_1, \ldots, q_m)$ then $q' \to (q'_1, \ldots, q'_m)$ with $(q_i, q'_i) \in R$ for $i \in [1, m]$.*

Given an NPA $\mathcal{A}$ and an equivalence $\equiv$ on the set of states which is a bisimulation, we define the quotient as $\mathcal{A}_{/\equiv} = \langle Q_{/\equiv}, \rightarrow_{/\equiv}, [q_0]_\equiv, \mathcal{F}_{/\equiv} \rangle$ where $[q]_\equiv \rightarrow_{/\equiv} ([q_1]_\equiv, \ldots, [q_m]_\equiv)$ if $q \rightarrow (q_1, \ldots, q_m)$ and $\mathcal{F}_{/\equiv} = (F_{0/\equiv}, \ldots, F_{h/\equiv})$. An NPA and its quotient accept exactly the same language.

Theorem 2 (language preservation). *Let $\mathcal{A}$ be an NPA and let $\equiv$ be an equivalence on the set of states which is a bisimulation. Then $L(\mathcal{A}_{/\equiv}) = L(\mathcal{A})$.*

When $\equiv$ is of finite index, the quotient $\mathcal{A}_{\mathcal{E},\varphi_{/\equiv}}$ is finite and, exploiting Theorems 1 and 2, we can verify whether $\mathcal{E} \models \varphi$ by checking the emptiness of the language accepted by $\mathcal{A}_{\mathcal{E},\varphi_{/\equiv}}$. Clearly a concrete algorithm will not first generate the infinite state NPA and then take the quotient, but it rather performs the quotient on the fly: whenever a new state would be equivalent to one already generated, the transition loops back to the existing state.

Whenever $\mathcal{E}$ is strongly regular, the future equivalence on states (see Definition 12) provides a bisimulation equivalence of finite index over $\mathcal{A}_{\mathcal{E},\varphi}$.

Lemma 1 ($\approx_f$ is a bisimulation). *Let $\mathcal{E}$ be a strongly regular* PES *and let φ be a closed formula in $\mathcal{L}_{hp}$. Then the future equivalence $\approx_f$ on $\mathcal{A}_{\mathcal{E},\varphi}$ is a bisimulation and it is of finite index.*

An obstacle towards the use of the quotiented NPA for model checking purposes is the fact that the future equivalence could be hard to compute (or even undecidable). In order to make the construction effective we need a decidable bisimulation equivalence on the NPA and the effectiveness of the set of successors of a state. This is further discussed in the next section.

4 Model Checking Petri Nets

We show how the model checking approach outlined before can be instantiated on finite safe Petri nets, a classical model of concurrency and distribution [32], by identifying a suitable effective bisimulation equivalence on the NPA.

4.1 Petri Nets and Their Event Structure Semantics

A *Petri net* is a tuple $\mathcal{N} = (P, T, F, M_0)$ where P, T are disjoint sets of *places* and *transitions*, respectively, $F : (P \times T) \cup (T \times P) \rightarrow \{0, 1\}$ is the *flow function*, and M_0 is the initial marking, i.e., the initial state of the net. We assume that the set of transitions is a subset of a fixed set $\mathbb{T}$ with a labelling $\lambda_N : \mathbb{T} \rightarrow \Lambda$.

A *marking* of $\mathcal{N}$ is a function $M : P \rightarrow \mathbb{N}$, indicating for each place the number of tokens in the place. A transition $t \in T$ is *enabled* at a marking M if $M(p) \geq F(p, t)$ for all $p \in P$. In this case it can be *fired* leading to a new marking M' defined by $M'(p) = M(p) + F(t, p) - F(p, t)$ for all places $p \in P$. This is written $M[t\rangle M'$. We denote by $\mathcal{R}(\mathcal{N})$ the set of markings reachable in $\mathcal{N}$ via a sequence of firings starting from the initial marking. We say that a marking M is *coverable* if there exists $M' \in \mathcal{R}(\mathcal{N})$ such that $M \leq M'$, pointwise. A net

$\mathcal{N}$ is *safe* if for every reachable marking $M \in \mathcal{R}(\mathcal{N})$ and all $p \in P$ we have $M(p) \leq 1$. Hereafter we will consider only safe nets. Hence markings will be often confused with the corresponding subset of places $\{p \mid M(p) = 1\} \subseteq P$. For $x \in P \cup T$ the *pre-set* and *post-set* are defined $^\bullet x = \{y \in P \cup T \mid F(y, x) = 1\}$ and $x^\bullet = \{y \in P \cup T \mid F(x, y) = 1\}$ respectively.

An example of Petri net can be found in Fig. 1b. Graphically places and transitions are drawn as circles and rectangles, respectively, while the flow function is rendered by means of directed arcs connecting places and transitions. Markings are represented by inserting tokens (black dots) in the corresponding places.

The concurrent behaviour of a Petri net can be represented by its unfolding $\mathcal{U}(\mathcal{N})$, an acyclic net constructed inductively starting from the initial marking of $\mathcal{N}$ and then adding, at each step, an occurrence of each enabled transition.

Definition 14 (unfolding). *Let $\mathcal{N} = (P, T, F, m_0)$ be a safe net. Define the net $U^{(0)} = (P^{(0)}, T^{(0)}, F^{(0)})$ as $T^{(0)} = \emptyset$, $P^{(0)} = \{(p, \bot) \mid p \in m_0\}$ and $F^{(0)} = \emptyset$, where $\bot$ is an element not belonging to P, T or F. The unfolding is the least net $\mathcal{U}(\mathcal{N}) = (P^{(\omega)}, T^{(\omega)}, F^{(\omega)})$ containing $U^{(0)}$ and such that*

- *if $t \in T$, the set of places $X \subseteq P^{(\omega)}$ is coverable and $\pi_1(X) = {}^\bullet t$, then $e = (t, X) \in T^{(\omega)}$;*
- *for any $e = (t, X) \in T^{(\omega)}$, the set $Z = \{(p, e) \mid p \in \pi_1(e)^\bullet\} \subseteq P^{(\omega)}$ where $\pi_1(u, v) = u$; moreover $^\bullet e = X$ and $e^\bullet = Z$.*

Places and transitions in the unfolding represent tokens and firing of transitions, respectively, of the original net. The projection π_1 over the first component maps places and transitions of the unfolding to the corresponding items of the original net $\mathcal{N}$. The initial marking is implicitly identified as the set of minimal places. For historical reasons transitions and places in the unfolding are also called *events* and *conditions*, respectively.

One can define *causality* $\leq_N$ over the unfolding as the transitive closure of the flow relation. *Conflict* is the relation $e \# e'$ if $^\bullet e \cap {}^\bullet e' \neq \emptyset$, inherited along causality. The events $T^{(\omega)}$ of the unfolding of a finite safe net, endowed with causality and conflict, form a PES, denoted $\mathcal{E}(\mathcal{N})$. The transitions of a configuration $C \in \mathcal{C}(\mathcal{E}(\mathcal{N}))$ can be fired in any order compatible with causality, producing a marking $C^\circ = (P^{(0)} \cup \bigcup_{t \in C} t^\bullet) \setminus (\bigcup_{t \in C} {}^\bullet t)$ in $\mathcal{U}(\mathcal{N})$; in turn, this corresponds to a reachable marking of $\mathcal{N}$ given by $\mathsf{M}(C) = \pi_1(C^\circ)$. As an example, the unfolding $\mathcal{U}(\mathcal{N})$ of the running example net $\mathcal{N}$ and the corresponding PES can be found in Figs. 1c and a.

4.2 Automata Model Checking for Petri Nets

The PES associated with a safe Petri net is known to be regular [27]. We next prove that it is also strongly regular and thus we can apply the theory developed so far for model checking $\mathcal{L}_{hp}$ over safe Petri nets.

Let $\mathcal{N} = \langle S, T, F, M_0 \rangle$ be a safe Petri net. A basic observation is that the residual of the PES $\mathcal{E}(\mathcal{N})$ with respect to a configuration $C \in \mathcal{C}(\mathcal{E}(\mathcal{N}))$ is uniquely determined by the marking produced by C. This correspondence can be extended to pointed configurations by considering markings which additionally record, for the events of interest in the past, the places in the marking which are caused by such events. This motivates the definition below.

Definition 15 (pointed marking). *Let $\mathcal{N} = \langle S, T, F, M_0 \rangle$ be a safe Petri net. Given a set X, a X-*pointed marking *is a pair $\langle M, r \rangle$ with $r : X \to 2^M$.*

A X-pointed configuration $\langle C, \zeta \rangle$ induces an X-pointed marking $\mathsf{M}(\langle C, \zeta \rangle) = \langle \mathsf{M}(C), r \rangle$ where $r(x) = \{\pi_1(b) \mid b \in C^\circ \ \wedge \ \zeta(x) < b\}$. Pointed configurations producing the same pointed marking have isomorphic pointed residuals.

Proposition 1 (pointed markings vs residuals). *Let $\mathcal{N} = \langle S, T, F, M_0 \rangle$ be a safe Petri net. Given a set X and two X-pointed configurations $\langle C_1, \zeta_1 \rangle$, $\langle C_2, \zeta_2 \rangle$ in $\mathcal{U}(\mathcal{N})$, if $\mathsf{M}(\langle C_1, \zeta_1 \rangle) = \mathsf{M}(\langle C_2, \zeta_2 \rangle)$ then $\mathcal{E}(\mathcal{N})[\langle C_1, \zeta_1 \rangle] \approx \mathcal{E}(\mathcal{N})[\langle C_2, \zeta_2 \rangle]$.*

By the previous result the PES associated with a finite safe Petri net is strongly regular. Indeed, the number of residuals of X-pointed configurations, up to isomorphism, by Proposition 1, is smaller than the number of X-pointed markings, which is clearly finite since the net is safe.

Corollary 1 (strong regularity). *Let $\mathcal{N}$ be finite safe Petri net. Then the corresponding* PES *$\mathcal{E}(\mathcal{N})$ is strongly regular.*

In order to instantiate the model checking framework to finite safe Petri nets, the idea is to take an equivalence over the infinite NPA by abstracting the (pointed) configurations associated with its states to pointed markings.

Definition 16 (pointed-marking equivalence on NPA). *Let $\mathcal{N}$ be a finite safe Petri net and let φ be a closed formula in $\mathcal{L}_{hp}$. Two states q_1, q_2 in the NPA $\mathcal{A}_{\mathcal{E}(\mathcal{N}),\varphi}$ are* pointed-marking equivalent, *written $q_1 \approx_m q_2$, if $q_i = \langle C_i, \eta_i, \psi \rangle$, $i \in \{1, 2\}$, for some $\psi \in \mathsf{sf}(\varphi)$ and $\mathsf{M}(\langle C_1, \eta_{1|fv(\psi)} \rangle) = \mathsf{M}(\langle C_2, \eta_{2|fv(\psi)} \rangle)$.*

Using Proposition 1 we can immediately prove that $\approx_m$ refines $\approx_f$. Moreover we can show that $\approx_m$ is a bisimulation in the sense of Definition 13.

Proposition 2 (marking equivalence is a bisimulation). *Let $\mathcal{N}$ be a finite safe Petri net and let φ be a closed formula in $\mathcal{L}_{hp}$. The equivalence $\approx_m$ on the automaton $\mathcal{A}_{\mathcal{E}(\mathcal{N}),\varphi}$ is a bisimulation and it is of finite index.*

Relying on Propositions 1 and 2 we provide an explicit construction of the quotient automaton $\mathcal{A}_{\mathcal{E}(\mathcal{N}),\varphi_{/\approx_m}}$. We introduce a convenient notation for transitions between pointed markings. Given the variables $\mathbf{x}$, $\mathbf{y}$, a set X such that $\mathbf{x} \cup \mathbf{y} \subseteq X$ and an X-pointed marking $\langle M, r \rangle$, we write $\langle M, r \rangle \xrightarrow{\mathbf{x}, \overline{\mathbf{y}} < t}_{\mathsf{a}, z} \langle M', r' \rangle$ if $M[t\rangle M'$, $\lambda_N(t) = \mathsf{a}$, for all $x \in \mathbf{x}$ we have $r(x) \cap {}^\bullet t \neq \emptyset$ and for all $y \in \mathbf{y}$ it holds $r(y) \cap {}^\bullet t = \emptyset$ and r' is defined by $r'(z) = t^\bullet$ and $r'(w) = (r(w) \cap M') \cup \{s \mid r(w) \cap {}^\bullet t \neq \emptyset \ \wedge \ s \in t^\bullet\}$, for $w \neq z$. In words, from the pointed marking $\langle M, r \rangle$ transition t is fired and "pointed" by variable z. Transition t is required to consume tokens caused by $\mathbf{x}$ and not to consume tokens caused by $\mathbf{y}$, in order to be itself caused by $\mathbf{x}$ and independent from $\mathbf{y}$. After the firing, variables which were causes of some $p \in {}^\bullet t$ become causes of the places in $t^\bullet$ and, clearly, z causes $t^\bullet$.

Construction 1 (quotient NPA). *Let $\mathcal{N}$ be a finite safe Petri net and let $\varphi \in \mathcal{L}_{hp}$ be a closed formula. The quotient NPA $\mathcal{A}_{\mathcal{E}(\mathcal{N}),\varphi_{/\approx_m}}$ is defined as follows. The set of states $Q = \{(M, r, \psi) \mid M \in \mathcal{R}(\mathcal{N}) \ \wedge \ r : fv(\psi) \to 2^M \ \wedge \ \psi \in \mathsf{sf}(\varphi)\}$. The initial state $q_0 = (M_0, \emptyset, \varphi)$. The transition relation is defined, for any state $q = (M, r, \psi) \in Q$, by:*

- *if $\psi = \mathsf{T}$ or $\psi = \mathsf{F}$, then $q \to (q)$*
- *if $\psi = \psi_1 \wedge \psi_2$, then $q \to (q_1, q_2)$ where $q_i = (M, r, \psi_i)$, $i \in \{1, 2\}$*
- *if $\psi = \psi_1 \vee \psi_2$, then $q \to (q_1)$ and $q \to (q_2)$ where $q_i = (M, r, \psi_i)$, $i \in \{1, 2\}$*
- *if $\psi = [\![\mathbf{x}, \overline{\mathbf{y}} < \mathsf{a}\, z]\!]\psi'$, let $S = \{(M', r'_{|fv(\psi')}) \mid \langle M, r\rangle \xrightarrow{\mathbf{x}, \overline{\mathbf{y}} < t}_{a,z} \langle M', r'\rangle\}$; if $S = \{(M_1, r_1), \ldots, (M_n, r_n)\} \neq \emptyset$ then $q \to (q_1, \ldots, q_n)$ where $q_i = (M_i, r_i, \psi')$ for $i \in [1, n]$, otherwise $q \to (q)$;*
- *if $\psi = \langle\!|\mathbf{x}, \overline{\mathbf{y}} < \mathsf{a}\, z|\!\rangle\psi'$, let $S = \{(M', r'_{|fv(\psi')}) \mid \langle M, r\rangle \xrightarrow{\mathbf{x}, \overline{\mathbf{y}} < t}_{a,z} \langle M', r'\rangle\}$; if $S = \{(M_1, r_1), \ldots, (M_n, r_n)\} \neq \emptyset$ then $q \to (q_i)$ where $q_i = (M_i, r_i, \psi')$ for $i \in [1, n]$, otherwise $q \to (q)$;*
- *if $\psi = \alpha X(\mathbf{x}).\psi'$ then $q \to (q')$ where $q' = (M, r, X(\mathbf{x}))$;*
- *if $\psi = X(\mathbf{y})$ and $\psi' \in \mathsf{sf}(\varphi)$ is the subformula such that $\psi' = \alpha X(\mathbf{x}).\psi''$ then $q \to (q')$ where $q' = (M, r[\mathbf{x} \mapsto r(\mathbf{y})], \psi'')$.*

The acceptance condition is as in Definition 10.

4.3 A Prototype Tool

The algorithm for model checking Petri nets outlined before is implemented in the prototype tool TCWB (*True Concurrency Workbench*) [33], written in Haskell. The tool inputs a safe Petri net $\mathcal{N}$ and a closed formula φ of $\mathcal{L}_{hp}$ and outputs the truth value of the formula on the initial marking of $\mathcal{N}$. The algorithm builds the quotient NPA $\mathcal{A}_{\mathcal{E}(\mathcal{N}),\varphi_{/\approx_m}}$ "on demand", i.e., the states of the automaton are generated when they are explored in the search of an accepting run. A path is recognised as successful when it includes a loop where a $\sqsubseteq_d^*$-maximal subformula is T, a $[\![\,]\!]$-subformula or a ν-subformula. In this way only the fragment of $\mathcal{A}_{\mathcal{E}(\mathcal{N}),\varphi_{/\approx_m}}$ relevant to decide the satisfaction of φ is built.

Given a net $\mathcal{N} = (P, T, F, M_0)$ and a formula φ, the number of states in the quotient automaton $\mathcal{A}_{\mathcal{E}(\mathcal{N}),\varphi_{/\approx_m}}$ can be bounded as follows. Recall that a state consists of a triple (M, r, ψ) where $\psi \in \mathsf{sf}(\varphi)$, M is a reachable marking and $r : fv(\psi) \to 2^M$ is a function. This leads to an upper bound $O(|\mathsf{sf}(\varphi)| \cdot |\mathcal{R}(\mathcal{N})| \cdot 2^{|P| \cdot v})$, where $v = max\{|fv(\psi)| : \psi \in \mathsf{sf}(\varphi)\}$ is the largest number of event variables appearing free in a subformula of φ. In turn, since $|\mathcal{R}(\mathcal{N})| \leq 2^{|P|}$, this is bounded by $O(|\mathsf{sf}(\varphi)| \cdot 2^{|P| \cdot (v+1)})$. The size of the automaton is thus exponential in the size of the net and linear in the size of the formula. Moving from the interleaving fragment of the logic (where $v = 0$) to formulae capable of expressing true concurrent properties thus causes an exponential blow up. However, note that the worst case scenario requires all transitions to be related by causality and concurrency to all places in any possible way, something that should be quite unlikely in practice. Indeed, despite the fact that the tool is very preliminary and more tweaks and optimisations could improve its efficiency, for the practical tests we performed the execution time seems to be typically well below than the theoretical worst case upper bound.

5 Conclusions

We introduced an automata-theoretic framework for the model checking of the logic for true concurrency $\mathcal{L}_{hp}$, representing the logical counterpart of a classical true concurrent equivalence, i.e., history preserving bisimilarity. The approach is developed abstractly for strongly regular PESs, that include regular trace PESs. A concrete model-checking procedure requires the identification of an effective bisimulation equivalence for the construction of the quotient automaton. We showed how this can be done for finite safe Petri nets. The technique is implemented in a proof-of-concept tool.

We proved that the class of regular trace PESs is included in that of strongly regular PESs which in turn is included in the class of regular PESs. The precise relation of strongly regular PESs with the other two classes is still unclear and interesting in view of [34] that recently showed that regular trace PESs are strictly included in regular PESs, disproving Thiagarajan's conjecture.

Several other papers deal with model checking for logics on event structures. In [35] a technique is proposed for model checking a CTL-style logic with modalities for immediate causality and conflict on a subclass of PESs. The logic is quite different from ours as formulae are satisfied by single events, the idea being that an event, with its causes, represents the local state of a component. The procedure involves the construction of a finite representation of the PES associated with a program which has some conceptual relation with our quotienting phase. In [19] the author shows that first order logic and Monadic Trace Logic (MTL), a restricted form of monadic second order (MSO) logic are decidable on regular trace event structures. The possibility of directly observing conflicts in MTL and thus of distinguishing behaviourally equivalent PESs (e.g., the PESs consisting of a single or two conflicting copies of an event), and the presence in $\mathcal{L}_{hp}$ of propositions which are non-monadic with respect to event variables, make these logics not immediate to compare. Still, a deeper investigation is definitively worth to pursue, especially in view of the fact that, in the propositional case, the mu-calculus corresponds to the bisimulation invariant fragment of MSO logic [36].

The work summarised in [18] develops a game theoretic approach for model-checking a concurrent logic over partial order models. It has been observed in [20] that such logic is incomparable to $\mathcal{L}_{hp}$. Preliminary investigations shows that our model-checking framework could be adapted to such a logic and, more generally, to a logic joining the expressive power of the two. Moreover, further exploring the potentialities of a game theoretic approach in our setting represents an interesting venue of further research.

Compared to our previous work [26], we extended the range of the technique to the full logic $\mathcal{L}_{hp}$, without limitations concerning the alternation depth of formulae. Relaxing the restriction to strongly regular PESs, instead, appears to be quite problematic unless one is willing to deal with transfinite runs which, however, would be of very limited practical interest.

The tool is still very preliminary. As suggested by its (wishful) name (inspired by the classical Edinburgh Concurrency Workbench [37]) we would like to bring the TCWB to a more mature stage, working on optimisations and adding an interface that gives access to a richer set of commands.

Acknowledgements. We are grateful to Perdita Stevens for insightful hints and pointers to the literature and to the anonymous reviewers for their comments.

References

1. Winskel, G.: Event structures. In: Brauer, W., Reisig, W., Rozenberg, G. (eds.) ACPN 1986. LNCS, vol. 255, pp. 325–392. Springer, Heidelberg (1987). https://doi.org/10.1007/3-540-17906-2_31
2. Winskel, G.: Events, causality and symmetry. Comput. J. **54**(1), 42–57 (2011)
3. Pichon-Pharabod, J., Sewell, P.: A concurrency semantics for relaxed atomics that permits optimisation and avoids thin-air executions. In: Bodík, R., Majumdar, R. (eds.) Proceedings of POPL 2016, pp. 622–633. ACM (2016)
4. Jeffrey, A., Riely, J.: On thin air reads towards an event structures model of relaxed memory. In: Grohe, M., Koskinen, E., Shankar, N. (eds.) Proceedings of LICS 2016, pp. 759–767. ACM (2016)
5. Dumas, M., García-Bañuelos, L.: Process mining reloaded: event structures as a unified representation of process models and event logs. In: Devillers, R., Valmari, A. (eds.) PETRI NETS 2015. LNCS, vol. 9115, pp. 33–48. Springer, Cham (2015). https://doi.org/10.1007/978-3-319-19488-2_2
6. Farzan, A., Madhusudan, P.: Causal atomicity. In: Ball, T., Jones, R.B. (eds.) CAV 2006. LNCS, vol. 4144, pp. 315–328. Springer, Heidelberg (2006). https://doi.org/10.1007/11817963_30
7. Baldan, P., Carraro, A.: A causal view on non-intereference. Fundamenta Informaticae **140**(1), 1–38 (2015)
8. van Glabbeek, R., Goltz, U.: Refinement of actions and equivalence notions for concurrent systems. Acta Informatica **37**(4/5), 229–327 (2001)
9. De Nicola, R., Ferrari, G.L.: Observational logics and concurrency models. In: Nori, K.V., Veni Madhavan, C.E. (eds.) FSTTCS 1990. LNCS, vol. 472, pp. 301–315. Springer, Heidelberg (1990). https://doi.org/10.1007/3-540-53487-3_53
10. Bednarczyk, M.A.: Hereditary history preserving bisimulations or what is the power of the future perfect in program logics. Technical report, Polish Academy of Sciences (1991)
11. Pinchinat, S., Laroussinie, F., Schnoebelen, P.: Logical characterization of truly concurrent bisimulation. Technical report 114, LIFIA-IMAG, Grenoble (1994)
12. Penczek, W.: Branching time and partial order in temporal logics. In: Time and Logic: A Computational Approach, pp. 179–228. UCL Press (1995)
13. Nielsen, M., Clausen, C.: Games and logics for a noninterleaving bisimulation. Nord. J. Comput. **2**(2), 221–249 (1995)
14. Bradfield, J., Fröschle, S.: Independence-friendly modal logic and true concurrency. Nord. J. Comput. **9**(1), 102–117 (2002)
15. Alur, R., Peled, D., Penczek, W.: Model-checking of causality properties. In: Proceedings of LICS 1995, pp. 90–100. IEEE Computer Society (1995)

16. Gutierrez, J., Bradfield, J.: Model-checking games for fixpoint logics with partial order models. In: Bravetti, M., Zavattaro, G. (eds.) CONCUR 2009. LNCS, vol. 5710, pp. 354–368. Springer, Heidelberg (2009). https://doi.org/10.1007/978-3-642-04081-8_24
17. Gutierrez, J.: Logics and bisimulation games for concurrency, causality and conflict. In: de Alfaro, L. (ed.) FoSSaCS 2009. LNCS, vol. 5504, pp. 48–62. Springer, Heidelberg (2009). https://doi.org/10.1007/978-3-642-00596-1_5
18. Gutierrez, J.: On bisimulation and model-checking for concurrent systems with partial order semantics. Ph.D. thesis, University of Edinburgh (2011)
19. Madhusudan, P.: Model-checking trace event structures. In: Proceedings of LICS 2013, pp. 371–380. IEEE Computer Society (2003)
20. Baldan, P., Crafa, S.: A logic for true concurrency. J. ACM **61**(4), 24:1–24:36 (2014)
21. Phillips, I., Ulidowski, I.: Event identifier logic. Math. Struct. Comput. Sci. **24**(2), 1–51 (2014)
22. Best, E., Devillers, R., Kiehn, A., Pomello, L.: Fully concurrent bisimulation. Acta Informatica **28**, 231–261 (1991)
23. Rabinovich, A.M., Trakhtenbrot, B.A.: Behaviour structures and nets. Fundamenta Informaticae **11**, 357–404 (1988)
24. Degano, P., De Nicola, R., Montanari, U.: Partial orderings descriptions and observations of nondeterministic concurrent processes. In: de Bakker, J.W., de Roever, W.-P., Rozenberg, G. (eds.) REX 1988. LNCS, vol. 354, pp. 438–466. Springer, Heidelberg (1989). https://doi.org/10.1007/BFb0013030
25. Jurdzinski, M., Nielsen, M., Srba, J.: Undecidability of domino games and hhp-bisimilarity. Inf. Comput. **184**(2), 343–368 (2003)
26. Baldan, P., Padoan, T.: Local model checking in a logic for true concurrency. In: Esparza, J., Murawski, A.S. (eds.) FoSSaCS 2017. LNCS, vol. 10203, pp. 407–423. Springer, Heidelberg (2017). https://doi.org/10.1007/978-3-662-54458-7_24
27. Thiagarajan, P.S.: Regular event structures and finite Petri nets: a conjecture. In: Brauer, W., Ehrig, H., Karhumäki, J., Salomaa, A. (eds.) Formal and Natural Computing. LNCS, vol. 2300, pp. 244–253. Springer, Heidelberg (2002). https://doi.org/10.1007/3-540-45711-9_14
28. Emerson, E.A., Jutla, C.S., Sistla, A.P.: On model checking for the μ-calculus and its fragments. Theor. Comput. Sci. **258**(1–2), 491–522 (2001)
29. Mostowski, A.W.: Regular expressions for infinite trees and a standard form of automata. In: Skowron, A. (ed.) SCT 1984. LNCS, vol. 208, pp. 157–168. Springer, Heidelberg (1985). https://doi.org/10.1007/3-540-16066-3_15
30. Klauck, H.: Algorithms for parity games. In: Grädel, E., Thomas, W., Wilke, T. (eds.) Automata Logics, and Infinite Games. LNCS, vol. 2500, pp. 107–129. Springer, Heidelberg (2002). https://doi.org/10.1007/3-540-36387-4_7
31. Abdulla, P.A., Kaati, L., Högberg, J.: Bisimulation minimization of tree automata. In: Ibarra, O.H., Yen, H.-C. (eds.) CIAA 2006. LNCS, vol. 4094, pp. 173–185. Springer, Heidelberg (2006). https://doi.org/10.1007/11812128_17
32. Petri, C.: Kommunikation mit Automaten. Schriften des Institutes für Instrumentelle Matematik, Bonn (1962)
33. Padoan, T.: True concurrency workbench. http://github.com/tpadoan/TCWB
34. Chalopin, J., Chepoi, V.: A counterexample to Thiagarajan's conjecture on regular event structures. In: Chatzigiannakis, I., Indyk, P., Kuhn, F., Muscholl, A. (eds.) Proceedings of ICALP 2017, LIPIcs, vol. 80, pp. 101:1–101:14, Schloss Dagstuhl - Leibniz-Zentrum fuer Informatik (2017)

35. Penczek, W.: Model-checking for a subclass of event structures. In: Brinksma, E. (ed.) TACAS 1997. LNCS, vol. 1217, pp. 145–164. Springer, Heidelberg (1997). https://doi.org/10.1007/BFb0035386
36. Janin, D., Walukiewicz, I.: On the expressive completeness of the propositional mu-calculus with respect to monadic second order logic. In: Montanari, U., Sassone, V. (eds.) CONCUR 1996. LNCS, vol. 1119, pp. 263–277. Springer, Heidelberg (1996). https://doi.org/10.1007/3-540-61604-7_60
37. Stevens, P., Stirling, C.: Practical model-checking using games. In: Steffen, B. (ed.) TACAS 1998. LNCS, vol. 1384, pp. 85–101. Springer, Heidelberg (1998). https://doi.org/10.1007/BFb0054166

12

Guarded Traced Categories

Sergey Goncharov(✉) and Lutz Schröder(✉)

Friedrich-Alexander-Universität Erlangen-Nürnberg, Erlangen, Germany
{Sergey.Goncharov,Lutz.Schroeder}@fau.de

Abstract. Notions of guardedness serve to delineate the admissibility of cycles, e.g. in recursion, corecursion, iteration, or tracing. We introduce an abstract notion of guardedness structure on a symmetric monoidal category, along with a corresponding notion of guarded traces, which are defined only if the cycles they induce are guarded. We relate structural guardedness, determined by propagating guardedness along the operations of the category, to geometric guardedness phrased in terms of a diagrammatic language. In our setup, the Cartesian case (recursion) and the co-Cartesian case (iteration) become completely dual, and we show that in these cases, guarded tracedness is equivalent to presence of a guarded Conway operator, in analogy to an observation on total traces by Hasegawa and Hyland. Moreover, we relate guarded traces to unguarded categorical uniform fixpoint operators in the style of Simpson and Plotkin. Finally, we show that partial traces based on Hilbert-Schmidt operators in the category of Hilbert spaces are an instance of guarded traces.

1 Introduction

In models of computation, various notions of *guardedness* serve to control cyclic behaviour by allowing only guarded cycles, with the aim to ensure properties such as solvability of recursive equations or productivity. Typical examples are guarded process algebra specifications [6,29], coalgebraic guarded (co-)recursion [27,33], finite delay in online Turing machines [9], and productive definitions in intensional type theory [1,30], but also contractive maps in (ultra-)metric spaces [24].

A highly general model for unrestricted cyclic computations, on the other hand, are *traced monoidal categories* [22]; besides *recursion* and *iteration*, they cover further kinds of cyclic behaviour, e.g. in Girard's *Geometry of Interaction* [4,14] and quantum programming [3,34]. In the present paper we parametrize the framework of traced symmetric monoidal categories with a notion of guardedness, arriving at *(abstractly) guarded traced categories*, which effectively vary between two extreme cases: symmetric monoidal categories (nothing is guarded) and traced symmetric monoidal categories (everything is guarded). In terms of the standard diagrammatic language for traced monoidal categories, we decorate input and output gates of boxes to indicate guardedness; the diagram governing trace formation would then have the general form depicted in Fig. 1 – that is, we can only form traces connecting guarded (black) output gates to input gates that are unguarded (black), i.e. not assumed to be already guarded.

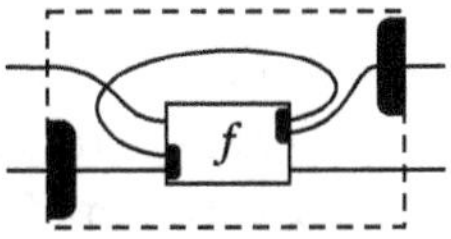

Fig. 1. Guarded trace

We provide basic structural results on our notion of abstract guardedness, and identify a wide array of examples. Specifically, we establish a geometric characterization of guardedness in terms of paths in diagrams; we identify a notion of *guarded ideal*, along with a construction of guardedness structures from guarded ideals and simplifications of this construction for the (co-)Cartesian and the Cartesian closed case; and we describe 'vacuous' guardedness structures where traces do not actually generate proper diagrammatic cycles. In terms of examples, we begin with the case where the monoidal structure is either product (Cartesian), corresponding to guarded recursion, or coproduct (co-Cartesian), for guarded iteration; the axioms for guardedness allow for a basic duality that indeed makes these two cases precisely dual. For total traces in Cartesian categories, Hasegawa and Hyland observed that trace operators are in one-to-one correspondence with *Conway fixpoint operators* [18,19]; we extend this correspondence to the guarded case, showing that guarded trace operators on a Cartesian category are in one-to-one correspondence with guarded Conway operators. In a more specific setting, we relate *guarded* traces in Cartesian categories to *unguarded* categorical uniform fixpoints as studied by Crole and Pitts [11] and by Simpson and Plotkin [37,38]. Concluding with a case where the monoidal structure is a proper tensor product, we show that the partial trace operation on (infinite-dimensional) Hilbert spaces is an instance of vacuous guardedness; this result relates to work by Abramsky, Blute, and Panangaden on traces over nuclear ideals, in this case over *Hilbert-Schmidt operators* [2].

Related Work. Abstract guardedness serves to determine definedness of a guarded trace operation, and thus relates to work on partial traces. We discuss work on nuclear ideals [2] in Sect. 6. In *partial traced categories* [17,26], traces are governed by a partial equational version (consisting of both strong and directed equations) of the Joyal-Street-Verity axioms; morphisms for which trace is defined are called *trace class*. A key difference to the approach via guardedness is that being trace class applies only to morphisms with inputs and outputs of matching types while guardedness applies to arbitrary morphisms, allowing for compositional propagation. Also, the axiomatizations are incomparable: Unlike for trace class morphisms [17, Remark 2.2], we require guardedness to be closed under composition with arbitrary morphisms (thus covering contractivity but not, e.g., monotonicity as in the modal μ-calculus); on the other hand, as noted by Jeffrey [21], guarded traces, e.g. of contractions, need not satisfy Vanishing II as a Kleene equality as assumed in partial traced categories. Some approaches treat traces as partial over objects [8,20]. In concrete algebraic categories, partial traces can be seen as induced by total traces in an ambient category of relations [5]. We discuss work on guardedness via endofunctors in Remark 23.

2 Preliminaries

We recall requisite categorical notions; see [25] for a comprehensive introduction.

Symmetric Monoidal Categories. A *symmetric monoidal category* $(\mathbf{C}, \otimes, I)$ consists of a category $\mathbf{C}$ (with object class $|\mathbf{C}|$), a bifunctor $\otimes$ (*tensor product*), and a *(tensor) unit* $I \in |\mathbf{C}|$, and coherent isomorphisms witnessing that $\otimes$ is, up to isomorphism, a commutative monoid structure with unit I. For the latter, we reserve the notation $\alpha_{A,B,C} : (A \otimes B) \otimes C \cong A \otimes (B \otimes C)$ (*associator*), $\gamma_{A,B} : A \otimes B \cong B \otimes A$ (*symmetry*), and $\upsilon_A : I \otimes A \cong A$ (*left unitor*); the *right unitor* $\hat{\upsilon}_A : A \otimes I \cong A$ is expressible via the symmetry. A symmetric monoidal category is *Cartesian* if the monoidal structure is finite product (i.e. $\otimes = \times$, and $I = 1$ is a terminal object), and, dually, *co-Cartesian* if the monoidal structure is finite coproduct (i.e. $\otimes = +$, and $I = \emptyset$ is an initial object). Coproduct injections are written $\mathsf{in}_i : X_i \to X_1 + X_2$ $(i = 1, 2)$, and product projections $\mathsf{pr}_i : X_1 \times X_2 \to X_i$. Various notions of algebraic tensor products also induce symmetric monoidal structures; see Sect. 6 for the case of Hilbert spaces. One has an obvious expression language for objects and morphisms in symmetric monoidal categories [36], the former obtained by postulating basic objects and closing under I and $\otimes$, and the latter by postulating basic morphisms of given profile and closing under $\otimes$, I, composition, identities, and the monoidal isomorphisms, subject to the evident notion of *well-typedness*. Morphism expressions are conveniently represented as *diagrams* consisting of boxes representing the basic morphisms, with input and output gates corresponding to the given profile. Tensoring is represented by putting boxes on top of each other, and composition by wires connecting outputs to inputs [36]. In a *traced symmetric monoidal category* one has an additional operation (*trace*) that essentially enables the formation of loops in diagrams, as in Fig. 1 (but without decorations).

Monads and (Co-)algebras. A(n F)-*coalgebra* for a functor $F : \mathbf{C} \to \mathbf{C}$ is a pair $(X, f : X \to FX)$ where $X \in |\mathbf{C}|$, thought of as modelling states and generalized transitions [33]. A *final coalgebra* is a final object in the category of coalgebras (with $\mathbf{C}$-morphisms $h : X \to Y$ such that $(Fh)f = gh$ as morphisms $(X, f) \to (Y, g)$), denoted $(\nu F, \mathsf{out} : \nu F \to F\nu F)$ if it exists. Dually, an F-*algebra* has the form $(X, f : FX \to X)$. A *monad* $\mathbb{T} = (T, \mu, \eta)$ on a category $\mathbf{C}$ consists of an endofunctor T on $\mathbf{C}$ and natural transformations $\eta : \mathrm{Id} \to T$ (*unit*) and $\mu : T^2 \to T$ (*multiplication*) subject to standard equations [25]. As observed by Moggi [31], monads can be seen as capturing *computational effects* of programs, with TX read as a type of computations with side effects from T and results in X. In this view, the *Kleisli category* $\mathbf{C}_{\mathbb{T}}$ of $\mathbb{T}$, which has the same objects as $\mathbf{C}$ and $\mathsf{Hom}_{\mathbf{C}_{\mathbb{T}}}(X, Y) = \mathsf{Hom}_{\mathbf{C}}(X, TY)$, is a category of side-effecting programs. A monad is *strong* if it is equipped with a *strength*, i.e. a natural transformation $X \times TY \to T(X \times Y)$ satisfying evident coherence conditions (e.g. [31]). A T-algebra (A, a) is an *(Eilenberg-Moore)* $\mathbb{T}$-*algebra* (for the *monad* $\mathbb{T}$) if additionally $a\eta = \mathsf{id}$ and $a(Ta) = a\mu_A$; the category of $\mathbb{T}$-algebras is denoted $\mathbf{C}^{\mathbb{T}}$.

3 Guarded Categories

We now introduce our notion of guarded structure. A standard example of guardedness are guarded definitions in process algebra. E.g. in the definition $P = a.P$, the right hand occurrence of P is guarded, ensuring unique solvability (by a process that keeps outputting a). A further example is contractivity of maps between complete metric spaces. We formulate abstract closure properties for *partial* guardedness where only some of the inputs and outputs of a morphism are guarded. Specifically, we distinguish *guarded outputs* and *guarded inputs* (D and B, respectively, in the following definition), with the intended reading that guarded outputs yield guarded data *provided* guarded data is already provided at guarded inputs, while unguarded inputs may be fed arbitrarily.

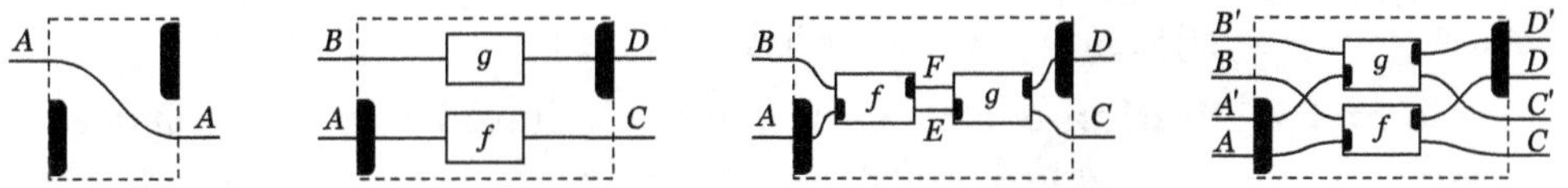

Fig. 2. Axioms of guarded categories

Definition 1 (Guarded category). An *(abstractly) guarded category* is a symmetric monoidal category $(\mathbf{C}, \otimes, I)$ equipped with distinguished subsets $\mathsf{Hom}^\bullet(A \otimes B, C \otimes D) \subseteq \mathsf{Hom}(A \otimes B, C \otimes D)$ of *partially guarded morphisms* for $A, B, C, D \in |\mathbf{C}|$, satisfying the following conditions:

(uni$_\otimes$) $\gamma_{I,A} \in \mathsf{Hom}^\bullet(I \otimes A, A \otimes I)$;
(vac$_\otimes$) $f \otimes g \in \mathsf{Hom}^\bullet(A \otimes B, C \otimes D)$ for all $f : A \to C$, $g : B \to D$;
(cmp$_\otimes$) $g \in \mathsf{Hom}^\bullet(A \otimes B, E \otimes F)$ and $f \in \mathsf{Hom}^\bullet(E \otimes F, C \otimes D)$ imply $fg \in \mathsf{Hom}^\bullet(A \otimes B, C \otimes D)$;
(par$_\otimes$) for $f \in \mathsf{Hom}^\bullet(A \otimes B, C \otimes D)$, $g \in \mathsf{Hom}^\bullet(A' \otimes B', C' \otimes D')$, the evident transpose of $f \otimes g$ is in $\mathsf{Hom}^\bullet((A \otimes A') \otimes (B \otimes B'), (C \otimes C') \otimes (D \otimes D'))$.

We emphasize that $\mathsf{Hom}^\bullet(A \otimes B, C \otimes D)$ is meant to depend individually on A, B, C, D and not just on $A \otimes B$ and $C \otimes D$.

One easily derives a *weakening* rule stating that if $f \in \mathsf{Hom}^\bullet((A \otimes A') \otimes B, C \otimes (D' \otimes D))$, then the obvious transpose of f is in $\mathsf{Hom}^\bullet(A \otimes (A' \otimes B), (C \otimes D') \otimes D)$.

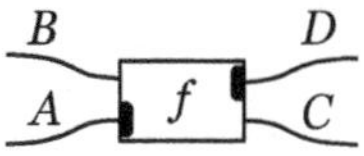

We extend the standard diagram language for symmetric monoidal categories (Sect. 2), representing morphisms $f \in \mathsf{Hom}^\bullet(A \otimes B, C \otimes D)$ by *decorated boxes* as shown on the right, with black bars marking the *unguarded input* gates A and the *guarded output* gates D. Weakening then corresponds to shrinking the black bars of decorated boxes. Figure 2 depicts the above axioms in this language. Solid boxes represent the assumptions, while dashed boxes represent the conclusions. The latter only occur in the derivation process and do not form part of the actual diagrams representing concrete morphisms. We silently identify object expressions and sets of gates in diagrams. Given a (well-typed) morphism expression e, a judgement $e \in \mathsf{Hom}^\bullet(A \otimes B, C \otimes D)$, called a *guardedness typing* of e, is *derivable* if it can be derived from the assumed guardedness typing of the constituent basic boxes of e using the rules in Definition 1. We have an obvious notion of (directed) *paths* in diagrams; a path is *guarded* if it passes some basic box f through an unguarded input gate and a guarded output gate (intuitively, guardedness is then introduced along the path as the passage through f will guarantee guarded output without assuming guarded input). We then have the following geometric characterization of guardedness typing:

Theorem 2. *For a well-typed morphism expression $e \in \mathsf{Hom}(A \otimes B, C \otimes D)$, the guardedness typing $e \in \mathsf{Hom}^\bullet(A \otimes B, C \otimes D)$ is derivable iff in the diagram of e, every path from an input gate in A to an output gate in D is guarded.*

Every symmetric monoidal category has both a largest ($\mathsf{Hom}^\bullet(A \otimes B, C \otimes D) = \mathsf{Hom}(A \otimes B, C \otimes D)$) and a least guarded structure:

Lemma and Definition 3 (Vacuous guardedness). *Every symmetric monoidal category is guarded under taking $f \in \mathsf{Hom}^\bullet(A \otimes B, C \otimes D)$ iff f factors as*

$$A \otimes B \xrightarrow{\mathsf{id}_A \otimes g} A \otimes E \otimes D \xrightarrow{h \otimes \mathsf{id}_D} C \otimes D$$

(eliding associativity) with $g : B \to E \otimes D$, $h : A \otimes E \to C$. This is the least guarded structure on $\mathbf{C}$, the vacuous guarded structure.

E.g. the natural guarded structure on Hilbert spaces (Sect. 6) is vacuous.

Remark 4 (Duality). The rules and axioms in Fig. 2 are stable under 180°-rotation, that is, under reversing arrows and applying the monoidal symmetry on both sides (this motivates decorating the *unguarded* inputs). Consequently, if $\mathbf{C}$ is guarded, then so is the dual category $\mathbf{C}^{op}$, with guardedness given by $f \in \mathsf{Hom}^\bullet_{\mathbf{C}^{op}}(A \otimes B, C \otimes D)$ iff the obvious transpose of f is in $\mathsf{Hom}^\bullet_{\mathbf{C}}(D \otimes C, B \otimes A)$.

In case $\otimes$ is coproduct, we can simplify the description of partial guardedness:

Proposition 5. *Partial guardedness in a co-Cartesian category $(\mathbf{C}, +, \emptyset)$ is equivalently determined by distinguished subsets $\mathsf{Hom}_\sigma(X, Y) \subseteq \mathsf{Hom}(X, Y)$ with σ ranging over coproduct injections $Y_2 \to Y_1 + Y_2 \cong Y$, subject to the rules on the right hand side of Fig. 3, where $f : X \to_\sigma Y$ denotes $f \in \mathsf{Hom}_\sigma(X, Y)$, with $f \in \mathsf{Hom}^\bullet(X_1 + X_2, Y_1 + Y_2)$ iff $(f \mathsf{in}_1) \in \mathsf{Hom}_{\mathsf{in}_2}(X_1, Y_1 + Y_2)$.*

We have used the mentioned rules for $\to_\sigma$ in previous work on guarded iteration [16] (with $(\mathbf{vac}_\times)$ called $(\mathbf{trv})$, and together with weakening, which as indicated above turns out to be derivable). By duality (Remark 4), we immediately have a corresponding description for the Cartesian case:

Corollary 6. *Partial guardedness in a Cartesian category $(\mathbf{C}, \times, 1)$ is equivalently determined by distinguished subsets $\mathsf{Hom}^\sigma(X, Y) \subseteq \mathsf{Hom}(X, Y)$ with σ ranging over product projections $X \cong X_1 \times X_2 \to X_1$, subject to the rules on the left hand side of Fig. 3, where $f : X \to^\sigma Y$ denotes $f \in \mathsf{Hom}^\sigma(X, Y)$, with $f \in \mathsf{Hom}^\bullet(X_1 \times X_2, Y_1 \times Y_2)$ iff $\mathsf{pr}_2 f \in \mathsf{Hom}^{\mathsf{pr}_1}(X_1 \times X_2, Y_2)$.*

$$(\mathbf{vac}_\times)\ \frac{f : X \to Z}{f\,\mathsf{pr}_1 : X \times Y \to^{\mathsf{pr}_2} Z} \qquad (\mathbf{vac}_+)\ \frac{f : X \to Z}{\mathsf{in}_1\, f : X \to_{\mathsf{in}_2} Z + Y}$$

$$(\mathbf{cmp}_\times)\ \frac{f : X \times Y \to^{\mathsf{pr}_2} Z \quad g : V \to^{\sigma} X \quad h : V \to Y}{f\,\langle g, h\rangle : V \to^{\sigma} Z} \qquad (\mathbf{cmp}_+)\ \frac{f : X \to_{\mathsf{in}_2} Y + Z \quad g : Y \to_{\sigma} V \quad h : Z \to V}{[g, h]\, f : X \to_{\sigma} V}$$

$$(\mathbf{par}_\times)\ \frac{f : X \to^{\sigma} Y \qquad g : X \to^{\sigma} Z}{\langle f, g\rangle : X \to^{\sigma} Y \times Z} \qquad (\mathbf{par}_+)\ \frac{f : X \to_{\sigma} Z \qquad f : Y \to_{\sigma} Z}{[f, g] : X + Y \to_{\sigma} Z}$$

Fig. 3. Axioms of Cartesian (left) and co-Cartesian (right) guarded categories

Remark 7. In a co-Cartesian category, vacuous guardedness (Lemma 3) can equivalently be described by $f \in \mathsf{Hom}^{\bullet}(A + B, C + D)$ iff f decomposes as $f = [\mathsf{in}_1 h, g]$ (uniquely provided that in_1 is monic), or in terms of the description from Proposition 5, $u \in \mathsf{Hom}_{\mathsf{in}_2}(X, Y + Z)$ iff u factors through in_1. Of course, the dual situation obtains in Cartesian categories.

Example 8 (Process algebra). Fix a monad $\mathbb{T}$ on $(\mathbf{C}, +, \emptyset)$ and an endofunctor $\Sigma : \mathbf{C} \to \mathbf{C}$ such that the generalized coalgebraic resumption transform $T_\Sigma = \nu\gamma.\, T(- + \Sigma\gamma)$ exists; we think of $T_\Sigma X$ as a type of processes that have side-effects in $\mathbb{T}$ and perform communication actions from Σ, seen as a generalized signature. The Kleisli category $\mathbf{C}_{\mathbb{T}_\Sigma}$ of $\mathbb{T}_\Sigma$ is again co-Cartesian. Putting

$$f : X \to_{\mathsf{in}_2} T_\Sigma(Y + Z) \iff \mathsf{out} f \in \{T(\mathsf{in}_1 + \mathsf{id})g \mid g : X \to T(Y + \Sigma T_\Sigma(Y + Z))\}$$

(cf. Sect. 2 for notation), we make $\mathbf{C}_{\mathbb{T}_\Sigma}$ into a guarded category [16]. The standard motivating example of finitely nondeterministic processes is obtained by taking $\mathbb{T} = \mathcal{P}_\omega$ (finite powerset monad) and $\Sigma = A \times -$ (action prefixing).

Example 9 (Metric spaces). Let $\mathbf{C}$ be the Cartesian category of metric spaces and non-expansive maps. Taking $f : X \times Y \to^{\mathsf{pr}_2} Z$ iff $\lambda y.\, f(x, y)$ is contractive for every $x \in X$ makes $\mathbf{C}$ into a guarded Cartesian category.

4 Guardedness via Guarded Ideals

Most of the time, the structure of a guarded category is determined by morphisms with only unguarded inputs and guarded outputs, which form an *ideal*:

Definition 10 (Guarded morphisms). A morphism $f : X \to Y$ in a guarded category is *guarded* (as opposed to only partially guarded) if $\upsilon_Y^{-1} f \hat{\upsilon}_X \in \mathsf{Hom}^{\bullet}(X \otimes I, I \otimes Y)$; we write $\mathsf{Hom}^{\blacktriangleright}(X, Y)$ for the set of guarded morphisms $f : X \to Y$.

Definition 11 (Guarded ideal). A family G of subsets $G(X, Y) \subseteq \mathsf{Hom}(X, Y)$ $(X, Y \in |\mathbf{C}|)$ in a monoidal category $(\mathbf{C}, \otimes, I)$ is a *guarded ideal* if it is closed under $\otimes$ and under composition with arbitrary $\mathbf{C}$-morphisms on both sides, and $G(I, I) = \mathsf{Hom}(I, I)$.

There is always a *least guarded ideal*, $G(X,Y) = \{gf \mid f : X \to I, g : I \to Y\}$. Moreover, as indicated above:

Lemma and Definition 12. *In a guarded category, the sets* $\mathsf{Hom}^{\blacktriangleright}(X,Y)$ *form a guarded ideal, the guarded ideal* induced *by the guarded structure.*

Conversely, it is clear that every guarded ideal *generates* a guarded structure by just closing under the rules of Definition 1.

Definition 13 (Ideally guarded category). A guarded category is *ideal* or *ideally guarded* (over G) if it is generated by some guarded ideal (G).

We give a more concrete description:

Theorem 14. *Let* $(\mathbf{C}, \otimes, I)$ *be ideally guarded over* G. *Then* $\mathsf{Hom}^{\bullet}(A \otimes B, C \otimes D)$ *consists of the morphisms of the form*

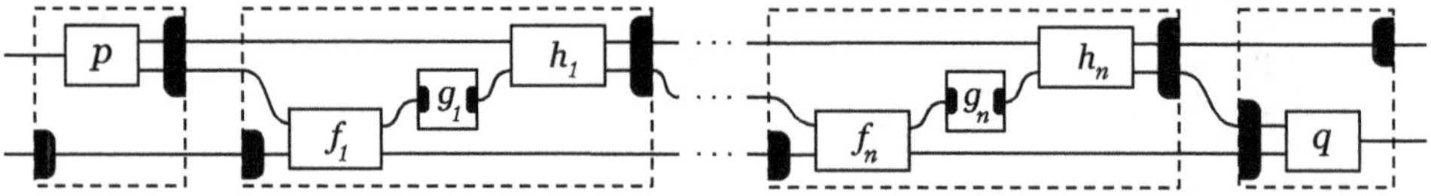

for g_i *in* G *and arbitrary* p, q, f_i, h_i.

The transitions between guarded ideals and guarded structures are not in general mutually inverse: The guarded structure generated the guarded ideal induced by a guarded structure may be smaller than the original one (Example 21), and the guarded ideal induced by the guarded structure generated by a guarded ideal G may be larger than G (Remark 16). We proceed to analyse details.

Proposition 15. *On every symmetric monoidal category, the least guarded structure (Lemma 3) is ideal.*

Remark 16. Vacuously guarded categories need not induce the least guarded ideal (although by the next results, this does hold in the Cartesian and the co-Cartesian case). In fact, by Lemma 3, the guarded ideal induced by the vacuous guarded structure consists of the morphisms of the form $(h \otimes \mathsf{id}_D)(\mathsf{id}_A \otimes g)$ (eliding associativity and the unitor) where $g : I \to E \otimes D$, $h : A \otimes E \to I$:

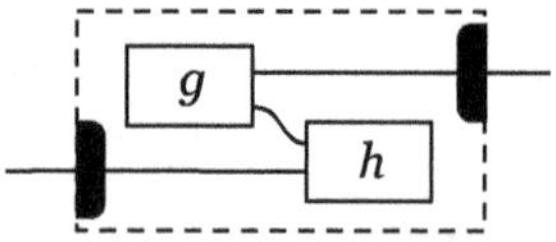

(1)

This ideal will resurface in the discussion of Hilbert spaces (Sect. 6).

The situation is simpler in the Cartesian and, dually, in the co-Cartesian case.

Lemma 17. *Let* $\mathbf{C}$ *be ideally guarded over* G, *and suppose that every* $f \in G(X \otimes Y, Z)$ *factors through* $\hat{f} \otimes \mathsf{id} : X \otimes Y \to V \otimes Y$ *for some* $\hat{f} \in G(X,V)$. *Then the guardedness structure of* $\mathbf{C}$ *induces* G.

If $\otimes = +$, the premise of the lemma is automatic, since $f \in G(X+Y,Z)$ can be represented as $[f\,\mathsf{in}_1, f\,\mathsf{in}_2] = [\mathsf{id}, f\,\mathsf{in}_2]\,(f\,\mathsf{in}_1 + \mathsf{id})$ where $f\,\mathsf{in}_1 \in G(X,Z)$ by the closure properties of guarded ideals. Hence, we obtain

Theorem 18. *The guarded structure generated by a guarded ideal G on a co-Cartesian category is equivalently described by* $\mathsf{Hom}_{\mathsf{in}_2}(X, Y+Z) = \{[\mathsf{in}_1, g]h \mid g \in G(W, Y+Z), h : X \to Y+W\}$, *and hence induces G.*

Corollary 19. *The guarded structure generated by a guarded ideal G on a Cartesian category is equivalently described by* $\mathsf{Hom}^{\mathsf{pr}_1}(X \times Y, Z) = \{h\,\langle g, \mathsf{pr}_2\rangle \mid g \in G(X \times Y, W), h : W \times Y \to Z\}$, *and hence induces G.*

The description can be further simplified in the Cartesian closed case.

Corollary 20. *Given a guarded ideal G on a Cartesian closed category, put $f : X \times Y \to^{\mathsf{pr}_1} Z$ iff* curry $f \in G(X, Z^Y)$. *This describes the guarded structure induced by G iff G is* exponential, *i.e. $f \in G(X,Y)$ implies $f^V \in G(X^V, Y^V)$.*

(We leave it as an open question whether a similar characterization holds in the monoidal closed case.) Natural examples of both ideal and non-ideal guardedness are found in metric spaces:

Example 21 (Metric spaces). The guarded structure on metric spaces from Example 9 fails to be ideal: It induces the guarded ideal of contractive maps, which however generates the (ideal) guarded structure described by $f : X \times Y \to^{\mathsf{pr}_2} Z$ iff $f(x,y)$ is *uniformly* contractive in y, i.e. there is $c < 1$ such that for every x, $\lambda y.\, f(x,y)$ is contractive with contraction factor c.

A large class of ideally guarded structures arises as follows.

Proposition 22. *Let $\mathbf{C}$ be a Cartesian category equipped with an endofunctor $\blacktriangleright : \mathbf{C} \to \mathbf{C}$ and a natural transformation* $\mathsf{next} : \mathrm{Id} \to \blacktriangleright$. *Then the following definition yields a guarded ideal in $\mathbf{C}$: $G(X,Y) = \{f\,\mathsf{next} \mid f : \blacktriangleright X \to Y\}$. The arising guarded structure is* $\mathsf{Hom}^{\mathsf{pr}_1}(X \times Y, Z) = \{f\langle \mathsf{next}, \mathsf{pr}_2\rangle \mid f : \blacktriangleright(X \times Y) \times Y \to Z\}$. *If moreover* $\mathsf{next} : X \times Y \to \blacktriangleright(X \times Y)$ *factors through* $\mathsf{next} \times \mathsf{id} : X \times Y \to \blacktriangleright X \times Y$, *then* $\mathsf{Hom}^{\mathsf{pr}_1}(X \times Y, Z) = \{f\,(\mathsf{next} \times \mathsf{id}) \mid f : \blacktriangleright X \times Y \to Z\}$.

Remark 23. Proposition 22 connects our approach to previous work based precisely on the assumptions of the proposition [28] (in fact, the term guarded traced category is already used there, with different meaning). A limitation of the approach via a functor $\blacktriangleright$ arises from the need to fix $\blacktriangleright$ globally, so that, e.g., the ideal guarded structure on metric spaces (Example 21) is not covered – capturing contractivity via $\blacktriangleright$ requires fixing a single global contraction factor.

The following instance of Proposition 22 has received extensive recent interest in programming semantics:

Example 24 (Topos of Trees). Let $\mathbf{C}$ be the *topos of trees* [7], i.e. the presheaf category $\mathbf{Set}^{\omega^{op}}$ where ω is the preorder of natural numbers (starting from 1) ordered by inclusion. An object X of $\mathbf{C}$ is thus a family $(X(n))_{n=1,2\ldots}$

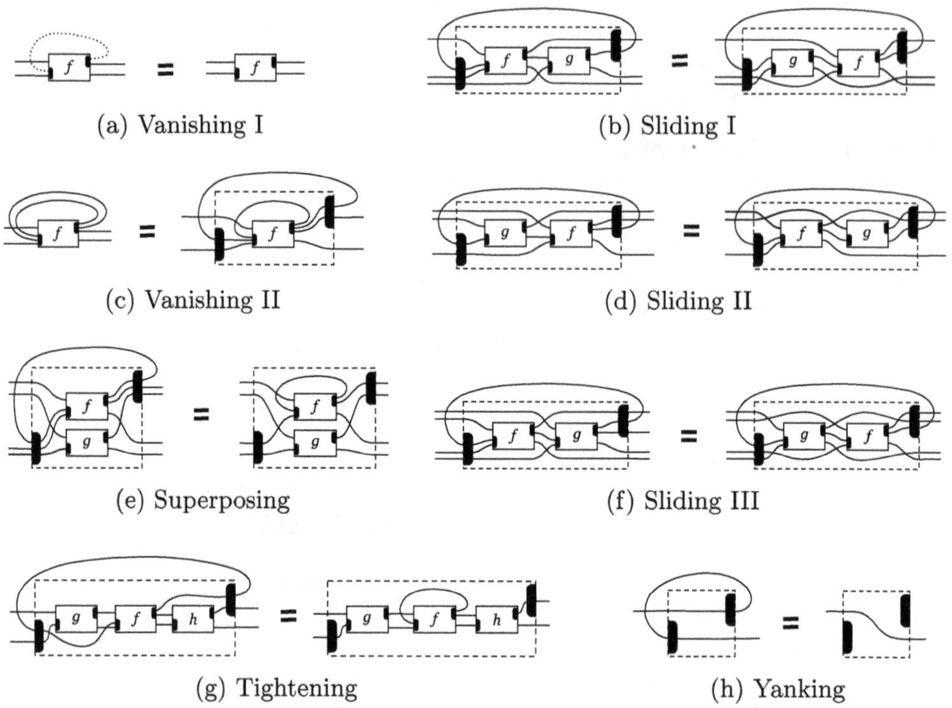

(a) Vanishing I (b) Sliding I (c) Vanishing II (d) Sliding II (e) Superposing (f) Sliding III (g) Tightening (h) Yanking

Fig. 4. Axioms of guarded traced categories

of sets with restriction maps $r_n : X(n+1) \to X(n)$. The *later*-endofunctor $\blacktriangleright : \mathbf{C} \to \mathbf{C}$ is defined by $\blacktriangleright X(1) = \{\star\}$ and $\blacktriangleright X(n+1) = X(n)$, and the natural transformation $\mathsf{next}_X : X \to \blacktriangleright X$ by $\mathsf{next}_X(1) = ! : X(1) \to \{\star\}$, $\mathsf{next}_X(n+1) = r_{n+1} : X(n+1) \to X(n)$. Guarded morphisms according to Proposition 22 are called *contractive*, generalizing the metric setup. Contractive morphisms form an exponential ideal, so partial guardedness is described as in Corollary 20, and hence agrees with contractivity in part of the input as in [7, Definition 2.2].

5 Guarded Traces

As indicated previously, the main purpose of our notion of abstract guardedness is to enable fine-grained control over the formation of feedback loops, viz, *traces.*

Definition 25 (Guarded traced category). We call a guarded category $(\mathbf{C}, \otimes, I)$ *guarded traced* if it is equipped with a *guarded trace operator*

$$\mathsf{tr}^U_{A,B,C,D} : \mathsf{Hom}^\bullet((A \otimes U) \otimes B, C \otimes (D \otimes U)) \to \mathsf{Hom}^\bullet(A \otimes B, C \otimes D),$$

visually corresponding to the diagram formation rule in Fig. 1, so that the adaptation of the Joyal-Street-Verity axiomatization of traced symmetric monoidal categories [22] shown in Fig. 4 is satisfied.

Remark 26. The versions of the sliding axiom in Fig. 4 differ in the way the loop is guarded. They are in line with duality (Remark 4): Sliding II arises from Sliding I by 180° rotation, and Sliding III is symmetric under 180° rotation.

We proceed to investigate the geometric properties of guarded traced categories, partly extending Theorem 2. The syntactic setting extends the one for guarded categories by additionally closing morphism expressions under the trace operator (interpreted diagrammatically as in Fig. 1), obtaining *traced morphism expressions.* Term formation thus becomes mutually recursive with guardedness typing: if e is a traced morphism expression such that $e \in \mathsf{Hom}^\bullet((A \otimes U) \otimes B, C \otimes (D \otimes U))$ is derivable, then $\mathsf{tr}_{A,B,C,D}(e)$ is a traced morphism expression, and $\mathsf{tr}_{A,B,C,D}(e) \in \mathsf{Hom}^\bullet(A \otimes B, C \otimes D)$ is derivable. *Traced diagrams* consists of finitely many (decorated) basic boxes and wires connecting output gates of basic boxes to input gates, with each gate attached to at most one wire; open gates are regarded as inputs or outputs, respectively, of the whole diagram. Of course, acyclicity is not required. We first note that the easy direction of Theorem 2 adapts straightforwardly to the setting with traces:

Proposition 27. *Let e be a traced morphism expression such that $e \in \mathsf{Hom}^\bullet(A \otimes B, C \otimes D)$ is derivable. Then in the diagram of e, all loops and all paths from input gates in A to output gates in D are guarded (p. 4).*

Remarkably, the converse of Proposition 27 in general fails in several ways:

Example 28. The left diagram below

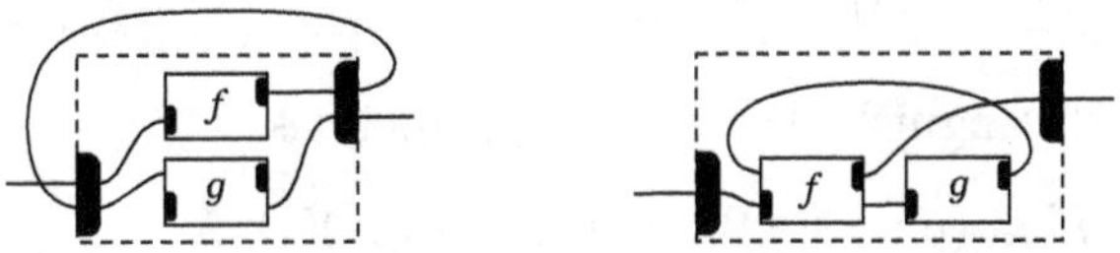

(2)

shows that guardedness typing is not closed under equality of traced morphism expressions: Write e for the expression inducing the dashed box. By Proposition 27, e, and hence $\mathsf{tr}(e)$, fail to type as indicated. However, $\mathsf{tr}(e) = gf$, for which the overall guardedness typing indicated is easily derivable.

Moreover, the diagram on the right above satisfies the necessary condition from Proposition 27 but is not induced by an expression for which the indicated guardedness typing is derivable, essentially because both ways of cutting the loop violate the necessary condition from Proposition 27.

However, if $\mathbf{C}$ is ideally guarded over a guarded ideal G, we do have a converse to Proposition 27: By Theorem 14, we can then restrict basic boxes in diagrams to be either *guarded*, i.e. have only black gates, or *unguarded*, i.e. have only white gates. We call the correspondingly restricted diagrams *ideally guarded.* (We emphasize that the guardedness typing of *composite* ideally guarded diagrams still needs to mix guarded and unguarded inputs and outputs.) A path in an ideally guarded diagram is guarded iff it passes through a guarded basic box.

The left-hand diagram in (2) is in fact ideally guarded, so guardedness typing fails to be closed under equality also in the ideally guarded case. However, for ideally guarded diagrams we have the following converse of Proposition 27.

Theorem 29. *Let Δ be an ideally guarded diagram, with sets of input and output gates disjointly decomposed as $A \uplus B$ and $C \uplus D$, respectively. If every loop in Δ and every path from a gate in A to a gate in D is guarded, then Δ is induced by a traced morphism expression e such that $e \in \mathsf{Hom}^\bullet(A \otimes B, C \otimes D)$ is derivable.*

We next take a look at the Cartesian and co-Cartesian cases. Recall that by Proposition 5, the definition of guarded category can be simplified if $\otimes = +$ (and dually if $\otimes = \times$). This simplification extends to guarded traced categories by generalizing Hyland-Hasegawa's equivalence between Cartesian trace operators and Conway fixpoint operators [18, 19].

Definition 30 (Guarded Conway operators). Let $\mathbf{C}$ be a guarded co-Cartesian category. We call an operator $(-)^\dagger$ of profile

$$f \in \mathsf{Hom}_{\sigma+\mathsf{id}}(X, Y + X) \mapsto f^\dagger \in \mathsf{Hom}_\sigma(X, Y) \tag{3}$$

a *guarded iteration operator* if it satisfies

- *fixpoint:* $f^\dagger = [\mathsf{id}, f^\dagger]\,f$ for $f : X \to_{\mathsf{in}_2} Y + X$;

and a *Conway iteration operator* if it additionally satisfies

- *naturality:* $g\,f^\dagger = ((g + \mathsf{id})\,f)^\dagger$ for $f : X \to_{\mathsf{in}_2} Y + X$, $g : Y \to Z$;
- *dinaturality:* $([\mathsf{in}_1, h]\,g)^\dagger = [\mathsf{id}, ([\mathsf{in}_1, g]\,h)^\dagger]\,g$ for $g : X \to_{\mathsf{in}_2} Y + Z$ and $h : Z \to Y + X$ or $g : X \to Y + Z$ and $h : Z \to_{\mathsf{in}_2} Y + X$;
- *(co)diagonal:* $([\mathsf{id}, \mathsf{in}_2]\,f)^\dagger = f^{\dagger\dagger}$ for $f : X \to_{\mathsf{in}_2+\mathsf{id}} (Y + X) + X$.

Furthermore, we distinguish the following principles:

- *squaring* [12]*:* $f^\dagger = ([\mathsf{in}_1, f]\,f)^\dagger$ for $f : X \to_{\mathsf{in}_2} Y + X$;
- *uniformity w.r.t. a subcategory* $\mathbf{S}$ *of* $\mathbf{C}$: $(\mathsf{id} + h)\,f = g\,h$ implies $f^\dagger = g^\dagger\,h$ for all $f : X \to_{\mathsf{in}_2} Z + X$, $g : Y \to_{\mathsf{in}_2} Z + Y$ and $h : Y \to X$ from $\mathbf{S}$;

and call $(-)^\dagger$ *squarable* or *uniform* if it satisfies squaring or uniformity, respectively.

Guarded (Conway) recursion operators $(-)_\dagger$ on guarded Cartesian categories are defined dually in a straightforward manner. We collect the following facts about guarded iteration operators for further reference.

Lemma 31. *Let $(-)^\dagger$ be a guarded iteration operator on $(\mathbf{C}, +, \emptyset)$.*

1. *If $(-)^\dagger$ is uniform w.r.t. some co-Cartesian subcategory of $\mathbf{C}$ and satisfies the codiagonal identity then it is squarable.*
2. *If $(-)^\dagger$ is squarable and uniform w.r.t. coproduct injections then it is dinatural.*
3. *If $(-)^\dagger$ is Conway then it is uniform w.r.t. coproduct injections.*

Proposition 32. *A guarded co-Cartesian category $\mathbf{C}$ is traced iff it is equipped with a guarded Conway iteration operator $(-)^\dagger$, with mutual conversions like in the total case [18, 19].*

Example 33 (Guarded Conway operators). We list some examples of guarded Conway iteration/recursion operators. In all cases except 2, Conwayness follows from uniqueness of fixpoints [16, Theorem 17].

1. In a vacuously guarded co-Cartesian category (Remark 7), $f : X \to_{\mathsf{in}_2} Y + Z$ iff $f = \mathsf{in}_1 g$ for some $g : X \to Y$. If coproduct injections are monic, then g is uniquely determined, and $f^\dagger = g$ defines a guarded Conway operator.
2. Every Cartesian category $\mathbf{C}$ is guarded under $\mathsf{Hom}^\pi(X, Y) = \mathsf{Hom}(X, Y)$ (making every morphism guarded). Then $\mathbf{C}$ has a guarded Conway recursion operator iff $\mathbf{C}$ is a *Conway category* [13], i.e. models standard total recursion.
3. The guarded Cartesian category of complete metric spaces as in Example 9 is traced: For $f : X \times Y \to^{\mathsf{pr}_2} Y$, define $f^\dagger(x)$ as the unique fixpoint of $\lambda y.\, f(x, y)$ according to Banach's fixpoint theorem.
4. Similarly, the topos of trees, ideally guarded as in Example 24, has a guarded Conway recursion operator obtained by taking unique fixpoints [7, Theorem 2.4].
5. The guarded co-Cartesian category $\mathbf{C}_{\mathbb{T}_\Sigma}$ of side-effecting processes (Example 8) has a guarded Conway iteration operator obtained by taking unique fixpoints, thanks to the universal property of the final coalgebra $T_\Sigma X$ [32].

Guarded vs. Unguarded Recursion. We proceed to present a class of examples relating guarded and unguarded recursion. For motivation, consider the category $(\mathbf{Cpo}, \times, 1)$ of complete partial orders (cpos) and continuous maps. This category nearly supports recursion via least fixpoints, except that, e.g., $\mathsf{id} : X \to X$ only has a least fixpoint if X has a bottom. The following equivalent approaches involve the *lifting monad* $(-)_\bot$, which adjoins a fresh bottom $\bot$ to a given $X \in |\mathbf{Cpo}|$.

Classical approach [38, 39]: Define a total recursion operator $(-)_\ddagger$ on the category $\mathbf{Cpo}_\bot$ of *pointed cpos* and continuous maps, using least fixpoints.

Guarded approach (cf. [28]): Extend $\mathbf{Cpo}$ to a guarded category: $f : X \times Y \to^{\mathsf{pr}_2} Z$ iff $f \in \{g(\mathsf{id} \times \eta) \mid g : X \times Y_\bot \to Z\}$ (see Proposition 22), and define a guarded recursion operator sending $f = g(\mathsf{id} \times \eta) : Y \times X \to^{\mathsf{pr}_2} X$ to $f_\dagger = g\langle \mathsf{id}, \hat{f}\rangle : Y \to X$ with $\hat{f}(y) \in X_\bot$ calculated as the least fixpoint of $\lambda z.\, \eta g(y, z)$.

Pointed cpos happen to be always of the form $X_\bot$ with $X \in |\mathbf{Cpo}|$, which indicates that $(-)_\ddagger$ is a special case of $(-)_\dagger$. This is no longer true in more general cases when the connection between $(-)_\ddagger$ and $(-)_\dagger$ is more intricate. We show that $(-)_\ddagger$ and $(-)_\dagger$ are nevertheless equivalent under reasonable assumptions.

Definition 34 ([11]). A *let-ccc with a fixpoint object* is a tuple $(\mathbf{C}, \mathbb{T}, \Omega, \omega)$, consisting of a Cartesian closed category $\mathbf{C}$, a strong monad $\mathbb{T}$ on it, an initial T-algebra (Ω, in) and an equalizer $\omega : 1 \to \Omega$ of $\mathsf{in}\, \eta : \Omega \to \Omega$ and $\mathsf{id} : \Omega \to \Omega$.

The key requirement is the last one, satisfied, e.g., for $\mathbf{Cpo}$ and the lifting monad. Given a monad $\mathbb{T}$ on $\mathbf{C}$, $\mathbf{C}^{\mathbb{T}}_{\star}$ denotes the category of $\mathbb{T}$-algebras and $\mathbf{C}$-morphisms (instead of $\mathbb{T}$-algebra homomorphisms).

Proposition 35 ([37, Theorem 4.6]). *Let $(\mathbf{C}, \mathbb{T}, \Omega, \omega)$ be a let-ccc with a fixpoint object. Then $\mathbf{C}^{\mathbb{T}}_{\star}$ has a unique $\mathbf{C}^{\mathbb{T}}$-uniform recursion operator $(-)_{\ddagger}$.*

By [38, Theorem 4], the operator $(-)_{\ddagger}$ in Proposition 35 is Conway, in particular, by Lemma 31, squarable, if $\mathbf{C}$ has a natural numbers object and $\mathbb{T}$ is an *equational lifting monad* [10], such as $(-)_{\perp}$. There are however further squarable operators obtained via Proposition 35, e.g. for the partial state monad $TX = (X \times S)^S_{\perp}$ [11]. By Lemma 31, the following result applies in particular in the setup of Proposition 35 under the additional assumption of squarability.

Theorem 36. *Let $\mathbb{T}$ be a strong monad on a Cartesian category $\mathbf{C}$. The following gives a bijective correspondence between squarable dinatural recursive operators $(-)_{\ddagger}$ on $\mathbf{C}^{\mathbb{T}}_{\star}$ and squarable dinatural guarded recursive operators $(-)_{\dagger}$ on $\mathbf{C}$ ideally guarded over $\mathsf{Hom}^{\blacktriangleright}(X,Y) = \{f\eta \mid f : TX \to Y\}$:*

$$(f : B \times A \to A)_{\ddagger} = a(\eta f(\mathsf{id} \times a))_{\dagger} \qquad \text{for } (A, a) \in |\mathbf{C}^{\mathbb{T}}_{\star}| \tag{4}$$

$$(f = g(\mathsf{id} \times \eta) : Y \times X \to X)_{\dagger} = g\langle \mathsf{id}, (\eta g)_{\ddagger}\rangle \tag{5}$$

(in (5) we call on a slight extension of $(-)_{\ddagger}$; the right hand side of (4) is defined because $\eta f(\mathsf{id} \times a)$ factors as $\eta f(\mathsf{id} \times a(Ta)\eta)$). Moreover, $(-)_{\dagger}$ is Conway iff so is $(-)_{\ddagger}$.

6 Vacuous Guardedness and Nuclear Ideals

We proceed to discuss traces in vacuously guarded categories (Lemma 3), and show that the partial trace operation in the category of (possibly infinite-dimensional) Hilbert spaces [2] in fact lives over the vacuous guarded structure. We first note that vacuous guarded structures are traced as soon as a simple rewiring operation satisfies a suitable well-definedness condition (similar to one defining traced nuclear ideals [2, Definition 8.14]):

Proposition 37. *Let $(\mathbf{C}, \otimes, I)$ be vacuously guarded. If for $f \in \mathsf{Hom}^{\bullet}(A \otimes B, C \otimes D)$ with factorization $f = (h \otimes \mathsf{id}_{D \otimes U})(\mathsf{id}_{A \otimes U} \otimes g)$ (eliding associativity), $g : B \to E \otimes D \otimes U$, $h : A \otimes U \otimes E \to C$ as per Lemma 3, the composite*

$$A \otimes B \xrightarrow{\mathsf{id}_A \otimes g} A \otimes E \otimes D \otimes U \cong A \otimes U \otimes E \otimes D \xrightarrow{h \otimes \mathsf{id}_D} C \otimes D \tag{6}$$

depends only on f, then $\mathbf{C}$ is guarded traced, with $\mathsf{tr}^U_{A,B,C,D}(f)$ defined as (6).

Diagrammatically, the trace in a vacuously guarded category is thus given by

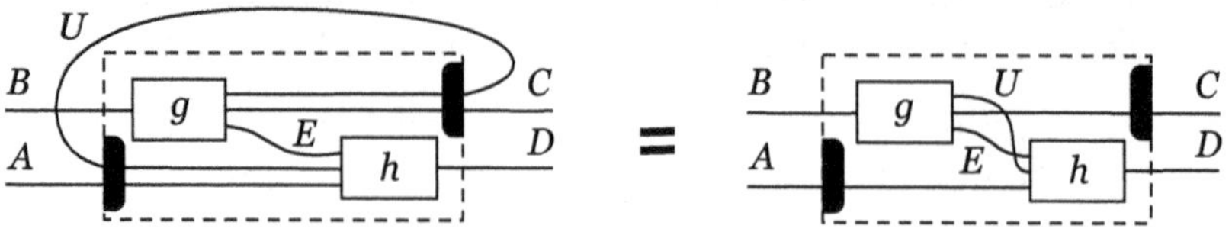

We proceed to instantiate the above to Hilbert spaces. On a more abstract level, a *dagger symmetric monoidal category* [35] (or *tensored $*$-category* [2]) is a symmetric monoidal category $(\mathbf{C}, \otimes, I)$ equipped with an identity-on-objects strictly involutive functor $(-)^\dagger : \mathbf{C} \to \mathbf{C}^{op}$ coherently preserving the symmetric monoidal structure. The main motivation for dagger symmetric monoidal categories is to capture categories that are similar to (dagger) compact closed categories in that they admit a canonical trace construction for certain morphisms, but fail to be closed, much less compact closed. The "compact closed part" of a dagger symmetric monoidal category is axiomatized as follows.

Definition 38 (Nuclear Ideal, [2]). A *nuclear ideal* N in a dagger symmetric monoidal category $(\mathbf{C}, \otimes, I, (-)^\dagger)$ is a family of subsets $\mathsf{N}(X, Y) \subseteq \mathsf{Hom}_{\mathbf{C}}(X, Y)$, $X, Y \in |\mathbf{C}|$, satisfying the following conditions:

1. N is closed under $\otimes$, $(-)^\dagger$, and composition with arbitrary morphisms on both sides;
2. There is a bijection $\theta : \mathsf{N}(X, Y) \to \mathsf{Hom}_{\mathbf{C}}(I, X^\dagger \otimes Y)$, natural in X and Y, coherently preserving the dagger symmetric monoidal structure.
3. (*Compactness*) For $f \in \mathsf{N}(B, A)$ and $g \in \mathsf{N}(B, C)$, the following diagram commutes:

$$\begin{array}{ccccc} A & \xrightarrow{\cong} & A \otimes I & \xrightarrow{\mathsf{id}_A \otimes \theta(g)} & A \otimes (B^\dagger \otimes C) \\ {\scriptstyle g f^\dagger}\downarrow & & & & \downarrow{\scriptstyle \cong} \\ C & \xleftarrow{\cong} & I \otimes C & \xleftarrow[(\theta(f))^\dagger \otimes \mathsf{id}_C]{} & (B^\dagger \otimes A) \otimes C \end{array}$$

The above definition is slightly simplified in that we elide a covariant involutive functor $\overline{(-)} : \mathbf{C} \to \mathbf{C}$, capturing, e.g. complex conjugation; i.e., we essentially restrict to spaces over the reals.

We proceed to present a representative example of a nuclear ideal in the category of Hilbert spaces. Recall that a *Hilbert space* [23] H over the field R of reals is a vector space with an *inner product* $\langle -, - \rangle : H \times H \to \mathsf{R}$ that is complete as a *normed space* under the induced *norm* $\|x\| = \sqrt{\langle x, x \rangle}$. Let **Hilb** be the category of Hilbert spaces and bounded linear operators.

Clearly, R itself is a Hilbert space; linear operators $X \to \mathsf{R}$ are conventionally called *functionals*. More generally, we consider *(multi-)linear* functionals $X_1 \times \ldots \times X_n \to \mathsf{R}$, i.e. maps that are linear in every argument. Such a functional is *bounded* if $|f(x_1, \ldots, x_n)| \leqslant c\|x_1\| \cdots \|x_n\|$ for some constant $c \in \mathsf{R}$. We can move between bounded linear operators and bounded linear functionals, similarly as we can move between relations and functions to the Booleans:

Proposition 39 ([23, Theorem 2.4.1]). *Given a bounded linear operator $f : X \to Y$, $f^\circ(x, y) = \langle fx, y \rangle$ defines a bounded linear functional f°, and every bounded linear functional $X \times Y \to \mathsf{R}$ arises in this way.*

Definition 40 (Hilbert-Schmidt operators/functionals). A bounded linear functional $f : X_1 \times \ldots \times X_n \to \mathsf{R}$ is *Hilbert-Schmidt* if the sum

$$\textstyle\sum_{x_1 \in B_1} \cdots \sum_{x_n \in B_n} (f(x_1, \ldots, x_n))^2$$

is finite for some, and then any, orthonormal bases $B_1, \ldots, B_n$ of $X_1, \ldots, X_n$, respectively. A bounded linear operator $f : X \to Y$ is *Hilbert-Schmidt* if the induced functional f° (Proposition 39) is Hilbert-Schmidt, equivalently if $\sum_{x \in B} \|fx\|^2$ is finite for some, and then any, orthonormal basis B of X. We denote by $\mathsf{HS}(X,Y)$ the space of all Hilbert-Schmidt operators from X to Y.

For $X, Y \in |\mathbf{Hilb}|$, the space of Hilbert-Schmidt functionals $X \times Y \to \mathsf{R}$ is itself a Hilbert space, denoted $X \otimes Y$, with the pointwise vector space structure and the inner product $\langle f, g\rangle = \sum_{x\in B}\sum_{y \in B'} f(x,y)g(x,y)$ where B and B' are orthonormal bases of X and Y, respectively. By virtue of the equivalence between f and f°, this induces a Hilbert space structure on $\mathsf{HS}(X,Y)$, with induced norm $\|f\|_2 = \sqrt{\sum_{x\in B}\|fx\|^2}$. The operator $\otimes$ forms part of a dagger symmetric monoidal structure on **Hilb**, with unit R. For a bounded linear operator $f : X \to Y$, $f^\dagger : Y \to X$ is the *adjoint operator* uniquely determined by equation $\langle x, f^\dagger y\rangle = \langle fx, y\rangle$. The tensor product of $f : A \to B$ and $g : C \to D$ is the functional sending $h : A \times C \to \mathsf{R}$ to $h(f^\dagger \times g^\dagger) : B \times D \to \mathsf{R}$. Given $a \in A$ and $c \in C$, let us denote by $a \otimes c \in A \otimes C$ the functional $(a', c') \mapsto \langle a, a'\rangle\,\langle c, c'\rangle$, and so, with the above f and g, $(f \otimes g)(a \otimes c) = f(a) \otimes g(c)$.

Proposition 41 ([2])**.** *The Hilbert-Schmidt operators form a nuclear ideal in* **Hilb** *with* $\theta : \mathsf{HS}(X,Y) \cong \mathsf{Hom}(\mathsf{R}, X^\dagger \otimes Y)$ *defined by*

$$\theta(f : X \to Y)(r : \mathsf{R})(x : X, y : Y) = r\,\langle fx, y\rangle.$$

A crucial fact underlying the proof of Proposition 41 is that $\mathsf{HS}(X,Y)$ is isomorphic to $X^\dagger \otimes Y$, naturally in X and Y. We emphasize that what makes the case of **Hilb** significant is that we do not restrict to finite-dimensional Hilbert spaces. In that case all bounded linear operators would be Hilbert-Schmidt and the corresponding category would be (dagger) compact closed [35]. In the infinite-dimensional case, identities need not be Hilbert-Schmidt, so HS is indeed only an ideal and not a subcategory.

Let $\mathsf{N}^2(X,Y) = \{g^\dagger h : X \to Y \mid h \in \mathsf{N}(X,Z), g \in \mathsf{N}(Y,Z)\}$ for any nuclear ideal N. The main theorem of the section now can be stated as follows.

Theorem 42. *1. The guarded ideal induced by the vacuous guarded structure on* **Hilb** *(see (1)) is precisely* HS^2*, and* **Hilb** *is guarded traced over* HS^2.

2. Guarded traces in **Hilb** *commute with* $(-)^\dagger$ *in the sense that if* $f \in \mathsf{Hom}^\bullet((A\otimes U)\otimes B, C \otimes (D \otimes U))$*, then* $\gamma_{B,A\otimes U} f^\dagger \gamma_{D\otimes U,C} \in \mathsf{Hom}^\bullet((D\otimes U)\otimes C, B \otimes (A\otimes U))$ *and* $\mathsf{tr}^U_{D,C,B,A}(\gamma_{B,A\otimes U} f^\dagger \gamma_{D\otimes U,C}) = \gamma_{A,B}\,(\mathsf{tr}^U_{A,B,C,D}(f))^\dagger\,\gamma_{C,D}$.

Clause 1 is a generalization of the result in [2, Theorem 8.16] to parametrized traces. Specifically, we obtain agreement with the conventional mathematical definition of trace: given $f \in \mathsf{HS}^2(X,X)$, $\mathsf{tr}(f) = \sum_i \langle f(e_i), e_i\rangle$ for any choice of an orthonormal basis $(e_i)_i$, and $\mathsf{HS}^2(X,X)$ contains precisely those f for which this sum is absolutely convergent independently of the basis.

7 Conclusions and Further Work

We have presented and investigated a notion of abstract *guardedness* and guarded *traces*, focusing on foundational results and important classes of examples. We have distinguished a more specific notion of *ideal guardedness*, which in many respects appears to be better behaved than the unrestricted one, in particular ensures closer agreement between structural and geometric guardedness. An unexpectedly prominent role is played by 'vacuous' guardedness, characterized by the absence of paths connecting unguarded inputs to guarded outputs; e.g., partial traces in Hilbert spaces [2] turn out to be based on this form of guardedness. Further research will concern a coherence theorem for guarded traced categories generalizing the well-known unguarded case [22, 34], and a generalization of the Int-construction [22], which would relate guarded traced categories to a suitable guarded version of compact closed categories. Also, we plan to investigate guarded traced categories as a basis for generalized Hoare logics, extending and unifying previous work [5, 15].

References

1. Abel, A., Pientka, B.: Wellfounded recursion with copatterns: a unified approach to termination and productivity. In: International Conference on Functional Programming, ICFP 2013, pp. 185–196. ACM (2013)
2. Abramsky, S., Blute, R., Panangaden, P.: Nuclear and trace ideals in tensored*-categories. J. Pure Appl. Algebra **143**, 3–47 (1999)
3. Abramsky, S., Coecke, B.: A categorical semantics of quantum protocols. In: Logic in Computer Science, LICS 2004, pp. 415–425. IEEE Computer Society (2004)
4. Abramsky, S., Haghverdi, E., Scott, P.: Geometry of interaction and linear combinatory algebras. Math. Struct. Comput. Sci. **12**(5), 625–665 (2002)
5. Arthan, R., Martin, U., Mathiesen, E., Oliva, P.: A general framework for sound and complete Floyd-Hoare logics. ACM Trans. Comput. Log. **11**, 7:1–7:31 (2009)
6. Baeten, J., Basten, T., Reniers, M.: Process Algebra: Equational Theories of Communicating Processes. Cambridge University Press, Cambridge (2010)
7. Birkedal, L., Møgelberg, R., Schwinghammer, J., Støvring, K.: First steps in synthetic guarded domain theory: step-indexing in the topos of trees. Log. Methods Comput. Sci. **8**(4:1), 1–45 (2012)
8. Blute, R., Cockett, R., Seely, R.: Feedback for linearly distributive categories: traces and fixpoints. J. Pure Appl. Algebra **154**, 27–69 (2000)
9. Book, R., Greibach, S.: Quasi-realtime languages. Math. Syst. Theory **4**(2), 97–111 (1970)
10. Bucalo, A., Führmann, C., Simpson, A.: An equational notion of lifting monad. Theoret. Comput. Sci. **294**, 31–60 (2003)
11. Crole, R., Pitts, A.: New foundations for fixpoint computations. In: Logic in Computer Science, LICS 1990, pp. 489–497. IEEE Computer Society (1990)
12. Ésik, Z.: Axiomatizing iteration categories. Acta Cybern. **14**(1), 65–82 (1999)
13. Ésik, Z.: Equational properties of fixed point operations in Cartesian categories: an overview. In: Italiano, G.F., Pighizzini, G., Sannella, D.T. (eds.) MFCS 2015. LNCS, vol. 9234, pp. 18–37. Springer, Heidelberg (2015). https://doi.org/10.1007/978-3-662-48057-1_2

14. Girard, J.-Y.: Towards a geometry of interaction. Contemp. Math. **92**(69–108), 6 (1989)
15. Goncharov, S., Schröder, L.: A relatively complete generic Hoare logic for order-enriched effects. In: Proceedings of 28th Annual Symposium on Logic in Computer Science (LICS 2013), pp. 273–282. IEEE (2013)
16. Goncharov, S., Schröder, L., Rauch, C., Piróg, M.: Unifying guarded and unguarded iteration. In: Esparza, J., Murawski, A.S. (eds.) FoSSaCS 2017. LNCS, vol. 10203, pp. 517–533. Springer, Heidelberg (2017). https://doi.org/10.1007/978-3-662-54458-7_30
17. Haghverdi, E., Scott, P.: Towards a typed geometry of interaction. Math. Struct. Comput. Sci. **20**, 473–521 (2010)
18. Hasegawa, M.: Recursion from cyclic sharing: traced monoidal categories and models of cyclic lambda calculi. In: de Groote, P., Roger Hindley, J. (eds.) TLCA 1997. LNCS, vol. 1210, pp. 196–213. Springer, Heidelberg (1997). https://doi.org/10.1007/3-540-62688-3_37
19. Hasegawa, M.: Models of Sharing Graphs: A Categorical Semantics of let and letrec. Distinguished Dissertations. Springer, London (1999). https://doi.org/10.1007/978-1-4471-0865-8
20. Jeffrey, A.: Premonoidal categories and flow graphs. In: Higher-Order Operational Techniques in Semantics, HOOTS 1997, vol. 10 of ENTCS, p. 51. Elsevier (1997)
21. Jeffrey, A.: LTL types FRP: linear-time temporal logic propositions as types, proofs as functional reactive programs. In: Programming Languages Meets Program Verification, PLPV 2012, pp. 49–60. ACM (2012)
22. Joyal, A., Street, R., Verity, D.: Traced monoidal categories. Math. Proc. Camb. Philos. Soc. **119**, 447–468 (1996)
23. Kadison, R., Ringrose, J.: Fundamentals of the Theory of Operator Algebras: Advanced Theory, vol. 2. AMS (1997)
24. Krishnaswami, N., Benton, N.: Ultrametric semantics of reactive programs. In: Logic in Computer Science, LICS 2011, pp. 257–266. IEEE Computer Society (2011)
25. MacLane, S.: Categories for the Working Mathematician. Springer, New York (1971). https://doi.org/10.1007/978-1-4612-9839-7
26. Malherbe, O., Scott, P.J., Selinger, P.: Partially traced categories. J. Pure Appl. Algebra **216**, 2563–2585 (2012)
27. Milius, S.: Completely iterative algebras and completely iterative monads. Inf. Comput. **196**, 1–41 (2005)
28. Milius, S., Litak, T.: Guard your daggers and traces: properties of guarded (co-)recursion. Fund. Inf. **150**, 407–449 (2017)
29. Milner, R.: Communication and Concurrency. Prentice-Hall Inc., Upper Saddle River (1989)
30. Møgelberg, R.: A type theory for productive coprogramming via guarded recursion. In: Computer Science Logic/Logic in Computer Science, CSL-LICS 2014, pp. 71:1–71:10. ACM (2014)
31. Moggi, E.: Notions of computation and monads. Inf. Comput. **93**, 55–92 (1991)
32. Piróg, M., Gibbons, J.: The coinductive resumption monad. In: Mathematical Foundations of Programming Semantics, MFPS 2014. ENTCS, vol. 308, pp. 273–288 (2014)
33. Rutten, J.: Universal coalgebra: a theory of systems. Theoret. Comput. Sci. **249**, 3–80 (2000)
34. Selinger, P.: Towards a quantum programming language. Math. Struct. Comput. Sci. **14**, 527–586 (2004)

35. Selinger, P.: Dagger compact closed categories and completely positive maps. In: Quantum Programming Languages, QPL 2005. ENTCS, vol. 170, pp. 139–163. Elsevier (2007)
36. Selinger, P.: A survey of graphical languages for monoidal categories. In: Coecke, B. (ed.) New Structures for Physics. Lecture Notes in Physics, vol. 813, pp. 289–355. Springer, Heidelberg (2010). https://doi.org/10.1007/978-3-642-12821-9_4
37. Simpson, A.: Recursive types in Kleisli categories. Technical report, University of Edinburgh (1992)
38. Simpson, A., Plotkin, G.: Complete axioms for categorical fixed-point operators. In: Logic in Computer Science, LICS 2000, pp. 30–41 (2000)
39. Winskel, G.: The Formal Semantics of Programming Languages. MIT Press, Cambridge (1993)

13

Depending on Session-Typed Processes

Bernardo Toninho[1,2(✉)] and Nobuko Yoshida[2]

[1] NOVA-LINCS, Departamento de Informática, FCT, Universidade Nova de Lisboa, Lisbon, Portugal
[2] Imperial College London, London, UK
b.toninho@imperial.ac.uk

Abstract. This work proposes a dependent type theory that combines functions and session-typed processes (with value dependencies) through a contextual monad, internalising typed processes in a dependently-typed λ-calculus. The proposed framework, by allowing session processes to depend on functions and vice-versa, enables us to specify and statically verify protocols where the choice of the next communication action can depend on specific values of received data. Moreover, the type theoretic nature of the framework endows us with the ability to internally describe and prove predicates on process behaviours. Our main results are type soundness of the framework, and a faithful embedding of the functional layer of the calculus within the session-typed layer, showcasing the expressiveness of dependent session types.

1 Introduction

Session types [14,24] are a typing discipline for communication protocols, whose simplicity provides an extensible framework that allows for integration with a variety of functional type features. One useful instance arising from the proof theoretic exploration of logical quantification is *value dependent session types* [25]. In this work, one can express properties of exchanged data in protocol specifications separately from communication, but *cannot* describe protocols where communication actions depend on the actual exchanged data (e.g. [16, Sect. 2]). Moreover, it does not allow functions or values to depend on protocols (i.e. sessions) or communication, thus preventing reasoning about dependent process behaviours, exploring the proofs-as-programs paradigm of dependent type theory, e.g. [8,17].

Our work addresses the limitations of existing formulations of session types by proposing a type theory that integrates dependent functions *and* session types using a *contextual monad*. This monad internalises a session-typed calculus within a dependently-typed λ-calculus. By allowing session types to depend on λ-terms *and* λ-terms to depend on typed processes (using the monad), we are able to achieve heightened degrees of expressiveness. Exploiting the former direction, we enable writing actual data-dependent communication protocols. Exploiting the latter, we can define and *prove* properties of linearly-typed objects (i.e. processes) within our intuitionistic theory.

To informally demonstrate how our type theory goes beyond the state of the art in order to represent data-dependent protocols, consider the following session type (we write $\tau \wedge A$ for $\exists x{:}\tau.A$ where x does not occur in A and similarly $\tau \supset A$ for $\forall x{:}\tau.A$ when x is not free in A), $T \triangleq \mathsf{Bool} \supset \oplus\{\mathtt{t} : \mathsf{Nat} \wedge \mathbf{1}, \mathtt{f} : \mathsf{Bool} \wedge \mathbf{1}\}$, representable in existing session typing systems. The type T denotes a protocol which first, inputs a boolean and then either emits the label t, which will be followed by an output of a natural number; or emits the label f and a boolean. The intended protocol described by T is to take the t branch if the received value is t and the f branch otherwise, which we can implement as Q with channel z typed by T as follows:

$$Q \triangleq z(x).\mathsf{case}\ x\ \mathsf{of}\ (\mathsf{true} \Rightarrow z.\mathtt{t}; z\langle 23\rangle.\mathbf{0},\ \mathsf{false} \Rightarrow z.\mathtt{f}; z\langle\mathsf{true}\rangle.\mathbf{0})$$

where $z(x).P$ denotes an input process, $z.\mathtt{t}$ is a process which selects label t and $z\langle 23\rangle.P$ is an output on z. However, since the specification is imprecise, process $z(x).\mathsf{case}\ x\ \mathsf{of}\ (\mathsf{false} \Rightarrow z.\mathtt{t}; z\langle 23\rangle.\mathbf{0},\ \mathsf{true} \Rightarrow z.\mathtt{f}; z\langle\mathsf{true}\rangle.\mathbf{0})$ is also a type-correct implementation of T that does not adhere to the intended protocol. Using our dependent type system, we can narrow the specification to guarantee that the desired protocol is precisely enforced. Consider the following definition of a session-type level conditional where we assume inductive definition and dependent pattern matching mechanisms (stype denotes the *kind* of session types):

$$\begin{array}{l} \mathtt{if} :: \mathsf{Bool} \rightarrow \mathsf{stype} \rightarrow \mathsf{stype} \rightarrow \mathsf{stype} \\ \mathtt{if}\ \mathsf{true}\, A\, B \ = \ A \qquad \mathtt{if}\ \mathsf{false}\, A\, B \ = \ B \end{array}$$

The type-level function above case analyses the boolean and produces its first session type argument if the value is true and the second otherwise. We may now specify a session type that faithfully implements the protocol:

$$T' \triangleq \forall x{:}\mathsf{Bool}.\mathtt{if}\ x\ (\mathsf{Nat} \wedge \mathbf{1})\ (\mathsf{Bool} \wedge \mathbf{1})$$

A process R implementing such a type on channel z is given below:

$$R \triangleq z(x).\mathsf{case}\ x\ \mathsf{of}\ (\mathsf{true} \Rightarrow z\langle 23\rangle.\mathbf{0},\ \mathsf{false} \Rightarrow z\langle\mathsf{true}\rangle.\mathbf{0})$$

Note that if we flip the two branches of the case analysis in R, the session is no longer typable with T', ensuring that the protocol is implemented faithfully.

The example above illustrates a simple yet useful data-dependent protocol. When we further extend our dependent types with a *process* monad [29], where $\{c \leftarrow P \leftarrow \overline{u_j}; \overline{d_i}\}$ is a functional term denoting a process that may be *spawned* by other processes by instantiating the names in $\overline{u_j}$ and $\overline{d_i}$, we can provide more powerful reasoning on processes, enabling refined specifications through the use of type indices (i.e. type families) and an ability to internally specify and verify predicates on process behaviours. We also show that *all* functional types and terms can be faithfully embedded in the process layer using the dependently-typed sessions and process monads.

Contributions. Section 2 introduces our dependent type theory, augmenting the example above by showing how we can reason about process behaviour using

$$
\begin{array}{lll}
\text{Kinds} & K, K' & ::= \mathsf{type} \mid \mathsf{stype} \mid \Pi x{:}\tau.K \mid \Pi t{:}K.K' \\
\text{Functional} & \tau, \sigma & ::= \Pi x{:}\tau.\sigma \mid \lambda x{:}\tau.\sigma \mid \tau\ M \mid \{\overline{u_j{:}B_j}; \overline{d_i{:}A_i} \vdash c{:}A\} \mid \lambda t :: K.\tau \mid \tau\ \sigma \\
\text{Sessions} & A, B & ::= !A \mid A \multimap B \mid A \otimes B \mid \forall x{:}\tau.A \mid \exists x{:}\tau.A \mid \mathbf{1} \\
 & & \mid\ \&\{\overline{l_i : A_i}\} \mid \oplus\{\overline{l_i : A_i}\} \mid \lambda x{:}\tau.A \mid A\ M \mid \lambda t{::}K.A \mid A\ B \\
\text{Terms} & M, N & ::= \lambda x{:}\tau.M \mid \{c \leftarrow P \leftarrow \overline{u_j}; \overline{d_i}\} \mid M\ N \mid x \\
\text{Processes} & P, Q & ::= \overline{c}\langle d\rangle.P \mid (\nu c)P \mid c(x).P \mid c\langle M\rangle.P \mid !c(x).P \\
 & & \mid\ c.\mathsf{case}\{\overline{l_i \Rightarrow P_i}\} \mid c.l; P \mid [c \leftrightarrow d] \mid \mathbf{0} \mid c \leftarrow M \leftarrow \overline{u_j}; \overline{d_i}; Q
\end{array}
$$

Fig. 1. Syntax of kinds, types, terms and processes

type families and dependently-typed functions (Sect. 2.3). We then establish the soundness of the theory (Sect. 2.4). Section 3 develops a faithful embedding of the dependent function space in the process layer (Theorem 3.4). Section 4 concludes with related work. Proofs, omitted definitions and additional examples can be found in [32].

2 A Dependent Type Theory of Processes

This section introduces our dependent type theory combining session-typed processes and functions. The theory is a generalisation of the line of work relating linear logic and session types [4,25,29], considering type-level functions and dependent kinds in an intensional type theory with full *mutual* dependencies between functions and processes. This generalisation enables us to express more sophisticated session types (such as those of Sect. 1) and also to define and *prove* properties of processes expressed as type families with proofs as their inhabitants. We focus on the new rules and judgements, pointing the interested reader to [5,25,26] for additional details on the base theory.

2.1 Syntax

The calculus is stratified into two mutually dependent layers of processes and terms, which we often refer to as the *process* and *functional* layers, respectively. The syntax of the theory is given in Fig. 1 (we use x, y for variables ranging over terms and t for variables ranging over types).

Types and Kinds. The process layer is able to refer to terms of the functional layer via appropriate (dependently-typed) communication actions and through a *spawn* construct, allowing for processes encapsulated as functional values to be executed. Dually, the functional layer can refer to the process layer via a *contextual* monad [29] that internalises (open) typed processes as opaque functional values. This mutual dependency is also explicit in the type structure on several axes: process channel usages are typed by a language of session types, which specifies the communication protocols implemented on the used channels, extended with two dependent communication operations $\forall x{:}\tau.A$ and $\exists x{:}\tau.A$, where τ is a functional type and A is a session type in which x may occur. Moreover, we also extend the language of session types with type-level λ-abstraction over terms

$\lambda x{:}\tau.A$ and session types $\lambda t :: K.A$ (with the corresponding elimination forms $A\,M$ and $A\,B$). As we show in Sect. 1, the combination of these features allows for a new degree of expressiveness, enabling us to construct session types whose structure depends on previously communicated values.

The remaining session constructs are standard, following [5]: $!A$ denotes a *shared* session of type A that may be used an arbitrary (finite) number of times; $A \multimap B$ represents a session offering to input a session of type A to then offer the session behaviour B; $A \otimes B$ is the dual operator, denoting a session that outputs A and proceeds as B; $\oplus\{\overline{l_i : A_i}\}$ and $\&\{\overline{l_i : A_i}\}$ represent internal and external labelled choice, respectively; $\mathbf{1}$ denotes the terminated session.

The functional layer is a λ-calculus with dependent functions $\Pi x{:}\tau.\sigma$, type-level λ-abstractions over terms and types (and respective type-level applications) and a *contextual monadic* type $\{\overline{u_j{:}B_j}; \overline{d_i{:}A_i} \vdash c{:}A\}$, denoting a (quoted) process offering session $c{:}A$ by using the *linear* sessions $\overline{d_i{:}A_i}$ and *shared* sessions $\overline{u_j{:}B_j}$ [29]. We often write $\{A\}$ for $\{\cdot;\cdot \vdash c{:}A\}$. The kinding system for our theory contains two base kinds type and stype of functional and session types, respectively. Type-level λ-abstractions require dependent kinds $\Pi x{:}\tau.K$ and $\Pi t :: K.K'$, respectively. We note that the functional connectives form a standard dependent type theory [11,21].

Terms and Processes. Terms include the standard λ-abstractions $\lambda x{:}\tau.M$, applications $M\,N$ and variables x. In order to internalise processes within the functional layer we make use of a monadic process wrapper, written $\{c \leftarrow P \leftarrow \overline{u_j}; \overline{d_i}\}$. In such a construct, the channels c, $\overline{u_j}$ and $\overline{d_i}$ are bound in P, where c is the session channel being offered and $\overline{u_j}$ and $\overline{d_i}$ are the session channels (linear and shared, respectively) being used. We write $\{c \leftarrow P \leftarrow \epsilon\}$ when P does not use any ambient channels, which we abbreviate to $\{P\}$.

The syntax of processes follows that of [5] extended with the monadic elimination form $c \leftarrow M \leftarrow \overline{u_j}; \overline{d_i}; Q$. Such a process construct denotes a term M that is to be evaluated to a monadic value of the form $\{c \leftarrow P \leftarrow \overline{u_j}; \overline{d_i}\}$ which will then be executed in parallel with Q, sharing with it a session channel c and using the provided channels $\overline{u_j}$ and $\overline{d_i}$. We write $c \leftarrow M \leftarrow \epsilon; Q$ when no channels are provided for the execution of M and often abbreviate this to $c \leftarrow M; Q$. The process $\overline{c}\langle d\rangle.P$ denotes the output of the *fresh* channel d along channel c with continuation P, which binds d; $(\boldsymbol{\nu} c)P$ denotes channel hiding, restricting the scope of c to P; $c(x).P$ denotes an input along c, bound to x in P; $c\langle M\rangle.P$ denotes the output of term M along c with continuation P; $!c(x).P$ denotes a replicated input which spawns copies of P; the construct $c.\mathsf{case}\{\overline{l_i \Rightarrow P_i}\}$ codifies a process that waits to receive some label l_j along c, with continuation P_j; dually, $c.l; P$ denotes a process that emits a label l along c and continues as P; $[c \leftrightarrow d]$ denotes a forwarder between c and d, which is operationally implemented as renaming; $P \mid Q$ denotes parallel composition and $\mathbf{0}$ the null process.

2.2 A Dependent Typing System

We now introduce our typing system, defined by a series of mutually inductive judgements, given in Fig. 2. We use Ψ to stand for a typing context for dependent

$\Psi \vdash$	Context Ψ is well-formed.
$\Psi; \Delta \vdash$	Context Δ is well-formed, under assumptions in Ψ.
$\Psi \vdash K$	K is a kind in context Ψ.
$\Psi \vdash \tau :: K$	τ is a (functional) type of kind K in context Ψ.
$\Psi \vdash A :: K$	A is a session type of kind K in context Ψ.
$\Psi \vdash M : \tau$	M has type τ in context Ψ.
$\Psi; \Gamma; \Delta \vdash P :: z{:}A$	P offers session $z{:}A$ when composed with processes offering sessions specified in Γ and Δ in context Ψ.
$\Psi \vdash K_1 = K_2$	Kinds K_1 and K_2 are equal.
$\Psi \vdash \tau = \sigma :: K$	Types τ and σ are equal of kind K.
$\Psi \vdash A = B :: K$	Session types A and B are equal of kind K.
$\Psi \vdash M = N : \tau$	Terms M and N are equal of type τ.
$\Psi \vdash \Delta = \Delta' :: \mathsf{stype}$	Contexts Δ and Δ' are equal, under the assumptions in Ψ.
$\Psi; \Gamma; \Delta \vdash P = Q :: z{:}A$	Processes P and Q are equal with typing $z{:}A$.

Fig. 2. Typing judgements

λ-terms (i.e. assumptions of the form $x{:}\tau$ or $t :: K$, not subject to exchange), Γ for a typing context for *shared* sessions of the form $u{:}A$ (implicitly subject to weakening and contraction) and Δ for a linear context of sessions $x{:}A$. The context well-formedness judgments $\Psi \vdash$ and $\Psi; \Delta \vdash$ require that types and kinds (resp. session types) in Ψ (resp. Δ) are well-formed. The judgments $\Psi \vdash K$, $\Psi \vdash \tau :: K$ and $\Psi \vdash A :: K$ codify well-formedness of kinds, functional and session types (with kind K), respectively. Their rules are standard.

Typing. An excerpt of the typing rules for terms and processes is given in Figs. 3 and 4, respectively, noting that typing enforces types to be of base kind type (respectively stype). The rules for dependent functions are standard, including the type conversion rule which internalises definitional equality of types. We highlight the introduction rule for the monadic construct, which requires the appropriate session types to be well-formed and the process P to offer $c{:}A$ when provided with the appropriate session contexts.

In the typing rules for processes (Fig. 4), presented as a set of right and left rules (the former identifying how to *offer* a session of a given type and the latter how to use such a session), we highlight the rules for dependently-typed communication and monadic elimination (for type-checking purposes we annotate constructs with the respective dependent type – this is akin to functional type theories). To offer a session $c{:}\exists x{:}\tau.A$ we send a term M of type τ and then offer a session $c{:}A\{M/x\}$; dually, to use such a session we perform an input along c, bound to x in Q, warranting a use of c as a session of (open) type A. The rules for the universal are dual. Offering a session $c{:}\forall x{:}\tau.A$ entails receiving on c a term of type τ and offering $c{:}A$. Using a session of such a type requires sending along c a term M of type τ, warranting the use of c as a session of type $A\{M/x\}$.

The rule for the monadic elimination form requires that the term M be of the appropriate monadic type and that the provided channels $\overline{u_j}$ and $\overline{y_i}$ adhere to the typing specified in M's type. Under these conditions, the process Q may then use the session c as session A. The type conversion rules reflect session type definitional equality in typing.

$$(\Pi I)\ \frac{\Psi \vdash \tau :: \mathsf{type} \quad \Psi, x{:}\tau \vdash M : \sigma}{\Psi \vdash \lambda x{:}\tau.M : \Pi x{:}\tau.\sigma} \qquad (\Pi E)\ \frac{\Psi \vdash M : \Pi x{:}\tau.\sigma \quad \Psi \vdash N : \tau}{\Psi \vdash M\, N : \sigma\{N/x\}}$$

$$(\{\}I)\ \frac{\forall i, j.\Psi \vdash A_i, B_j :: \mathsf{stype} \quad \Psi; \overline{u_j{:}B_j}; \overline{d_i{:}A_i} \vdash P :: c{:}A}{\Psi \vdash \{c \leftarrow P \leftarrow \overline{u_j}; \overline{d_i}\} : \{\overline{u_j{:}B_j}; \overline{d_i : A_i} \vdash c{:}A\}} \qquad (\mathsf{Conv})\ \frac{\Psi \vdash M : \tau \quad \Psi \vdash \tau = \sigma :: \mathsf{type}}{\Psi \vdash M : \sigma}$$

Fig. 3. Typing for terms (Excerpt – See [32])

$$(\exists \mathsf{R})\ \frac{\Psi \vdash M{:}\tau \quad \Psi; \Gamma; \Delta \vdash P :: c{:}A\{M/x\}}{\Psi; \Gamma; \Delta \vdash c\langle M \rangle_{\exists x:\tau.A}.P :: c{:}\exists x{:}\tau.A} \qquad (\exists \mathsf{L})\ \frac{\Psi \vdash \tau :: \mathsf{type} \quad \Psi, x{:}\tau\ ; \Gamma; \Delta, c{:}A \vdash Q :: d{:}D}{\Psi\ ; \Gamma; \Delta, c{:}\exists x{:}\tau.A \vdash c(x{:}\tau).Q :: d{:}D}$$

$$(\forall \mathsf{R})\ \frac{\Psi \vdash \tau :: \mathsf{type} \quad \Psi, x{:}\tau\ ; \Gamma; \Delta \vdash P :: c{:}A}{\Psi; \Gamma; \Delta \vdash c(x{:}\tau).P :: c{:}\forall x{:}\tau.A} \qquad (\forall \mathsf{L})\ \frac{\Psi \vdash M{:}\tau \quad \Psi; \Gamma; \Delta, c{:}A\{M/x\} \vdash Q :: d{:}D}{\Psi; \Gamma; \Delta, c{:}\forall x{:}\tau.A \vdash c\langle M \rangle_{\forall x:\tau.A}.Q :: d{:}D}$$

$$(\{\}E)\ \frac{\Delta' = \overline{d_i : B_i} \quad \overline{u_j{:}C_j} \subseteq \Gamma \quad \Psi \vdash M : \{\overline{u_j{:}C_j}; \overline{d_i{:}B_i} \vdash c{:}A\} \quad \Psi; \Gamma; \Delta, c{:}A \vdash Q :: z{:}C}{\Psi; \Gamma; \Delta', \Delta \vdash c \leftarrow M \leftarrow \overline{u_j}; \overline{y_i}; Q :: z{:}C}$$

$$(\mathsf{ConvR})\ \frac{\Psi; \Gamma; \Delta \vdash P :: z{:}A \quad \Psi \vdash A = B :: \mathsf{stype}}{\Psi; \Gamma; \Delta \vdash P :: z{:}B} \qquad (\mathsf{ConvL})\ \frac{\Psi; \Gamma'; \Delta' \vdash P :: z{:}A \quad \Psi; \Gamma'; \Delta' = \Psi; \Gamma; \Delta}{\Psi; \Gamma; \Delta \vdash P :: z{:}A}$$

$$(\mathsf{cut})\ \frac{\Psi; \Gamma; \Delta \vdash P :: c{:}A \quad \Psi; \Gamma; \Delta', c{:}A \vdash Q :: d{:}D}{\Psi; \Gamma; \Delta, \Delta' \vdash (\boldsymbol{\nu} c)(P \mid Q) :: d{:}D}$$

Fig. 4. Typing for processes (Excerpt – See [32])

Definitional Equality. The crux of any dependent type theory lies in its *definitional equality*. Type equality relies on equality of terms which, by including the monadic construct, necessarily relies on a notion of *process* equality.

Our presentation of an intensional definitional equality of terms follows that of [12], where we consider an intrinsically typed relation, including β and η conversion (similarly for type equality which includes β and η principles for the type-level λ-abstractions). An excerpt of the rules for term equality is given in Fig. 5. The remaining rules are congruence rules and closure under symmetry, reflexivity and transitivity. Rule ($\mathsf{TMEq}\beta$) captures the β-reduction, identifying a λ-abstraction applied to an argument with the substitution of the argument in the function body (typed with the appropriately substituted type). We highlight rule ($\mathsf{TMEq}\{\}\eta$), which codifies a general η-like principle for arbitrary terms of monadic type: We form a monadic term that applies the monadic elimination form to M, forwarding the result along the appropriate channel, which becomes a term equivalent to M.

(TMEqβ)
$$\frac{\Psi \vdash \tau :: \mathsf{type} \quad \Psi, x{:}\tau \vdash M : \sigma \quad \Psi \vdash N : \tau}{\Psi \vdash (\lambda x{:}\tau.M)\, N = M\{N/x\} : \sigma\{N/x\}}$$

(TMEqη)
$$\frac{\Psi \vdash M : \Pi x{:}\tau.\sigma \quad x \notin fv(M)}{\Psi \vdash \lambda x{:}\tau.M\, x = M : \Pi x{:}\tau.\sigma}$$

(TMEq$\{\}\eta$)
$$\frac{\Psi \vdash M : \{\overline{u_j{:}B_j}; \overline{d_i{:}A_i} \vdash c{:}A\}}{\Psi \vdash \{c \leftarrow (y \leftarrow M; \overline{u_j}; \overline{d_i}; [y \leftrightarrow c]) \leftarrow \overline{u_j}; \overline{d_i}\} = M : \{\overline{u_j{:}B_j}; \overline{d_i{:}A_i} \vdash c{:}A\}}$$

Fig. 5. Definitional equality of terms (Excerpt – See [32])

$$(\mathsf{PEqRed})\ \frac{\Psi; \Gamma; \Delta \vdash P :: z{:}A \quad P \rightarrow Q \quad \Psi; \Gamma; \Delta \vdash Q :: z{:}A}{\Psi; \Gamma; \Delta \vdash P = Q :: z{:}A}$$

$$(\mathsf{PEq}\forall\eta)\ \frac{}{\Psi; \Gamma; d{:}\forall x{:}\tau.A \vdash c(x).d\langle x\rangle.[d \leftrightarrow c] = [d \leftrightarrow c] :: c{:}\forall x{:}\tau.A}$$

$$(\mathsf{PEqCC}\forall)\ \frac{\Psi; \Gamma; \Delta \vdash P :: d{:}B \quad \Psi, x{:}\tau; \Gamma; \Delta', d{:}B \vdash Q :: c{:}A}{\Psi; \Gamma; \Delta, \Delta' \vdash (\boldsymbol{\nu} d)(P \mid c(x).Q) = c(x).(\boldsymbol{\nu} d)(P \mid Q) :: c{:}\forall x{:}\tau.A}$$

Fig. 6. Definitional equality of processes (Excerpt – See [32])

Definitional equality of processes is summarised in Fig. 6. We rely on process reduction defined below. Definitional equality of processes consists of the usual congruence rules, (typed) reductions and the commutting conversions of linear logic and η-like principles, which allows for forwarding actions to be equated with the primitive syntactic forwarding construct. Commutting conversions amount to sound observational equivalences between processes [22], given that session composition requires name restriction (embodied by the (cut) rule): In rule (PEqCC$\forall$), either process can only be interacted with via channel c and so postponing actions of P to after the input on c (when reading the equality from left to right) cannot impact the process' observable behaviours. While P can in general interact with sessions in Δ (or with Q), these interactions are unobservable due to hiding in the (cut) rule.

Operational Semantics. The operational semantics for the λ-calculus is standard, noting that no reduction can take place inside monadic terms. The operational (reduction) semantics for processes is presented below where we omit closure under structural congruence and the standard congruence rules [4,25,29]. The last rule defines spawning a process in a monadic term.

$$c\langle M\rangle.P \mid c(x).Q \rightarrow P \mid Q\{M/x\} \qquad \overline{c}\langle x\rangle.P \mid c(x).Q \rightarrow (\boldsymbol{\nu} x)(P \mid Q)$$
$$!c(x).P \mid \overline{c}\langle x\rangle.Q \rightarrow\ !c(x).P \mid (\boldsymbol{\nu} x)(P \mid Q) \qquad c.\mathsf{case}\{\overline{l_i \Rightarrow P_i}\} \mid c.l_j; Q \rightarrow P_j \mid Q \quad (l_j \in \overline{l_i})$$
$$(\boldsymbol{\nu} c)(P \mid [c \leftrightarrow d]) \rightarrow P\{d/c\} \qquad c \leftarrow \{c \leftarrow P \leftarrow \overline{u_j}; \overline{d_i}\} \leftarrow \overline{u_j}; \overline{d_i}; Q \rightarrow (\boldsymbol{\nu} c)(P \mid Q)$$

2.3 Example – Reasoning About Processes Using Dependent Types

The use of type indices (i.e. type families) in dependently typed frameworks adds information to types to produce more refined specifications. Our framework enables us to do this at the level of session types.

Consider a session type that "counts down" on a natural number (we assume inductive definitions and dependent pattern matching in the style of [21]):

$$\begin{array}{ll} \mathsf{countDown} & :: \Pi x{:}\mathsf{Nat}.\mathsf{stype} \\ \mathsf{countDown}\,(\mathsf{succ}(n)) & = \exists y{:}\mathsf{Nat}.\mathsf{countDown}(n) \\ \mathsf{countDown}\ \mathsf{z} & = \mathbf{1} \end{array}$$

The type family $\mathsf{countDown}(n)$ denotes a session type that emits exactly n numbers and then terminates. We can now write a (dependently-typed) function that produces processes with the appropriate type, given a starting value:

$$\begin{array}{ll} \mathsf{counter} & : \Pi x{:}\mathsf{Nat}.\{\mathsf{countDown}(x)\} \\ \mathsf{counter}\ (\mathsf{succ}(n)) & = \{c \leftarrow c\langle \mathsf{succ}(n)\rangle.\, d \leftarrow \mathsf{counter}(n);\, [d \leftrightarrow c]\} \\ \mathsf{counter}\ \mathsf{z} & = \{c \leftarrow \mathbf{0}\} \end{array}$$

Note how the type of counter, through the type family countDown, allows us to specify exactly the number of times a value is sent. This is in sharp contrast with existing recursive (or inductive/coinductive [18,30]) session types, where one may only specify the general iterative nature of the behaviour (e.g. "send a number and then recurse or terminate").

The example above relies on session type indexing in order to provide additional static guarantees about processes (and the functions that generate them). An alternative way is to consider "simply-typed" programs and then *prove* that they satisfy the desired properties, using the language itself. Consider a simply-typed version of the counter above described as an inductive session type:

$$\begin{array}{l} \mathsf{simpleCounterT} :: \mathsf{stype} \\ \mathsf{simpleCounterT} = \oplus\{\mathsf{dec} : \mathsf{Nat} \wedge \mathsf{simpleCounterT}, \mathsf{done} : \mathbf{1}\} \end{array}$$

There are many processes that correctly implement such a type, given that the type merely dictates that the session outputs a natural number and recurses (modulo the dec and done messages to signal which branch of the internal choice is taken). A function that produces processes implementing such a session, mirroring those generated by the counter function above, is:

$$\begin{array}{ll} \mathsf{simpleCounter} & : \mathsf{Nat} \to \{\mathsf{simpleCounterT}\} \\ \mathsf{simpleCounter}\ (\mathsf{succ}(n)) & = \{c \leftarrow c.\mathsf{dec};\, (\boldsymbol{\nu} d)(d\langle \mathsf{succ}(n)\rangle.\mathbf{0} \mid d(x).c\langle x\rangle. \\ & \quad d \leftarrow \mathsf{simpleCounter}(n);\, [d \leftrightarrow c])\} \\ \mathsf{simpleCounter}\ \ \mathsf{z} & = \{c \leftarrow c.\mathsf{done}; \mathbf{0}\} \end{array}$$

The process generated by simpleCounter, after emiting the dec label, spawns a process in parallel that sends the appropriate number, which is received by the parallel thread and then sent along the session c. Despite its simplicity, this example embodies a general pattern where a computation is spawned in parallel (itself potentially spawning many other threads) and the main thread then waits for the result before proceeding.

While such a process is typable in most session typing frameworks, our theory enables us to *prove* that the counter implementation above indeed counts down from a given number by defining an appropriate (inductive) type family, indexed by *monadic* values (i.e. processes):

$$\begin{array}{lll} \mathsf{corrCount} & :: & \Pi x{:}\mathsf{Nat}.\Pi y{:}\{\mathsf{simpleCounterT}\}.\mathsf{type} \\ \mathsf{corr}_z & : & \mathsf{corrCount}\,\mathsf{z}\,\{c \leftarrow c.\mathsf{done}; \mathbf{0}\} \\ \mathsf{corr}_n & : & \Pi n{:}\mathsf{Nat}.\Pi P{:}\{\mathsf{simpleCounterT}\}.\mathsf{corrCount}\,n\,P \rightarrow \\ & & \mathsf{corrCount}\,(\mathsf{succ}(n))\,\{c \leftarrow c.\mathsf{dec}; c\langle \mathsf{succ}(n)\rangle.d \leftarrow P; [d \leftrightarrow c]\} \end{array}$$

The type family corrCount, indexed by a natural number and a monadic value implementing the session type simpleCounter, is defined via two constructors: corr_z, which specifies that a correct 0 counter emits the done label and terminates; and corr_n, which given a monadic value P that is a correct n-counter, defines that a correct $(n+1)$-counter emits $n+1$ and then proceeds as P (modulo the label emission bookkeeping).

The proof of correctness of the simpleCounter function above is no more than a function of type $\Pi n{:}\mathsf{Nat}.\mathsf{corrCount}\,n\,(\mathsf{simpleCounter}(n))$, defined below:

$$\begin{array}{lll} \mathsf{prf} & & :\ \Pi n{:}\mathsf{Nat}.\mathsf{corrCount}\,n\,(\mathsf{simpleCounter}(n)) \\ \mathsf{prf} & \mathsf{z} & = \mathsf{corr}_z \\ \mathsf{prf} & (\mathsf{succ}(n)) & = \mathsf{corr}_n\,n\,(\mathsf{simpleCounter}(n))\,(\mathsf{prf}\,n) \end{array}$$

Note that in this scenario, the processes that index the corrCount type family are not syntactically equal to those generated by simpleCounter, but rather *definitionally* equal.

Typically, the processes that index such correctness specifications tend to be distilled versions of the actual implementations, which often perform some additional internal computation or communication steps. Since our notion of definitional equality of processes includes reduction (and also commuting conversions which account for type-preserving shuffling of internal communication actions [26]), the type conversion mechanism allows us to use the techniques described above to generally reason about specification conformance.

2.4 Type Soundness of the Framework

The main goal of this section is to present type soundness of our framework through a subject reduction result. We also show that our theory guarantees progress for terms and processes. The development requires a series of auxiliary results (detailed in [32]) pertaining to the functional and process layers which are ultimately needed to produce the inversion properties necessary to establish subject reduction. We note that strong normalisation results for linear-logic based session processes are known in the literature [3, 26, 30], even in the presence of impredicative polymorphism, restricted corecursion and higher-order data.

Such results are directly applicable to our work using appropriate semantics preserving type erasures.

In the remainder we often write $\Psi \vdash \mathcal{J}$ to stand for a well-formedness, typing or definitional equality judgment of the appropriate form. Similarly for $\Psi; \Gamma; \Delta \vdash \mathcal{J}$. We begin with the substitution property, which naturally holds for both layers, noting that the dependently typed nature of the framework requires substitution in both contexts, terms and in types.

Lemma 2.1 (Substitution). *Let* $\Psi \vdash M : \tau$*:*

1. *If* $\Psi, x{:}\tau, \Psi' \vdash \mathcal{J}$ *then* $\Psi, \Psi'\{M/x\} \vdash \mathcal{J}\{M/x\}$*;*
2. *If* $\Psi, x{:}\tau, \Psi'; \Gamma; \Delta \vdash \mathcal{J}$ *then* $\Psi, \Psi'\{M/x\}; \Gamma\{M/x\}; \Delta\{M/x\} \vdash \mathcal{J}\{M/x\}$

Combining substitution with a form of functionality for typing (i.e. that substitution of equal terms in a well-typed term produces equal terms) and for equality (i.e. that substitution of equal terms in a definitional equality proof produces equal terms), we can establish validity for typing and equality, which is a form of internal soundness of the type theory stating that judgments are consistent across the different levels of the theory.

Lemma 2.2 (Validity for Typing). (1) *If* $\Psi \vdash \tau :: K$ *or* $\Psi \vdash A :: K$ *then* $\Psi \vdash K$*;* (2) *If* $\Psi \vdash M : \tau$ *then* $\Psi \vdash \tau :: \mathsf{type}$*; and* (3) *If* $\Psi; \Gamma; \Delta \vdash P :: z{:}A$ *then* $\Psi \vdash A :: \mathsf{stype}$.

Lemma 2.3 (Validity for Equality)

1. *If* $\Psi \vdash M = N : \tau$ *then* $\Psi \vdash M : \tau$, $\Psi \vdash N : \tau$ *and* $\Psi \vdash \tau :: \mathsf{type}$
2. *If* $\Psi \vdash \tau = \sigma :: K$ *then* $\Psi \vdash \tau :: K$, $\Psi \vdash \sigma :: K$ *and* $\Psi \vdash K$
3. *If* $\Psi \vdash A = B :: K$ *then* $\Psi \vdash A :: K$, $\Psi \vdash B :: K$ *and* $\Psi \vdash K$
4. *If* $\Psi \vdash K = K'$ *then* $\Psi \vdash K$ *and* $\Psi \vdash K'$
5. *If* $\Psi; \Gamma; \Delta \vdash P = Q :: z{:}A$ *then* $\Psi; \Gamma; \Delta \vdash P :: z{:}A$, $\Psi; \Gamma; \Delta \vdash Q :: z{:}A$ *and* $\Psi \vdash A :: \mathsf{stype}$.

With these results we establish the appropriate inversion and injectivity properties which then enable us to show unicity of types (and kinds).

Theorem 2.4 (Unicity of Types and Kinds)

1. *If* $\Psi \vdash M : \tau$ *and* $\Psi \vdash M : \tau'$ *then* $\Psi \vdash \tau = \tau' :: \mathsf{type}$
2. *If* $\Psi \vdash \tau :: K$ *and* $\Psi \vdash \tau :: K'$ *then* $\Psi \vdash K = K'$
3. *If* $\Psi; \Gamma; \Delta \vdash P :: z{:}A$ *and* $\Psi; \Gamma; \Delta \vdash P :: z{:}A'$ *then* $\Psi \vdash A = A' :: \mathsf{stype}$
4. *If* $\Psi \vdash A :: K$ *and* $\Psi \vdash A :: K'$ *then* $\Psi \vdash K = K'$.

All the results above, combined with the process-level properties established in [5, 26, 27] enable us to show the following:

Theorem 2.5 (Subject Reduction – Terms). *If* $\Psi \vdash M : \tau$ *and* $M \rightarrow M'$ *then* $\Psi \vdash M' : \tau$.

Theorem 2.6 (Subject Reduction – Processes). *If* $\Psi; \Gamma; \Delta \vdash P :: z{:}A$ *and* $P \rightarrow P'$ *then* $\exists Q$ *such that* $P' \equiv Q$ *and* $\Psi; \Gamma; \Delta \vdash Q :: z{:}A$.

Theorem 2.7 (Progress – Terms). *If $\Psi \vdash M : \tau$ then either M is a value or $M \to M'$.*

As common in logical-based session type theories, typing enforces a strong notion of *global* progress which states that closed processes that are waiting to perform communication actions cannot get stuck (this relies on a notion of *live* process, defined as $\mathsf{live}(P)$ iff $P \equiv (\boldsymbol{\nu}\tilde{n})(\pi.Q \mid R)$ for some process R, sequence of names $\tilde{n}$ and a non-replicated guarded process $\pi.Q$). We note that the restricted typing for P is without loss of generality, due to the (cut) rule.

Theorem 2.8 (Progress – Processes). *If $\Psi; \cdot; \cdot \vdash P :: c{:}\mathbf{1}$ and $\mathsf{live}(P)$ then $\exists Q$ such that $P \to Q$.*

3 Embedding the Functional Layer in the Process Layer

Having introduced our type theory and showcased some of its informal expressiveness in terms of the ability to specify and *statically* verify true data dependent protocols, as well as the ability to prove properties of processes, we now develop a formal expressiveness result for our theory, showing that the process level type constructs are able to encode the dependently-typed functional layer, faithfully preserving type dependencies.

Specifically, we show that (1) the type-level constructs in the functional layer can be represented by those in the process layer combined with the contextual monad type, and (2) all term level constructs can be represented by session-typed processes that exchange monadic values. Thus, we show that both λ-abstraction and application can be eliminated while still preserving non-trivial type dependencies. Crucially, we note that the monadic construct *cannot* be fully eliminated due to the cross-layer nature of session type dependencies: In the process layer, simply-kinded dependent types (i.e. types with kind stype) are of the form $\forall x{:}\tau.A$ where τ is of kind type and A of kind stype (where x may occur). Operationally, such a session denotes an input of some term M of type τ with a continuation of type $A\{M/x\}$. Thus, to faithfully encode type dependencies we cannot represent such a type with a non-dependently typed input (e.g. a type of the form $A \multimap B$).

3.1 The Embedding

A first attempt. Given the observation above, a seemingly reasonable option would be to attempt an encoding that maintains monadic objects solely at the level of type indices and then exploits Girard's encoding [9] of function types $\tau \to \sigma$ as $![\![\tau]\!] \to [\![\sigma]\!]$, which is adequate for session-typed processes [28]. Thus a candidate encoding for the type $\Pi x{:}\tau.\sigma$ would be $\forall x{:}\{[\![\tau]\!]\}.![\![\tau]\!] \multimap [\![\sigma]\!]$, where $[\![-]\!]$ denotes our encoding on types. If we then consider the encoding at the level of terms, typing dictates the following (we write $[\![M]\!]_z$ for the process encoding of $M : \tau$, where z is the session channel along which one may observe the "result" of the encoding, typed with $\llbracket \tau \rrbracket$):

$$\begin{array}{ll} \llbracket \lambda x{:}\tau.M \rrbracket_z & \triangleq z(x).z(x').\llbracket M \rrbracket_z \\ \llbracket M\, N \rrbracket_z & \triangleq (\boldsymbol{\nu} x)(\llbracket M \rrbracket_x \mid x\langle\{\llbracket N \rrbracket_y\}\rangle.\overline{x}\langle x'\rangle.(!x'(y).\llbracket N \rrbracket_y \mid [x \leftrightarrow z]) \end{array}$$

However, this candidate encoding breaks down once we consider definitional equality. Specifically, compositionality (i.e. the relationship between $\llbracket M\{N/x\} \rrbracket_z$ and the encoding of N substituted in that of M) requires us to relate $\llbracket M\{N/x\} \rrbracket_z$ with $(\boldsymbol{\nu} x)(\llbracket M \rrbracket_z\{\{\llbracket N \rrbracket_y\}/x\} \mid !x'(y).\llbracket N \rrbracket_y)$, which relies on reasoning up-to *observational equivalence* of processes, a much stronger relation than our notion of definitional equality. Therefore it is *fundamentally* impossible for such an encoding to preserve our definitional equality, and thus it cannot preserve typing in the general case.

A faithful embedding. We now develop our embedding of the functional layer into the process layer which is compatible with definitional equality. Our target calculus is reminiscent of a higher-order (in the sense of higher-order processes [23]) session calculus [19]. Our encoding $\llbracket - \rrbracket$ is inductively defined on kinds, types, session types, terms and processes. As usual in process encodings of the λ-calculus, the encoding of a term M is indexed by a result channel z, written $\llbracket M \rrbracket_z$, where the behaviour of M may be observed.

$$\begin{array}{ll} \llbracket \lambda x{:}\tau.M \rrbracket_z & \triangleq z(x).z(x').\llbracket M \rrbracket_z \\ \llbracket M\, N \rrbracket_z & \triangleq (\boldsymbol{\nu} x)(\llbracket M \rrbracket_x \mid x\langle\{\llbracket N \rrbracket_y\}\rangle.\overline{x}\langle x'\rangle.(!x'(y).\llbracket N \rrbracket_y \mid [x \leftrightarrow z]) \end{array}$$

Kind:

$$\begin{array}{llll} \llbracket \mathsf{type} \rrbracket & \triangleq \mathsf{stype} & \llbracket \mathsf{stype} \rrbracket & \triangleq \mathsf{stype} \\ \llbracket \Pi x{:}\tau.K \rrbracket & \triangleq \Pi x{:}\{\llbracket \tau \rrbracket\}.\llbracket K \rrbracket & \llbracket \Pi t :: K_1.K_2 \rrbracket & \triangleq \Pi t{::}\llbracket K_1 \rrbracket.\llbracket K_2 \rrbracket \end{array}$$

Functional:

$$\begin{array}{llll} \llbracket \Pi x{:}\tau.\sigma \rrbracket & \triangleq \forall x{:}\{\llbracket \tau \rrbracket\}.\llbracket \sigma \rrbracket & \llbracket \{\overline{u_j{:}B_j}; \overline{d_i{:}B_i} \vdash c{:}A\} \rrbracket & \triangleq \overline{!\llbracket B_j \rrbracket} \multimap \overline{\llbracket B_i \rrbracket} \multimap \llbracket A \rrbracket \\ \llbracket \lambda x{:}\tau.\sigma \rrbracket & \triangleq \lambda x{:}\{\llbracket \tau \rrbracket\}.\llbracket \sigma \rrbracket & \llbracket \tau\, M \rrbracket & \triangleq \llbracket \tau \rrbracket\, \{\llbracket M \rrbracket_c\} \\ \llbracket \lambda t{::}K.\tau \rrbracket & \triangleq \lambda t{::}\llbracket K \rrbracket.\llbracket \tau \rrbracket & \llbracket \tau\, \sigma \rrbracket & \triangleq \llbracket \tau \rrbracket\, \llbracket \sigma \rrbracket \end{array}$$

Session:

$$\begin{array}{llll} \llbracket \forall x{:}\tau.A \rrbracket & \triangleq \forall x{:}\{\llbracket \tau \rrbracket\}.\llbracket A \rrbracket & \llbracket \exists x{:}\tau.A \rrbracket & \triangleq \exists x{:}\{\llbracket \tau \rrbracket\}.\llbracket A \rrbracket \\ \llbracket \lambda x{:}\tau.A \rrbracket & \triangleq \lambda x{:}\{\llbracket \tau \rrbracket\}.\llbracket A \rrbracket & \llbracket A\, M \rrbracket & \triangleq \llbracket A \rrbracket\, \{\llbracket M \rrbracket_c\} \end{array}$$

Terms:

$$\begin{array}{ll} \llbracket \lambda x{:}\tau.M \rrbracket_z \triangleq z(x{:}\{\llbracket \tau \rrbracket\}).\llbracket M \rrbracket_z & \llbracket M\, N \rrbracket_z \triangleq (\boldsymbol{\nu} x)(\llbracket M \rrbracket_x \mid x\langle\{\llbracket N \rrbracket_y\}\rangle.[x \leftrightarrow z]) \\ \llbracket x \rrbracket_z \triangleq y \leftarrow x; [y \leftrightarrow z] & \llbracket \{z \leftarrow P \leftarrow \overline{u_j}; \overline{d_i}\} \rrbracket_z \triangleq z(u_0).\ldots.z(u_j).z(d_0).\ldots.z(d_n).\llbracket P \rrbracket \end{array}$$

Processes:

$$\begin{array}{ll} \llbracket (\boldsymbol{\nu} x)(P \mid Q) \rrbracket & \triangleq (\boldsymbol{\nu} x)(\llbracket P \rrbracket \mid \llbracket Q \rrbracket) \quad \llbracket \mathbf{0} \rrbracket \triangleq \mathbf{0} \quad \llbracket \overline{x}\langle y\rangle.(P \mid Q) \rrbracket \triangleq \overline{x}\langle y\rangle.(\llbracket P \rrbracket \mid \llbracket Q \rrbracket) \\ \llbracket x\langle M\rangle.P \rrbracket & \triangleq x\langle\{\llbracket M \rrbracket_y\}\rangle.\llbracket P \rrbracket \quad \llbracket x(y).P \rrbracket \triangleq x(y).\llbracket P \rrbracket \\ \llbracket c \leftarrow M \leftarrow \overline{u_j}; \overline{y_i}; Q \rrbracket & \triangleq (\boldsymbol{\nu} c)(\llbracket M \rrbracket_c \mid \overline{c}\langle v_1\rangle.(\overline{u_1}\langle a_1\rangle.[a_1 \leftrightarrow v_1] \mid \cdots \mid \\ & \quad \overline{c}\langle d_1\rangle.([y_1 \leftrightarrow d_1] \mid \cdots \mid \overline{c}\langle d_n\rangle.([y_n \leftrightarrow d_n] \mid \llbracket Q \rrbracket)\ldots) \end{array}$$

Fig. 7. An embedding of dependent functions into processes

The embedding is presented in Fig. 7, noting that the encoding extends straightforwardly to typing contexts, where functional contexts $\Psi, x{:}\tau$ are mapped to $\{[\![\Psi]\!]\}, x{:}\{[\![\tau]\!]\}$. The mapping of base kinds is straightforward. Dependent kinds $\Pi x{:}\tau.K$ rely on the monad for well-formedness and are encoded as (session) kinds of the form $\Pi x{:}\{[\![\tau]\!]\}.[\![K]\!]$. The higher-kinded types in the functional layer are translated to the corresponding type-level constructs of the process layer where all objects that must be type-kinded rely on the monad to satisfy this constraint. For instance, $\lambda x{:}\tau.\sigma$ is mapped to the session-type abstraction $\lambda x{:}\{[\![\tau]\!]\}.[\![\sigma]\!]$ and the type-level application $\tau\, M$ is translated to $[\![\tau]\!]\,\{[\![M]\!]_c\}$. Given the observation above on embedding the dependent function type $\Pi x{:}\tau.\sigma$, we translate it directly to $\forall x{:}\{[\![\tau]\!]\}.[\![\sigma]\!]$, that is, functions from τ to σ are mapped to sessions that input *processes* implementing $[\![\tau]\!]$ and then behave as $[\![\sigma]\!]$ accordingly. The encoding for monadic types simply realises the contextual nature of the monad by performing a sequence of inputs of the appropriate types (with the shared sessions being of ! type).

The mutually dependent nature of the framework requires us to extend the mapping to the process layer. Session types are mapped homomorphically (e.g. $[\![A \multimap B]\!] \triangleq [\![A]\!] \multimap [\![B]\!]$) with the exception of dependent inputs and outputs which rely on the monad, similarly for type-level functions and application.

The encoding of λ-terms is guided by the embedding for types: the abstraction $\lambda x{:}\tau.M$ is mapped to an input of a term of type $\{[\![\tau]\!]\}$ with continuation $[\![M]\!]_z$; application $M\, N$ is mapped to the composition of the encoding of M on a fresh name x with the corresponding output of $\{[\![N]\!]_y\}$, which is then forwarded to the result channel z; monadic expressions are translated to the appropriate sequence of inputs, as dictated by the translation of the monadic type; and, the translation of variables makes use of the monadic elimination form (since the encoding enforces variables to always be of monadic type) combined with forwarding to the appropriate result channel.

The mapping for processes is mostly homomorphic, using the monad constructor as needed. The only significant exception is the encoding for monadic elimination which must provide the encoded monadic term $[\![M]\!]_c$ with the necessary channels. Since the session calculus does not support communication of free names this is achieved by a sequence of outputs of fresh names combined with forwarding of the appropriate channel. To account for replicated sessions we must first trigger the replication via an output which is then forwarded accordingly.

We can illustrate our encoding via a simple example of an encoded function (we omit type annotations for conciseness):

$$\begin{array}{l}
[\![(\lambda x.x)\,(\lambda x.\lambda y.y)]\!]_z = (\boldsymbol{\nu} c)([\![\lambda x.x]\!]_c \mid c\langle\{[\![\lambda x.\lambda y.y]\!]_w\}\rangle.[c \leftrightarrow z]) \\
= (\boldsymbol{\nu} c)(c(x).y \leftarrow x; [y \leftrightarrow c] \mid c\langle\{w(x).w(y).d \leftarrow y; [d \leftrightarrow w]\}\rangle.[c \leftrightarrow z]) \\
\rightarrow^{+} z(x).z(y).d \leftarrow y; [d \leftrightarrow z] \;=\; [\![\lambda x.\lambda y.y]\!]_z
\end{array}$$

3.2 Properties of the Embedding

We now state the key properties satisfied by our embedding, ultimately resulting in type preservation and operational correspondence. For conciseness, in the statements below we list only the cases for terms and processes, omitting those for types and kinds (see [32]). The key property that is needed is a notion of compositionality, which unlike in the sketch above no longer falls outside of definitional equality.

Lemma 3.1 (Compositionality)

1. $\Psi; \Gamma; \Delta \vdash [\![M\{N/x\}]\!]_z = [\![M]\!]_z\{\{[\![N]\!]_y\}/x\} :: z{:}[\![A\{N/x\}]\!]$
2. $\Psi; \Gamma; \Delta \vdash [\![P\{M/x\}]\!] :: z{:}[\![A\{M/x\}]\!]$ *iff* $\Psi; \Gamma; \Delta \vdash [\![P]\!]\{\{[\![M]\!]_c\}/x\} :: z{:}[\![A]\!]\{\{[\![M]\!]_c\}/x\}$.

Given the dependently typed nature of the framework, establishing the key properties of the encoding must be done simultaneously (relying on some auxiliary results – see [32]).

Theorem 3.2 (Preservation of Equality)

1. *If* $\Psi \vdash M = N : \tau$ *then* $\{[\![\Psi]\!]\}; \cdot; \cdot \vdash [\![M]\!]_z = [\![N]\!]_z :: z{:}[\![\tau]\!]$
2. *If* $\Psi; \Gamma; \Delta \vdash P = Q :: z{:}A$ *then* $\{[\![\Psi]\!]\}; [\![\Gamma]\!]; [\![\Delta]\!] \vdash [\![P]\!] = [\![Q]\!] :: z{:}[\![A]\!]$.

Theorem 3.3 (Preservation of Typing)

1. *If* $\Psi \vdash M : \tau$ *then* $\{[\![\Psi]\!]\}; \cdot; \cdot \vdash [\![M]\!]_z :: z{:}[\![\tau]\!]$
2. *If* $\Psi; \Gamma; \Delta \vdash P :: z{:}A$ *then* $\{[\![\Psi]\!]\}; [\![\Gamma]\!]; [\![\Delta]\!] \vdash [\![P]\!] :: z{:}[\![A]\!]$.

Theorem 3.4 (Operational Correspondence). *If* $\Psi; \Gamma; \Delta \vdash P :: z{:}A$ *and* $\Psi \vdash M : \tau$ *then:*

1. (a) *If* $P \rightarrow P'$ *then* $[\![P]\!] \rightarrow^+ Q$ *with* $\{[\![\Psi]\!]\}; [\![\Gamma]\!]; [\![\Delta]\!] \vdash Q = [\![P']\!] :: z{:}[\![A]\!]$ *and*
   (b) *if* $[\![P]\!] \rightarrow P'$ *then* $P \rightarrow^+ Q$ *with* $\{[\![\Psi]\!]\}; [\![\Gamma]\!]; [\![\Delta]\!] \vdash P' = [\![Q]\!] :: z{:}[\![A]\!]$
2. (a) *If* $M \rightarrow M'$ *then* $[\![M]\!]_z \rightarrow^+ N$ *with* $\{[\![\Psi]\!]\}; \cdot; \cdot \vdash N = [\![M']\!]_z :: z{:}[\![\tau]\!]$ *and*
   (b) *if* $[\![M]\!]_z \rightarrow P$ *then* $M \rightarrow N$ *with* $\{[\![\Psi]\!]\}; \cdot; \cdot \vdash [\![N]\!]_z = P :: z{:}[\![\tau]\!]$.

In Theorem 3.4, (a) is commonly referred to as operational completeness, with (b) establishing soundness. As exemplified above, our encoding satisfies a very precise operational correspondence with the original λ-terms.

4 Related and Future Work

Enriching Session Types via Type Structure. Exploiting the linear logical foundations of session types, [25] considers a form of value dependencies where session types can state properties of exchanged data values, while the work [29] introduces the contextual monad in a simply-typed setting. Our development not only subsumes these two works, but goes beyond simple value dependencies by extending to a richer type structure and integrating dependencies with the contextual monad. Recently, [1] considers a non-conservative extension of linear logic-based session types with sharing, allowing true non-determinism. Their work includes dependent quantifications with shared channels, but their type syntax does *not* include free type variables, so the actual type dependencies do not arise (see [1, 37:8]). Thus none of the examples in this paper can be represented in [1]. The work [16] studies gradual session types. To the best of our knowledge, the main example in [1, Sect. 2] is *statically* representable in our framework as in the example of Sect. 1, where protocol actions depend on values that are communicated (or passed as function arguments).

In the context of multiparty session types, the theory of multiparty indexed session types is studied in [7], and implemented in a protocol description language [20]. The main aim of these works is to use indexed types to represent an arbitrary number of session *participants*. The work [31] extends [25] to multiparty sessions in order to treat value dependency across multiple participants. Extending our framework to multiparty [15] or non-logic based session types [14] is an interesting future topic.

Combining Linear and Dependent Types. Many works have studied the various challenges of integrating linearity in dependent functional type theories. We focus on the most closely related works. The work [6] introduced the Linear Logical Framework (LLF), integrating linearity with the LF [11] type theory, which was later extended to the Concurrent Logical Framework (CLF) [33], accounting for further linear connectives. Their theory is representable in our framework through the contextual monad (encompassing full intuitionistic linear logic), depending on linearly-typed processes that can express dependently typed functions (Sect. 3).

The work of [17] integrates linearity with type dependencies by extending LNL [2]. Their work is aimed at reasoning about imperative programs using a form of Hoare triples, requiring features that we do not study in this work such has proof irrelevance and computationally irrelevant quantification. Formally, their type theory is extensional which introduces significant technical differences from our intensional type theory, such as a realisability model in the style of NuPRL [10] to establish consistency.

Recently, [8] proposed an extension of LLF with first-class contexts (which may contain both linear and unrestricted hypotheses). While the contextual aspects of their theory are reminiscent of our contextual monad, their framework differs significantly from ours, since it is designed to enable higher-order abstract syntax (commonplace in the LF family of type theories), focusing on a type system for canonical LF objects with a meta-language that includes contexts and context manipulation. They do not consider additives since their integration with first-class contexts can break canonicity.

While none of the above works considers processes as primitive, their techniques should be useful for, e.g. developing algorithmic type-checking and integrating inductive and coinductive session types based on [18, 26, 30].

Dependent Types and Higher-Order π-calculus. The work [35] studies a form of dependent types where the type of processes takes the form of a mapping Δ from channels x to channel types T representing an interface of process P. The dependency is specified as $\Pi(x{:}T)\Delta$, representing a channel abstraction of the environment. This notion is extended to an existential channel dependency type $\Sigma(x{:}T)\Delta$ to address fresh name creation [13, 34]. Combining our process monad with dependent types can be regarded as an "interface" which describes explicit channel usages for processes. The main differences are (1) our dependent types are more general, treating full dependent families including terms and processes in types, while [13,34,35] study only channel dependency to environments (i.e. neither terms nor processes appear in types, only channels); and (2) our calculus emits only fresh names, not needing to handle the complex scoping mechanism treated in [13,34]. In this sense, the process monad provides an elegant framework to handle higher-order computations and assign non-trivial types to processes.

Acknowledgements. The authors would like to thank the anonymous reviews for their comments and suggestions. This work is partially supported by EPSRC EP/K034413/1, EP/K011715/1, EP/L00058X/1, EP/N027833/1, EP/N028201/1 and NOVA LINCS (UID/CEC/04516/2013).

References

1. Balzer, S., Pfenning, F.: Manifest sharing with session types. PACMPL **1**(ICFP), 37:1–37:29 (2017)
2. Benton, P.N.: A mixed linear and non-linear logic: proofs, terms and models. In: Pacholski, L., Tiuryn, J. (eds.) CSL 1994. LNCS, vol. 933, pp. 121–135. Springer, Heidelberg (1995). https://doi.org/10.1007/BFb0022251
3. Caires, L., Pérez, J.A., Pfenning, F., Toninho, B.: Behavioral polymorphism and parametricity in session-based communication. In: Felleisen, M., Gardner, P. (eds.) ESOP 2013. LNCS, vol. 7792, pp. 330–349. Springer, Heidelberg (2013). https://doi.org/10.1007/978-3-642-37036-6_19
4. Caires, L., Pfenning, F.: Session types as intuitionistic linear propositions. In: Gastin, P., Laroussinie, F. (eds.) CONCUR 2010. LNCS, vol. 6269, pp. 222–236. Springer, Heidelberg (2010). https://doi.org/10.1007/978-3-642-15375-4_16
5. Caires, L., Pfenning, F., Toninho, B.: Linear logic propositions as session types. Math. Struct. Comput. Sci. **26**(3), 367–423 (2016)
6. Cervesato, I., Pfenning, F.: A linear logical framework. Inf. Comput. **179**(1), 19–75 (2002)
7. Deniélou, P., Yoshida, N., Bejleri, A., Hu, R.: Parameterised multiparty session types. Log. Methods Comput. Sci. **8**(4), 1–46 (2012). https://doi.org/10.2168/LMCS-8(4:6)2012
8. Georges, A.L., Murawska, A., Otis, S., Pientka, B.: **LINCX**: a linear logical framework with first-class contexts. In: Yang, H. (ed.) ESOP 2017. LNCS, vol. 10201, pp. 530–555. Springer, Heidelberg (2017). https://doi.org/10.1007/978-3-662-54434-1_20
9. Girard, J.: Linear logic. Theor. Comput. Sci. **50**, 1–102 (1987)
10. Harper, R.: Constructing type systems over an operational semantics. J. Symbolic Comput. **14**(1), 71–84 (1992)
11. Harper, R., Honsell, F., Plotkin, G.D.: A framework for defining logics. J. ACM **40**(1), 143–184 (1993)
12. Harper, R., Pfenning, F.: On equivalence and canonical forms in the LF type theory. ACM Trans. Comput. Log. **6**(1), 61–101 (2005)
13. Hennessy, M., Rathke, J., Yoshida, N.: safeDpi: a language for controlling mobile code. Acta Inf. **42**(4–5), 227–290 (2005)

14. Honda, K., Vasconcelos, V.T., Kubo, M.: Language primitives and type discipline for structured communication-based programming. In: Hankin, C. (ed.) ESOP 1998. LNCS, vol. 1381, pp. 122–138. Springer, Heidelberg (1998). https://doi.org/10.1007/BFb0053567
15. Honda, K., Yoshida, N., Carbone, M.: Multiparty asynchronous session types. J. ACM **63**(1), 9:1–9:67 (2016). https://doi.org/10.1145/2827695
16. Igarashi, A., Thiemann, P., Vasconcelos, V.T., Wadler, P.: Gradual session types. PACMPL **1**(ICFP), 38:1–38:28 (2017)
17. Krishnaswami, N.R., Pradic, P., Benton, N.: Integrating linear and dependent types. In: POPL 2015, pp. 17–30 (2015)
18. Lindley, S., Morris, J.G.: Talking bananas: structural recursion for session types. In: ICFP 2016, pp. 434–447 (2016)
19. Mostrous, D., Yoshida, N.: Two session typing systems for higher-order mobile processes. In: Della Rocca, S.R. (ed.) TLCA 2007. LNCS, vol. 4583, pp. 321–335. Springer, Heidelberg (2007). https://doi.org/10.1007/978-3-540-73228-0_23
20. Ng, N., Yoshida, N.: Pabble: parameterised scribble. Serv. Oriented Comput. Appl. **9**(3–4), 269–284 (2015)
21. Norell, U.: Towards a practical programming language based on dependent type theory. Ph.D. thesis, Department of Computer Science and Engineering, Chalmers University of Technology (2007)
22. Pérez, J.A., Caires, L., Pfenning, F., Toninho, B.: Linear logical relations for session-based concurrency. In: Seidl, H. (ed.) ESOP 2012. LNCS, vol. 7211, pp. 539–558. Springer, Heidelberg (2012). https://doi.org/10.1007/978-3-642-28869-2_27
23. Sangiorgi, D., Walker, D.: The Pi-calculus: A Theory of Mobile Processes. C.U.P, Cambridge (2001)
24. Takeuchi, K., Honda, K., Kubo, M.: An interaction-based language and its typing system. In: Halatsis, C., Maritsas, D., Philokyprou, G., Theodoridis, S. (eds.) PARLE 1994. LNCS, vol. 817, pp. 398–413. Springer, Heidelberg (1994). https://doi.org/10.1007/3-540-58184-7_118
25. Toninho, B., Caires, L., Pfenning, F.: Dependent session types via intuitionistic linear type theory. In: PPDP 2011, pp. 161–172 (2011)
26. Toninho, B.: A logical foundation for session-based concurrent computation. Ph.D. thesis, Carnegie Mellon University and New University of Lisbon (2015)
27. Toninho, B., Caires, L., Pfenning, F.: Dependent session types via intuitionistic linear type theory. Technical report CMU-CS-11-139, School of Computer Science, Carnegie Mellon University (2011)
28. Toninho, B., Caires, L., Pfenning, F.: Functions as session-typed processes. In: Birkedal, L. (ed.) FoSSaCS 2012. LNCS, vol. 7213, pp. 346–360. Springer, Heidelberg (2012). https://doi.org/10.1007/978-3-642-28729-9_23
29. Toninho, B., Caires, L., Pfenning, F.: Higher-order processes, functions, and sessions: a monadic integration. In: Felleisen, M., Gardner, P. (eds.) ESOP 2013. LNCS, vol. 7792, pp. 350–369. Springer, Heidelberg (2013). https://doi.org/10.1007/978-3-642-37036-6_20
30. Toninho, B., Caires, L., Pfenning, F.: Corecursion and non-divergence in session-typed processes. In: Maffei, M., Tuosto, E. (eds.) TGC 2014. LNCS, vol. 8902, pp. 159–175. Springer, Heidelberg (2014). https://doi.org/10.1007/978-3-662-45917-1_11
31. Toninho, B., Yoshida, N.: Certifying data in multiparty session types. J. Log. Algebraic Methods Program. **90**(C), 61–83 (2017)

32. Toninho, B., Yoshida, N.: Depending on session-typed processes. CoRR abs/1801.08114 (2017). https://arxiv.org/abs/1801.08114
33. Watkins, K., Cervesato, I., Pfenning, F., Walker, D.: A concurrent logical framework: the propositional fragment. In: Berardi, S., Coppo, M., Damiani, F. (eds.) TYPES 2003. LNCS, vol. 3085, pp. 355–377. Springer, Heidelberg (2004). https://doi.org/10.1007/978-3-540-24849-1_23
34. Yoshida, N.: Channel dependent types for higher-order mobile processes. In: Proceedings of the 31st ACM SIGPLAN-SIGACT Symposium on Principles of Programming Languages, POPL 2004, Venice, Italy, 14–16 January 2004, pp. 147–160 (2004)
35. Yoshida, N., Hennessy, M.: Assigning types to processes. Inf. Comput. **174**(2), 143–179 (2002)

Permissions

All chapters in this book were first published by Springer; hereby published with permissic under the Creative Commons Attribution License or equivalent. Every chapter publish in this book has been scrutinized by our experts. Their significance has been extensive debated. The topics covered herein carry significant findings which will fuel the growth the discipline. They may even be implemented as practical applications or may be referr to as a beginning point for another development.

The contributors of this book come from diverse backgrounds, making this book a tru international effort. This book will bring forth new frontiers with its revolutionizing resear information and detailed analysis of the nascent developments around the world.

We would like to thank all the contributing authors for lending their expertise to make t book truly unique. They have played a crucial role in the development of this book. Witho their invaluable contributions this book wouldn't have been possible. They have made vit efforts to compile up to date information on the varied aspects of this subject to make th book a valuable addition to the collection of many professionals and students.

This book was conceptualized with the vision of imparting up-to-date information ar advanced data in this field. To ensure the same, a matchless editorial board was set u Every individual on the board went through rigorous rounds of assessment to prove the worth. After which they invested a large part of their time researching and compiling t most relevant data for our readers.

The editorial board has been involved in producing this book since its inception. They ha spent rigorous hours researching and exploring the diverse topics which have resulted the successful publishing of this book. They have passed on their knowledge of decad through this book. To expedite this challenging task, the publisher supported the team every step. A small team of assistant editors was also appointed to further simplify t editing procedure and attain best results for the readers.

Apart from the editorial board, the designing team has also invested a significant amou of their time in understanding the subject and creating the most relevant covers. Th scrutinized every image to scout for the most suitable representation of the subject ar create an appropriate cover for the book.

The publishing team has been an ardent support to the editorial, designing and productic team. Their endless efforts to recruit the best for this project, has resulted in t accomplishment of this book. They are a veteran in the field of academics and their po of knowledge is as vast as their experience in printing. Their expertise and guidance h proved useful at every step. Their uncompromising quality standards have made this boc an exceptional effort. Their encouragement from time to time has been an inspiration f everyone.

The publisher and the editorial board hope that this book will prove to be a valuable pie of knowledge for researchers, students, practitioners and scholars across the globe.

List of Contributors

nela Dardha and Simon J. Gay
ıool of Computing Science, University of ısgow, Glasgow, UK

arco Devesas Campos and Paul Blain Levy
hool of Computer Science, University of rmingham, Birmignham, UK

uilhem Jaber
NS de Lyon, Université de Lyon, LIP, Lyon, ance

ikos Tzevelekos
ıeen Mary University of London, London, ıgland

erre Clairambault
ıiv Lyon, CNRS, ENS de Lyon, UCB Lyon LIP, Lyon, France

nathan Hayman and Glynn Winskel
omputer Laboratory, University of ımbridge, Cambridge, UK

ıin-ya Katsumata
ıtional Institute of Informatics, Tokyo, pan

ément Jacq and Paul-André Melliès
stitut de Recherche en Informatique ndamentale, Université Paris Diderot, ris, France

ıca Aceto
an Sasso Science Institute, L'Aquila, Italy
hool of Computer Science, Reykjavik ıiversity, Reykjavik, Iceland

mon Castellan
ıperial College London, London, UK

Antonis Achilleos and Anna Ingólfsdóttir
School of Computer Science, Reykjavik University, Reykjavik, Iceland

Adrian Francalanza
Department of Computer Science, ICT, University of Malta, Msida, Malta

Xinxin Liu, Tingting Yu and Wenhui Zhang
State Key Laboratory of Computer Science, Institute of Software, CAS, University of Chinese Academy of Sciences, Beijing, China

Paolo Baldan and Tommaso Padoan
Dipartimento di Matematica, Università di Padova, Padua, Italy

Étienne Miquey
Équipe Gallinette, Inria, LS2N (CNRS), Université de Nantes, Nantes, France
Équipe πr2, Inria, IRIF (CNRS), Université Paris-Diderot, Paris, France

Hugo Herbelin
Équipe πr2, Inria, IRIF (CNRS), Université Paris-Diderot, Paris, France

Bernardo Toninho
NOVA-LINCS, Departamento de Informática, FCT, Universidade Nova de Lisboa, Lisbon, Portugal Imperial College London, London, UK

Nobuko Yoshida
Imperial College London, London, UK

Index

T

V

Printed in the USA
CPSIA information can be obtained
at www.ICGtesting.com
JSHW061214131223
53612JS00023B/55